THE MAVERICK GUIDE TO MALAYSIA AND SINGAPORE

mav·er·ick (mav'er-ik), *n* 1. an unbranded steer. Hence [colloq.] 2. a person not labeled as belonging to any one faction, group, etc., who acts independently. 3. one who moves in a different direction than the rest of the herd—often a nonconformist. 4. a person using individual judgment, even when it runs against majority opinion.

MAVERICK GUIDE TO
MALAYSIA AND SINGAPORE

Len Rutledge

Researched by
Phensri Athisumongkhon

ALL NEW 2ND EDITION

PELICAN PUBLISHING COMPANY
GRETNA 1994

ISBN: 0-88289-990-2

The word "Pelican" and the depiction of a pelican are trademarks of Pelican Publishing Company, Inc., and are registered in the U.S. Patent and Trademark Office.

Information in this guidebook is based on authoritative data available at the time of printing. Prices and hours of operation of businesses listed are subject to change without notice. Readers are asked to take this into account when consulting this guide.

Maps by Len Rutledge

Manufactured in the United States of America
Published by Pelican Publishing Company, Inc.
1101 Monroe Street, Gretna, Louisiana 70053

Contents

LIST OF MAPS

ACKNOWLEDGMENTS

One of the joys of travel writing is the people you meet along the way. There are scores of people who helped in the preparation of this book. I would particularly like to acknowledge the following:

Belvinder Kaur, Jane Vong, Wendy Lee, Kevin Dragon, Lee Geok Suan, Pearl Sequerah, Siewyong Gnanalingam, Robert Kaling, Roland Ng, Maria Wee, Celina Chin, T. Markland Blaiklock, Beatrice Lee, Jesse Chevrez, Elizabeth Chan, Selana Oh, Phensri Athisumongkhon, Malcolm Longstaff, and Dennis Pile.

THE MAVERICK GUIDE TO MALAYSIA AND SINGAPORE

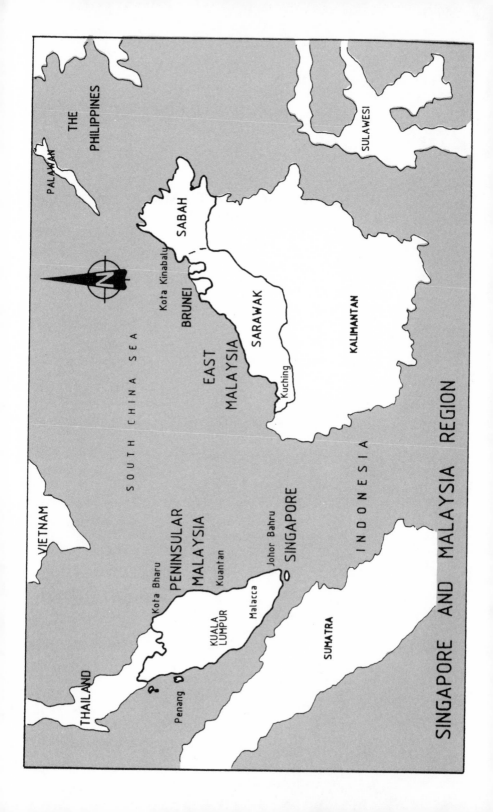

SINGAPORE AND MALAYSIA REGION

1

Why Go to Malaysia and Singapore?

It would be hard to find two countries sitting side by side that are more different yet completely complementary than Malaysia and Singapore. For a short time they belonged to the same federation, but now they coexist and cooperate while going along their independent paths.

At times they are competitors, at other times partners. Sometimes they cooperate, sometimes they fight. There are strange love-hate undercurrents that pervade many aspects of their relationship, yet the visitor normally sees none of this. Both countries encourage visitors and no long-distance international traveller should visit one without also seeing the other.

As a vacation destination, Malaysia and Singapore have almost everything you could want. There is sun, sand, and sea. There are mountains, forests, fine rivers, waterfalls, and national parks. Ultramodern cities contrast with remnants from the past. There is luxury and high adventure. You can meet computer-literate international businessmen, as well as jungle tribesmen still hunting with blowguns.

The contrasts mean that almost every type of vacationer can be satisfied. Consider this: if you are a "city person" tired of shopping in Los Angeles or New York, you can try Singapore or Kuala Lumpur. There are sophisticated shopping complexes equal to any at home, but there are also bazaars, markets, shop-houses, and handicraft outlets the likes of which you will never see in the West. Maybe you like ethnic artifacts. The interior of Sabah and Sarawak will provide you with offerings at a quarter of the price you will pay back home.

Perhaps islands are your thing. A visit to Tioman, Pangkor, Penang, or Langkawi will take you to paradise. But there are more options. Why not combine a stay on Singapore's Sentosa Island, with all its man-made attractions, with a visit to the unspoiled coral islands of the Tunku Abdul Rahman National Park, or the world-famous dive location of Sipadan.

If you are the outdoor adventurer type, you can climb to the top of southeast Asia's highest peak, raft rapid-filled rivers through steamy tropical jungles, explore the largest caves in the world, or fish for the superb fighting mahseer fish while staying in safari lodges deep in the interior.

Animal lovers can have breakfast with an orangutan at the Singapore Zoo in civilized comfort, or see these wonderful animals in their natural state in isolated jungle reserves. You can visit national park animal preserves to see tapir and deer, have late-night walks on faraway beaches to watch giant turtles come ashore to lay their eggs, or observe hornbills, proboscis monkeys, and two-meter-long monitor lizards in Sabah and Sarawak.

Man was inhabiting the Niah Caves 40,000 years ago, yet the sites of today's major cities were deserted 200 years ago. Malaysia and Singapore are at once ancient and modern. If you brought ancient man to modern Singapore, with its ultramodern underground railway stations, its cloud-scraping high-rise buildings, and its state-of-the-art port and airport, it would be like putting you or me on Jupiter. But perhaps the same result could be achieved if you brought to Kuala Lumpur the present-day *orang asli* people, whom you can meet in the Cameron Highlands or in the foothills of Pahang.

The beauty of Malaysia and Singapore is that all this diversity is available within a relatively small area. Additionally, because tourism is vital to the economy of both countries, a sound infrastructure is there so that all can see and experience this collage of culture, nature, and twentieth-century materialism.

The people are diverse, as well. About 50 percent are ethnic Malays, about 10 percent are Malay-related ethnic tribespeople, 32 percent are Chinese, and about 8 percent are Indian and other races. The Malays are the largest group in Malaysia, and the Chinese are the largest group in Singapore. As you travel about, you will meet sophisticated city dwellers, simple fishermen, farmers and rural folk, and tribal people who retain many elements of their ancient culture.

To meet them all, you will need to visit Singapore, Kuala Lumpur, some of the other major tourist centers, and some of the more remote locations. Fortunately you will find that you can do this without sacrificing too much comfort, and without danger. There are reasonable hotels, transportation, and eating facilities throughout Singapore and peninsular Malaysia, and in the major centers in Sabah and Sarawak. The facilities deteriorate, but the adventure builds, as you explore the more remote areas of Sabah and Sarawak. Maybe these remote areas are more for the traveller than the tourist, but if you understand the problems and the rewards, you will probably decide that these areas were the highlights of your visit.

Malaysia and Singapore are like nowhere else. They are not a substitute for any other destination. You will not find their special attractions elsewhere. If you want a safe, clean, sophisticated destination, you will be well satisfied with Singapore, Kuala Lumpur, or Penang. If you want the adventure, romance, and thrill of Asia as it once was, you can find all of that in Malacca, Sabah, and Sarawak. Wherever you go, you are unlikely to be disappointed. Millions of people visit this region every year. Most return for more.

Tourist Malaysia/Singapore in Summary

- Malaysia and Singapore are multiracial countries of considerable cultural diversity.
- Tourism is important to both countries, so infrastructures are well developed.
- Costs are cheap when compared to the United States, Europe, or much of the South Pacific.
- Singapore is one of the most sophisticated cities in Asia. It has great shopping opportunities, an ultramodern transportation system, a range of man-made visitor attractions, and good sporting opportunities.
- The hotel and restaurant facilities in Singapore are the best and most extensive in southeast Asia.
- The hill resorts of Cameron Highlands and Fraser's Hill provide a wonderful respite from the heat of the region while offering excellent sight-seeing and sporting opportunities.
- Penang is the most developed island in the region, with excellent facilities for visitors looking for a beach-oriented holiday.
- Other islands such as Langkawi, Pangkor, Tioman, and Tinggi provide lovely beaches, a relaxed atmosphere, and modern facilities to help you enjoy the sea and sun.
- The east coast of peninsular Malaysia is almost one continuous

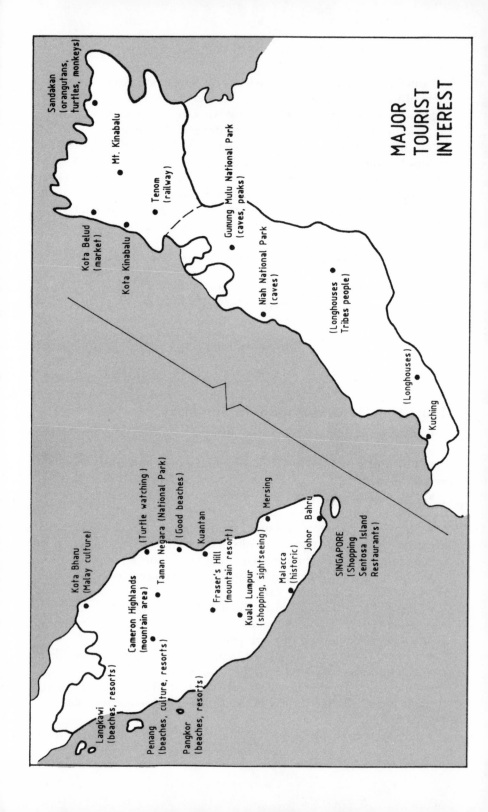

MAJOR TOURIST INTEREST

Sandakan (orangutans, turtles, monkeys)

Mt. Kinabalu

Tenom (railway)

Kota Belud (market)

Kota Kinabalu

Gunung Mulu National Park (caves, peaks)

Niah National Park (caves)

(Longhouses Tribes people)

(Longhouses)

Kuching

Kota Bharu (Malay culture)

(Turtle watching)

Taman Negara (National Park)

(Good beaches)

Kuantan

Cameron Highlands (mountain area)

Fraser's Hill (mountain resort)

Langkawi (beaches, resorts)

Penang (beaches, culture, resorts)

Pangkor (beaches, resorts)

Kuala Lumpur (shopping, sightseeing)

Malacca (historic)

Mersing

Johor Bahru

SINGAPORE (Shopping Sentosa Island Restaurants)

beach, with long stretches of totally undeveloped white sand and a few isolated resorts. This area also provides a great opportunity to see some traditional Malay culture and to buy some handicrafts.

• The national parks of Malaysia provide some wonderful chances to return to nature while walking, climbing, caving, or flora and fauna watching.

• Sabah and Sarawak are home to some of the world's last remaining virgin rainforest, and to some people who are living a life-style little changed by the twentieth century.

• Malaysia is home to some of the world's rarest and most endangered animal species.

The Confessional

Unlike many other guidebooks, this one contains no advertising, either overt or covert. The opinions expressed—and there are many— are mine. As with other books in the series, no one can use friendship or favors to influence the coverage of personal commercial interests. You may not agree with my opinion, but you will know that it is based on my personal experience and is given openly and honestly.

It is physically impossible for anyone to experience all the thousands of components that make up the "Visitor's Malaysia." I first visited Singapore and Malaysia in 1970 and have been a regular visitor ever since. When I was commissioned to write this book I made five visits specifically to obtain the latest information on everything of interest to a visitor. During these visits I deliberately stayed in a wide range of accommodations, ate at a wide variety of restaurants and street stalls, experienced some guided tours, investigated the shopping opportunities, and tried out the nightlife. At no time did I ask members of the tourism industry to subsidize this research.

On two occasions I did accept offers of help from the government-owned tourist organizations in both Singapore and Malaysia so that I could visit places outside my own financial resources, and make my research as complete as possible. I did this on the firm understanding that neither organization could approve or disapprove of anything I wrote. There was no argument from either the Singapore Tourist Promotion Board or the then Tourist Development Corporation of Malaysia, and for this I am very grateful to them. In both cases their reaction was, "Once you have seen our product, we are happy for you to write about it, provided it is accurate. We think you will be impressed." In most cases I was.

For this second edition I have made a further four visits. One of these was supported by the Singapore Tourist Promotion Board and the Malaysia Tourism Promotion Board.

It has not been possible to stay in every hotel that a visitor can use, but the book covers a good range from luxury to basic. Likewise with restaurants, night spots, and shops—you will end up eating at, or visiting, some places not mentioned in this book. If they are particularly good, cheap, friendly, or interesting, please let me know about them so that I can visit them before completing the next edition of the guide. This edition has benefitted greatly from comments made by readers of the previous edition.

This old guy has been a travel writer for more than twenty years, ever since I was owner and editor of a small newspaper in Australia in 1969. I have had the opportunity since then of travelling throughout the world, and in some ways it has helped to keep me young at heart. At the same time I think my travel experiences have made me a more tolerant, aware, and appreciative person. I ask the same of you. Don't visit Malaysia and Singapore expecting everything to be a duplication of things at home. Try not to complain if the beer tastes "different," or the people sometimes walk on the "wrong" side of the sidewalk. Accept that in some parts of the globe, time has less meaning to locals than it does to "busy" tourists. See these things as a broadening of your experience, and as an insight into a new culture that may just have as many plusses as your own.

Getting the Most Out of This Book

This guide is arranged in a pattern similar to that of the other Maverick Guides. It is a tried and tested format that has been used for more than ten years and it enables you to get a good feel for the country and its people while at the same time getting the specifics that are so necessary when you are travelling.

After a chapter on how to reach Singapore and Malaysia, how to travel around when you get there, and how to smooth the basics of government requirements and travel practicalities, I have split the book into two sections. In each I have two chapters on the land and the people, and then I follow with specific area chapters.

The chapters need not be read in that sequence, of course. I suggest, however, that if you are using the book to plan your trip, you should read all sections so that you can decide which areas you will and will not be able to visit.

Each of the area chapters is divided into twelve numbered sections, and after you become familiar with them in one chapter you will know where to look for these same subjects in each of the other sections. The categories are as follows:

1. **The General Picture**
2. **Getting There**
3. **Local Transportation**
4. **The Hotel Scene**
5. **Dining and Restaurants**
6. **Sight-seeing**
7. **Guided Tours**
8. **Culture**
9. **Sports**
10. **Shopping**
11. **Entertainment and Nightlife**
12. **The Address List**

The book has been set up to be used in two ways. First, you should look through it thoroughly before you leave home. Make some plans on the basis of this reading. Decide where you would like to visit and what you would like to do when you are there. Select some hotels, decide if there are some specific restaurants or night spots that you will visit, consider which tours have appeal, and make a list of the things you would like to buy while in Singapore and Malaysia. Then go and talk to your travel agent.

Remember that while travel agents are well qualified to advise on airfares and some package tours, it is unrealistic to expect them to be familiar with details of all destinations around the world. A good agent will appreciate your making informed suggestions, and will benefit from the contact names and telephone numbers found inside this guide.

The book is also designed to be used when you are in Singapore and Malaysia. The recommendations on sight-seeing tours, hotels, restaurants, and shopping will help in your quest for smooth, fun travelling. The information on sight-seeing, culture, and sports will help broaden your horizons and encourage you to explore things that most visitors are forced to ignore. All the sections will help you save time and money as you travel through Singapore and Malaysia.

I have included many maps in this volume because it seems to me that a guidebook without good maps is somewhat of a misnomer. The city and town maps will help you orientate yourself quickly and will help to show you where hotels and sight-seeing attractions are situated. The regional maps are useful in planning itineraries, and to follow as you travel through the area by road or rail.

Some Quick Comments

As well as a great source of information, I hope you find this book a good read. It has been written so you can pick it up and put it down as time permits. Even if you know very little about Singapore and Malaysia, you should gain a good appreciation of the countries, the people, and the cultures by reading the descriptive chapters. After reading them, you will know more about life in Singapore and Malaysia than many tourists who have been there on a brief, fully escorted package tour.

If you are serious about getting the most out of your proposed visit, be sure to take advantage of the good literature available from the Singapore Tourist Promotion Board and the Malaysia Tourism Promotion Board. Both organizations have a range of top-quality material that can help you. Don't forget the two national airlines, Singapore Airlines and Malaysia Airlines. Both also have some useful information and some holiday package ideas. Telephone, fax, or write to the offices most convenient to you. The addresses are listed under "Tourist Information" in the next chapter.

Write or fax also to other addresses you'll find throughout this book and tell them you are planning a visit. If you tell them you are using the Maverick Guide, they should recognize you as an informed potential customer, and respond with a useful amount of up-to-date literature and information.

This book is crammed full of telephone numbers that you will skip over during your initial reading. It is a different story when you get to Singapore and Malaysia and need this information. Use the telephone when you can. In Singapore everyone will be able to speak English with you. In Malaysia, you will have little trouble in calling the places listed in this book.

Prices in the book are all quoted in Singaporean or Malaysian currency. S$100 means 100 Singapore dollars. M$50 means 50 Malaysian ringgit. It is a good idea to become familiar with their values before you arrive in each country because all prices will be quoted to you in these local currencies. If you are a serious shopper, you should check out home prices, convert them to Singaporean and Malaysian currency, and then write them down in a notebook that you take with you. You will then know instantly which are the true bargains. Never let anyone tell you that the "dollar price" quoted you is in U.S., Canadian, Australian, or New Zealand dollars. Learn that a dollar in Singapore is a Singapore dollar and nothing else. There are many stories of Americans paying US$20 when they should be paying S$20 (i.e., about US$10).

Finally, after you have made your trip, would you please write to me (care of the publisher) and tell me about it? The travelling experiences of persons such as you will help me tremendously in preparing the next edition of this guidebook. This in turn will help future readers, and will also reward the owners of places in Singapore and Malaysia that you recommend.

Use either the enclosed letter/envelope form, or if that's not enough space, copy the address onto your own envelope and include as many pages as you like. Your reactions to both the book and the destinations are earnestly solicited and will be warmly appreciated.

Good travelling,
LEN RUTLEDGE

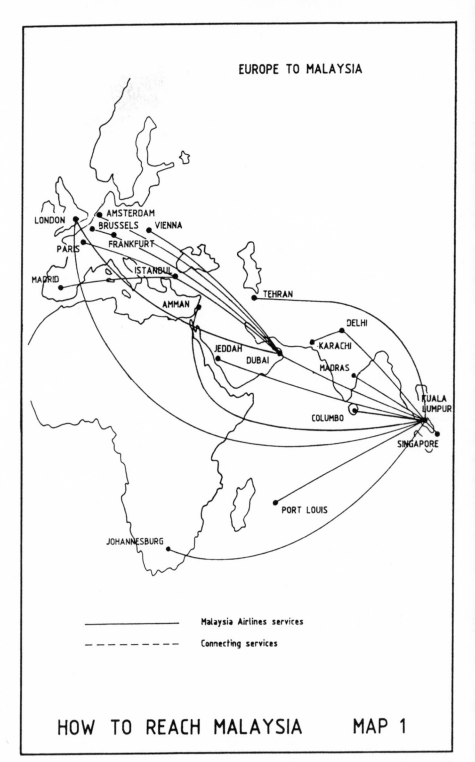

EUROPE TO MALAYSIA

HOW TO REACH MALAYSIA   MAP 1

2

Happy Landings

How to Get There

The only practical way to reach Singapore and Malaysia from most parts of the world is to go by air. Fortunately, Singapore and Kuala Lumpur are served by dozens of airlines and they can both be reached without problems from almost every corner of the globe. These days there are nonstop flights from Europe, Australia, New Zealand, and many places in Asia to both Singapore and Malaysia. Many North American flights have become one-stop affairs.

The distance from Europe and North America precludes Singapore and Malaysia from being a budget flight destination. Regular first, business, and economy class airfares are relatively expensive. Fortunately, however, there are several other options in the way of excursion fares, circle Pacific fares, off-peak fares, and so on. If you aim to get the cheapest possible fare—rather than choose a particular airline or a particular route—you need to find a good travel agent who can sift through all the options available.

It pays to carefully consider all the options, though, as the lowest airfare is not necessarily the cheapest or the best for you in the long run. Consider the route, the stopovers, and the convenience. Do you have to change aircraft at some strange foreign airport with long delays? Maybe you would like to combine several regional destinations in the one vacation. If any of these considerations has an interest for you, please quiz and brief your travel agent about your particular concerns.

A travel agency should be able and willing to take the time to tailor your arrangements to what you want. I strongly suggest that you use this Maverick Guide to help you choose your facilities and activities, and to decide which areas you want to visit. Then take these plans to a good agent who can put them into operation. Take this book into the travel agency if you wish; that has brought excellent results in the past.

All airlines give you fare options. The comfort and service usually deteriorate as you move down-market, but so does the price. Your perception of what is the best level for you will be determined by your finances and activities at home. Some travellers insist that first class is the only way to avoid jet lag and some of the other problems associated with modern travel. Others study the situation and determine that the large savings to be made by flying economy or excursion fares are better spent on activities at their destination. Others of us have no choice in the matter and take what we can afford. That travel decision is a very individual one and I will have no part in the making of it for you.

Both Singapore and Malaysia have national airlines, so naturally these provide excellent services to the region. North American, European, Australian, New Zealander, and other airlines also fly in. Here is a quick rundown on the birds that can get you there.

Malaysia Airlines is a young airline, but its history dates back to 1937, when it was formed as **Malayan Airways Ltd.** (MAL). The company took ten years to become airborne and it started modestly with a five-seater Airspeed Consul.

In 1958 the airline became a public limited company, owned by a British and an Australian airline and the governments of Malaya, Singapore, and the Borneo Territories. MAL acquired a DC3 aircraft in 1947 and a DC4 in 1958, then added Viscount propjets, a Lockheed Super Constellation, and a Bristol Britannia in quick succession. It entered the jet age in 1962 with British Comet aircraft.

With the formation of Malaysia, the airline was renamed **Malaysia Airways Ltd.**, and in 1966 the governments of Malaysia and Singapore acquired majority control. In 1967 it had a further change to **Malaysia-Singapore Airlines** (MSA), but even this did not last long.

As a result of differences in the national aspirations of the parties in MSA, it was decided in 1971 that the governments of Malaysia and Singapore would operate their own national carriers. With this decision, **Malaysian Airline System** (MAS) was formed as Malaysia's airline. In 1987 it changed its name to **Malaysia Airlines**.

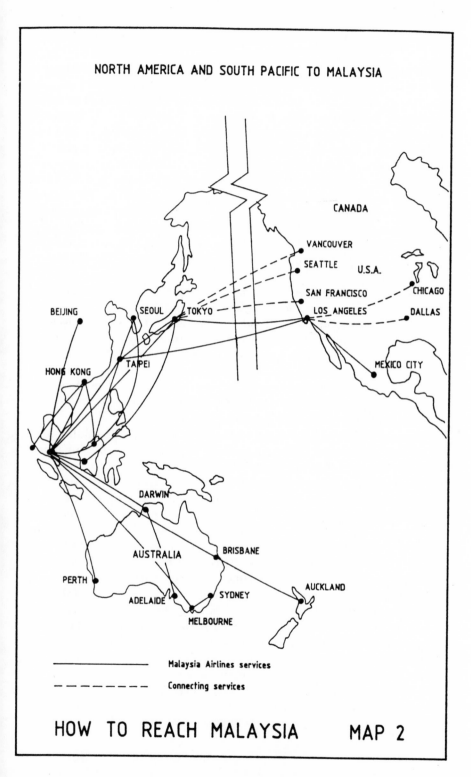

NORTH AMERICA AND SOUTH PACIFIC TO MALAYSIA

CANADA

VANCOUVER
SEATTLE   U.S.A.
SAN FRANCISCO   CHICAGO
LOS ANGELES   DALLAS

BEIJING   SEOUL   TOKYO

HONG KONG   TAPEI   MEXICO CITY

DARWIN

AUSTRALIA   BRISBANE

PERTH   AUCKLAND

ADELAIDE   SYDNEY
MELBOURNE

—————————— Malaysia Airlines services

— — — — — — Connecting services

HOW TO REACH MALAYSIA   MAP 2

Today, Malaysia Airlines flies to eighty-two destinations worldwide with a fleet of Boeing 747s, including the B747-400, McDonnell Douglas DC10s, Airbus A-300s, Boeing 737-400s, and Fokker 50s. The airline has an enviable record for courtesy and in-flight service. This is seen on all flights, but is best appreciated on the long-distance services from Los Angeles, Honolulu, London, Brussels, Paris, Amsterdam, Frankfurt, Vienna, Zurich, Auckland, and the various Australian ports.

For many visitors, their first introduction to Malaysia is the *selamat datang* greeting they receive from *kebaya*-clad stewards or stewardesses in *songket*-trimmed suits as they enter a Malaysia Airlines jet on a flight to Malaysia, and in fact the whole ambience of each flight reflects the warmth and hospitality that are inherent in the Malaysian persona. The airline has earned a reputation for "Enchanting Service," and it is easy to see why.

Singapore Airlines has one of the most extensive international flight networks of any Asian/Pacific airline. In addition, the airline has in recent years negotiated several code-sharing and other agreements with other airlines that effectively extend the network even farther. From the United States, the airline operates daily services from San Francisco to Singapore via Hong Kong, daily Los Angeles to Singapore services via Tokyo, and some Los Angeles to Singapore services via Honolulu and Taipei. A code-sharing system with Delta Airlines provides a daily connection from Dallas/Fort Worth to Los Angeles.

There are services from many European, Asian, New Zealander, and Australian ports and a few connections to Africa. In all, Singapore Airlines serves fifty-eight cities worldwide.

Other carriers fly in from around the world. From North America, **Northwest Airlines** flies to both Kuala Lumpur and Singapore, and **United** services Singapore. **Qantas** has services from numerous points in Australia to Singapore, and a lesser number of flights to Kuala Lumpur, while **Air New Zealand** has direct services to Singapore. Major European carriers such as **British Airways, KLM, Lufthansa, Aeroflot**, and **Czechoslovak Airlines** connect many European cities with both Kuala Lumpur and Singapore. Currently **SAS, Swissair, Sabina, Air France**, and **Olympic** serve Singapore, but not Malaysia.

All the major regional carriers—**Thai Airways International, Philippine Airlines, Garuda International, Air India, Cathay Pacific, China Airlines,** and **Japan Airlines**—have services to both Singapore and Kuala Lumpur, and some also serve Penang and Kota Kinabalu. A number of smaller regional carriers—**Pelangi Air, Royal Brunei, and Air Lanka**—also have services.

The occasional cruise liner visits Singapore and some Malaysian ports as part of a world, Pacific, or Asian cruise, but this is not the way to visit and see some of the country.

It is possible to reach Malaysia by road and rail from Thailand, and this is a popular route with the backpacker and long-term-traveller market. There is a daily international express train from Bangkok, and frequent buses link southern Thailand with northern Malaysia.

Transportation Within Malaysia

If you wish to visit both peninsular Malaysia and Borneo, you have no option but to take a plane between the two. Even within peninsular Malaysia there are some advantages in flying between some centers. In Borneo, most visitors fly some sectors because of the distances involved and the lack of practical alternatives.

Air: Malaysia Airlines has an extensive network that covers most of Malaysia and links Singapore with several Malaysian cities. The network is centered in Kuala Lumpur, but Penang, Kuching, and Kota Kinabalu are other major hubs. The system is operated with DC10s, A300B airbuses, Boeing B737s, Fokker 50s, and DHC-6 Twin Otter aircraft. The Twin Otters operate to small airfields in Sabah and Sarawak, the Fokkers operate some domestic services within peninsular Malaysia, Sabah, and Sarawak, while jets operate all the major routes. Frequency is excellent. There are at least ten services daily linking Kuala Lumpur and Singapore, fourteen on the Kuala Lumpur-Penang route, and eight on the Kuala Lumpur-Kota Kinabalu route.

There are a variety of special fares within Malaysia that ease the cost of travel. Many of these are available to international visitors. Your travel agent will be able to find out further details. These fares include night tourist fares, excursion fares, advance purchase excursion fares, special local selling fares, family fares, student fares, disabled passenger fares, military fares, common interest group fares, and so on. They all have restrictions on them, but some are very useful if you have a little flexibility in your travel plans.

Another option worth investigating is the *Discover Malaysia Pass*. The pass can only be used in conjunction with international travel that includes at least one sector into or out of Malaysia on Malaysia Airlines, and it applies only to economy-class/Fokker flights on Malaysia Airlines' domestic services.

For US$138 (1993 price) you can travel up to five sectors within the Malay peninsula, within Sabah (including Labuan), or within Sarawak. In addition, a pass holder is eligible for a 50-percent discount on the normal sector fares between K.L. and Kota Kinabalu or Kuching,

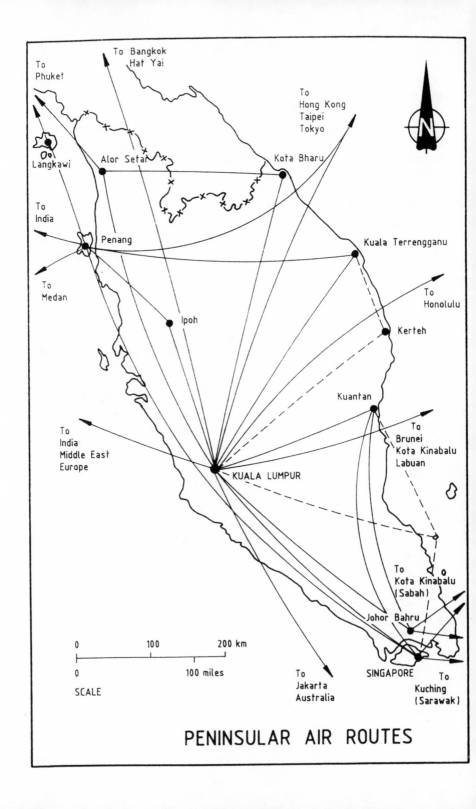

PENINSULAR AIR ROUTES

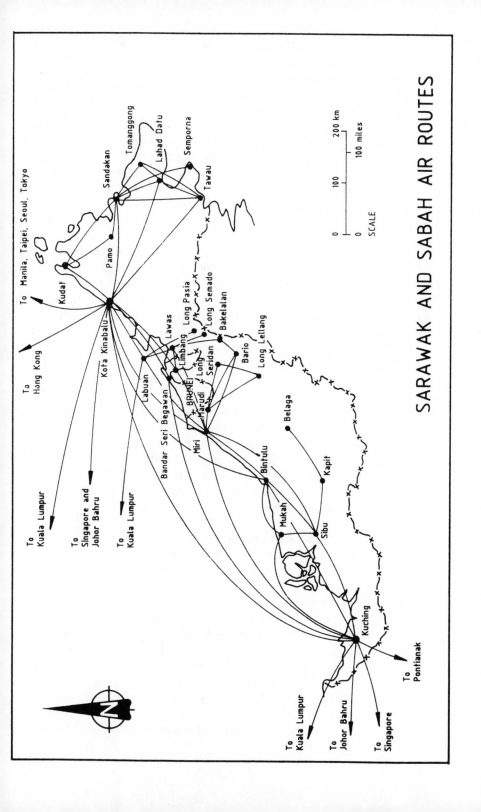

SARAWAK AND SABAH AIR ROUTES

between Kota Kinabalu and Kuching, Miri, or Bintulu, or between Labuan and Kuching or Miri.

Passes may be purchased from any MAS office in your home country or within fourteen (14) days of arrival into Malaysia.

Scheduled air services are also operated by **Pelangi Air**, a subsidiary of Malaysia Airlines. These link Kuala Lumpur with a number of centers in the Malay peninsula, but there are also some flights from Singapore (to Malacca, Pangkor, and Tioman), and some services linking smaller centers not served by Malaysia Airlines.

Rail: Peninsular Malaysia has a fairly extensive rail network of about 1600 kilometers. Sabah has a section of about 130 kilometers. The passenger services in the Malay peninsula have been upgraded in recent years and there are good facilities between Singapore, Kuala Lumpur, Butterworth, and Thailand. The other major line is from Gemas, through Tembeling and Kota Bharu, to Tumpat near the Thai border. A branch line links with the Thailand rail system at Sungai Golok, although no passenger trains use this sector.

There are three classes of rail travel, but in practice many trains only operate two classes. The major train services that will appeal to visitors are the fast services between Singapore, Kuala Lumpur, and Butterworth. The **Ekspress Rakyat** is a daily through-service from Singapore to Butterworth and vice versa. It leaves Singapore at 7:45 A.M., reaches Kuala Lumpur at 2:30 P.M., and arrives in Butterworth at 9:10 P.M. The southbound service follows a similar schedule. This train offers three-class service, with first and second being air-conditioned.

The **Ekspress Sinaran Pagi** consists of *two* trains that leave Kuala Lumpur for Butterworth and Singapore simultaneously at 7:30 P.M. The **Ekspress Sinaran Petang** leaves Butterworth at 2:15 P.M. and reaches Kuala Lumpur at 8:15 P.M., while from Singapore it leaves at 2:45 P.M., arriving in Kuala Lumpur at 9:35 P.M. This offers first- and second-class service only, in modern air-conditioned carriages.

The **Langkawi Express** runs a daily night service. It departs K.L. at 11:00 P.M. and arrives at Arau, where there are direct bus connections to Kuala Perlis for the Langkawi ferry.

As well as these services there is an ordinary day mail train from K.L. to Butterworth, and an ordinary night train, both of which have second- and third-class facilities. A **Timuran Express** train operates from Singapore to Tumpat near the Thai border on the east coast. Departures are three times a week at 8:00 A.M.

If you love rail travel and plan to see every corner of Malaysia, you should consider a *Visit Malaysia Pass*. These are only available to visitors with foreign passports and give unlimited travel on all trains. They do

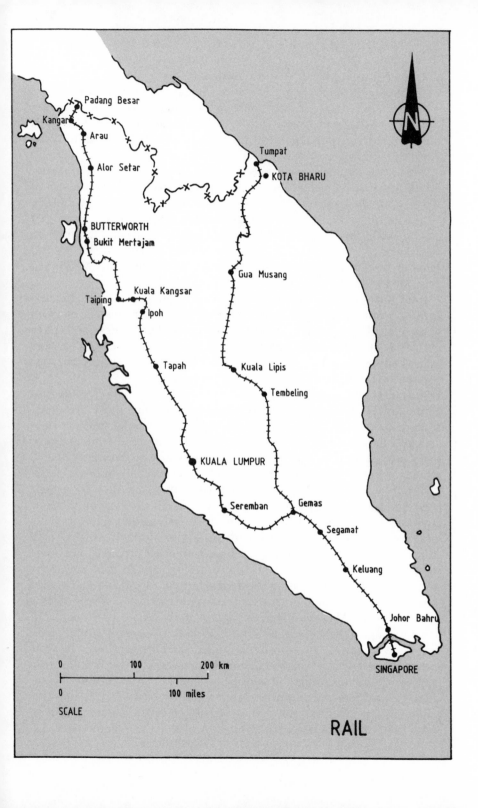

Padang Besar
Kangar
Arau
Alor Setar
Tumpat
KOTA BHARU
BUTTERWORTH
Bukit Mertajam
Gua Musang
Kuala Kangsar
Taiping
Ipoh
Tapah
Kuala Lipis
Tembeling
KUALA LUMPUR
Seremban
Gemas
Segamat
Keluang
Johor Bahru
SINGAPORE

N

| 0 | 100 | 200 km |
| 0 | 100 miles | |

SCALE

RAIL

not cover sleeping berth charges. Both a 10-day and a 30-day pass are available. The passes are purchased in Singapore or Malaysia.

In tandem with the trains, there are **railbus services** (bus services operated by Malayan Railways) that connect various centers. The major ones are K.L. to Ipoh, Ipoh to Butterworth, and Butterworth to Arau. Fares are similar to third-class rail.

There are various concessions available to family groups, students, handicapped persons, senior citizens, and others. For more details of these, you can write to the Director of Commerce, Malayan Railway, Kuala Lumpur. Typical rail fares are: Kuala Lumpur to Singapore—1st class M$50, 2nd class M$31, 3rd class M$15; Kuala Lumpur to Butterworth—1st class M$50, 2nd class M$25, 3rd class M$15; Rakyat/Sinaran fares K.L. to Singapore—1st class M$60, 2nd class M$33, 3rd class M$19.

Bus: Buses operate all over Malaysia and they provide the cheapest form of public transportation. Bus services are provided by both government and private operators on schedules, routes, and fares approved by the government. On many routes there are local services as well as express services. Many of the express services are air-conditioned, but the majority of local services are not.

Where there is a rail service available (e.g., Kuala Lumpur to Butterworth), I would prefer to travel by train, but there are many routes where bus is the only public transportation option. Services such as Kuala Lumpur to Kuantan, and K.L. to the Cameron Highlands are particularly useful. As the north-south expressway progressively opens, the attraction of bus travel in this corridor will certainly improve. Until it is fully operational, however, bus travel will be haunted by a high accident rate caused by some of the most antisocial driving you will find anywhere. In Sabah and Sarawak the situation is rather different, and local services are an excellent way of getting around.

The subject of **car rental** provides me with a big problem. Theoretically, peninsular Malaysia should be a great place to rent a car. In general the roads are reasonable, rental facilities are good, and traffic outside some of the major urban centers is not too heavy. The problem, however, is the Malaysian drivers. On my most recent 4000-kilometer drive through the Malay peninsula, I devised a new set of road rules that many Malaysian transport, bus, and taxi drivers obviously have to learn before they are allowed behind the wheel. Typical rules are: Double white lines mean you *must* pass someone, either on the left or right. Speed limits in built-up areas are to be doubled, then used as the minimum speed you can travel. Playing chicken with oncoming traffic is compulsory at least every five minutes. And there are many more.

The result of this type of driving is that Malaysia has an appalling traffic safety record when you consider the size of the country and the number of vehicles on the roads. But as you can see, I have survived a number of extended periods on Malaysian roads and the odds are that you can, too. Just drive with care, and do not ever try to emulate the locals.

Most of the major international car rental companies—**Avis, Hertz, Thrifty, National,** and **Budget**—are represented in Singapore and Kuala Lumpur, and some have offices in other centers as well. There are some Malaysia-wide rental companies such as **SMAS Rent a Car,** and also many local operators just represented in one or two places. This latter group tends to be cheaper but is not recommended if you plan to do country-wide touring. Typical daily rates (unlimited mileage) for the major companies are from M\$120-400. Weekly rates are around M\$700-2400. Fuel is more expensive than in the United States, but cheaper than in Europe.

The cheapest car to rent is often the locally made Proton Saga, which comes with a 1.3- or 1.5-liter engine. Traffic drives on the left in both Singapore and Malaysia. Always ask about special deals such as week-end rates, tourist rates, and so on.

Long-distance taxis are something you will quickly become familiar with if you do any travel by road. These taxis operate a town-to-town service almost like a bus service. They line up at the "teksi" stand in a town, then leave as soon as four passengers arrive. On popular routes the wait for passengers will not be long. Taxi fares are about twice the bus fare for the same route, but they are certainly more convenient and often more comfortable. You may find, however, if you are the front-seat passenger, that you will end up with your eyes closed for much of the trip to ease the stress caused by some very original driving.

Travel Facts and Figures

Here are some essential facts to make planning your trip a little easier, and to make visiting Singapore and Malaysia as enjoyable as it should be. If you are a frequent traveller, you may choose to skip over this section, but there could even be a hint or two for you.

Weather and Climate: Singapore and Malaysia are situated within the tropics, so temperatures are always high, except at night in the mountain areas. Humidity is high all year-round. The average temperature throughout the year is 25-27 degrees C. or around 80 degrees F. Maximum temperatures rarely reach over 32 degrees C. (90 degrees F.).

There is no marked wet or dry season but Singapore, the east coast of peninsular Malaysia, and northeastern Sabah receive the most rain in the November to February period, while the west coast of peninsular Malaysia has a particularly wet period in April and May. It is generally best to avoid these specific areas at these times.

Packing and Wearing: It has become boring to repeat the phrase "travel light," yet you still see people dragging around assorted suitcases, bags, and parcels at the start of their trip. I do not understand how they survive. Perhaps halfway through their vacation they throw everything away and start over. No matter who you are, there is one basic rule: if you can't carry your own bags through an airport terminal, a railway station, or up the hotel elevator, you have too much.

In Singapore and Malaysia there is no excuse for having heavy baggage when you arrive, although when you leave it is a different matter. What you need are light, casual clothes. For business meetings and at some hotels and restaurants you will need a long-sleeved shirt and tie, or its female equivalent, and at night in the highlands you will need a sweater. The rest of the time you will need light summer clothing (preferably cottons) and comfortable footwear.

Common travel items such as medications, sunscreen, toothpaste, film, videotape, and so on are readily available in Singapore and in the major centers of Malaysia. Go into a supermarket and you will recognize many of the brand names, but you are also likely to see their local, cheaper equivalents. If you get caught needing extra clothing for some reason, clothes are readily available and prices are reasonable. There may be a minor problem if you need extra-large sizes in anything because the local population is much smaller than the average in the West.

Asians in general, and in this case the Malays in particular, tend to be more conservative than many people in the West. Keep that in mind if you are tempted to parade that micro-bikini or that way-out set of bikie gear. Follow the lead of the locals and you will not go far wrong.

Mail and Telephone Services: Singapore and Malaysia have efficient and reliable telephone and postal services. Singapore Telecom offers mail, telephone, fax, telex, and other services. In Malaysia, postal services are operated by the Malaysian Postal Service Department, and telecommunications are provided by a private company called Syarikat Telekom Malaysia.

Singapore is a country in love with the telephone. There are about 1.5 million telephones in the country. That's more than one for every two people. You'll think that most of these must be mobile telephones from the number of people who walk down the street with a telephone firmly to the ear. Surprisingly, there are some 27,000 public payphones in the country. That's 11 per 1000 people, the highest penetration rate in the world. Many of these take credit cards and can be used for making overseas calls.

While Malaysia does not have this same penetration, the service is well organized, and many areas have international subscriber dialing (ISD), mobile telephone service, and other facilities. If you wish to book an international call with the operator, you dial 108. Calls can be booked in advance, but in most cases they can be connected without any long delay. There are 24-hour international telephones at the Central Telegraph Office, Bukit Mahkamah, Kuala Lumpur, and a 16-hour service at the international airport.

Some telephone numbers in this book have been listed without area codes because most will be made locally. If, however, you are making long-distance calls within Malaysia and Singapore, you must dial the area code before the local number. All area codes start with zero. If you are dialing from outside the country you drop the zero. To dial Singapore from overseas, you dial the country code (65), no area code, then the number. To dial Kuala Lumpur you dial the country code (60), then the area code (3), then the number. Area codes for calls made within Malaysia are:

Singapore—02
Kuala Lumpur region—03
Northwest (Penang, Langkawi, Perlis, Kedah)—04
Central west (Ipoh, Taiping, Pangkor, Cameron Highlands)—05
South central coast (Malacca, Port Dickson, Seremban)—06
The South (Johor Bahru, Desaru)—07
East Coast (Kuantan, Kuala Terengganu, Kota Bharu)—09
Southern Sarawak (Kuching)—082
Sri Aman region, Sarawak—083
Sibu region, Sarawak (Sibu, Sarikei, Kapit, Belaga)—084
Miri region, Sarawak (Miri, Limbang)—085
Central region, Sarawak (Bintulu)—086
Labuan Island—087
West Sabah (Kota Kinabalu, Ranau, Kudat)—088
East Sabah (Sandakan, Tawau)—089

Metrics and Electrics

Both Malaysia and Singapore now use the metric system, although there are a few instances where reminders of the imperial system remain. If you are not familiar with metrics, you can quickly learn a few conversions that will help you through the strange terms. The important measures for most visitors are temperature, distance, and volume.

How hot will it be? In most instances at home we are not really interested in whether the maximum temperature will be 82 degrees F. or 83 degrees F. It's the same with metrics. All you need to know is whether it is going to be hot or cold. Try and remember these Celsius numbers and most of your problems will be solved. Ten degrees Celsius equals 50 degrees Fahrenheit, 20 degrees Celsius equals 68 degrees Fahrenheit, and 30 degrees Celsius equals 86 degrees Fahrenheit. It also helps if you know zero degrees Celsius is the freezing point of water, and 100 degrees Celsius is the boiling point.

How far is it? Is it close by or a long way? Will it take 2 hours or 5 hours? These are the questions travellers ask and the answers are relatively easy. All distances shown on signboards will be in kilometers. To convert roughly to miles, remember that 5 kilometers approximates 3 miles, 10 kilometers equals 6 miles, and 100 kilometers is roughly 60 miles.

For small distances, remember 5 centimeters equals 2 inches, 30 cm. equals 1 foot, and a meter and a yard are roughly equal.

Volumes and Weight: You will only need to know anything about volumes if you are buying gasoline or milk. Both are sold by the liter. It's close enough to equate a liter to an American quart, so there are roughly four liters in a gallon. Some knowledge of weight is useful in the market. For practical purposes a pound is approximately equal to half a kilogram, so cut your order in half if shopping by weight in Singapore or Malaysia.

Electricity: Voltages, amperages, and cycles are a total mystery to most people, so don't worry too much about that. What you need to know is that electric current is supplied at 220-230 volts. European and Australian appliances will work on this current, but American and Canadian ones will fry. Then there is the question of power outlets. The Malaysian and Singaporean systems resemble the British, so Australian and European appliances can not be plugged in without an adaptor. If all this sounds too hard, I agree. I recommend you leave all your electrical appliances at home and use what you can find in the local hotels. Many hotels will provide you with an iron and a hairdryer on request.

Money and Prices

While they were once interchangeable, because of different values for each currency, you now have to use only Malaysian ringgit in Malaysia and only Singaporean dollars in Singapore. That is a nuisance to visitors only spending a few days in each place, but there is nothing you can do about it. The Singaporean and Malaysian notes and coins look quite different, but fortunately they come in similar denominations, and they have the value clearly marked.

Coins in use in both Singapore and Malaysia have values of 1c, 5c, 10c, 20c, and 50c. In Singapore there is also a S$1 coin. Notes in both countries come in $1, $5, $10, $20, $50, $100, $500, and $1000 denominations. Singapore also has a $2 note. Brunei notes are interchangeable with Singapore currency, so you will occasionally see these being used.

Banking hours vary considerably through the region. In Singapore banks open from 10 A.M. to 3 P.M. on weekdays, and most are open on Saturdays between 11 A.M. and 4:30 P.M. Orchard Road branches of some banks also open Sundays from 9:30 A.M. to 3 P.M. In Sabah, Sarawak, Johor, Melaka, Negeri Simbilan, Pahang, Perak, Penang, Selangor, and the Federal Territory, the schedule is 10 A.M. to 3 P.M. Monday through Friday and 9:30 A.M. to 11:30 A.M. on Saturday. In Kedah, Perlis, Kelantan, and Terengganu, hours are 10 A.M. to 3 P.M. Saturdays through Wednesdays, and from 9:30 A.M. to 11:30 A.M. on Thursdays.

Exchange rates vary from time to time, but at the time of this writing, one U.S. dollar was worth about S$1.65 and M$2.60, an Australian dollar would buy about S$1.10 and M$1.80, a Canadian dollar S$1.30 and M$2.10, and a New Zealand dollar about S$0.90 and M$1.50.

It's a good idea to pick up a little overseas money before you leave home so that you can become familiar with it and also to check on the current exchange rates. Your travel agent or bank will help you with this. For those who don't take this advice, there are banks at the Singapore and Kuala Lumpur airports that will accept your home country money.

Most international credit cards are accepted in Singapore and Malaysia. As with your home country, there are fewer takers of plastic in the rural areas than in the cities, but even in Sabah and Sarawak you will find that American Express, Diners Club, MasterCard, and Visa are accepted in many hotels and some restaurants and shops.

Traveller's checks are accepted at banks, department stores, hotels, and some other outlets. The best exchange rate is obtained from banks and on most occasions the rate will be a few percentage points higher than it is for cash. Cash can be exchanged at private money changers and you will sometimes find that they will give a slightly better rate than the banks. They will certainly be quicker. Money changers often will not change traveller's checks.

Malaysia and Singapore prices have appeal. If you take the time, you can find accommodations, restaurants, and shopping items much cheaper than they are at home. But it doesn't happen automatically. Prices in some "tourist areas" are substantially higher than you will pay a kilometer away in the "local area." It just takes time and some effort to find these other places.

If saving money is a high priority, take public transportation, eat in local restaurants or at the hawker stalls, shop in the markets rather than the boutiques, and avoid anywhere that cries out "tourist." Duty-free shopping in Singapore and Malaysia has traditionally been one of the big attractions, and it is still a good value. Just compare before you buy and know what prices are back home.

Singapore and Kuala Lumpur regularly rate towards the bottom of Asian cities in cost surveys, and rural Malaysia is cheaper still, so don't be put off by stories of high prices. It's almost a case of paying what you want to pay. There are luxury and budget prices to suit most pockets.

Governmental Fiddle-Faddle

Passports and Visas: You'll need a passport to enter Malaysia and Singapore and get back into your own country. You should ask your travel agent, passport office, or post office for information about obtaining a passport.

Entry conditions into Singapore and Malaysia are different because each is an independent country and sets its own rules. In practice, however, there is little difference for most tourists who plan short-term visits. Visas are not needed to enter Singapore if you come from Australia, Bangladesh, Brunei, Canada, Hong Kong, Malaysia, the Netherlands, New Zealand, Sri Lanka, Switzerland, the United King-dom, or the United States. Nationals of many other countries do not require a visa if their stay is shorter than 90 days. These countries include Austria, Belgium, Denmark, France, Germany, Italy, Japan, South Korea, Norway, Pakistan, Spain, and Sweden.

For Malaysia, most Commonwealth citizens (including Australians, New Zealanders, Canadians, British, and Singaporeans), and citizens of Ireland, Switzerland, the Netherlands, San Marino, and Lichtenstein do not need a visa. United States citizens do not require a visa for social or business visits. Nationals of many other countries do not require a visa for social or business visits not exceeding three months. These include Austria, Belgium, Denmark, Finland, France, Germany, Ireland,

Italy, Japan, Luxembourg, Norway, South Korea, Sweden, and Tunisia. Citizens of ASEAN countries do not need a visa for a visit not exceeding three months.

As regulations may change from time to time, it is worth checking with your travel agent or the nearest Singaporean or Malaysian tourist office or embassy at the time you are planning your trip.

Health: No health certificates are required for smallpox or cholera, but a yellow fever vaccination certificate is required if you are coming from an endemic zone. This includes most areas of tropical Africa and South America.

Both Malaysia and Singapore are considered to be malaria-free, but I strongly recommend you take some anti-malarial drugs if you are planning to go off the beaten track in Sabah or Sarawak. You should also take action to keep mosquitoes away from you—long-sleeve shirts, insect repellents, mosquito nets, and so on.

Drinking tap water in Singapore and the major Malaysian cities and towns is considered to be safe; at least the locals do it. In smaller places and particularly if you are staying in *kampungs* (Malay villages), I suggest that you ensure the water has been boiled. Remember that a visitor has less immunity to local problems than a local, so you should take more precautions.

Malaysia and Singapore both enjoy good standards of health care, and cleanliness is high on the priority list of each country. In the major cities you can safely eat in virtually any street food stall. If you need a doctor you will find that all the major hospitals have some excellent foreign-trained staff, and many private doctors (who are listed in the telephone book under medical practitioners) are also competent and, by North American standards, inexpensive.

Travel seems to give minor problems to some people and constipation or minor diarrhea are fairly common. This is partly induced by time zone changes, different water, and different food. In the tropics there are some other health problems that you should note. The tropical sun can be a hazard, so do not sunbathe between the hours of 11 A.M. and 3 P.M. unless you are well used to the outdoor life. Even when touring you should wear a hat, and drink more than normal so that you do not become dehydrated.

Everyone is susceptible to prickly heat, an itchy rash that often occurs on the buttocks; heat stroke, which is a serious condition caused when the body's heat-regulating mechanism breaks down; fungal infections, such as athlete's foot; and typhoid fever, cholera, and hepatitis, which are rare but extremely dangerous if not treated. Your local physician is best able to recommend precautions.

Customs: Most visitors will complete a customs form that allows them to pass through the "Nothing to Declare" gates at the Singapore or Kuala Lumpur airports. If you travel solely with the normal tourist or business articles, you should have no problem. It is still, however, wise to be aware of the customs requirements, because spot checks are made, and a false declaration is regarded very seriously by officials.

There are several items that are prohibited by both countries. These include controlled drugs, obscene materials, seditious and treasonable materials, and endangered species of wildlife and their by-products. You should avoid these at all costs. Penalties are severe.

Singapore allows duty-free concessions to travellers so you can bring personal effects, small quantities of food preparations (chocolates, etc.), 1 liter of spirits, 1 liter of wine, 1 liter of beer, and 200 cigarettes or the equivalent in cigars or tobacco into the country without payment of duty. As electronic and electrical goods, cosmetics, cameras, clocks, watches, jewelry, footwear, and arts and crafts are non-dutiable, you can also take these items in without a problem.

Malaysia has a much more restrictive list, but in practice I have not heard of any bona fide visitor having a problem with normal items. The official Malaysian duty-free concessions are: 1 liter of wine or spirits, 200 cigarettes, 100 matches, 3 pieces of wearing apparel, 1 pair of footwear, 1 unit of portable electric appliance for personal care and hygiene, small quantities of food preparations, small quantities of cosmetics and soap in open containers, and souvenirs and gifts not exceeding M$200. You should note that taped videocassettes require customs clearance. Any plants, seeds, insects, or soil must be declared to the customs officers.

Illegal Drugs: Severe penalties apply to drug abusers and traffickers in both countries. Possession can mean a long jail sentence and those caught with larger quantities can face a death sentence. Several foreigners have been executed in the last five years. The simple answer is *don't,* under any circumstances.

There have been stories about innocent travellers caught with drugs that were placed in their possession by "unknown persons." If these stories are true, you should carefully go through your belongings prior to entering or leaving each country, then ensure that you don't leave your bags anywhere that would allow others access to them.

Despite all the penalties, you may still be approached by trishaw drivers, street peddlers, and others in some parts of Malaysia. Don't even stop to listen to their story. Certainly under no circumstances should you accept anything from them—not even a name or address.

Other Laws to Note: It is an offense to litter in both Singapore and

Malaysia. One of the reasons Singapore is so clean is that the laws are rigidly applied. If you drop a piece of paper or a cigarette butt in the street, you face a fine of S$1000. In Malaysia it can be M$500. Singapore also has a law against pedestrians crossing a road within 50 meters of a pedestrian crossing, overhead bridge, or underpass. Break this law and you can be fined S$50.

The Singapore government is also waging a campaign against smoking in public places. It is now against the law to smoke in public buses, elevators, theaters, cinemas, government offices, restaurants, and air-conditioned shopping centers. The fine is S$500.

Airport and Departure Tax: You pay an airport tax of S$15 every time you depart from Singapore's Changi Airport. Coupons for the international departure tax can be purchased from hotels, airline offices, and travel agents.

In Malaysia the charges are: international flights—M$15; domestic flights—M$3; and Singapore flights—M$5.

Traveller's Guide

Safety: Singapore and Malaysia are countries where you should not worry about your safety. The streets in the major cities are much safer at night than many U.S. or European cities, and women can safely walk alone in most areas at any time of the day or night. After saying this, I will still recommend that you ask your hotel receptionist about local conditions just to be wise.

Female travellers should also be aware of the Muslim view of women that applies in some areas. Particularly on the east coast of peninsular Malaysia, women should be discreet in dress and behavior. I have received a few reports from women of minor harassment, particularly if they are travelling alone. Several travellers have reported that they have felt distinctly uncomfortable on the beach when a crowd has gathered to watch every move.

Business Hours: In Singapore, government offices open Monday through Friday from around 8 A.M. to 5 P.M., with a midday break for lunch. There is a very sensible policy of staggering office hours to reduce the morning and afternoon peak, so some staff start at 7:30 A.M. while others do not start until 9:30 A.M. Most government offices also work Saturday morning.

Shops also operate varying hours. Some are open from 9 A.M. to 6 P.M., and others are open from 10 A.M. to 9 P.M. Many operate seven days a week.

In Malaysia, government offices in Perlis, Kedah, Terengganu, Kelantan, and Johor operate Saturday to Wednesday from 8 A.M. to 12:45 P.M. and 2 P.M. to 4:15 P.M., and 8 A.M. to 12:45 P.M. on Thursday. Elsewhere the hours are Monday to Thursday 8 A.M. to 12:45 P.M. and 2 P.M. to 4:15 P.M., Friday 8 A.M. to 11:30 A.M. and 2:30 P.M. to 4:45 P.M. Shopping complexes are open 10 A.M. to 10 P.M. daily, while some small shops open 9 A.M. to 6 P.M.

Tipping: This is discouraged in hotels and restaurants that impose a service charge, and is not expected at local restaurants or eating stalls. It is totally banned at airports throughout Malaysia and Singapore. Please leave your own tipping practices at home.

Tourist Information: The Singapore Tourist Promotion Board (STPB) is a government agency established to develop and promote Singapore as a tourist destination and to look after the needs of tourists and other visitors to Singapore. It has its main office on the 36th floor of Raffles City Tower, 250 North Bridge Road, Singapore, but has two information centers that are designed specifically to help foreigners in Singapore. These are at

● Level 1, Raffles City Shopping Center, 250 North Bridge Road, Singapore. Hours are 8:30 A.M. to 6 P.M. daily. Tel: 330-0432.

● Level 2, Scotts Shopping Center, 6 Scotts Road, Singapore. Hours are 9:30 A.M. to 9:30 P.M. daily. Tel: 738-3778.

The STPB also has a number of offices worldwide that will provide much useful information about Singapore. These are the main offices in North America, Europe, and the South Pacific:

● 8484 Wilshire Boulevard, Beverly Hills, CA 90211, USA	Tel: 213-852-1901 Fax: 213-852-0129
● 590 Fifth Avenue, New York, NY 10036, USA	Tel: 212-302-4861 Fax: 212-302-4801
● 333 North Michigan Ave. Chicago, IL 60601, USA	Tel: 312-220-0099 Fax: 312-220-0020
● 175 Bloor St. East, North Tower, Toronto, M4W 3R8, Canada	Tel: 416-323-9139 Fax: 416-323-3514
● Carrington House, 126 Regent St., London WIR5FE, UK	Tel: 071-437-0033 Fax: 071-734-2191
● 2 Place du Palais-Royal, 75044 Paris Cedex 01, France	Tel: 01-4297-1616 Fax: 01-4297-1617
● Poststrasse 2-4 D-6000 Frankfurt/Main, Germany	Tel: 069-231-456 Fax: 069-233-924
● Hochstrasse 48 CH-8044 Zurich, Switzerland	Tel: 01-252-5454 Fax: 01-252-5303
● Westpac Plaza, 60 Margaret St., Sydney, Australia	Tel: 02-241-3771 Fax: 02-252-3586

- 16 St. George's Terrace,   Tel: 09-325-8578
  Perth 6000, Australia   Fax: 09-221-3864
- Dataset House, 143 Nelson Street, Tel: 09-358-1191
  Auckland 1, New Zealand   Fax: 09-358-1196

The **Malaysia Tourism Promotion Board (MTPB)** serves a similar purpose in Malaysia. It has a head office in Kuala Lumpur and regional offices in several centers in Malaysia. In Kuala Lumpur there are several tourist information centers as well. Here are the main offices within Malaysia.

- Head Office, World Trade Center,   Tel: 03-293-5188
  Jalan Tun Ismail, 50480 K.L.   Fax: 03-293-5884
- Information complex,   Tel: 03-243-4929
  109 Jalan Ampang, 50450
  Kuala Lumpur
- 2243 Tingkat Bawah,   Tel: 09-621-433
  J.S. Zainal Abidin,
  20000 Kuala Terengganu
- 10 J.T. Syed Barakbah,   Tel: 04-619-067
  10200 Pulau Pinang
- Kompleks Tun Razak,   Tel: 07-223-590
  J. Wong Ah Fook,
  80000 Johor Bahru
- Wing On Life Bld. J. Sagunting,   Tel: 088-248-698
  88000 Kota Kinabah, Sabah
- AlA Bld. J. Song Thian Cheok,   Tel: 082-246-575
  93100 Kuching, Sarawak

The MTPB has a network of offices worldwide to help people plan and execute a visit to Malaysia. These are the main offices in North America, Europe, and the South Pacific.

- 818 West Seventh St.,   Tel: 213-689-9702
  Los Angeles, CA 90017, USA   Fax: 213-689-1530
- 830 Burrard Street,   Tel: 604-689-8899
  Vancouver BC, V6Z2K4, Canada   Fax: 604-689-8804
- 57 Trafalgar Square,   Tel: 01-930-7932
  London WC 2N 5DU, UK   Fax: 01-930-9015
- Rossmark 11, 6000   Tel: 069-283-782
  Frankfurt Am Main, Germany   Fax: 069-285-215
- 29 Rue des Pyramides,   Tel: 4297-4171
  75001 Paris, France   Fax: 4297-4169
- 65 York Street, Sydney 2000,   Tel: 02-299-4441

Australia   Fax: 02-262-2026
- 56 William Street, Perth 6000,   Tel: 09-481-0400
Australia   Fax: 09-321-1421

Embassies and Consulates: Singapore and Kuala Lumpur are very much international cities, and as capitals they are home to representatives of the world's governments. There are also some consular representatives in Penang, Kota Bharu, Kuching, and Kota Kinabah, and some of these are noted in those individual chapters.

The following foreign missions are in *Singapore*.

Argentina—Tong Bld., 302 Orchard Road	Tel: 235-4231
Australia—25 Napier Road	737-9311
Austria—Shaw Center, 1 Scotts Road	235-4088
Bangladesh—United Square, 101 Thomson Road	255-0075
Belgium—International Plaza, 10 Anson Road	220-7677
Brazil—Tong Building, 302 Orchard Road	734-3435
Britain—Tanglin Road	473-9333
Brunei—7A Tanglin Hill	474-3393
Bulgaria—Thong Teck Building, 15 Scotts Road	737-1111
Canada—IBM Towers, 80 Anson Road	225-6363
Chile—The Octagon, 105 Cecil Street	223-8577
China—70 Dalvey Road	734-3273
Cyprus—6 Kung Chong Road	474-8473
Denmark—United Square, 101 Thomson Road	250-3383
Egypt—75 Grange Road	737-1811
Finland—United Square, 101 Thomson Road	254-4042
France—5 Gallop Road	466-4866
Germany—Far East Center, 545 Orchard Road	737-1355
Greece—Anson Center, 51 Anson Road	220-8622
Honduras—10 Anson Road	227-2170
Hungary—United Square, 101 Thomson Road	250-4424
India—31 Grange Road	737-6777
Indonesia—7 Chatsworth Road	737-7422
Ireland—Liat Towers, 541 Orchard Road	732-3430
Israel—58 Dalvey Road	235-0966
Italy—United Square, 101 Thomson Road	250-6022
Japan—16 Nassim Road	235-8855
Korea (North)—7500A Beach Road	299-1650
Korea (South)—United Square, 101 Thomson Road	256-1188
Malaysia—301 Jervois Road	235-0111
Myanmar—15 St. Martin Drive	235-8704

Netherlands—Liat Towers, 541 Orchard Road	737-1155
New Zealand—13 Nassim Road	235-9966
Norway—Hong Leong Building, 16 Raffles Quay	220-7122
Pakistan—20A Nassim Road	737-6988
Panama—16 Raffles Quay	221-8677
Papua New Guinea—11 Dhoby Ghaut	336-7677
Peru—Edale Block, 7 Brookvale Drive	467-0497
Philippines—20 Nassim Road	737-3977
Poland—Shaw Towers, 100 Beach Road	294-2513
Romania—48 Jalan Harom Setangkai	468-3424
Russia—51 Nassim Road	235-1834
Saudi Arabia—10 Nassim Road	734-5878
Spain—4 Shenton Way	227-8310
Sri Lanka—Goldhill Plaza, 51 Newton Road	254-4595
Sweden—PUB Building, 111 Somerset Road	734-2771
Switzerland—1 Swiss Club Link	468-5788
Thailand—370 Orchard Road	737-2644
Turkey—20B Nassim Road	732-9211
U.S.A.—30 Hill Street	338-0251

The following is a list of the foreign missions in *Kuala Lumpur.*

Argentina—3 Jalan Semanta, 2 Damansara Heights	Tel: 255-0176
Australia—6 Jalan Yap Kwan Seng, 50450	242-3122
Austria—MUI Plaza Building, Jalan P. Ramlee	248-4277
Bangladesh—204-1 Jalan Ampang, 50450	242-3271
Belgium—12 Lorong Yap Kwan Seng, 50450	248-5733
Brazil—22 Persiaran Damansara Endah, 50490	254-8020
Brunei—Plaza MBF, Jalan Ampang 50450	261-2800
Canada—MBF Plaza, 172 Jalan Ampang	261-2000
China—229 Jalan Ampang, 50450	242-8495
Czechoslovakia—32 Jalan Mesra, 55000, off J. Damai	242-7185
Denmark—Bangunan Angkasa Raya, 123 Jalan Ampang	241-6088
Egypt—28 Lingkungan u Thant, off J. U Thant	456-8184
Fiji—Wisma Equity, 150 Jalan Ampang	242-8422
Finland—Plaza MBf. Jalan Ampang 50450	261-1008
France—192 Jalan Ampang 50450	248-4122
Germany—3 Jalan U Thant 55000	242-9666
India—Wisma Selangor Dredging, 142C Jalan Ampang	261-7000
Indonesia—233 Jalan Tun Razak 50400	984-2011
Iran—1 Lorong U Thant	451-8424

Iraq—2 Jalan Langgark Gold, off J. Tun Razak	248-0555
Ireland—Straits Trading Bldg., 4 Leboh Pasar Besar	298-5111
Italy—99 Jalan U Thant	456-5122
Japan—11 Persiaran Stonor, off J. Tun Razak	242-7044
Korea (North)—11A Jalan Delima	984-7007
Korea (South)—Wisma MCA	262-2377
Kuwait—229 Jalan Tun Razak	984-6033
Libya—6 Jalan Madge, off Jalan U Thant	248-2112
Luxembourg—12 Lorong Yap Kwan Seng	248-5733
Myanmar—5 Taman U Thant 1, 55000	242-3062
Netherlands—4 Jalan Mesra, off Jalan Ampang	242-6844
New Zealand—193 Jalan Tun Razak	248-6422
Norway—Bangunan Angkasaraya, Jalan Ampang	243-1044
Oman—24 Lingkungan U Thant	457-5011
Pakistan—132 Jalan Ampang	241-8877
Papua New Guinea—1 Lorong Ru Kedua, off Jalan Ampang	457-4203
Philippines—1 Changkat Kia Peng 40540	248-4233
Poland—495, 4½ mile Jalan Ampang	457-6733
Romania—114 Jalan Damai, off Jalan Ampang	2 12-3072
Russia—5 Lorong Damai	241-5214
Saudi Arabia—7 Jalan Kedondong, off J. Ampang Hilir	457-9433
Singapore—209 Jalan Tun Razak	261-6277
Spain—200 Jalan Ampang 50450	248-4868
Sri Lanka—18 Lorong Yap Kwan Seng	242-3094
Sweden—Wisma Angkasa Raya, 123 Jalan Ampang	248-5981
Switzerland—16 Persiaran Madge, 55000	248-0622
Thailand—206 Jalan Ampang, 50450	248-8222
Turkey—118 Jalan U Thant, 55000	457-2225
United Kingdom—185 Jalan Ampang, 50450	248-2122
U.S.A.—376 Jalan Tun Razak, 50450	248-9011
Vietnam—4 Persiaran Stonor, 50450	248-4036
Yugoslavia—300 Batu 4½, Jalan Ampang	456-4561

Visit the Region

Singapore and Malaysia are well placed to be a base for further Asian touring. Malaysia Airlines serves 20 Asian cities outside Malaysia, so there is no problem in combining some of these with your visit to Malaysia. Visitors should be aware that they will require visas to enter some of these countries and it can take several days to have these

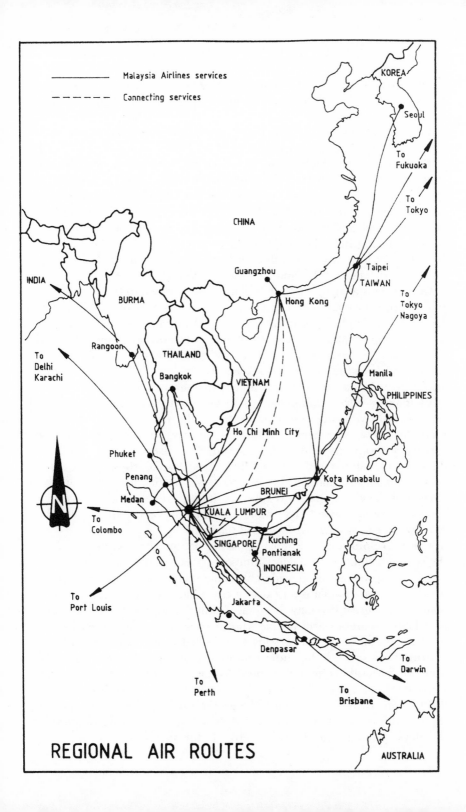

Malaysia Airlines services

Connecting services

REGIONAL AIR ROUTES

issued. You should obtain as many of these as possible before you leave home, or allow a week in Kuala Lumpur before you wish to travel to a country requiring a visa.

You could consider including one or more of the following in your Singapore and Malaysian vacation.

Thailand borders Malaysia to the north and Malaysia Airlines flies to Bangkok, Phuket, and Had Yai. Visitors can freely cross the border for tourist purposes and this destination is sufficiently different to add considerably to any vacation. There are some beautiful beaches, islands, and spectacular scenery in the south, and lovely mountain country with fascinating hill-tribe people in the north. Bangkok, the capital, is a booming, exciting city quite different from Singapore or Kuala Lumpur. For more details on Thailand, see the *Maverick Guide to Thailand.*

Indonesia is a string of 13,000 islands once known to the West as the fabled Spice Islands. The capital, Jakarta, is situated on the island of Java, a fertile land of live volcanoes, misty mountains, paddy fields, and ancient temples. Major tourist development has occurred on the island of Bali, where a succession of festivals, dances, gentle people, handicrafts, and breathtaking beaches keep visitors happy. Malaysia Airlines also flies to Medan in Sumatra, and Pontianak in Kalimantan.

Vietnam is encouraging tourists to visit, but opportunities are still limited. Most visits are restricted to the southern city of Ho Chi Minh, formerly known as Saigon. All visitors require visas and these may be refused without any reason being given. Tour arrangements are handled by the state-run Vietnam Tourism. Despite these difficulties, Vietnam is an unusual and fascinating travel destination, reflecting an ancient history and great creative traditions, and with an interesting French colonial period. For more information on Vietnam, see the *Maverick Guide to Vietnam, Laos, and Cambodia.*

The Philippines is an English-speaking nation where visitors can see the strong influence of Malay, Chinese, Spanish, and American periods of history as well as the considerable achievements of the modern independent nation. Manila is an exciting city, while the archipelago of 7000 islands has a great diversity of ethnic, cultural, and geographic features. The Filipinos are a warm people who welcome visitors and their love of music, color, dancing, and partying ensures that visitors have a great time.

Brunei is a small, independent country surrounded by the Malaysian state of Sarawak. The population is made up of Malays, Chinese, Europeans, and local tribal people, and the major industry is oil production. Brunei lays claim to being the world's richest country per capita. Although it is not recognized as a major tourist destination, a few days in Brunei can be very enjoyable for any visitor.

3

The Land and Life of Singapore

For a country that has only 626 square kilometers (240 square miles) of land area, Singapore has made a remarkably big splash on the world scene.

The country consists of the island of Singapore and some 58 islets within its territorial waters. The main island is about 42 kilometers long and 23 kilometers at its widest part. It has a coastline of about 140 kilometers.

Singapore is about 135 kilometers (80 miles) north of the equator, closer than any other city in Asia. Its immediate neighbors are Malaysia to the north and east, and Indonesia to the east, west, and south. It is linked to peninsular Malaysia by a 1000-meter-long causeway that carries a road, a railway, and a water pipeline across the Straits of Johor.

The main island can be roughly divided into three regions. The central hilly area of igneous rock, which appears in such places as Bukit Timah (Timah Hill) and Bukit Panjang, is perhaps the most interesting to the visitor. Then there is the western region of sedimentary rocks that forms a series of low hill-lines and valleys northeast of Jurong. Finally there is the relatively flat eastern region of sand and gravel deposits that extends from the northeastern edge of the central city all the way to Changi in the east.

Singapore's northern edge along the Straits of Johor is a collection of

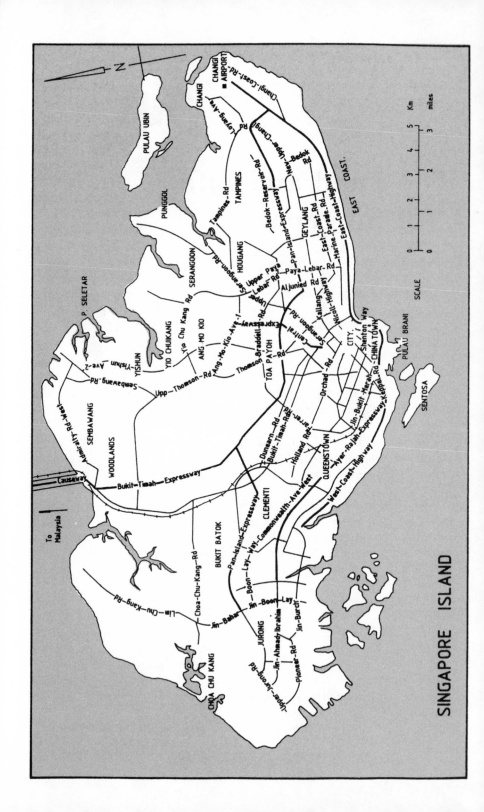

SINGAPORE ISLAND

mangrove swamps, low-lying beaches, and patches of scrub and jungle. In contrast, the southern coastline is either man-made or man-improved with a series of beaches, parks, wharves, container terminals, and industrial estates.

Hot, Wet, and Sticky

When it rains in Singapore, it really rains. None of this drizzle or mist that you get in some parts, but real downpours that wet you to the skin and wash everything else bright and clean. It can rain anytime of the year.

The annual rainfall is around 2.4 meters (about 95 inches) and most of it occurs in sudden showers. The wettest months are November to January during the first half of the northeast monsoon season, but be prepared for rain at any time. Thunderstorms with spectacular lightning displays are frequent during April, May, October, and November.

When it's not raining, it's hot. The average daily temperature is 26.6 degrees C. (80 F.) with a mean maximum of 30.7 degrees C. (87 F.) and mean minimum of 23.8 degrees C. (75 F.). Relative humidity often exceeds 90 percent at night, and the average daily humidity is a sticky 84.5 percent. The humidity makes the temperatures seem hotter than they are.

Singapore is not in the cyclone (typhoon) belt, so wind speeds are usually light. This further aggravates the feeling of heat and humidity. Late on a still-humid afternoon, most visitors seek refuge in an air-conditioned lounge, with a long, cool drink.

The People

Singapore's three million people live under the banner of "many races, one people," as the government carefully tries to weave the fabric of Singapore's society from many multicultural threads. While most Singaporeans have a strong sense of national pride, they also have cultural roots that stretch to China, India, Malaysia, and Europe.

The Chinese constitute 76 percent of the population, Malays 15 percent, Indians 6.5 percent, and other ethnic groups the remaining 2.5 percent. The history of how these nationalities contributed to the development of Singapore, is a fascinating story, and we touch on it in the next chapter.

The Chinese: The first junk from Amoy, China, arrived in 1821 and since that time the Hokkiens from Fukien province have been the major Chinese group in Singapore. They were soon followed by other

One of the few sections of modern-day rural Singapore. (Courtesy of the Singapore Tourist Promotion Board)

The Singapore skyline with the Central Business District and the Singapore River.

groups, each of whom clanned together in certain districts, and specialized in particular trades. Many Chinese also came from Malacca where "Straits Chinese" had been settled for a hundred years.

Most Chinese were humble, anonymous laborers and craftsmen and most remained so, but there were a few rags-to-riches stories that led to the rise of influential businessmen, property owners, and later, politicians.

In the mid and late 1800s, the Chinese community was a violent place. Secret clan societies grew strong and the rivalry brought bloody clashes. Opium, gambling, and prostitution were major elements in early Singapore, as Chinese without families and with growing affluence sought a relief from work.

The 1800s saw flamboyant characters emerge like Hoo Ah Kay, or Whampoa as he was called. He built one of Singapore's finest homes at the time, gave fabulous dinner parties, acted simultaneously as consul for Russia, China, and Japan, and was decorated by Queen Victoria. Later, merchants like Lee Kong Chian were equally successful. Lee landed barefoot in Singapore and through sheer hard work became a rubber magnate, and chancellor of Singapore University.

The Chinese have contributed much to the unique Singapore lifestyle from the Confucian morals to the vast range of regional cuisines. You see it too in art forms as diverse as intricate cloisonné, and elegantly simple calligraphy.

Singapore has mellowed with age but much of the old influence remains. For centuries, the Chinese have believed in ghosts, spirits, and multiple gods; and today there is still widespread belief in the powers of the gods, and an unwavering faith in old herbal remedies and the word of the priest.

The Malays: Singapore's second largest ethnic group were the ones who were here first. The Malays are mainly Muslims and they take their strict religious teachings and traditional values very seriously.

A century ago most of Singapore's Malays lived in *kampungs* (villages) of timber houses built on stilts. Each family would share fruit trees, chicken coops, and vegetable gardens with others in the village. Life was open, communal, and easy.

Today most of the *kampungs* have gone and many Malays have melted into the mainstream of Singapore life. Many now live in high-rise apartments, rubbing shoulders with non-Muslims in the work and home environment. Some work hard at being Singaporean rather than Malay and this sometimes causes a conflict with the older generation.

Despite this, you will see a definite "Malayness" about Singapore. Some women still wear traditional dress and in some areas of the city the sounds and smells are purely Malay. While English is the language

Stately Alkaff Mansion provides fine food in luxurious surroundings.

Nineteenth-century glamour with modern shopping and dining at the Festival Market.

of industry, commerce, and tourism, Bahasa Malaysian is still the official language of Singapore, and the national anthem is sung in Malay.

The Indians: If a first-time visitor were driven straight from the airport to Serangoon Road, he could be forgiven if he thought he had arrived in Madras, India.

From 1825, the British brought in large numbers of Indian laborers and prisoners to drain swamps, construct roads and bridges, and erect public buildings. They were quickly followed by clerks, teachers, traders, and money lenders. Many brought Hinduism with them so today you can see the elaborate temples and hear the music of their faith.

A second wave of immigrants arrived late in the century when it was discovered that rubber trees were a license to print money if they could find people prepared to work in the tropical heat for low wages. The Tamils from South India were the answer and many of the tappers have since stayed on in Singapore.

Much of the classical Indian culture can still be seen in Singapore, but hand in hand with this are the young professionals whom you will meet in the gleaming hotels and office buildings, and the policemen, security guards, and bus drivers who help in keeping the Singapore machine oiled and running.

The Europeans: The European community includes families descendant from Singapore's British colonial pioneers, as well as Jews, Armenians, and others from many countries around the world.

A look at a Singapore map reveals the diversity of her European pioneers. British, Americans, Belgians, Dutch, French, and Portuguese are all remembered in street names and localities.

Today's Europeans have either taken Singaporean citizenship or are working here as "expatriate" visitors on contract.

A subgroup of importance are the Eurasians—some part English, Dutch, Portuguese, but also part Chinese, Malay, Indian, Filipino, or Thai. Physically some of these people are stunning, while culturally they are almost impossible to classify.

While it may be possible to categorize the population on paper, in practice the distinctions blur and the emerging Singaporean can be white, tan, or dark brown. The future of Singapore is its people and they share a destiny shaped by a common purpose. "Many races, one people" has almost become a reality in modern Singapore.

The Government

Singapore has a president as constitutional head of state and an elected parliament to govern the country. Parliament has a maximum

The future of Singapore lies with its well-educated young people.

life of five years from the date of its first sitting. Every citizen 21 years of age or older is, subject to certain qualifications, eligible for election to parliament. Voting is compulsory.

The president of the Republic of Singapore is elected by parliament for a term of four years. The president in turn appoints as prime minister, the member of parliament who commands the confidence of the majority of the members of that body.

Since 1959, the People's Action Party (PAP) has been firmly in charge of parliament, and this is still the case. There are currently 82 members of parliament and 80 are members of the PAP.

Sittings of parliament are presided over by the speaker who is elected by parliament from among its own members. During sittings, members may speak in Malay, Mandarin, Tamil, or English and simultaneous interpretation is provided. Sittings are open to the public.

One unusual aspect of government is the Presidential Council for Minority Rights. This consists of a chairman, not more than ten members appointed for life, and not more than ten other members each appointed for three years. When bills have been passed by parliament they are required to be submitted to the council before they are presented to the president. The council's function is to draw attention to any bill or legislation, which in its opinion will be disadvantageous to any racial or religious group. In this way, minority interests are safeguarded.

The government operates through 14 ministries that employ about 64,000 people. The Ministry of Education, Ministry of Health, and Ministry of Home Affairs are by far the largest departments, employing about 75 percent of the total.

The Economy

Someone once remarked that Singapore had no resources other than human. There is much truth in this statement and it is certainly amazing to many that Singapore has been economically so successful. But anyone who looks a little deeper will see that Singapore's success is not just a matter of luck. Hard work, excellent government planning, and a natural entrepreneurial flair have steered the economy down a course that has resulted in spectacular growth and great stability.

During the late 1980s the Singapore economy expanded at an average rate of 10 percent a year. This also coincided with a change from manufacturing to financial and business services as the leading sector of the economy. Singapore is emerging as a major Asian financial market, and in some areas it is taking business away from Hong

Kong. There has been a large recent increase in the activities of banks and in the Asian Dollar Market, the stock market, the foreign exchange market, and in fund management.

About 140 different banks operate in Singapore with a total of 420 offices. Thirty-five of these have full licences and 13 are locally incorporated. In addition about 70 merchant banks are also in operation. The Development Bank of Singapore is the largest bank in the country. It is jointly owned by the Singapore government and private shareholders.

The Singapore foreign exchange market is the second largest in Asia after Tokyo. Turnover is growing at an amazing rate. The Stock Exchange of Singapore has shown similar growth.

Manufacturing industry was the prime catalyst for the remarkable growth in Singapore's economy during the 1970s and 1980s and it continues to be the area involving most investment, employment, and diversity.

Major sections of the industry are shipbuilding and overhaul facilities; electronic products and components such as computers, transistors, semi-conductors and printed circuit boards; fabricated metal products; electrical machinery; petroleum products; chemicals; and printing and publishing. All these sectors have enjoyed strong growth in recent years and up to 80 percent of the investment in these industries is foreign.

The government has established an Economic Development Board that is responsible for planning, developing, and promoting investment in manufacturing and related service industries. The board operates 17 international offices in the United States, Europe, Japan, and the Asia-Pacific to generate investor interest in Singapore and to service existing investors. It is currently focusing its efforts on the development of local small and medium enterprises that meet the technological, skill, and employment needs of Singapore's future economic development.

Although Singapore has a small area and high population density, the government attempts to ensure a regular supply of meat, eggs, fish, and vegetables for domestic consumption. The Primary Production department develops and manages agrotechnology parks, and carries out research and development work. The parks are leased to individuals and companies for livestock production, horticulture, freshwater fisheries, and marine prawn/fish breeding.

The rapid modernization and industrialization of Singapore has benefitted almost all segments of Singapore's population. In 1992 the unemployment rate ran at 2.3 percent, which in effect means full employment. The government, in fact, has difficulty getting sufficient labor in some occupations and allows Thais, Filipinos, and others to enter the country on contract employment permits.

Employees generally work a 44-hour week with one rest day, although in certain industries this has dropped to 40 hours and a 5½-day working week. The total labor force is around 1.3 million and about 0.2 million are members of trade unions.

Singapore is certainly not a socialist welfare state but it does have a contributory social service scheme that provides for a member's retirement, home ownership, and health care needs. The scheme receives wide community support and is the cornerstone of savings for most people. Both the employer and employee contribute to the fund on a sliding scale depending on age. It is structured so that it encourages the continued employment of older workers.

While the scheme was originally set up to provide workers with financial protection in their old age, a significant component now is the ability to use accumulated funds to buy a government apartment or private residence, to pay hospitalization expenses, to invest in approved shares and unit trusts, and to purchase non-residential properties.

It is a form of compulsory saving that is benefitting the individual and the country in many ways.

Religion

Singapore has no state religion and its people enjoy total freedom of worship. The main religions are Islam, Buddhism, Christianity, Hinduism, and Sikhism. You will find places of worship and devotion of all these faiths in central Singapore. And there are organizations such as the Muslim Religious Council and the Singapore Buddhist Federation that attend to affairs of their particular faith.

A body called the Inter-Religious Organisation exists to promote good will among the leaders and followers of the different religions. It conducts multireligious services for some public and private functions and helps to promote harmony, peace, and goodwill within multilingual, multireligious, and multicultural Singapore.

Many Christian denominations are represented in the city, although only a small percentage of the population is Christian. The Anglican and Roman Catholic congregations have long-established cathedrals near Raffles City, but there are also significant numbers of Methodists, Presbyterians, Lutherans, Syrian Christians, Salvation Army, and Seventh Day Adventists.

Language

The official languages in Singapore are Malay, Chinese (Mandarin), Tamil, and English. Malay is the national language, but English is the language of administration and business.

There are three Chinese, two English, one Malay, and one Indian daily newspapers published in the city. The most famous of the papers is the English-language *Straits Times*, which commenced publication in 1845. In contrast, the afternoon *New Paper* only began publication in 1988.

Radio programs are broadcast in four languages through seven services. All stations operate FM services and some have AM and short-wave services as well. English language programs are found on Radio 1, Radio 5, and Radio 10. There is also a private cable service.

There are three television services. Channels 5 and 8 have programs in the four official languages including about 35 percent of local Singapore-produced programs. Channel 12 telecasts mainly in English.

Leisure

Singapore is a small country with only one land link to a neighbor, so it is not surprising that some Singaporeans feel restricted and in need of wider space. The government is aware of this problem and it has embarked on a program to develop cultural and recreational opportunities to help overcome this feeling.

It may come as a surprise to many that the Singapore government can say with confidence that there were 1600 activities in the 1990 cultural calendar. The truth is that it can speak with such authority because it controls and involves itself in most of these events. It categorizes each event into music, drama, dance, art exhibitions, and others. Drama events were the most numerous.

Most of the major events are directly organized by the Ministry of Community Development. There is now a Singapore music festival, a drama festival, and a dance festival. For some years there has been an annual Young People's Theatre and the Traditional Theatre Festival.

One of the most successful cultural organizations has been the Singapore Symphony Orchestra, which was formed about 14 years ago. As the only professional music body, it plays an active part in the musical life of the country. So too, does the National Theatre Trust although it no longer has a national theater to manage. It now promotes cultural programs and activities in Singapore and presents good quality shows by foreign and local artists.

In sports, the government has established the Singapore Sports

Council to promote sports and physical fitness and to develop and maintain public sports facilities. The council manages the National Stadium, the Singapore Indoor Stadium, 13 other stadia, a practice track, a swimming lagoon, and a collection of sports halls; swimming pools; fitness parks; netball, tennis, and squash courts; and numerous multipurpose fields.

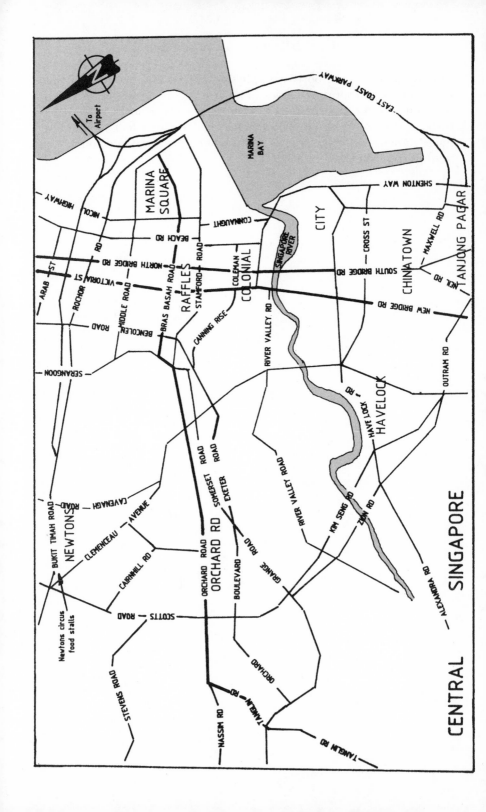

4

The Singaporeans—
Who and How?

It is extremely difficult to find accurate information about Singapore's early history. One of the first recorded references to the island is in a third-century Chinese book that describes it as "an island at the end of a peninsula."

It is assumed that the first residents of the island were *orang asli*—aboriginals who probably originally came from southern China. At some time these people were replaced by Malays, and it is likely that Chinese and Indian traders had contact with the island in the early centuries after the death of Christ.

Records of actual events in Singapore did not appear until about the fourteenth century and by this time the island was a small but flourishing center of trade. It had acquired the Javanese name of Temasek, or Sea Town, by the mid-fourteenth century, but control of the island swung between the Javanese, the Siamese, and the Indians. By the end of the fourteenth century its Sanskrit name, Singapura, or Lion City, was being commonly used.

Singapore became prominent about 1390 when Iskandar, a prince from Sumatra, was granted asylum on the island. He is said to have promptly murdered his host, the chieftain, and installed himself as the new ruler. He didn't last long, however, and was probably driven out by the Javanese forces of the Majapahit Empire. What is known with more certainty is that he fled north to Malaya and founded what eventually became Malacca.

Singapore was a Siam vassal state in the early fifteenth century but it was too remote for Siam to properly control, and the Malacca sultanate extended its authority over the island. After the Portuguese seizure of Malacca in 1511, the Malay admiral fled initially to Singapura, then he built a new capital at Johor Lama close by on peninsular Malaya. The Portuguese destroyed Johor Lama in 1587 and then in 1613 reported burning down a Malay outpost at the mouth of the river. That was the end of Singapore for 200 years.

Sir Stamford Raffles

The major European powers had control over much of south and southeast Asia by the eighteenth century. The Dutch had ousted the Portuguese and represented a major presence in the East Indies, while the British exercised control of India and were expanding their trade with China.

With the Spanish firmly in command of the Philippines and the French becoming increasingly troublesome in Europe, the stage was set for a clash of powers. In 1818 the British saw the need of a halfway house to refit, stock, and protect its merchant fleet operating from India to China. It would also forestall any further advance by the Dutch. Late that year, Lord Hastings, Governor-General of India, gave tacit approval to Sir Stamford Raffles to establish a trading station at the southern end of the Malay peninsula.

On January 29, 1819, Raffles landed on Singapore island and concluded a preliminary treaty with the territorial chief of the southern part of the Malay peninsula, Temeggong Abdu'r Rahman. A few weeks later he signed a somewhat doubtful formal treaty with Sultan Hussein of Johor.

Raffles held the position of Lieutenant-Governor of Bencoolen in Sumatra and could not remain in residence in Singapore, so he appointed Major William Farquhar as the first Resident of Singapore. Farquhar ordered the clearing of the jungle and the erection of buildings and soon the settlement gained a reputation as a bustling center of trade.

Raffles returned to Singapore in October 1822 and was disturbed to find that Farquhar had allowed the town to develop haphazardly. Raffles immediately appointed a committee to draw up development plans for the city. The north bank of the Singapore River was reserved for government building; an area on the southwest bank was allocated as a commercial area for merchants; land to the west of the river became Chinatown; and the Malay, Arab, and Indian populations were allocated sites for their settlements. The shape of modern Singapore was set and in fact all these sites still exist today.

Raffles left Singapore for the last time in June 1823. He returned to England in 1824 and died in 1826, at age 45.

The Straits Settlements

In 1824, Singapore's status as a British possession was formalized by two new treaties. Under the Anglo-Dutch Treaty, the Dutch withdrew all objections to British occupation of Singapore in return for the British handing over Bencoolen. The British then signed another treaty with Sultan Hussein and Temeggong Abdu'r Rahman, in which they received total ownership of the island in return for increased cash payments and pensions.

The first official census was held in 1824 and the 11,000 inhabitants included Malays, Chinese, Indians, Europeans, Armenians, and Arabs. Already Singapore multiculturalism was underway.

In 1826, Singapore, together with Malacca and Penang, the two British settlements in the Malay peninsula, became the Straits Settlements, under the control of British India. Not long afterwards, Britain withdrew the monopoly of the East India Company's trade with China. While this caused some initial consternation, there were many long-term benefits.

Early agricultural experiments had generally failed so Singapore remained very much a trade center. Boats arrived from throughout the Malay archipelago, from India and the Middle East, and from Siam and China. They brought tea, silk, ebony, ivory, pepper, rattan, cloth, opium, and nutmegs.

Many of the early inhabitants had come with plans to make quick money then return home, but by the mid-nineteenth century there was a feeling of permanency on the island. Chinese residents had opened up businesses. Indians arrived as laborers but often became traders. Prosperous Europeans built lavish houses on sprawling grounds. The Malays tended to suffer in comparison and remained as fishermen, boatmen, or woodcutters. By 1860, Singapore's population was approaching 100,000.

A Crown Colony

The Straits Settlement was given a boost in 1867 when it became a Crown Colony, under the Colonial Office in London. The next few years saw dramatic development.

With the advent of the steamship and the opening of the Suez Canal in 1869, Singapore became a major port of call for ships plying between Europe and East Asia. A few years later, the director of the Singapore Botanic Gardens planted some rubber trees and thus started a huge industry. By the 1880s Singapore had become the world's main sorting and exporting center of the commodity.

Tin was being mined in Malaya and much of this was shipped through Singapore. By 1903, Singapore had become one of the world's ten most important ports. Raffles' little settlement had arrived.

Population growth continued. By now the Chinese clearly outnumbered all other races combined. A new generation of Chinese who had been born in Singapore had emerged. Because there was still a chronic shortage of Chinese women, many of these young Chinese married Malays, or at least had some relationship with female Malays. They became known as Straits Chinese or Babas, and incorporated Malay food, fashion, and culture in their life-styles.

The Babas became a significant force in the colony and in 1900 formed the Straits Chinese British Association. This became a stabilizing force as it maintained good relations with the British, and gave the Chinese a forum in which to air their views. The Babas, as British subjects, preferred to speak English, and acquired a taste for British culture, sports, and civic institutions.

By 1911, the population had passed 250,000 and this period saw electric light introduced, cars become a common sight, new hospitals and schools opened, and a concentration on the "good life." There was also the first signs of discontent in the local Asian population.

Japanese Occupation

More than 100 years of peace and prosperity came to an end when Japanese aircraft bombed the city on December 8, 1941. At the same time a large Japanese force landed in North Malaya and started a march south. The Japanese met only limited resistance and quickly established air superiority.

On February 15, 1942, after a short resistance by the British forces and local volunteers, Singapore fell to the Japanese forces. For three and a half years the country (renamed Syonan, "Light of the South") suffered enormously under the Japanese occupation.

The Japanese immediately made all Europeans military prisoners and civilian internees. All Chinese males were ordered to report to registration centers where they were imprisoned and "cleansed" of

Western influence. Those who were well dressed or could write their names in English were singled out and many were executed.

Schools were reopened and children were forced to attend. Each day started with the pupils facing towards Japan and singing the Japanese national anthem. Compulsory classes were held in the Japanese language and Singapore clocks were synchronized to match Tokyo time.

As the occupation progressed, Singapore's once prosperous economy collapsed. There was chronic inflation and food shortages. Many people died from hunger and malnutrition, and morale sank to an all-time low. The prison camps that continued to hold many Europeans became infamous for their brutality and appalling conditions. The worst was Changi Prison where hundreds died.

But the end was near for Japan. The Japanese surrendered to allied forces on August 21, 1945, and the Japanese commander formally surrendered the island to Britain's Admiral Lord Mountbatten in September of that year.

Self-Government

British forces occupied Singapore until March 1946 while Singapore came under the British Military Administration. On April 1, 1946, the administration ended, the Straits Settlements was dissolved, and Singapore became a separate British Crown Colony.

Constitutional powers were initially vested in the governor who had an advisory council of officials and non-officials. This evolved into separate executive and legislative councils in July 1947. Provision was made for the election of six members of the legislative council and Singapore's first election was held on March 20, 1948.

At the same time, the Communist Party of Malaya made a bid to take over Malaya and Singapore by force. A state of emergency was declared that lasted for 12 years. In 1954, proposals made by a commission under Sir George Rendel were accepted, and these formed the basis of a new constitution giving Singapore a greater measure of self-government.

The 1955 election saw the realization of a flurry of political activity. The election was won by the Labor Front, and flamboyant lawyer David Marshall became Singapore's first Chief Minister in a coalition government of his own Labor Front, the United Malays National Organisation, and the Malayan Chinese Association. The election was also significant because the newly formed People's Action Party, which had fielded four candidates, won three seats.

Marshall resigned in 1956 in a disagreement with Britain over full internal self-government and was replaced by his deputy, Lim Yew

Hock. Lim lead a mission to London and succeeded in obtaining the main terms of a new Singapore constitution. Self-government was attained in 1959 and Singapore's first general election was held to choose 51 representatives to the first fully elected legislative assembly. The People's Action Party won 43 seats with 53 percent of the total vote.

The governor, Sir William Goode, proclaimed the new constitution and became the first Head of State. The first government of the State of Singapore was sworn in on June 5, with Lee Kuan Yew as Prime Minister. While this obviously was a big moment for the People's Action Party, it was seen by the prime minister as just a step towards merger with the newly independent state of Malaya and full independence for Singapore.

The People's Action Party had come to power in a united front with the Communists but it was an uneasy alliance. It soon became clear that the objectives of each were quite different. In the case of the moderate PAP, it was to obtain full independence for Singapore as part of a non-Communist Malaya. The Communists, however, were aiming for a take-over of Singapore. In 1961, the alliance split with the Communists forming a new political party. For the Communists, it was the beginning of the end.

A Nation Is Born

In 1961, the Malayan Prime Minister, Tunku Abdul Rahman, proposed closer political and economic cooperation between the Federation of Malay, Singapore, Sarawak, North Borneo, and Brunei. A 1962 referendum in Singapore overwhelmingly supported the proposal and on September 16, 1963, Malaysia was formed consisting of the Federation of Malaya, Singapore, Sarawak, and North Borneo (now Sabah). At the last moment, oil-rich Brunei refused to join.

The creation of Malaysia was the signal for problems to emerge. The Philippines laid claim to Sabah, Indonesia laid claim to the whole area, and the local Communists set about a campaign of destabilization. The most serious threat came from Sukarno-lead Indonesia. Indonesian forces crossed the borders from Kalimantan (Indonesia Bornea) into Sarawak and Sabah, and landings were made in Singapore and peninsular Malaysia. A three-year "confrontation" began.

Within Malaysia problems had also emerged. The British had attempted to ensure that Malaysia would have a majority of Malays in the population and although this had occurred, it was clear that the Chinese controlled the economy. In Malaya, the Malays held a privileged position but Singapore refused to extend this situation to Malays in Singapore. With growing disagreement between Singapore and the Malay-dominated parts of Malaysia, Singapore was forced out.

On August 9, 1965, Singapore became a sovereign, independent nation. International recognition followed quickly. It was admitted to the United Nations in September and became a member of the Commonwealth of Nations in October. In December, it became a republic with Yusof bin Ishak as the first president.

The Quest for Identity

With its political status finally determined, Singapore set about nation-building. A massive industrialization program was launched and an act of parliament was passed to promote industrial peace and discipline of the work force.

The British government made a sudden decision in 1967 to withdraw its armed forces from Singapore by the end of 1971. There was some initial consternation, but then Singapore set out to build its own defense forces. Compulsory national service was introduced, an Armed Forces Training Institute was established, and an Air Defense Command and a Maritime Command commenced. Singapore also concluded a Five-Power Defense Agreement with Malaysia, Britain, Australia, and New Zealand.

In 1967, Singapore joined Indonesia, Malaysia, the Philippines, and Thailand to form the Association of Southeast Asian Nations.

With its basic economic, defense, and trading relationships in place, Singapore looked inward. Education policies were modified by expanding technology and computer education, financial incentives were offered to industrial enterprises, and a productivity movement was launched. Public housing was given top priority and new towns established. While nearly 75 percent of the population was Chinese, the government continued to emphasize that all races were Singaporeans. A concerted attempt was made to treat all people equally when it came to housing, education, and health. Different races were quartered in the same housing blocks and shared schools, the work place, and shopping facilities.

The economic and social policies proved to be outstandingly successful. For year after year, Singapore recorded almost 10-percent annual growth. At the same time there was social harmony in the community. By the late 1970s, Singapore had become the second most prosperous country in Asia, with a stable government and a strong sense of democracy. Some concern was expressed by outsiders because the 1968 election brought about a one-party parliament when the People's Action Party won all seats. This achievement was repeated in 1972, 1976, and 1980 but by then most of the concern had gone. Since then it has continued to dominate at each election.

In much of the world, this apparent easy win would be highly suspicious but in modern Singapore it hardly raises any eyebrows. The reason appears to be that the government is seen as being highly successful, fair in its dealings with all races, and generally above corruption. That's not to say that it has been totally liberal. Soon after the country's independence, Lee Kuan Yew took action against radicals in his country with long periods of detention. In the 1970s, Singapore had strong policies against antisocial behavior, which extended to such things as males wearing their hair too long. Critics called these policies dictatorial campaigns but most had wide support within the community and fell within Lee Kuan Yew's declared intention to develop a tough country where enterprise, hard work, and social concern were the cornerstones of policy.

It is impossible to play down the role of Lee Kuan Yew in the development of Singapore and the creation of a national identity. He has firmly controlled the country's destiny for 30 years and despite his stepping down in late 1990 as Prime Minister of Singapore, it is generally conceded that he still has much authority.

I believe the judgment of history will see Lee as almost a unique figure in world politics. He left office as the world's longest-serving elected prime minister and the last of Asia's great post-colonial leaders. He started his career in a coalition with Communists, initially embraced socialism, then decided that enterprise and the operation of a free market were what Singapore needed. By hard work and shrewd planning, Lee was able to steer a whole nation in a new direction and at the same time build one of Asia's most dynamic economies from almost nothing. It was a great achievement.

The prime minister, Mr. Goh, is a new generation politician. He is too young to have taken part in pre-independence activity and has grown up through years of constant stable growth. He is a product of the new Singapore with its emphasis on academic achievement, economic growth, and social stability.

What is clear is that his country is well placed to meet the changes and challenges of the 1990s. From my discussions with Chinese, Malays, Indians, Filipinos, and Europeans in Singapore, I conclude that they all agree. There is no longer a need for a quest for identity—Singapore has indeed become "many races, one people."

5

Singapore Profile

1. The General Picture

Located at the southern tip of the Asian mainland, just a few kilometers from the equator, Singapore is an amazing island city-state. No one ever finds Singapore as he imagined it would be. It is unique.

When you touch down at Singapore's gleaming Changi Airport (now called Airtropolis), you will experience the luxury and efficiency of one of the world's best gateways. As you ride by bus or taxi towards the city, you will be surrounded by lush greenery unequalled by most other places in the world. Your first glimpse of the city skyline will remind you more of New York or Chicago than any mind pictures you may have of the East. A short sight-seeing tour will allow you to appreciate the refreshing cleanliness of this orderly and reassuringly safe city. The exuberance of Singapore's foliage and climate can envelope and over-power you by day, but at night the island air is velvety and balmy, a true tropical paradise.

But don't be fooled into believing you have come to grips with the complete Singapore. Certainly with its luxurious hotels, superb shopping centers, excellent communications and transportation, Singapore offers the visitor all the comforts of the West in a lush and exotic tropical setting. At the same time the Asian factor is alive and well with an interesting blend of Chinese, Malay, and Indian cultures; a constant round of colorful festivals; and an endless array of irresistible cuisines.

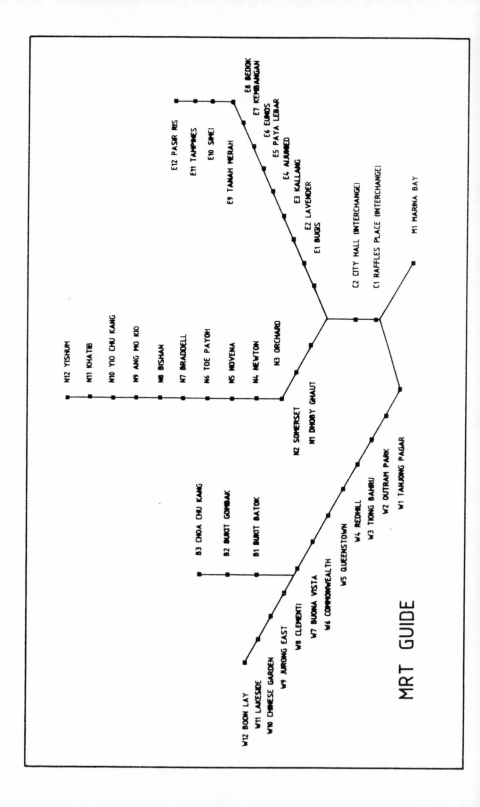

MRT GUIDE

It is not entirely sanitized, homogenized, and high-rise. Singapore fortunately still has a split personality.

In the late 1980s Singapore gained a reputation among some travellers as being boring. Perhaps the super organization and efficiency that existed did give that impression, but it was not true. If you take the time to dig below the surface, you will find all the variety you want. Nevertheless, the Singapore government took the criticism seriously and in the last few years there has been a concerted drive to increase the interests and attractions in the city. At the same time the mad rush to pull down the old and clean up every corner has halted—emphasis now is on restoration. It happened just in time.

Now many first-time visitors find that they have not left enough time to do all the interesting things that Singapore offers. Repeat visitors discover many new attractions that can provide days of fun and excitement. They also discover that Singaporeans are proud of their city-state, and enjoy the cosmopolitan interaction between locals and foreign visitors. Singapore indeed is a city for the civilized man or woman.

2. Getting There

Singapore's Changi Airport is widely regarded by many travellers as the most efficient and user-friendly facility in the world. The airport was opened in 1981 and since then has almost been in a constant state of expansion. It is built on land taken from the sea, a swamp, and a sleepy stretch of beach. Singapore has become a major world aviation hub with more than 15 million passengers using the terminal in 1992. That number is expected to continue to rise during the 1990s with Terminal 2, now giving the airport a passenger handling capacity of more than 20 million a year.

One of the major operational features of the terminals is the automated high-speed passenger transit system—the Changi Skytrain, which links the two terminals in one minute compared to a walking time of 15 minutes. The 100-passenger carpeted and air-conditioned trains operate at 1½-minute intervals from 6 A.M. to midnight then "on call" to passengers by the press of a button.

Singapore is served by more than 60 scheduled airlines with links to 55 countries. The country has two scheduled airlines—Singapore Airlines, which has a worldwide network of services to 37 countries, and Silkair, which was established as an air charter company but that now operates as a regional airline in southeast Asia.

While the Changi terminal complex is vast, it is not impersonal. Shops, banks, telephones, restrooms, lounges, bars, and so on are conveniently arranged and easy to find. There are several information desks with helpful personnel, and excellent signs in English clearly showing the way to customs, baggage areas, and city transportation. Free local telephone calls can be made from several centers, while there are facilities to make calls through your own country operator and charge on a collect basis.

The airline that you are travelling will determine whether you arrive at Terminal 1 or 2. Singapore Airlines, Swissair, Silkair, Air France, Myanmar Airways, Malaysia Airlines, Royal Brunei Airlines, Philippine Airlines, Finnair, and Olympic Airways use Terminal 2. All other flights are from Terminal 1. Both terminals have a garden-like setting that is the perfect introduction to the "Garden City."

Passing through Changi Airport is simple. Aircraft nose into landing bridges and passengers emerge into wide concourses with moving walkways that lead to a central spine. Arriving passengers descend by escalator to a large reception area decorated by waterfalls and orchids, before passing through immigration. There is a chance to make some duty-free purchases before you move into the baggage collection area. Large monitors inform you where baggage from specific flights can be found. It's not unusual to find your luggage enjoying a ride on the carousel by the time you reach it.

Most passengers will pass through the customs gates without interruption and then enter the public arrivals hall where there are banking, postal, hotel reservation, information, car rental, and telephone services. If you are meeting someone, large signs point to a public meeting area while other signs direct you to taxis, bus services, and the parking lot.

Transport from the airport to the city is by public bus (No. 390) or by taxi. The bus fare is S$0.90 (normal) and S$1.30 (air-conditioned). It takes about 45 minutes to the Orchard Road hotel area. A taxi will cost about S$16, including a S$3 surcharge that applies to all departures from the airport. The drive into the city along the tree-lined expressway, with the modern skyline and busy harbor as a backdrop, makes for a lasting favorable impression of the island.

Of course, not all passengers arrive by air. Singapore is one of the world's busiest ports and, while passenger shipping services are not numerous, there are regularly scheduled services from Indonesia and Thailand, and cruise ships visit from around the world. A modern cruise terminal has recently opened at Singapore's World Trade Centre providing aerobridge links to the air-conditioned arrival and departure lounges. There are duty-free shops, modern baggage handling services, banking and telecommunication facilities, and restaurants and shops.

Then there are land arrivals. Although Singapore is surrounded by water, it is connected by road and rail with Malaysia via a causeway. There are several daily rail services from Kuala Lumpur, the Malaysian capital, and it is possible to travel by International Express all the way from Bangkok, Thailand.

Trains arrive at the Keppel Road railway station while long-distance buses from Malaysia arrive at the Lavender Street bus terminal.

3. Local Transportation

Singapore has one of the world's best transport networks. An excellent system of roads and expressways crisscross the main island while the Mass Rapid Transit system (MRT), and bus network, are outstanding.

The S$5 billion **MRT system** is Singapore's largest urban development project and one of the most technologically advanced railway systems in the world. The system extends to three corners of the main island and travels overland as well as underground. There are 42 stations along a 67-kilometer route with two main lines that interconnect at City Hall and Raffles Place stations.

The MRT offers a speedy and completely safe way of getting around the city but you should pick up the free guide book that's available from all MRT stations if you want to get the most from the system. There are single-trip tickets and stored-value tickets available. If you are staying for more than a few days in Singapore, the convenience of the stored ticket makes it a good buy.

You will need coins to buy your single-trip ticket from the ticket machines. There are machines that convert paper S$1 notes into S$1 coins. A list of destinations above the machines will tell you how much your journey will cost. You can feed the ticket machines the correct fare in coins, or insert dollar coins and receive a ticket and any change. You gain entry to the train area by "posting" your ticket into the barrier machine. Wait for it to reappear because you will need it to exit at your destination.

Escalators take you to the platform and train destinations are clearly marked. Trains operate about 18 hours daily and at peak periods there is a 3-4 minute service. All trains and underground stations are air-conditioned and spotlessly clean. It really is one of the best systems in the world.

After your trip, follow the exit signs and you will find yourself in the main concourse of the station. Here you "post" your ticket into the machine that operates the barrier. Each single ticket is time-coded so you are advised not to spend more than 30 minutes in addition to your

The Mass Rapid Transit (MRT) train makes travel in Singapore more comfortable, convenient, and fast.

travel time because your ticket can expire. There are station control rooms at every stop, should you lose your ticket or have other problems. Fares range from S$0.60 to S$1.50.

Buses are another transport option that you should try. The network is extensive and the view from the front seat on the upper level of the London-style buses is, to me, one of the best value rides in Asia. You can buy a copy of the Singapore Bus Guide for details of the bus routes and services. It is available from most bookshops as well as bus depots at a cost of S$0.70. Buses run from 6 A.M. to 11:30 P.M. and fares range from S$0.50 to S$1 for the normal non-air-conditioned services. There are a growing number of air-conditioned buses at a slightly higher charge. Note that bus drivers do not give change. The sights to be found on the buses reveal the true character of Singapore, which is far more colorful and refreshingly eccentric than its government might like to admit. If you want to see the "real" Singapore, don't ignore the buses.

If you are planning to squeeze all your sight-seeing into a few days, you should consider buying a one-day or three-day Explorer Bus Ticket. With this ticket you can travel anywhere on the island on any bus service operated by Singapore Bus Service (SBS)—the red and white buses—and Trans Island Bus Service (TIBS)—the orange and yellow buses. You can break your journey wherever you wish, make as many trips as you like, and not have to worry about the right fare or the right change. When you buy your ticket (they are available at most hotels), you will receive a bus map showing bus stops and major points of interest. Special signboards have also been erected at some stops showing nearby sight-seeing attractions.

The one-day ticket costs S$5 and the three-day ticket S$12. For more details, telephone 287-2727.

The following is a guide to a few selected bus services from the Orchard Road area, which is where most visitors will be staying.

To Changi Airport: Bus No. 390, Orchard Road.

To Jurong Bird Park: Bus No. 198 from Penang Road to Jurong Bus. Interchange then Bus No. 250 or 253 to Park.

To Chinatown: Bus No. 124, 143, 167, or 174 and alight at New Bridge Road, opposite People's Park.

To Clifford Pier: Bus No. TIBS 850.

To Sentosa Island: Bus No. 143 to World Trade Centre then cable car or ferry service.

To Zoological Gardens: Bus No. 171 from Scotts Road or Orchard Boulevard.

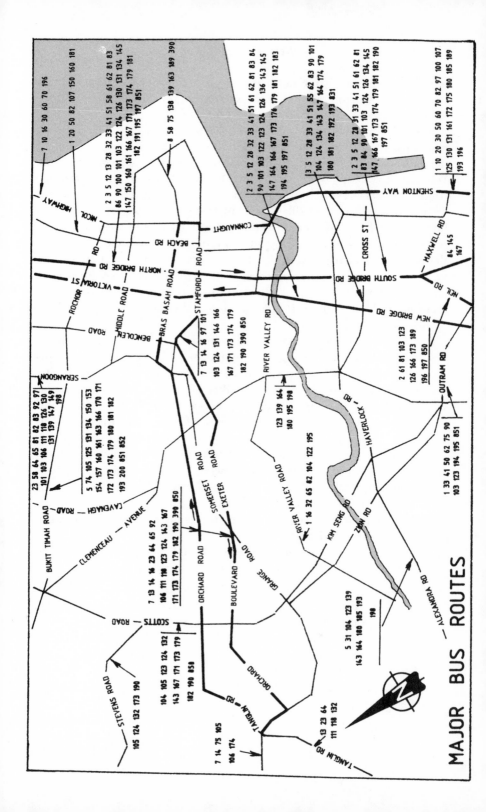

MAJOR BUS ROUTES

Taxis are plentiful (except when it is wet) and relatively inexpensive. Cabs are air-conditioned and all have meters that are used. Each taxi can carry a maximum of four adult passengers. Flag fall is S$2.20 for the first 1.5 kilometers or less, with S$0.10 for every subsequent 250 meters travelled. Every 45 seconds or less of waiting time is S$0.10. It's sometimes hard to hail a cab on the street, but they are readily available at hotels and taxi stands.

Before starting off, make sure the driver knows your exact destination and that the meter is flagged at S$2.20. When the trip is over, you're obliged to pay only the metered fare plus any of the following extras:

—a S$3 surcharge for trips from Changi Airport.

—a S$2 surcharge for calling a taxi by telephone.

—a S$3 surcharge for bookings exceeding 30 minutes in advance.

—a 50 percent surcharge on the metered fare for journeys made between midnight and 6 A.M.

—a S$1 surcharge for all trips departing the Central Business District between 4 P.M. and 7 P.M. Monday to Friday and 12 noon and 3 P.M. on Saturday.

—a S$3 surcharge for travelling into the Central Business District between 7:30 A.M. to 10:15 A.M. and 4:30 P.M. to 7 P.M. Monday to Friday and 7:30 A.M. to 10:15 A.M. on Saturday.

Almost all taxi drivers can speak English and I have found them to be honest and reasonably helpful. All taxis are numbered and any complaints or commendations can be made in writing to the Registry of Vehicles, Sin Ming Drive, Singapore. Taxi drivers do not expect to be tipped.

Trishaws still ply the streets of some areas of the city, but they are now mainly a tourist attraction for visitors. They are a remnant of the past and revive memories of the early 1900s when there were about 9,000 rickshaws on the island serving as taxis. After World War II, the rickshaw gradually gave way to the trishaw but today only about 500 registered drivers remain. You will see some in Chinatown, in Little India, and outside Raffles City.

Settle the price before you head off. Tell the driver where you want to go and he will quote you a price. Don't pay the first asking price. Negotiate a discount of about 25 percent. This will still be more than the locals would pay but it will be worth the cost.

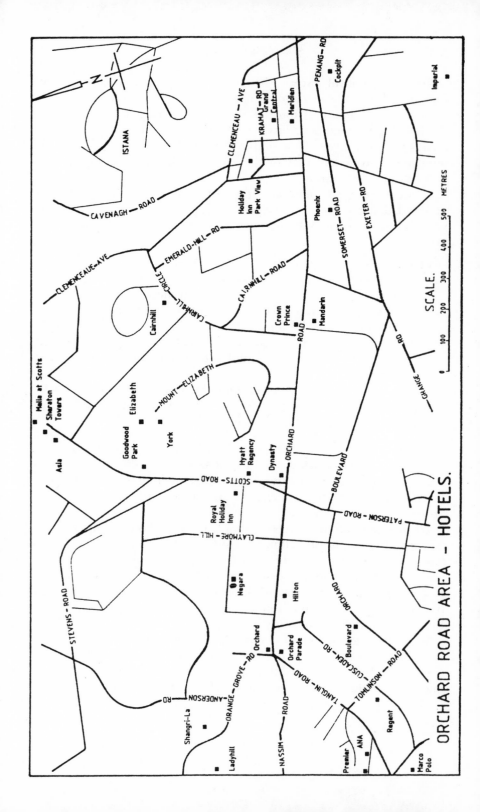

ORCHARD ROAD AREA - HOTELS.

4. The Hotel Scene

Singapore has hotels priced to suit every pocket. There are vast glass and marble palaces, hotels where ceiling fans stir up memories of bygone colonial splendor, hotels with tiny entrances and rooms that have known better days, and others where adequate facilities are matched by very reasonable prices.

Hotels are clustered primarily in two areas—Orchard Road, and Raffles City/Marina Square. Each of these areas has its particular attractions, but with Singapore's great transportation facilities, it is not difficult to get from one area to another.

Singapore has about 70 gazetted hotels with more than 50 rooms. Of these more than 25 are top-quality hotels and there are an equal number that aim for the upper midmarket clientele. Below this range, there is still reasonable choice but the total number of rooms in the lower midmarket and budget sections of the market are less than you would find in many other major cities. The following is a personal selection that is by no means complete but I believe you will be satisfied with these, once you decide which level of luxury you need.

EXPENSIVE HOTELS

Many people still consider the **Shangri-La Hotel Singapore** (Tel: 737-3644) to be the city's best business traveller's hotel and one of the best in the world. I say "still" because the hotel has held this reputation for close to 20 years and that is quite an achievement. In that time, the hotel has added two new sections and has been constantly upgrading facilities to match or surpass that offered at newer properties.

The charm of the Shangri-La Hotel is its position and its service. It is situated in a tranquil district, removed from the mainstream hustle and bustle, yet it remains a mere five-minute walk from Orchard Road. The hotel spreads across six hectares (15 acres) of lush, landscaped greenery in three wings—Tower, Garden, and Valley. It is an excellent choice for those looking for extensive amenities, peace, comfort, and a little excitement.

The hotel's extensive recreational facilities include a golf-putting green, tennis and squash courts, a health club, and indoor and outdoor swimming pools. Food and beverage outlets include the Coffee Garden; a 24-hour cafe; the delightfully situated outdoor Waterfall Cafe; the Restaurant Latour, which serves Continental food; the well-known and popular Shang Palace for Cantonese cuisine; and the Nadaman Restaurant for Japanese food. For entertainment, there's the Peacock Bar, the Lobby Court, and the Xanadu Discotheque.

The lobby of a luxury hotel in Singapore.

Inn of Happiness, Hilton International Singapore. (Courtesy of the Hilton International Singapore)

Given a choice, I would stay in the Garden Wing because of the greenery that almost invades the room and the outdoors atmosphere, which is a great contrast to the hectic pace of shopping and sight-seeing elsewhere in the city. (Reserve through the Shangri-La organization or contact the hotel at 22 Orange Grove Road, Singapore 1025; Fax: 65-733-7220/733-1029.) You are unlikely to be disappointed in this fine hotel.

The **Sheraton Towers Singapore** (Tel: 737-6888) is a different type of hotel from the Shangri-La but it achieves similar standards and has become acknowledged as an outstanding business person's property. The 21-story hotel is within walking distance of the Scotts and Orchard Road shopping areas. The outside of the hotel is plain, but as you enter the lobby you are greeted by soaring marble columns, a spectacular waterfall, and huge glass walls that look out on dramatic rock gardens and further plunging water.

Readers familiar with the Sheraton Towers floor concept at other Sheraton hotels will understand the appeal of this all-towers hotel. There are individual check-in desks, butler service, complimentary à-la-carte breakfast and a concierge to handle all special arrangements. All bedrooms have writing desks.

Restaurants include the Domvs, featuring Western cuisine; Li Bai, with its spectacular black and silver decor and variations on traditional Cantonese cuisine; and the Terazza, which provides all-day, cosmopolitan fare with cascading waterfalls and greenery as a feast for the eyes. There is also a bar with a live band, and a disco for fun night-time entertainment. A business center, private offices, and boardroom are available for business or private purposes. The health club offers a gymnasium, sauna, and massage, with a swimming pool and poolside snack bar.

You get the feeling that you are being completely looked after without being overwhelmed. It is an art that is not easy to acquire. (Reserve through the Sheraton organization or contact the hotel at 39 Scotts Road, Singapore 0922; Fax: 65-737-1072.) This is a thoroughly smooth operation. Room rates are around S$400 a night.

The **Goodwood Park Hotel** (Tel: 727-7411) is just down the road a bit from the Sheraton Towers, yet the two hotels are a world apart in appearance and style. Unlike the high-rise towers, it's low-slung, all wings and courtyards and a turret that's fashioned after a German nineteenth-century Rhineland make-believe castle. The Goodwood Park Hotel began in 1899 as the Teutonia Club for the German community in Singapore. The distinctive architecture that reflects that period has been well preserved. The building became a hotel after World War I

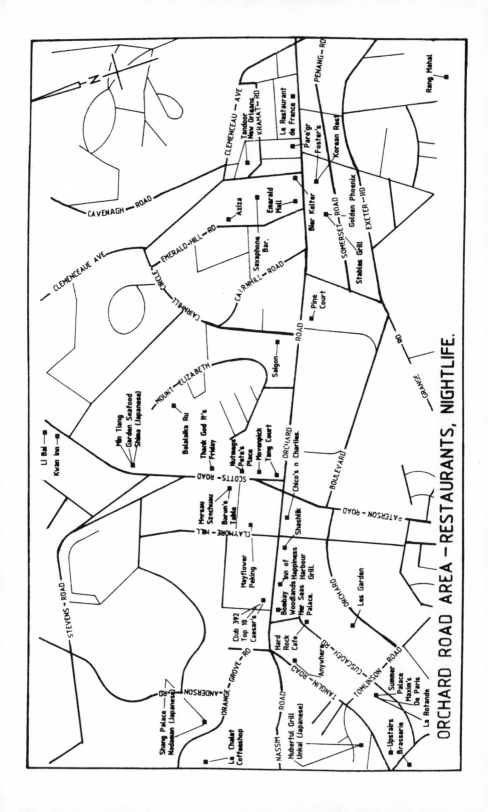

ORCHARD ROAD AREA – RESTAURANTS, NIGHTLIFE.

and today the 231-room property sits on six hectares (15 acres) of hill land just a short distance from Orchard Road. The flavor is neither Chinese, nor international modern, nor British colonial, but a strong, sometimes eccentric, blend of all three.

The hotel's coffee lounge is decorated in traditional eighteenth-century English style and serves a wide choice of food. The Gordon Grill specializes in Continental food, while Japanese cuisine is available at the Shima Restaurant. At the Minx Jiang Sichuan Restaurant you can savor spicy Sichuan dishes or you may prefer seafood or *dim sum* in the Garden Seafood Restaurant. As you can see, the hotel has food outlets far in excess of what you would expect in a medium-sized hotel.

Further choices are available. To eat out under the stars, try the seafood barbecues at the poolside. At Cafe L'Espresso, you can choose from more than a dozen blends of coffee, or you may want to drink and relax at the Highland Bar. Both are adjacent to the bright lobby that looks out on one of the two swimming pools.

Most rooms, decorated in muted tones, have garden views. They have all the usual features. Prices start at S$400 a night. An alternative for longer stays are the delightful self-contained Parklane Suites, which rent at S$4500 for a 30-day period. (Reserve through the SRS reservation organization or contact the hotel at 22 Scotts Road, Singapore 0922; Fax: 65-732-8558.) If you need a business center, shops, babysitting services, or a tour and car rental desk, they are all here.

The **Westin Plaza** (Tel: 338-8585), a 28-story hotel with 796 rooms, including 40 suites designed in various ethnic themes, is aimed primarily at the discriminating business traveller. That doesn't mean, however, that it is not suitable for the vacationer. In fact, together with its sister hotel—the 73-story Western Stamford—the Raffles City office tower, the Raffles City Convention Center, and a huge shopping center, it makes up Raffles City, Singapore's largest international tourist, commercial, and convention complex.

The hotel houses eight restaurants and lounges while the whole complex offers at least another 10 dining or drinking opportunities. You could stay here for a week and never eat in the same restaurant twice. Top of the list is the elegant Palm Grill, which serves French haute cuisine; there are two Chinese restaurants, the Szechuan Court and the Canton Garden; Inagiku, a Japanese restaurant; the Tea Room, a 24-hour coffee shop; Somerset Bar; and Scandals, a space-age disco.

The hotel is quite different from the Goodwood Park Hotel. Nothing is older than 10 years. Glass and marble substitute for tradition and green lawns, but in its own way, this is a very fine hotel. My only complaint is that it's easy to get caught up with too much public traffic before reaching the elegant lobby. Other hotel facilities include a fully equipped health club—the largest in Singapore—that comprises two free-form swimming pools, six tennis courts, four air-conditioned squash courts, a gymnasium, a sauna, a jacuzzi, and exercise and massage rooms. Do you need any more? (Reserve through the Westin organization or contact the hotel at 2 Stanford Place, Singapore 0617; Fax: 65-338-2862.) Raffles City probably has more transportation facilities, including an underground railway station, than any other area of the city. Room rates start at about S$350 a night.

Then there is **Raffles** (Tel: 337-1886). Dating back to 1887, Raffles Hotel is one of the few remaining great nineteenth-century hotels in all of Asia. It was declared a National Monument by the Singapore government in 1987.

The hotel was closed for two years while it underwent a complete restoration. When it reopened in 1991 it immediately created a new market niche for itself. Frankly there is nothing else like it anywhere in Asia. The hotel has 104 suites, each a showpiece in its own right. The original 14-foot ceilings with their grand arches and ceiling fans maintain the spacious, airy feeling. Elegant period furnishings—including oriental carpets arranged on the teak, marble, and tile floors—ensure that each suite exudes warmth and character.

Each of the suites is divided into four rooms: a living room, complete with a lounge and dining table, leads to the bedroom and beyond to the dressing room and bathroom. Natural sunlight filters in through the verandah windows while central air conditioning keeps everything cool and quiet. Naturally, personal valets attend to each suite.

The distinctive restaurants and bars within the hotel recall the atmosphere of a bygone era. Old-timers will tell you about the time that a tiger hid under the billiard table and the management had to call in an experienced hunter to get rid of it. The Tiffin Room is the main dining room, Raffles Grill the fine dining room, while the Writers Bar continues to pay tribute to the novelists and travel writers who have become part of the Raffles tradition. The new adjacent area known simply as Raffles is integrated into the restored hotel and provides 60 shops, a ballroom, indoor and outdoor function areas, the Long Bar where the famous Singapore Sling was created, the Empire Cafe, and the Empress Room, serving fine Cantonese cuisine.

Jubilee Hall, the recreation of a nineteenth-century playhouse, features audio-visual presentations, plays, and recitals. Raffles Museum is a showcase of memorabilia, period photographs, and other mementos of Colonial Singapore. Raffles' pool is found on the third-floor deck adjacent to a bar and health club. A 24-hour business center operates in the main building. (Book with the hotel at 11 Beach Road, Singapore 0718; Fax 65-339-7650.) Room prices start at S$650.

By international standards all of these hotels are a good value and many visitors will be tempted to splurge during a short stay in Singapore. If, however, the bank balance dictates a slight moderation to this splurge while still allowing you to enjoy full five-star luxury, one of the following may fit the bill.

The **Holiday Inn Park View Singapore** (Tel: 733-8333) is just off Orchard Road facing the parklike grounds of the Presidential Palace. The hotel is ultramodern, fully equipped, and super smooth. There is an executive floor with a private lounge. First-class restaurants include the Loong Yuen Chinese restaurant; the Tandoor, offering North Indian fare; and the New Orleans Restaurant, serving Southern U.S.A.-style food.

Besides a health studio and rooftop swimming pool, there is a lively lobby bar and a shopping arcade. (Reserve through the Holiday Inn organization or direct with the hotel at 11 Cavenagh Road, Singapore 0922; Fax: 65-734-4593.)

The **Hyatt Regency Singapore** (Tel: 733-1188) is on Scotts Road just off Orchard Road. The 21-story hotel consists of the main tower that was built about 20 years ago and the newer Regency Terrace, which features spacious rooms with separate bathrooms, dressing areas, and enclosed balconies. The hotel has several Regency Club floors where there is butler service, complimentary breakfast, and cocktails in the evening.

The Hyatt is alive with activity both day and night. There are two outdoor swimming pools, tennis and squash courts, and a fitness center complete with gymnasium, whirlpool, sauna, steam room, and massage and beauty facilities. Restaurants include Nutmegs for seafood, steaks and jazz; Ruyi for Cantonese cuisine; Pete's Place, a friendly pizzeria in the cellar; and The Cafe restaurant for international and local fare. (Reserve through the Hyatt organization or contact the hotel at 10 Scotts Road, Singapore 0922; Fax: 65-732-1696.) After-dark choices can be made from Scotts, the lobby bar; the lounge; the Chinoiserie discotheque; and Brannigan's, the fun pub.

Le Meridian, Singapore (Tel: 733-8855) is a hotel with a distinctive French atmosphere. The hotel is situated on Orchard Road but it is inward-looking rather than imposing from the outside. There is a vast lobby and atrium that is distinctive, but guests appear divided on their opinion of the effectiveness of this feature.

The 400 rooms are tastefully decorated and there are five restaurants and a piano bar: the Restaurant de France, renowned for its French cuisine; La Brasserie Georges, a lively restaurant serving European fare; the Cafe La Terrasse, a 24-hour coffee shop; Nusa Dua Lagon, a poolside Indonesian restaurant; and Cafe Etoile. (Reserve through the Meridian Group or direct with the hotel at 100 Orchard Road, Singapore 0923; Fax: 732-7886.) There is a business center, a swimming pool, a fitness center, and a shopping arcade.

The **Mandarin Singapore** (Tel: 737-4411) has long been a landmark in Orchard Road and is one of Singapore's best-known buildings. The 1200-room hotel has twin towers that rise 40 stories, and the style and character is a blend of international with the subtle splendor of China. In the lobby, canopies decorate the high ceiling with its waterfall of crystal chandeliers cascading downwards. Precious Chinese antiques greet the guest on arrival.

The hotel has a wide array of dining and entertaining areas including five restaurants featuring European, Chinese, French, English, and Japanese cuisine; a coffee house; five cocktail bars; and the Kasbah nightclub. There is also a swimming pool, tennis and squash courts, a minigolf course, and a fitness center. (Reserve through the Mandarin Group or direct with the hotel at 333 Orchard Road, Singapore 0923; Fax: 65-732-2361.) This hotel is surrounded by shopping opportunities; your only problem will be in deciding where to go.

The **Marina Mandarin** (Tel: 338-3388) is one of three hotels in the Marina Square complex. This area was developed about 10 years ago on reclaimed land on the waterfront. The original scheme was overly optimistic at the time but the area has now developed into a major tourist center.

The hotel has rooms with balconies and three specialty restaurants: Ristorante Bologna with Italian fare; House of Blossoms for Teochen meals; and the Brasserie Tatler for local, Japanese, and European cuisine. In addition, there is a coffee house, two cocktail lounges, and a disco-club. (Contact the hotel at 6 Raffles Boulevard, Marina Square, Singapore 0103; Fax: 65-339-4977.) There are the usual swimming pool, fitness center, and tennis and squash courts plus good bus connections to other parts of the city and to the MRT station.

The **Oriental Singapore** (Tel: 338-0066) is the second of the Marina Square Hotels. The distinctive 21-story triangular-shaped hotel is built around an 18-story atrium and there is an impressive array of food and beverage outlets.

Fourchettes is the hotel's premier Continental restaurant while the Captains Bar is a delightful venue for roast beef lunches or for international night-time entertainment. The Cafe Palm offers light,

Western, and local specialities while the Cherry Garden has spicy Sichuan and Hunan Chinese cuisine. L'Appetit Lounge serves afternoon tea and day and night drinks, while the Atrium Lounge is a popular venue for cocktails. (Contact the hotel at 5 Raffles Avenue, Marina Square, Singapore 0103; Fax: 65-339-9537.)

The **Regent Singapore** (Tel: 733-8888) may not be as well known as its Hong Kong or Bangkok counterparts but it is a fine 440-room hotel with a degree of understated elegance. It has been recently totally refurbished to bring it to top Regent standard. Cantonese cuisine is prepared at the Summer Palace restaurant while authentic French cuisine is served at Maxim's de Paris. Local dishes are available at Capers.

The health center adjacent to the swimming pool terrace features all the usual equipment and services while the hotel has a small shopping arcade and a modern business center. (Reserve through the Regent Group or direct with the hotel at 1 Cuscaden Road, Singapore 1024; Fax: 65-732-8838.)

The **Hilton International Singapore** (Tel: 737-2233), 435 rooms, has long been a favorite among visitors and locals and it is easy to see why. The hotel is in a marvelous position in the heart of the Orchard Road shopping and entertainment area and is within easy walking distance of the Orchard MRT station. On a recent visit I was also impressed with the helpful and friendly attitude of the staff, something that unfortunately can not always be said of all Singaporeans. The hotel has a rooftop swimming pool together with exotic food stalls, a French restaurant, the Cantonese Inn of Happiness, and a coffee shop. There is a health club, three executive floors with a lounge and business center, numerous meeting rooms, and an up-market shopping arcade. This is a thoroughly enjoyable hotel with room rates from S$360. Nonsmoking floors are available. (Reserve with the Hilton organization or direct with the hotel at 581 Orchard Road, Singapore 0923; Fax: 65-732-2917.) An added bonus is the nighttime entertainment both in the hotel and in the surrounding area.

All the previous hotels have been large, international-style properties. **The Duxton** (Tel: 227-7678) is quite different. The 49 rooms and suites have been converted from what were once homes to merchants. It is cozy, charming, and intimate. Each room is unique. Both the split-level deluxe suites and the garden suites, where French windows open onto a landscaped patio, are particularly charming. Meals are served at the L'Aigle d'Or, an affiliate of the celebrated Parisian restaurant. The service and cuisine are outstanding. For those who enjoy a small boutique hotel, The Duxton is perfect. While it is quite a

The 435-room deluxe Hilton International Singapore enjoys a vantage point on fashionable Orchard Road. (Courtesy of the Hilton International Singapore)

distance from Orchard Road, the Tanjong Pagar area where it is located has its own appeal and transport is readily available close by. I thoroughly enjoyed a recent stay. Room rates are from S$300. (Book with the hotel at 83 Duxton Road, Singapore 0208; Fax: 65-227-1232.)

This by no means exhausts the list of top class hotels in Singapore. There are many more and the number continues to grow. Some of the remaining are new properties still establishing a firm identity; others are older hotels built in the first major hotel building boom 20 years ago; while still others are just outside the main hotel and tourist areas and are thus marginally less convenient than some of the major hotels listed above. None of this means that you will be disappointed with any of the following. In fact some of these hotels are on my own "better hotels" list.

The **Boulevard Hotel** (Tel: 737-2911) is a 530-room hotel close to Orchard Road that is particularly popular with business people and up-market groups. There is a choice of three restaurants serving American, Cantonese, and Japanese cuisine, as well as a 24-hour coffee shop. Two pools, a fitness club, a discotheque, and a lounge help with relaxation periods. (Reserve with the hotel at 200 Orchard Boulevard, Singapore, 1024; Fax: 65-737-8449.)

The **Carlton Hotel** (Tel: 339-8333) is located close to Raffles Hotel and Raffles City. The 420-room hotel is newish and modern with a choice of 24-hour coffee shop; The Carlton Brasserie, a Continental restaurant; the Woh Lok, a Cantonese restaurant; and a wine bar. (Reserve with the hotel at 76 Bras Basah Road, Singapore 0718; Fax: 65-339-6866.)

The **ANA Hotel** (Tel: 732-1222), with a turn-of-the-century ambience and charm, is a modern hotel situated in an area about a 10-minute walk from Orchard Road. The 456 rooms are surrounded by tropical greenery and the public areas have tapestries and antiques to add to the elegance. American, Continental, and Japanese food is available in various outlets and there are bars, a discotheque, a pool, a business center, and shops. Room prices are from S$350. (Reserve through the ANA Hotels organization, 213-646-2170 in the U.S.A., or direct with the hotel at 16 Nassim Hill, Singapore, 1025; Fax: 65-235-1516.)

The **Melia at Scotts** (Tel: 732-5885), 250 rooms, is operated by the Spanish Melia Hotels Group. It is near a MRT station and the open-air food center at Newton Circus. Food outlets include the Goya Restaurant, which specialises in Spanish fare; and a 24-hour coffee house. There is also a health center, a business center, and a swimming pool. The hotel has one of the cheeriest lobbies and the nicest flowers in

Singapore. Room prices start just below S$300. (Reserve with the hotel at 45 Scotts Road, Singapore 0922; Fax: 65-732-1332.)

The **Dynasty Singapore** (Tel: 734-9900), 400 rooms, is one of the more spectacular hotels with a 30-story octagonal tower topped by a green-tiled, Chinese pagoda-style roof. The architecture and furnishings are unmistakably Eastern but the facilities are as modern as any in Singapore. There is a Chinese restaurant, a Continental restaurant, a coffee house, two lounges, bars, a pool, and a health club. Room rates start at around S$280. (Reserve with the hotel at 320 Orchard Road, Singapore 0923; Fax: 65-733-5251.)

The **Concorde Hotel** (Tel: 733-0188) is equally distinctive. The 27-story glass tower thrusts into the sky around a huge atrium that brings filtered sunlight into the heart of the building. There are six glass elevators that bring color and movement to the lobby, a coffee shop, the Hide-Q Japanese restaurant, and a Chinese restaurant. The hotel has a large shopping center adjacent to it but there are several vacant spaces and some anxious faces around. The hotel in conjunction with other hotels in the area operates a shuttle bus service to Orchard Road. (Reserve with the hotel at 317 Outram Road, Singapore 0316; Fax: 65-733-0989.)

The **Harbour View Dai-Ichi Hotel** (Tel: 224-1133) is Asian in character and appeals to both the business and vacation market. The hotel is in the business district within walking distance of a MRT station. There is a Japanese restaurant, a Cantonese restaurant, and a coffee house. (Reserve with the hotel at 81 Anson Road, Singapore 0207; Fax: 65-222-0749.)

The **Hotel New Otani Singapore** (Tel: 338-3333) is a 408-room hotel with a cozy atmosphere on the banks of the Singapore River. There is a coffee shop, Japanese and Chinese restaurants, and Trader Vic's of San Francisco. The hotel is adjacent to a large shopping complex but is some distance from Orchard Road and the MRT system. An unusual touch is the chicken noodle soup with the tea and coffee in the bedrooms. (Reserve with the hotel at 117A River Valley Road, Singapore 0617; Fax: 65-339-2854.)

The **Omni Marco Polo** (Tel: 474-7141), 600 rooms, is an old-time favorite with landscaped gardens, a swimming pool, and Clark Hatch fitness center. The new-look 300-room Continental wing features European-style decor and several excellent European restaurants. Special emphasis has been given to the needs of the business traveller with big working desks, teletext, and a well-equipped business center. Room prices start at S$360. (Reserve with the hotel at 247 Tanglin Road, Singapore 1024; Fax: 65-471-0521.)

The recently renovated **Novotel Orchid Singapore** (Tel: 250-3322) is a semi-resort hotel with a relaxed ambience. There are two hectares (five acres) of garden, a business center, a health center, a swimming pool, cycling and jogging facilities, and a golf-putting green. There is a nonstop bus service to and from Orchard Road to help overcome the relative isolation of the site. (Reserve with the hotel at 214 Dunearn Road, Singapore 1129; Fax: 65-250-9292.)

The **Orchard Hotel** (Tel: 734-7766) is a 350-room hotel with a striking glass lobby, located right on Orchard Road adjacent to the main shopping and entertainment district. There is a choice of restaurants and bars, tennis and squash courts, nighttime entertainment, and a rooftop swimming pool. (Reserve with the hotel at 442 Orchard Road, Singapore 0923; Fax: 65-733-5482.)

Almost directly across the road is the recently renovated **Orchard Parade Hotel** (Tel: 737-1133), previously called the Ming Court. The 270 rooms have standard facilities and there are restaurants serving Chinese, Japanese, local, and Western food. The Jade Lounge has evening entertainment. (Book with the hotel at 1 Tanglin Road, Singapore 1024; Fax: 65-733-0242.)

The 800-room **Pan Pacific Hotel** (Tel: 336-8111), with its 37-story-high atrium, is the largest of the three hotels in Marina Square. There are Japanese, Chinese, and Polynesian restaurants, a grill room, a sidewalk cafe, and several bars and lounges. The rooftop restaurant has stunning views while the gymnasium, health club, tennis courts, and swimming pool help keep guests active. (Reserve with the hotel at 7 Raffles Boulevard, Singapore 0103; Fax: 65-339-1861.)

There is no other hotel quite like the **Westin Stamford** (Tel: 338-8585). The 72 stories make it the world's tallest hotel and allow for 1250 rooms and 80 suites, numerous restaurants, and other facilities. The Compass Rose Restaurant and Bar sits on the 70th and 71st floors, offering a spectacular vista of Singapore. (Reserve with the Westin Group or the hotel at 2 Stamford Road, Singapore 0617; Fax: 65-337-1554.)

The list still goes on but I know little about the following. Perhaps readers will provide comments that will help with the next edition of the guide.

Allson Hotel, 412 rooms, at 101 Victoria Street, Singapore 0718; Tel: 336-0811; Fax: 339-7019.

Amara Hotel, 332 rooms, at 163 Tanjong Pagar Road, Singapore 0208; Tel: 224-4488; Fax: 224-3910.

Crown Prince Hotel, 288 rooms, at 270 Orchard Road, Singapore 0923; Tel: 732-1111; Fax: 732-7018.

Excelsior Hotel, 274 rooms, at 5 Coleman Street, Singapore 0617; Tel: 338-7733; Fax: 339-3847.

Garden Hotel, 209 rooms, at 14 Balmoral Road, Singapore 1025; Tel: 235-3344; Fax: 235-9730.

Imperial Hotel, 561 rooms, at 1 Jalan Rumbia, Singapore 0923; Tel: 542-7700; Fax: 737-4761.

Le Meridian Changi, 272 rooms, at 1 Netheravon Road, Singapore 1750; Tel: 542-7700; Fax: 512-5295.

Plaza Hotel, 350 rooms, at 7500A Beach Road, Singapore 0719; Tel: 298-0011; Fax: 296-3600.

York Hotel, 324 rooms, at 21 Mount Elizabeth, Singapore 0922; Tel: 737-0511; Fax: 732-1217.

MEDIUM-PRICE HOTELS

The following establishments, which will cost about S$150-$250 for two, are each considered an excellent value and will satisfy most people who have to keep to a reasonable budget. All have attached bathrooms, color TV, bar and restaurant facilities, and so forth. Some will have rooms with refrigerators, some even run to minibars, but the building will be older or situated in a slightly less popular area, the rooms may be smaller, or it may be that the ambience is more of a family-run establishment than of a slick hotel. It could well be that for those planning a longer stay in Singapore, one of these hotels could be a first choice.

Several excellent hotels just squeeze into this category or just miss out depending on your point of view. In fact they fall somewhere between the expensive and midmarket category and they should be listed here. I can recommend:

Golden Landmark Hotel, 387 rooms, at 390 Victoria Street, Singapore 0718; Tel: 297-2828; Fax: 298-2038.

Hotel Equatorial, 195 rooms, at 429 Buket Timah Road, Singapore 1025; Tel: 732-0431; Fax: 737-9426.

Hotel Phoenix, 300 rooms, at Orchard/Somerset Road, Singapore 0923; Tel: 737-8666; Fax: 732-2024.

Kings Hotel, 316 rooms, at Havelock Road, Singapore 0316; Tel: 733-0011; Fax: 732-5764.

Lady Hill Hotel, 174 rooms, at 1 Ladyhill Road, Singapore 1025; Tel: 737-2111; Fax: 737-4606.

Sea View Hotel, 435 rooms, at Amber Close, Singapore 1543; Tel: 345-2222; Fax: 348-4335.

Singapore Paramount Hotel, 250 rooms, at Marine Parade Road, Singapore 1544; Tel: 344-5577; Fax: 447-4131.

Singapore Peninsula Hotel, 306 rooms, at 3 Coleman Street, Singapore 0617; Tel: 337-2200; Fax: 339-3580.

One of the best value hotels at the moment is the **Cairnhill Hotel** (Tel: 743-6622), a 222-room property in a good residential area only a five-minute walk from Orchard Road. The 12-story hotel looks rather plain from the outside, but the rooms are nice and most have good views. There is a 24-hour coffee shop, a Chinese restaurant, a swimming pool, a health and fitness center, and live entertainment in the cocktail lounge. The hotel has a shopping arcade but some of the best shopping in Singapore is available within walking distance so look around before you buy. Prices start at around S$190 for a standard room. (Reserve with the hotel at 19 Cairnhill Circle, Singapore 0922; Fax: 65-235-5598.) Excellent service plus good position make this hotel a good choice.

The **Apollo Hotel** (Tel: 733-2081) also represents excellent value. The hotel is situated in the Havelock Road area near the Concorde Hotel and is not far from the Singapore River. It's a long walk to Orchard Road but there is a MRT station about 10 minutes away and there is a shuttle bus to Orchard Road from the hotel. The rather small lobby is enhanced by a miniatrium and spiral staircase that leads to the 24-hour restaurant. The 19-story hotel building houses 317 rooms, and a four-story annex has a shopping arcade and a branch of the big Japanese Isetan department store. There are three restaurants serving Chinese, Japanese, and Indonesian food, plus a disco for late-night entertainment. (Reserve with the hotel at 405 Havelock Road, Singapore 0316; Fax: 65-733-1588.) This hotel is very popular with Asian visitors, but there is no reason why you can't enjoy the value as well.

The **Furama Hotel** (Tel: 533-3888) is a futuristic, curvilinear hotel in the center of Chinatown. In many ways it is totally incongruous with the century-old Chinese shop houses that stand nearby. The lobby has rich carpet, marble and sandstone, and polished brass columns. The food outlets offer Chinese, Japanese, and Western food. The Heritage Bar has cocktails and entertainment. The hotel has three levels of shops and is connected to the huge People's Park complex via a sheltered walkway. There is a pool, a gymnasium, and a business center. All the 352 rooms have a TV, minibar, and refrigerator. (Reserve with the hotel at 10 Eu Tong Sen Street, Singapore 0105; Fax: 65-534-1489.) This hotel will give you a different perspective on Singapore compared to those in Orchard Road.

The 476-room **River View Hotel** (Tel: 732-9922) is a gleaming landmark on the banks of the Singapore River. The clean lines of the building are a reflection of what is inside—a functional, no-nonsense hotel with five restaurants, a swimming pool, a fitness center, a business center, and the largest disco in Singapore. The Havelock Road area is not my personal choice for location if my Singapore stay is short, but shopping and entertainment opportunities are improving and public transportation facilities are now good. (Reserve with the hotel at 382 Havelock Road, Singapore 0316; Fax: 65-732-1034.)

The **Hotel Asia** (Tel: 737-8388) shares a Scotts Road frontage close to the Sheraton Towers, within walking distance of Newtons Circus hawkers' food center, and the MRT station. The hotel has 146 well-equipped rooms with TV, telephone, and refrigerator. There is a Chinese restaurant and a cocktail bar with live entertainment. The accommodation is adequate rather than fancy, but the hotel is friendly and there is 24-hour room service. (Reserve with the hotel at 37 Scotts Road, Singapore 0922; Fax: 65-733-3563.) If you can find money for a splurge, there are plenty of opportunities close by.

An unusual alternative is the boutique **Inn of the Sixth Happiness** (Tel: 223-3266), nestled up against Chinatown in the Telok Ayer conservation area. The 40 shop houses and one four-story building that make up the hotel have been restored to their traditional wood-beamed ceilings and shuttered windows, with iron lamps and Chinese works of art. Ground-floor suites are grouped around an internal glass-roofed, air-conditioned courtyard. Room rates start at S$160 a night. (Reserve with the hotel at Erskine Road, Tanjong Pagar, Singapore 0106; Fax: 65-223-7951.)

The remaining recommendations fall into two categories—reasonably modern hotels situated some distance from the center of the city, and a group of older buildings in Bencoolen Street close to all the action. Both groups, price-wise, come into the lower end of the midmarket hotels but all would be adequate for many travellers who need to keep to a budget.

The **Broadway Hotel** (Tel: 292-4661) is situated in a local shopping area about 15 minutes away from the city. The 62 rooms are clean and have color TV. There is 24-hour room service and a coffee shop serving Chinese and Western food. (Address: 195 Serangoon Road, Singapore 0812; Fax: 65-291-6414.)

The **Duke Hotel** (Tel: 345-3311) is midway between the airport and the city. The 170-room hotel is opposite a park and the hotel has a swimming pool. Rooms have color TV and radio, and there is a Chinese restaurant and a 24-hour coffee shop. (Address: 42 Meyer Road, Singapore 1543; Fax: 65-345-4025.)

The **Great Eastern Hotel** (Tel: 284-8244) has 155 rooms with color

TV and telephone. Refrigerators are available on request. There is a Chinese restaurant and a coffee shop, while a nightclub offers performances by local artists. (Address: 401 Macpherson Road, Singapore 1336; Fax: 65-284-8335.)

The **Bayview Inn** (Tel: 337-2882) is probably the best of the Bencoolen area hotels. The 117 rooms are neat and clean and there is a swimming pool, a Chinese restaurant, a coffee house, and a bar with nightly entertainment. Prices start at S$160. (Address: 30 Bencoolen Street, Singapore 0718; Fax: 65-338-2880.) This area is convenient to many of Singapore's attractions, and public transportation is excellent.

The **Strand Hotel** (Tel: 338-1866) is also of good standard. The 125 rooms have color TV, video movies, and telephone. Chinese and Western meals are served in the coffee house while the bar lounge has live music most nights. (Address: 25 Bencoolen Street, Singapore 0718; Fax: 65-336-3147.)

Just a few doors away is the 69-room **Hotel Bencoolen** (Tel: 336-0822). Again there is color TV and the hotel has a rooftop garden and restaurant *cum* bar with Chinese and Western food. (Address: 47 Bencoolen Street, Singapore 0718; Fax: 65-336-4304.)

In the same general area, the **Metropole Hotel** (Tel: 336-3611) is a nice property offering "family-style" hospitality in its 54 rooms on eight stories. There are two restaurants, a cocktail lounge, and room service till 11 P.M. (Address: 41 Seah Road, Singapore 0718; Fax: 65-339-3610.)

Also worth trying is the **New 7th Storey Hotel** (Tel: 337-0251), which is among old shop houses but it has 38 nice rooms, and a restaurant and bar on the top floor with good views. (Address: 229 Rochor Road, Singapore 0718; Fax: 65-334-3550.)

At the other end of Orchard Road, the **Hotel Negara** (Tel: 737-0811) has 101 reasonable rooms, a restaurant, swimming pool, and roof garden. (Address: 15 Claymore Drive, Singapore 0922; Fax: 65-737-9075.)

There are several YMCAs in Singapore and a highly recommended YWCA. Top of the list is the **YMCA of Singapore** (Tel: 336-6000), which has air-conditioned rooms from S$75, a fitness center, a swimming pool, squash and badminton courts, and a fast-food outlet. The rooms are tastefully furnished with showers, color TV, and telephone, and are an outstanding value for the money. (Address: 1 Orchard Road, Singapore 0923; Fax: 65-337-3140.)

The **YWCA Hostel** (Tel: 336-3150) is located close by. There are dormitory and private rooms, some with air conditioning. The hostel only takes women or couples and it provides a safe and secure place for lone female travellers. (Address: 6 Fort Canning Road, Singapore 0617.)

Another place worth considering is the **Hotel Premier** (Tel: 733-9811). This is operated by the Singapore Hotel Association Training and Educational Center. All 30 rooms are air-conditioned with attached bathrooms and there are two restaurants. The standard of this and the Ys is well above all other budget accommodation in the city. (Address: 22 Nassim Hill, Singapore 1025; Fax: 65-733-5595.)

BUDGET ACCOMMODATIONS

The Bencoolen area is where I would start looking for really basic accommodation. You can go way down-market to micro room spaces that have been created by subdividing existing apartments. The **Hawaii Hotel** (Tel: 338-4187), at 171 Bencoolen Street, is clean and friendly and has small air-conditioned and carpeted rooms from S$25. There are hot and cold showers and free tea and coffee. **Why Not Homestay** (Tel: 338-8838), at 127 Bencoolen Street, is an air-conditioned bed-and-breakfast place with dormitory accommodations from S$10 and small rooms from S$25.

There are numerous small Chinese-run hotels that are one step up from the micro spaces. An outlay of S$35-$50 will get you a sparsely furnished room with wash basin and fan. Some have rooms with air conditioning. In the Bencoolen area some of the better places are **San Wah** (Tel: 336-2428), 11 rooms, at 36 Bencoolen Street, with a small open courtyard out front; the **Trong Hoa** (Tel: 338-4522) at 4 Prinsen Street, basic but just a few steps from Orchard Road; the **South-East Asia Hotel** (Tel: 338-2394) at 190 Waterloo Street, which is actually a 50-room air-conditioned budget hotel with basic attached bathrooms; and the very friendly **Sun Sun Hotel** (Tel: 338-4911), 20 rooms, at 260 Middle Road, which has spacious rooms from S$40 (a few even have balconies). You find the office at the top of the stairs on the second floor. There is a nice restaurant on the ground floor.

Other budget hotels elsewhere include the 24-room air-conditioned but "olde world" **Majestic Hotel** (Tel: 222-3377), which is in a quiet street near Chinatown (some rooms have a balcony) (Address: 31 Bukit Pasoh Road, Singapore 0208.); the **Cameron Hotel** (Tel: 545-1816), with 24 rooms out towards the airport at 547 Upper Changi Road; the **Min Hwa Boarding House** (Tel: 741-8553), with 26 rooms near the Aljuried MRT station at 19A Larong, 22 Geylang Road; and the **Lai Meng Hotel** (Tel: 744-2038) in the same area at 432 Geylang Road.

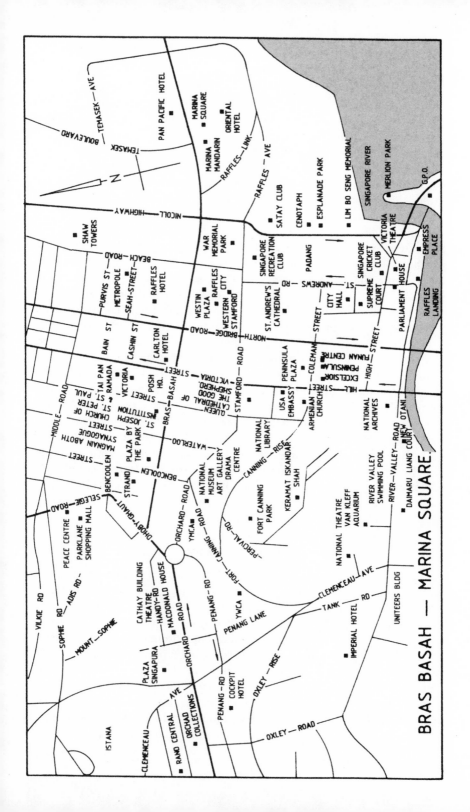

BRAS BASAH — MARINA SQUARE

5. Dining and Restaurants

Visitors would be forgiven if they concluded that many Singaporeans live for food. Eating, it seems, is a cross between a hobby, a passion, and a necessity. Certainly it is something very close to the hearts of most Singaporeans who seem to relish it almost as much as they enjoy making money. It seems that food is the most common topic of conversation among the locals (the stable weather hardly makes for interesting conversation) and the newest restaurants are given critical reviews by everyone.

Many Singaporeans believe food is something to be experienced, not just eaten, and the correct interpretation of each dish is a passion. The result, of course, is that Singapore has a huge number of fine restaurants, some that cost an arm and a leg and others that cost next to nothing. The variety is amazing—from Chinese, Malay, Indian, and Thai to some unique local dishes, Western fast food, and European "nouvelle cuisine" or hearty favorites from Germany and Austria.

I have agonized over how to adequately cover the Singapore food scene and have decided that the best way is to categorize the food type after I have discussed hawkers' food and hotel food. Singapore is one of Asia's cleanest cities so I have no problem with recommending the street stalls or the food centers. Likewise even the most basic Chinese restaurant will be safe and some of the food from these places is more tasty than that in the semi-sanitized Western-style restaurants. You will find that after a few days you will wander around until you see something that appeals. Don't be at all surprised to find yourself in a restaurant that you would not have ventured into on your first day. You will then have discovered what every Singaporean already knows—appearance counts for little, the food counts for everything.

HAWKERS' FARE

Not so long ago, all kinds of food hawkers trundled their carts through the streets of Singapore, selling as they went. Today, they are victims of the modern world. But all is not lost. Many of the original hawkers now operate from nonmobile stalls clustered together in food centers. They have been joined by other entrepreneurs to produce vast open-air kitchens and dining areas that are an experience that shouldn't be missed. Prices here are rock-bottom while the interest level is high. Local food favorites are frequently stir-fried and usually spiced.

Some food centers cater to visitors (and some locals), while others aim solely at locals. First-time visitors should probably first try one that encourages tourists such as those at Newton Circus, the Satay Club, or

Enjoy the eating experience of a modern hawkers' center.

Market stalls provide a fascinating insight into another side of Singapore.

the Cuppage Center. But once you are familiar with the food and the system, it is fun to eat at the more local centers and do some people-watching in the process. For a pure sight and sound experience along with an eating adventure, these centers must not be missed. Part of the fun is trying new dishes and part is sharing a table with other people—preferably locals. Who knows what friendships are made over a bowl of noodles?

The food centers all have communal seating. You can wander around and order from different stalls and the food will be brought to the table where you are sitting. The key is to find a table, then leave one of the party there while the rest select their food. It's a real wonder how the various operators find their customers, keep track of their crockery and cutlery, and ensure that they get paid at the end of the meal. Some places have overcome this latter problem by introducing a pay-as-you-go system.

Food centers are great because of the variety of food—most have Chinese, Malay, Indian, and Western food; the low cost—between S$2 and S$4; and the chance it gives you to get close to the local people. If you are two people sitting at a table with four chairs, the locals will assume that the other two seats are vacant and will use them. That's a good chance to get a conversation going.

There are hawkers' centers all over Singapore and none will disappoint. The following, however, are some of the more popular ones in the areas where the visitor is likely to be.

Newtons Circus holds the premier position among hawkers' centers. The complex is a round-the-clock affair near one of Singapore's major intersections—Bukit Timah Road and Clemenceau Avenue. You can reach it by MRT (alighting at Newton) and it's within walking distance of many of the major Orchard Road/Scotts Road hotels. This place really moves in the evenings with frenzied activity from about 100 stalls. There are so many good meal possibilities that particular recommendations are redundant. Prices are probably a little higher here than some other places but the atmosphere is great.

At the other end of the city, the **Satay Club** is another favorite. This area has seen much development in recent years and the Satay Club suffered access and other problems. The fact that it survived at all speaks volumes for its food. Here *satay* is king but close by there is also a great spot for steamboat.

The **Cuppage Street Center** in Orchard Road is frequented by many visitors but it is also a popular place with locals who are shopping in the huge centers in this area. There is less atmosphere here but the Chinese stalls have great food. Nearby, there is the opportunity to enjoy a garden atmosphere and some fine restaurants in Cuppage Terrace and Peranakan Place.

The **Lau Pa Sat Festival Market** in Shenton Way is a renovated Victorian cast-iron building with food stalls, shops, and strolling performers. The building is more than a hundred years old and has great atmosphere. The Boon Tat Street market operates next door each evening from 7 P.M. on weekdays and 5 P.M. on weekends. The food available at both locations is excellent, reasonably priced, and recommended.

People's Park is a huge shopping complex on the edge of Chinatown. The food center is large, jammed with locals and is cheap.

Bugis Square Food Center is very much a local center and the food here is perhaps more authentic than elsewhere, but it is a long way from the popular hotel areas. Another alternative is the **Albert Center**, which is popular with visitors staying in the Bencoolen area.

Marina South Food Center is modern, attractive, and more structured than most of the other centers. You have to make a specific decision to go to Marina South and getting there takes a bit of an effort. That doesn't seem to stop thousands of Singaporeans from going there, so that on weekend evenings the place is really jumping. There is a good range of food at attractive prices that you share with young families and many young couples. The huge 24-hour bowling alleys are an added attraction to the area and the adjacent Marina Village provides a unique range of up-market European bars and restaurants. Take the MRT to Marina Bay, then feeder bus No. 400 to Marina South.

HOTEL RESTAURANTS

As you would expect, many of Singapore's fine hotels also have fine restaurants. Visitors will inevitably eat at some of these during their stay and in most cases they will not be disappointed. There is no need to dwell on these restaurants as you can locate them much easier than the unique local food haunts, but I have tried to list some of my favorite hotel restaurants with an indication of their food style.

Please do not think that because I haven't listed a restaurant in your hotel, it is not worthy of a listing. It just probably means that I haven't yet eaten there or I regard others as being a better value.

I can recommend all of the following and I list them by the type of food they serve. Note that in some cases the bill will be large, but the food, service, and atmosphere will be excellent.

Cantonese fare is undoubtedly the most popular Chinese food for

Western visitors. There are two outstanding food and value restaurants and many others that are excellent in most aspects. The **Majestic Restaurant** (Tel: 223-5111) at the old Majestic Hotel has long been regarded as a classic. It has the best suckling pig, roast chicken, and noodles that you will find anywhere, and the yams with prawns and shark's fin omelette is highly recommended. It's best to go with a party of people so you can share dishes. The restaurant is large, air-conditioned, and reasonably priced. It is open for lunch and dinner. Average price is S$300 for a table for 10 people.

The **Shang Palace** (Tel: 737-3644) at the Shangri-La Hotel is a classic in a totally different vein. It is pretentious and showy and the food is reminiscent of Chinese food found in a Western restaurant. Most visitors will love it and I am amazed how many locals end up here as well. Lunch can cost S$20-30 per person and dinner from S$35 on up.

For the best shredded duck you have ever tasted, I recommend the **Summer Palace** (Tel: 733-8888) in the Regent Hotel. The duck is served with melon and a sweet plum sauce. Another good choice is the stir-fried fresh scallops, and the palace also serves a delicious shark's fin soup. Lunch is S$30-50 per person with dinner S$50-75. Similar prices and standards are found at the **Li Bai Restaurant** (Tel: 737-6888) at the Sheraton Towers. Recommended dishes are the baked crab meat served in a shell, steamed red garoupa, or fried lobster in black bean paste. Li Bai opens for lunch and dinner.

So too does the **Tang Court** (Tel: 734-9900) in the Dynasty Hotel, where you should try the sliced whelk sauteed with roasted ham (average price S$40 a head), or the cheaper but charming **Inn of Happiness** (Tel: 737-2233) on the top floor of the Hilton International. I have had some fine meals here without emptying my wallet. Another popular choice is the **Lei Garden Restaurant** (Tel: 235-8122) at the Boulevard Hotel.

The **Empress Room** at Raffles serves superb Cantonese cuisine in classic surroundings. Old China is the inspiration for the decor of rich wood finishes and muted colors. The staff is attired in uniforms reminiscent of Shanghai in the 1930s. It opens for lunch and dinner.

Sichuan food is hotter and more robust, but easily appreciated. The **Golden Phoenix Restaurant** (Tel: 732-0431) at the Hotel Equatorial is considered by many to be the best in town. A selection of prawns with dried red chillies, lobster salad, fresh abalone with vegetables, and smoked duck makes a delicious meal. Lunch is around S$40 per person with dinner S$50-60. Other experts favor the **Min Jiang Restaurant** (Tel: 737-7411) at the Goodwood Park Hotel. There certainly are some delightful dishes on the menu. Try the bean curd with minced meat and chilli, the steamed meat dumpling, or the hot and sour Sichuan soup. The average price is S$70-80 per couple. The **Meisan Sichuan Restaurant** (Tel: 737-7966) at the Royal Holiday Inn provides a cheaper alternative.

So too does the **Dragon City** (Tel: 254-7070) at the Novotel Orchid Inn where prawns with dried chillies, and smoked boneless duck are two specialities. A meal here should cost no more than S$25-30.

Other *regional Chinese dishes* are obtained in several other hotel restaurants. The best Hunan fare is available at the **Cherry Garden** (Tel: 338-0066) in the Oriental Hotel. The honey-glazed ham is excellent and the minced pigeon with dried scallops in a bamboo tube is a challenge. **Pine Court** (Tel: 737-4411) at the Mandarin Hotel is excellent for Beijing food. The marinated lamb and the Beijing (Peking) duck should be on your menu. Cost will be about S$25-35 for lunch and S$40-60 for dinner.

Most restaurants have a variety of *seafood* but the **Garden Seafood Restaurant** (Tel: 737-7411) at the Goodwood Park Hotel is hard to beat for variety and freshness. No matter what else you have, don't miss the steamed prawns with wine, or the prawn rolls. Cost will be S$30-45 per person unless you go overboard with your selection.

Nonya food is available at the **Luna Coffee House** (Tel: 733-2081) at the Apollo Hotel. This operates both a buffet lunch and a buffet dinner.

Two *Indian* restaurants stand out from the crowd. The **Tandoor Restaurant** (Tel: 733-8333) at the Holiday Inn Parkview is one of the city's favorites. Lamb soup, tandoori soup, vegetable pilau, and roast leg of lamb are some of the specialties. Cost is around S$30 a head. The alternative is the **Rang Mahal Restaurant** (Tel: 737-1666) at the Hotel Imperial where North Indian dishes such as the tandoori specialities are the big attraction.

You probably should find the best *Japanese* restaurants in the Japanese-controlled hotels but two that I particularly enjoy are the **Nadaman Restaurant** (Tel: 737-3644) in the Shangri-La Hotel and the **Shima Restaurant** (Tel: 734-6281) in the Goodwood Park Hotel. Both operate for lunch and dinner. The Nadaman has the usual *sushi, sashimi,* and *teppan-yaki* favorites while the Shima has *shabu-shabu* and *yakiniki* as specialties. Prices are about S$40 per person. Two others worth trying are the **Hoshigaoka Restaurant** (Tel: 733-2081) in the Apollo Hotel and the **Unkai Restaurant** (Tel: 732-1222) in the ANA Singapore Hotel.

I have always believed that it was difficult to find top Western food in Asia but after experiencing some of Singapore's best Western hotel restaurants, I have changed my mind. It would be hard to find better hotel American or European food anywhere. My particular favorite for American food is the **New Orleans Restaurant** (Tel: 733-8333) at the Holiday Inn Park View. That is because I particularly enjoy Creole cuisine, and the barbecue shrimp and seafood jambalaya are difficult to fault. The restaurant opens for lunch and dinner but is closed on Sundays.

Another delightful restaurant is **Nutmegs** (Tel: 733-1188) at the Hyatt Regency Hotel. My favorites here are the grilled lobster, the Philadelphia pepper pot, and the rotisserie duckling. Lunch is around S$25 and dinner S$40-60 per person. I'm not quite sure where to position the **Hubertus Grill** (Tel: 732-1222) at the ANA Hotel. It has prime rib of U.S. beef but also has European specialties such as cheese and onion pie with crab meat, avocado and cucumber cream soup, and a selection of game dishes.

There is no doubt at all where **La Brasserie** (Tel: 474-7141) at the Omni Marco Polo Hotel fits in the market. This Parisian-style brasserie is pure *French*. You won't find better lemon mousse crepes outside France. Lunch is around S$30 and dinner S$50-60 per person. Then there is **Le Restaurant de France** (Tel: 733-8855) at the Hotel Le Meridien. It opens for lunch on weekdays and dinner daily and specializes in salad with foie gras, lobster cream soup, roast rack of lamb, and an assortment of seafood. The aim here is to produce a top-class French restaurant and it succeeds. Lunch is around S$40 and dinner S$75 and up per person.

The same aim is achieved at **Maxim's de Paris** (Tel: 733-8888) at the Regent. It opens for lunch on weekdays and dinner daily. There is no doubt that fricassee of frogs' legs, and snails with garlic and herb sauce are French dishes. So too are the tournedos Rossini, and the poached scallops in ginger and lime cream sauce. Expect to pay S$40 for lunch and S$60-80 for dinner per person.

French provincial cooking is best enjoyed at **L'Aigle d'Or** (Tel: 227-4388) at The Duxton Hotel. This delightful restaurant has excellent food and impeccable service together with an extensive wine list of French and Australian varieties. The special Sunday lunch is a particularly good value. Then there is the uninspiredly named **Harbour Grill** (Tel: 737-2233) at the Hilton International. There is nothing uninspiring about the restaurant, however—fine French cuisine, a great salad bar, and dinner prices around S$80-90 per person.

Raffles Grill at Raffles is the hotel's most exclusive restaurant. It is formal, elegant, and its architecture features the details of the original hotel. French doors provide a picturesque view of the Palm Court while inside there are Chippendale furnishings and period landscape paintings. An extensive menu offers a range of Continental specialities.

Other European cuisines are also available. *Italian* is probably the most popular with at least three excellent choices. **Bologna** (Tel: 338-3388) in the Marina Mandarin Hotel is reasonably priced but top quality. It has excellent calamari, veal, and a good range of pastas. You will also be tempted by the pistachio ice cream. The price is about S$30 for lunch and S$50-60 for dinner.

The **Ristorante Italiano Prego** (Tel: 338-8585, ext. 16310) at the Westin Stanford Hotel aims at good food at reasonable prices. It opens for lunch and dinner but is closed on Mondays. Italian seafood stew, linguini, and scallopine are some of the specialties. Prices are about S$20 for lunch and S$30-35 for dinner. **Pete's Place** (Tel: 733-1188) at the Hyatt Regency is a fun place for spaghetti or pizza at lunch or dinner. With care you can enjoy a meal for S$15-20 per person.

For *German cuisine*, head straight for the **Baron's Table** (Tel: 737-7966) at the Royal Holiday Inn. All the German and Austrian favorites are available at lunch and dinner.

English fare is the rage at **Stables Grill Room** (Tel: 737-4411) in the Mandarin Hotel. Roast beef, a selection of pies, and fish and chips are all available. For *Swiss food*, nothing beats **Le Chalet** (Tel: 737-2111) in the Lady Hill Hotel. This has authentic Swiss cuisine and some of the best fondues you will find anywhere. While at the Lady Hill Hotel, drop into the poolside **coffee shop** for a range of Western and local food at attractive prices.

If *vegetarian food* is what you crave, **Kwan Im** (Tel: 336-2389) at the South East Asia Hotel is bound to appeal. Most of the food is Asian but there are a few Western dishes. Prices are reasonable. For a more sophisticated vegetarian dining environment, settle in among the bronze figurines, carved teak chairs, tables and wall panels, and vegetable-dyed canvas paintings at **Annalakshm's** at the Excelsior Hotel. The restaurant was founded by an Indian monk and today it is staffed completely by volunteers. There is a selection of North and South Indian dishes that should be topped off with the homemade yogurt ice cream.

CHINESE FOOD

In most Western countries, Chinese food equates to Cantonese cuisine. In fact each province of China has its own distinctly different cuisine and most of these are available in Singapore. The reason is quite simple. When the Chinese started flocking into Singapore at the start of the nineteenth century, the British colonial government decided on a divide-and-rule policy so that the various races and dialect groups could not unite and rebel.

It was not long before the Hokkiens from Fujian province were settled in the labyrinth of roads around Hokkien Street, the Teochews congregated in Carpenter and Teochew Street, the Cantonese were settled towards the center of what we call Chinatown, and the Hainanese had an enclave around Raffles Hotel. Time has blurred many of these provincial differences but when it comes to food, these areas still specialize in their regional foods.

The following restaurants are good for sampling some of the best regional Chinese food available in Singapore. Most will have an English menu and, if they do not, there will be someone who can help you choose.

Cantonese food is considered the finest of China's multifaceted cuisines and because many visitors are already familiar with some dishes, it is a good place to start. Stir frying, steaming, and roasting are most employed in this kitchen. Flavor comes from a light touch of soy and oyster sauces.

The **Hillman Restaurant** (Tel: 221-5073) at 159 Cantonment Road is a great example of a Singapore restaurant. It is unpretentious with an old streetside coffee shop atmosphere, takes no credit cards, and is not particularly tidy or spick-and-span but the food can challenge the best. You can enjoy a full banquet with a group of people or select individual dishes from a menu. The restaurant is famous for its clay pot dishes— try the pot prawns, or select the fried pork chop Chinese-style, and the crabmeat with braised vegetables. This is food for those with expensive tastes but more moderate means.

Much more up-market is the **Tung Lok Shark's Fin Restaurant** (Tel: 336-6022) at 177 River Valley Road. This restaurant specializes in Hong Kong Cantonese nouvelle cuisine for dinner at between S$30-50 per person. At lunch they have an excellent *dim sum* selection. *Dim sum* is a meal of small dishes served from trolleys. Each dish contains three or four small mouth-sized pieces of food that have been either steamed or fried. You stop a trolley as it passes your table and point at your choice. At the end of the meal, the empty plates or steamer trays on your table are counted for your bill. Lunch should cost no more than S$20.

Then there is the **Mayflower Peking Restaurant** (Tel: 737-1224) at the International Building on Orchard Road. This huge air-conditioned and carpeted cavern specializes in *dim sum* for lunch, and exotic dishes like drunken prawns, and steamed treasures of the sea for dinner. Lunch will not cost more than S$15 and dinner will be in the S$25-35 range. Good value for quality food. A similar comment can be made of Mitzi (Tel: 222-8281) at 24/26 Murray Street. If you are in the area you should try it.

The **Paramount Chinese Restaurant** (Tel: 440-3233) is almost in a class by itself. This luxury restaurant is in a backwater shopping center in Katong and its decor is almost like Disneyland. The restaurant is in a double-height room decorated as a courtyard surrounded by Peranakan-style houses sporting balconies, balustrades, arches, and a skylight. There is a good à-la-carte menu with dishes at S$10-20. A delightful place to sit is the private balcony on the second floor.

Hainanese cuisine is simple and the specialty—chicken rice—is a good example. Chicken is tenderly boiled, then moist rice is steamed in the stock. The result is delicious. Two recommended restaurants are **Yet Con Restaurant** (Tel: 337-6819) at 25 Purvis Road, and the nearby **Swee Kee Restaurant** (Tel: 337-0314) at 51 Middle Road. Both are close to Raffles Hotel and are unpretentious local restaurants without air conditioning. A basic chicken rice dish will only cost around S$4 and a whole meal is S$10-15. Both restaurants have been around for a long time. The decor at Yet Con is very much like what Somerset Maugham would have encountered earlier this century. Both of these restaurants also specialize in steamboat and this should not cost more than S$20 a head.

Teochew cuisine is another Chinese regional fare popular in Singapore. The cuisine is famous for its light, clear broth; the aim is to preserve and enhance the natural flavors. It is homely, simple cooking, bordering on blandness but at the really fine restaurants it has a subtle, delicious flavor. A traditional Chinatown shop front restaurant **Ban Sing** (Tel: 431-471) at 79 New Bridge Road has what many consider to be the best Teochew cuisine in the city. The atmosphere and food have changed little over the years but it has retained its popularity because it delivers fine food at a reasonable price. Try the mutton soup, and the steamed lobster if they happen to be on the menu when you visit. They are excellent. Your credit card won't be much use here but a meal will only cost about S$15 a head.

Just around the corner at 49 Mosque Street is **Chui Wah Lin Restaurant** (Tel: 223-3721) where fine food is served in basic surroundings. There is no extensive menu but you will find that one of the staff will speak English and offer helpful suggestions about the day's meal.

The **Delicious Kitchen Restaurant** (Tel: 226-0607) is quite different. This is in the Tanjong Pagar restoration area and while other restaurants in this area have opted for exotic decor, here there is a simple no-nonsense approach that lets you concentrate on the food.

There are several other cuisines worth trying. For good *Hakka* food it is hard to beat the **Moi Kong Restaurant** (Tel: 221-7758) at 22 Murray Street near the Maxwell Road/South Bridge Road intersection. Hakka food is normally frugal but this restaurant has a few dishes that are a little more exotic. Try the soup with red wine, a rich broth that includes a variety of tidbits. The steamed chicken is also good—cubes of chicken that have been steamed in wine.

Right next door at 20 Murray Street is one of the better *Hokkien* restaurants in the city. The **Beny Hiang Restaurant** (Tel: 221-6684) serves some of the traditional oily, hearty food of this region but there are also some other traditional dishes that should have great appeal. Try the oyster omelette fried with onions, or the turtle soup, and don't miss the Hokkien *mee*, a delicious mixture of thick yellow noodles, cooked with prawns, squid, beansprouts, lime, and chillies. A meal will cost around S$20.

Vegetarian food lovers should visit one of the **Kingsland Vegetarian Restaurants** where the chefs are not only masters of cooking but are also skilled artists. The outlets are at Whampoa West, People's Park Complex, and Albert Complex, and each offers more than 100 Chinese vegetarian dishes. Many dishes are molded and shaped to resemble prawns, liver, spare ribs, cuttlefish, and chicken, and they are served with plum, sweet and sour, and chilli sauces. Dishes range in price from S$4-10.

A further option is the **Wan Sea Palace** (Tel: 227-7156), at 2 Craig Road, where the food and service are both better than average.

MALAY AND INDONESIAN FOOD

If you are a newcomer to this cuisine, the place to start is with *satay*. These skewers of seasoned beef, chicken, or mutton are grilled over charcoal and served with a bowl of spicy peanut gravy. It's better to eat *satay* outdoors where you can see the chef grill the skewers and you can savor the aroma, but other dishes are ideal for restaurant fare. Another popular dish is *nasi goreng* (fried rice) loaded with meat, prawns, egg, and onion. Then there is *mee rebus*, a hearty dish of thick noodles in a rich, spicy sauce, or *tahu goreng*, deep-fried beancurd with beansprouts. For those into fiery food, try *beef rendang* or *nasi padang*.

Malay and Indonesian restaurants are scattered throughout the city. The **Jawa Timur Restaurant** (Tel: 337-5532) on the ninth floor of the Chiat Hong Building, 110 Middle Road, has that unbeatable combination of cheerful surroundings, reasonable prices, and excellent cooking. The Javanese cooks prepare dishes in a spotless stainless steel kitchen, and the service is basic but friendly. Malay and Indonesian food is best enjoyed with a group sharing dishes, but at Jawa Timur there are several alternatives that are suitable for one. Ask for advice. Cost is around S$15 per person.

Aziza's Restaurant (Tel: 235-1130) at 36 Emerald Hill Road off Orchard Road is one of the few restaurants serving true Malay food. It opens for lunch and dinner every day except Sunday lunch. Specialties of the house are ox tail soup, *udang goreng merah* (fried prawn), and *beef rendang*, tender beef coated with a thick, piquantly spiced gravy. The average price of a meal here is S$20 and all major credit cards are accepted.

Downtown at Centrepoint on Orchard Road, **Sanur** (Tel: 734-2192) is very popular with the local crowd because of its good prices and quality food.

Tambuah Mas (Tel: 733-3333) in the Tanglin Shopping Center is a longtime favorite that just gets more popular as the years go by. All the most popular ethnic dishes are available here and they are served without fuss in pleasant surroundings. A similar recommendation can be made for the **Rajah Inn Restaurant** (Tel: 235-5100) in the Concorde Hotel shopping complex. It opens from 11:30 to 2:30 for lunch and from 6 to 9:30 for dinner.

At this point, I think it is appropriate to mention **Alkaff Mansion**, the turn-of-the-century home of one of Singapore's founding families. The house specialty, *rijstaffel*, is a veritable banquet of spicy dishes and condiments. To order the dish is to summon up a procession of 10 women, dressed in colorful *batik* sarongs, each bearing delicious delicacies. In addition to *rijstaffel*, Alkaff serves both Western and Asian dishes. Extensive verandahs, imposing twin towers, stained-glass windows, carved eaves, and intricately tiled floors all contribute to an ambience unparalleled in Singapore. Alkaff is open from 8 A.M. to midnight daily. It is well worth a visit.

NONYA FOOD

Nonya food is the result of the intermarriage of Malay and Chinese cultures in Singapore to form the Peranakan society. The cuisine is full of surprises but these are some masterpieces. In *laksa lemak*, the Chinese love of noodles is superbly complemented by the Malay love of spices to achieve a rich spicy coconut-based soup with rice noodles laced with herbs. Then there is *mee siam*, with rice vermicelli, boiled egg, beanspouts, and even a few prawns in a sweet-soup gravy with a hint of chilli. Some bite-sized food suggestions are *poh piah*, a savory roll filled with shredded turnip, bamboo shoots, beancurd, prawns, and strips of pork, and *kueh pie tee*, crispy savories filled with crunchy vegetables and topped with prawn and chilli.

Nonya cooking remains very much a domestic art so there are few true Nonya restaurants. However, it is worth seeking out one to enjoy this unique blend of flavors. One of the best-known Nonya restaurants is the **Nonya and Baba Restaurant** (Tel: 734-1382) at 262 River Valley Road. This no-nonsense restaurant opens for lunch then stays open until late evening. Dishes start at S$4 and a full meal can be enjoyed for S$10-15. Start your meal with a soup such as *itek tim*, duck with salted vegetables and preserved plums, then try *sanibal udang*, a dish of shelled prawns fried with a spice paste of chillies, shrimp paste, shallots, and candlenuts given a sweet-and-sour flavor by a dash of sugar and tamarind juice.

Another alternative is to head out East Coast Road till you reach Katong, one of the original Peranakan suburbs. Here you will find the **Guan Hoe Soon Restaurant** (Tel: 440-5650) at 241 Joo Chiat Road, and the **Peranaken Inn** (Tel: 440-6194) at 210 East Coast Road. These are restaurants for the locals, and there are no credit facilities but you will enjoy genuine Nonya delights without frills or hype.

A further alternative is the **Oleh Sayang Food** (Tel: 468-9859), a home-cooked Peranakan restaurant at 25 Lorang Liput in Holland Village. This one opens from 11 A.M. to 3 P.M. and from 5:30 to 10 P.M. but is closed on Mondays.

INDIAN FOOD

Think of Indian food and most Westerners conjure up images of hot curries. But really that is only part of the picture. Indian food has much more subtlety than that. Naturally you find many of the best Indian restaurants in Little India, that area around Race Course Road and Serangoon Road. Race Course Road has developed into a "curry" street with more than 10 restaurants congregated in North Bridge Road.

Once you reach these areas it is not difficult to decide which restaurant suits your purse and mood. You would make a good choice if you selected one of the following. For Indian vegetarian food try **Komala Vilas Restaurant** (Tel: 293-6980) at 76 Serangoon Road or **Annapoorna's Vegetarian East Food Restaurant** (Tel: 291-4693) in Serangoon Plaza, 320 Serangoon Road. Both open for breakfast and remain open all day. Prices are from S$3 to S$5 per dish. An alternative is **Ananda Bhavan** at 219 Selegie Road, which is staffed only by males, because an ancient

Indian custom did not approve of beautiful young Indian women serving food in public where they would be seen by many men. Cutlery is available but do as the locals do and eat with the fingers of the right hand.

For nonvegetarian food in Race Course Road, try **Our Makan Shop** (Tel: 292-9475) at number 74, **Muthu's Curry** (Tel: 293-2309) next door at number 76 or **Banana Leaf Apollo** (Tel: 298-5054) at number 56. Two excellent cheap, non-air-conditioned North Indian restaurants in North Bridge Road are **Singapore Restaurant** (Tel: 298-6320) at number 697, and **Victory Restaurant** (Tel: 298-6320) at number 701. Both are open from 6 A.M. to midnight. Neither has credit facilities.

Then there are the more up-market Indian restaurants. Several have a good reputation. Top of the list is probably **Moti Mahal Restaurant** (Tel: 221-4338) at 18 Murray Street off Maxwell Road. There they serve superb Kashmiri, Punjabi, and Muchlai Indian cuisine prepared by chefs from India. The extensive menu is somewhat overwhelming with more than 130 choices, so I recommend the Tandoori chicken, kebabs, or the fish *noor jahani*. Rice is served in several ways but there are also some exquisite fresh breads that you should sample. Wash the whole meal down with sweet or salty *lassi*, a yogurt drink. A meal here will cost S$20-25.

Up-market from here (although the food in my opinion is not better) is the **Omar Khayyam Restaurant** (Tel: 336-1515) at 55 Hill Street, almost opposite the U.S. Embassy. This is a world of lush carpeting, low lighting, and soft music. The food is northern Indian with recipes from the Moghul palaces brought via Kashmir. One of the specialties is tandoori chicken, which has been marinated in yogurt and spices for 12 hours before being cooked in a clay oven. Other popular dishes are the rajah prawns, and the shish kebabs. Most of the dishes are not overly hot and each has a blended spice sauce to add flavor and color. You can finish with *kulfi* or pistachio ice cream. Prices per person are S$15 and up.

For those visitors reluctant to venture far from Orchard Road, a branch of the Indian Woodlands chain of restaurants can be found in Forum Galleria next to the Hilton Hotel. The **Bombay Woodlands Restaurant** (Tel: 235-2712) at 583 Orchard Road claims to serve the healthiest, tastiest, and greatest Indian vegetarian delicacies in Singapore. What else can I say? It opens for lunch and dinner seven days a week.

OTHER ASIAN FOOD

It should be no surprise that a cosmopolitan city such as Singapore has a wide range of other Asian cuisines available for the visitor. Hot, spicy Thai food; delicate, eye-catching Japanese food; Chinese-based, highly seasoned Vietnamese food; and distinctive Korean food are all available. Here are some suggestions.

Several *Thai* restaurants are in Joo Chiate Road with perhaps the **Haadyai Beefball Restaurant** (Tel: 344-3234) at number 467 being one of the best. Specialities are seafood *tom yum* (a delicious soup), pineapple rice, and deep-fried fish in Thai chilli sauce. Average cost is S$20 per person. For seafood lovers **Her Seas Palace Restaurant** (Tel: 732-5688) in the Forum Galleria at 583 Orchid Road has chilli crab, lobster salad, and fish soup, Thai style. They also have some excellent Thai desserts. The cost here per person is S$30 and up. The **Siang World Thai Restaurant** (Tel: 227-8983) at 14 Murray Street is good value for good food.

The **Chao Phaya Seafood Restaurant** at Holland Village is a convenient place to have a good, inexpensive Thai meal if you are in this district. It opens from 11:30 A.M. to 2:30 P.M. and from 6:30 to 10:30 P.M. and has the option of a set menu at S$9 for one person or S$25 for two or three. The **Ria Aneka**, in the same area, has a good selection of Thai/Asian spicy food. Likewise the **Rim Nam Thai Restaurant** (Tel: 250-2324) at United Square is a good place to go for a quick business lunch or with the family for dinner. Dishes such as the *tang hoon* prawn in clay pot represent fine examples of Thai-Chinese cooking.

Japanese restaurants tend to be fairly pricey but at most the food is quite authentic. At many you can watch a Japanese chef cook the food at your table, as he juggles his utensils at lightning speed. Most also have *tatami* rooms where you can sit Japanese-style on cushions and mats. The **Restaurant Suntory** (Tel: 732-5111) at 402 Orchard Road opens for lunch and dinner and has the full range of Japanese favorites from *sushi*, *teppan-yaki*, and *shabu-shabu* to traditional banquet style meals. Prices start at about S$30 per person. Another popular restaurant is **Kobe** (Tel: 734-6796) on the fourth floor of the Tanglin Shopping Center. Try their *sashini*; it is particularly good.

Vietnamese restaurants cater mainly to visitors so the food is perhaps a little milder than you will find in Saigon. Nevertheless, the unique mixture of Chinese styles and the more highly seasoned and fragrant food of southeast Asia is still there. **Pare'gu Restaurant** (Tel: 733-4211) at Orchard Plaza, 150 Orchard Road opens from noon until 3 A.M. and has a wide choice of food. One favorite, which is delicious, is the barbecued prawns on sugar cane. Prices start at about S$20 per person. The **Saigon Restaurant** (Tel: 235-0626) in Cairnhill Place, 15 Cairnhill Road, just off Orchard Road, is another restaurant with authentic cuisine. The Vietnamese spring rolls are the best available in Singapore and you will find all the usual favorites on the menu. Meal prices average about S$20 per person. Credit cards are accepted.

Korean food is popular in Singapore. It is hotter and more spicy than most Chinese food with ginseng chicken soup (*sumgay tang*), spicy preserved cabbage soup with pork (*kimchi chegay*), and sliced barbecued beef (*bulgogi*) some of the favorites. For seafood lovers, barbecued prawns marinated in spices (*seawoo bulgogi*), and king oyster fried in egg (*gul jean*) are recommended. You can try the Korean buffet barbecue at the **Seoul Garden Restaurant** (Tel: 345-1339) at Parkway Parade Shopping Center, 80 Marine Parade Road. In the Orchard Road area try the **Korean Restaurant** (Tel: 235-0018) in the Specialists' Shopping Center.

WESTERN FOOD

Many readers will be delighted to hear that McDonald's, Kentucky Fried Chicken, Dunkin' Donuts, Pizza Hut, and many more are all located in Singapore. Western fast-food outlets have some prestige attached to them in the minds of many young Singaporeans so the number of outlets has grown dramatically. You will find one close to you in most areas of Singapore.

Apart from these outlets, there are many restaurants providing Western food of all types. For steak you would try **Jack's Place Steakhouse** (Tel: 235-7361) at Yen San Building, 268 Orchard Road and at 117A Killiney Road (Tel: 737-7028). As well as steak they have a four-course set lunch from S$7 and a five-course set dinner from S$20. If French cuisine is your choice, you should be satisfied with the **Frisco Restaurant** (Tel: 220-3777) in the Hong Kong Bank Building, Collyer Quay.

English breakfasts, pie and pudding lunches, and high tea are available from the **Upstairs Restaurant** (Tel: 732-3922) in Tudor Court, Tanglin Road, while **Fosters** (Tel: 737-8939) in the Specialists' Shopping Center, Orchard Road, continues a tradition for man-sized English meals with good beer and wine that has been part of Singapore since World War II. Mouth-watering steaks cost S$23-29, cottage pie S$16, fish and chips S$18, and a ploughmans' lunch just S$10. Light meals are served between 11 A.M. and 6 P.M. with mushrooms on toast S$6, and beef pies S$6, being two recommendations. I must also mention the homemade apple pie, which is absolutely delicious. There is a choice of nine teas and several coffees, and it is a great place to take a break from that Orchard shopping. Dinner reservations on weekends are essential.

Several other Western restaurants are worth a brief mention. **Movenpick**

(Tel: 275-8700) in Scotts Shopping Center, 6 Scotts Road, opens from 11 A.M. to midnight every day and serves a fascinating range of Swiss food. **Chico's n Charlie's** (Tel: 734-1753) at Liat Towers, Orchard Road, is my pick for Mexican food, while the **Shashlik Restaurant** (Tel: 732-6401) just next door at the Far East Shopping Center is great for Russian food. **Casablanca** (Tel: 235-9328), at 7 Emerald Hill Road, is a wine bar with good food and atmosphere. **Oscar's Brasserie** (Tel: 223-4033), at 30 Robinsons Road, is another wine bar that opens for lunch and dinner.

For excellent food at bargain prices visit the two restaurants at **SHATEC** (Tel: 235-9533) at 24 Nassim Hill. This is a training school operated by the Singapore Hotel Association and you will find the food excellent and the service friendly. Lunch price is about S$10 at the coffee house and S$18 at the fine dining restaurant with dinner about S$15 and S$25, respectively.

Da Paolo's Ristorante Italiano (Tel: 224-7081) is oozing with romance. Situated in a restored shop house at 66 Tanjong Pagar Road, the restaurant is often filled with the beautiful people of Singapore. The upstairs dining room with its white walls, pastel tablecloths, and rich patina of weathered wood, is quite stunning. Fresh pasta is made on the premises, and I am told it offers the best *risotto* in town. A meal for two will cost S$60-70. **Parta Brava** at 11 Craig Road is a worthwhile cheaper alternative close by.

If opulence is more your style, you will love **Windows Restaurant** (Tel: 294-5169) in Beach Road. There are carved Regency chairs, a grand piano, and comfortable armchairs. Despite the grandeur, the set lunch will only cost S$15. À-la-carte prices are French onion soup S$6, filet steak bathed in chanterelle sauce S$33, lobster thermidor S$28, and crepes suzettes S$6. At night there is a pianist and singer.

I like the atmosphere at **Bob's Tavern** (Tel: 467-2419) at Holland Village. This bar and restaurant is run by Robert Lim who was food and beverage manager for 16 years at the Tanglin Club. Opening hours are midday to midnight, and lunches and dinners are served. On weekends you will need to make a reservation. The bar is excellent and food prices very attractive. Bob's BBQ spare ribs are S$12, while a green peppercorn steak is S$16.50.

Then there is **Emmerson's Steak and Seafood Restaurant** (Tel: 227-7518) at 51 Neil Road, run by The Raffles Company. Traditional favorites such as chicken curry are still there, but now there is a wide range of steaks, lamb, pork, veal, and seafood to enjoy in a delightful atmosphere.

Finally if outdoor dining under tropical nights is your idea of heaven, call into **Emerald Mall** at Peranakan Place, Orchard Road. It's Singapore's equivalent of a Parisian sidewalk cafe. They have fresh seafood and cold beer, together with other options. Even the plastic chairs and tables can't totally take away the great atmosphere.

SEAFOOD RESTAURANTS

The **Ng Tiong Choon Sembawang Seafood Restaurant** (Tel: 257-7939) is something you would expect to find in Malaysia or Thailand rather than Singapore. This is far from the rush of city life and is a side of Singapore that most visitors never see. The restaurant is situated beside a fishing pond in the country on the north side of the island. An air-conditioned bus operates from the Hotel Grand Central or you can take the MRT to Yishun station and catch a minibus from there. You need to check with the restaurant for times. Specialties include deep-fried scallops with bananas, and baked crab with pepper.

For a more conventional venue you should head out the East Coast Parkway to the **UDMC Seafood Center**. Here six restaurants cater to almost all tastes. On week nights you can arrive without a reservation and look around to see which one appeals to you. There are crabs, fish, squid, prawns, clams, and more, served steamed, fried, or barbecued, proving true that the Chinese will eat almost anything that moves. Most of it is delicious, although you may not be sure what it is. Try chilli crab, Singapore's most popular seafood dish. You get chunks of crab still in the shell coated with a zesty, spicy rich tomato-chilli sauce. Another recommendation is *har loke*—fresh prawns fried in their shells in soya sauce and a host of tantalizing seasonings.

Other specialties include crispy fried baby squid in a sweet black sauce, and drunken prawns, cooked in ginseng after the prawns have been given an overdose of Chinese wine. No visitor should leave Singapore without trying the seafood.

6. Sight-seeing

Many Western tourists have a perversity towards the "romantic East" that Singaporeans find most baffling. We demand all the comforts and luxuries of the best "Western" hotels, then expect to find our own private Eastern fantasy when we step outside of the air-conditioned lobby. The reality is something quite different. Singapore has some of the world's best and most modern hotels and much of the surrounding urban environment is similar. A visitor to Singapore must arrive with the knowledge that the business and tourist centers of the city are as modern as any city on earth. Once you accept this, you can start enjoying the city for the myriad attractions that it offers. Please do not arrive expecting a romantic 1920s experience. That has gone forever. Fortunately Singapore has now subdued an insanity that would have made it a barren cultural and architectural desert from its once-charming beauty.

There are plenty of sights, sounds, and happenings that you will never experience at home, and the harder you look, the more you find. Beside every track that seems to be beaten bare by the tourist, there is always one running parallel containing marvelous surprises. To get started you need to remember a few fundamentals about the island and the city. When you look at a map of the island, Changi Airport is at the extreme eastern end; the causeway to Malaysia is at the north; and Jurong, the major industrial area, is to the west.

Whether you enter Singapore city from the airport or from the Malaysian causeway, your first impression will be one of greenery, cleanliness, and planning. Very little in Singapore happens by chance and it shows. In the city, it is helpful if you remember a basic L-shape with Orchard Road and North/South Bridge Road forming the two legs. Orchard Road is the address of a large number of international hotels and shopping centers while North/South Bridge Road borders on colonial Singapore, the business center, and Chinatown.

I strongly recommend that you pick up a copy of the excellent, free American Express Map of Singapore. It is available at the airport, at hotels, and at the Singapore Tourist Promotion Board offices. Further local information about Singapore is available from the Tourist Information Center at Raffles City Shopping Center where North Bridge Road joins Bras Basah Road (an extension of Orchard Road), and at the desk at Scotts Center in Scotts Road.

Don't be put off when some people tell you there is little to see in Singapore. That is simply not true. There is in fact great variety. Most people would not dream that in Singapore you can visit a rubber plantation and a Malay *kampong* village, or that you can trek through primary jungle, pole a longboat among the steamy mangrove swamps, or walk a stretch of deserted beach. But this is another side of Singapore far removed from the shops and the skyscrapers.

Unfortunately Singapore's city attractions are so spread out and numerous that it is impossible to visit them all in a short time. The best you can hope to do is visit one area of the city then catch some transportation to the next area of interest, and so on until your time runs out. Within each area, the only way to fully appreciate the whole picture is to walk. Let us start with areas close to where most visitors will be staying.

ORCHARD ROAD AREA

The Orchard Road area has become the major hotel and shopping precinct. It is the area where the majority of visitors will spend most of their time, yet you need to get away from here to see the variety within the city. We will begin our sight-seeing where Orchard Road starts at the junction of Tanglin Road and Orange Grove Road. The area to the west of here contains many beautiful homes and a large number of embassies—including those of Australia, New Zealand, Britain, Japan, the U.S.S.R., Pakistan, and the Philippines. This is a great area for a late afternoon stroll.

Orchard Road is a broad thoroughfare lined by major hotels and shopping centers. It is a walker's delight with a well-paved pedestrian boulevard clear of the heavy one-way vehicular traffic flow. It will take you six minutes or half a day to reach the first major intersection of Scotts Road, depending on your inclination to shop or look. Scotts Road itself has become an important hotel and shopping street so many visitors will be tempted off to the left into the modern shopping plazas and high-class boutiques.

If this happens to you, wander the few extra meters up the rise to have a quick look at the Goodwood Park Hotel—a classic from days gone-by but now one of Singapore's top hotels. It offers a famous high tea which you might enjoy. If you go far enough (about one kilometer) you will reach Newton Circus and the site of one of the best hawkers' centers.

Back on Orchard Road you can either plunge underground into the Orchard MRT station for the 1½-kilometer ride to Dhoby Ghaut station, or continue walking. Before you do that, however, step into the lobby of the Dynasty Hotel and admire the huge woodcarvings that grace the walls. The next half kilometer of Orchard Road is much the same as before—more shopping centers, more high-rise hotels. **Peranakan Place** changes that—here on the corner of Emerald Hill Road, six old-fashioned shop houses now bloom in pastel tones with decorative moldings and traditional tiles. This is our first look at old Singapore and you will like what you see. There are quaint shops and restaurants, antique furnishings, and plenty of atmosphere. The adjacent Emerald Mall is a great place for a snack, a drink, or a full meal in a delightful outdoor setting. It is open from 8 A.M. till 1 A.M.

It can be hard going from here. There is another three-quarters of a kilometer of shopping centers and hotels before you pass the Dhoby Ghaut railway station and come to the eastern end of Orchard Road. Just before you reach here, it is worth going one block to the right along Clemenceau Avenue to see the **House of Tan Yeok Nee**, which was built in 1885 and is a fine example of an architectural style then popular in South China. It is now the headquarters of the Salvation Army and is open to the public Monday through Friday 8:30 A.M.-4:30 P.M.

At the end of Orchard Road turn half right into Stamford Road, take a quick look at the small Presbyterian Church, and the equally small Wesley Church in Fort Canning Road, then head for the **National Museum and Art Gallery**. This gracious Victorian building was originally opened in 1887 as the Raffles Museum. The building has been extensively renovated and improved in recent years and it is now a treasure house of history, art, and ethnology of Singapore and southeast Asia. There is a wide collection of articles relating to Sir Stamford Raffles including his manuscripts, and the Revere Bell donated to the original St. Andrew's Church in 1843 by the daughter of the American patriot, Paul Revere.

The museum now holds the fabulous 380-piece Haw Par Jade Collection and this alone is worth the visit for some people. The art collection is not outstanding, but there are some interesting contemporary works by local painters as well as some historically important canvases. You can buy cards, prints and books at the museum shop. The museum and art gallery open every day except Sundays and public holidays: art gallery 9 A.M.-4:30 P.M., admission free; museum 9 A.M.-5:30 P.M., admission S$1 for adults and S$0.50 for children.

Behind the museum you will find **Fort Canning Park**. This was once the ancient fortress of Malay kings called the Forbidden Hill, then later it was an important British fort. White stone Gothic entrance gates lead you up to an old Christian cemetery where you'll find the gravestones of Singapore's first European settlers dating from 1820. You can see the remains of the fort in massive metal gates, a derelict guardhouse and earthworks. It was from this point that guns were fired daily to mark dawn, noon, and night for the young colony.

LITTLE INDIA

Your goal now is an area known as Little India, so to reach it by foot, you have to retrace your path to the end of Orchard Road then head off along Dhoby Ghaut and Selegie Road until you eventually reach Serangoon Road (about 0.75 kilometers). This is a long, straight street pushing its way through an area of older, sometimes crumbling shop houses punctuated here and there by a few high-rise buildings.

Serangoon Road is an adventure of color, sounds, and smells. It is a world apart from the Orchard Road area we have just left. Gone are the pop songs and music of the West. In their place are the lyrical *sitar* or the plaintive high voice of a well-known Indian singer. This is no stage for tourists; it is India in the raw. There are beggars, vendors in stark white *dhotis*, young housewives with jewels glittering from their nostrils, and shirtless Tamil men washing down the sidewalks. It is totally foreign for most visitors, but not at all daunting.

Many of the buildings here have seen better days; the plaster on their arched arcades is cracked and peeling, weeds poke out of gutters and from holes in the sidewalk, and tiles are missing from roofs. But there is plenty of life in the people passing by—women in brightly colored *saris* off to the temple or the market, men in white cotton *dhotis* or safari suits off to work, young people hailing taxis or waiting impatiently at bus stands.

You have to see this area on foot. Apart from the temples and street action, you need to venture into strange little stores, take an Indian coffee at a corner coffee shop, and savor the smell from the curry houses. Most of Serangoon Road is arcaded so walking is fine in just about any weather, but don't be afraid to venture into some of the side streets as well. As in India, a great deal of commerce takes place on the sidewalks and under the arcades.

See the small *sari*, garland, and sound equipment shops along Buffalo Road. Mannequins with chipped plaster smiles are draped in beautiful silk saris from India and polyester ones from Japan. Look above the doorways and you will see strings of dried mango leaves, a customary Indian sign of blessing and good fortune. Check out the market stalls selling prawn crackers, rice, and dried beans side by side with tinkling trinkets and plastic toys in Clive Street and solid gold chains and jewelry in long, narrow, old-fashioned shops. Bargaining is an accepted part of each transaction. This is no place for impulse, casual shopping.

This area has numerous temples. The **Sri Veeramakaliamman Temple** on Serangoon Road is dedicated to "Kali the Courageous," a ferocious incarnation of Siva's wife. Over on Chander Street, the four-story **Shree Lakshminarayan Temple** is the only Northern Hindu temple in Singapore. In Tai Gin Road the new **Burmese Buddhist Temple** houses a 10-meter-high Buddha carved from a 10-ton block of white marble from Mandalay. Back on Senangoon Road the **Sri Srinivasa Perumal Temple** has a 20-meter-high monumental gateway with intricate sculptures depicting fine manifestations of Vishnu the Preserver. Along a little farther is the **Central Sikh Temple**, a modern three-storied temple with a unique injection of the traditional. The temple has an impressive 13-meter-wide dome, and a prayer hall with the holy book as its centerpiece.

Perhaps the most interesting temple of all is the **Temple of 1000 Lights** on Race Course Road. The temple is dominated by a brightly painted 15-meter-high seated figure of the Buddha that is surrounded by countless lights. If you have seen Buddhist temples in Thailand or Burma you will recognize that this has far more Chinese influence than others. There is a huge mother-of-pearl Buddha footprint and many other intriguing religious relics from the Buddha's life. Directly across the road is the charming Chinese **Leong San See** containing a main altar dedicated to Kuan Yin. The temple entrance is impressive with stone lions, carved wooden lotus flowers, and beautiful frescos.

ARAB STREET

The Arab Street area is a direct result of Raffles' decision to allot different areas of the new colony for commercial and residential purposes, thus ensuring that people of similar origins and trade congregated together. When Arab traders flocked to Singapore it was natural that they should head to the Muslim areas near the palace of the Malay ruler. Today there are few ethnic Arabs here, since most of them intermarried with local Malay or Indian Muslims, but the area is still completely dominated by the Muslim community of Singapore.

The mantle of Islam hangs almost palpably over the Arab Street area with prayer rugs hanging on the wood-panelled walls of many of the textile shops, and prayer shawls, caps, and special money belts available almost everywhere. When the call goes out from the mosque that there is no other god but Allah, the whole region seems to vibrate in agreement.

From Little India, you walk southeastward, cross the Rochor Canal, and you are quickly in the heart of the area. You'll find streets with names straight from the Middle East—Baghdad, Muscat, Kandahar, and others taken direct from Malay—Jalan Pisang, Jalan Pinang, and Jalan Kubor. At Sultan Gate you can see the Sultan's once-grand mansion behind two imposing old gateposts. In Jalan Sultan, the Sultan Plaza houses many traditional Arab, Indonesian, Malay, and Muslim-Indian cloth traders. Here *batiks*, sarongs, flower essences, and rattan goods go hand in hand. Here too are some excellent Muslim restaurants, so stop for a meal.

Very few remnants of "Old Singapore" remain. Typical shop houses on Arab Street.

Precious works of art and jewelry are popular buys in Singapore.

The **Sultan Mosque** is the most impressive building in this area. The present imposing building was completed in 1928. It replaced the first mosque that was built on this site in the early 1820s with a cash grant from the East India Company as part of the treaty with the Sultan of Johore. The gold-domed building is open to visitors from 5 A.M. to 8:30 P.M. daily. If you are here at dawn, 12:30 P.M., 4 P.M., sunset, or 8:15 P.M., you will hear the Bilal calling the faithful to prayer. The **Hajjah Fatimah Mosque** on Beach Road is also worth seeing. A wealthy Muslim woman commissioned a British architect to build this delightful mosque in 1845. Its leaning minaret is reputedly modelled on the spire of the original St. Andrew's Church. There are two historic Muslim burial grounds in the Arab Street area, one of which contains the graves of several Malay princes.

COLONIAL SINGAPORE

As Singapore becomes more and more high-rise, its colonial-era architecture and town planning become very precious commodities. For the visitor, they are a reminder of how Singapore came to be—and fortunately the government has recognized the value to both visitors and residents alike. Sir Stamford Raffles would undoubtedly be startled to see the current profile of his swampy, tropical island but nevertheless, he would recognize many of the features of the area south from Bras Basah Road.

The perfect starting point is **Raffles Hotel**. It's just a short stroll along Beach Road from the Arab Street area. It is said that the world knew Raffles Hotel better than Singapore at one time. Colonial gentlemen retired to the bar for that Raffles invention, the Singapore Sling, and a steady flow of overseas celebrities decorated its corridors. The French Renaissance building became the focal point of Singapore social life in the early 1900s and its reputation spread far and wide. Today Raffles Hotel provides thoroughly modern facilities but its colonial charm remains. At enormous cost the old hotel has been completely restructured and it once more provides the best in Singapore. You simply cannot visit Singapore without a visit to Raffles Hotel.

Many people would say the same about **Raffles City**. Certainly nothing represents modern Singapore better than this area. The soaring skyscrapers contain two huge hotels, a state-of-the-art shopping complex, a modern office tower that houses the headquarters of the Singapore Tourist Promotion Board, and an entrance to the City Hall MRT station. You will probably find yourself here at some time during your stay.

The Sultan Mosque in Singapore.

Of more immediate interest are three Christian churches in this general area. If you plan to visit all three, select the **Cathedral of the Good Shepherd** first. This is Singapore's Catholic cathedral and was completed in 1846 with funds collected by a French priest. You will find it in Bras Basah Road. Now walk down Victoria Street and Hill Street, past the U.S. Embassy, to the delightful **Armenian Church of St. Gregory the Illuminator**. This beautiful building was built in 1835 and is Singapore's oldest church. It is still used for services and has been preserved as a national monument. The Armenians were just one of the minority groups who came to Singapore in the early days. The church was built with funds contributed by just a few families who commissioned George Coleman as their architect. The result is one of his finest works. You can also explore the churchyard with its many weathered tombstones.

Now walk down Coleman Street and enter the grounds of **St. Andrews Cathedral** from North Bridge Road. In 1823, Raffles earmarked this site for a church. The present fine early English Gothic-style Anglican cathedral was built between 1856 and 1861, largely by Indian convict labor. The cathedral's interior walls are coated with a rock-hard plaster called "Madras Chunam," an extraordinary mixture of shell lime, egg whites, and sugar. If you are hungry or thirsty, the ladies of St. Andrews thoughtfully provide light refreshments within the church building for a nominal cost.

If you exit to St. Andrew's Road, there before you lies the bright green lawns of the **Padang**. This long, immaculate green is still home to weekend cricket matches. Parasol-shaded colonial ladies and white-jacketed gentlemen used to stroll the length of the green, meeting to exchange news that apparently was spicy enough to give the place the nickname "Scandal Point." At that time "sport" on the Padang was considered almost mandatory and it is said that many a civil servant or company director was hired more for his proficiency at cricket or rugby than for his academic or professional powers. Today the Padang is a delightful place to spend a few moments with your memories.

There are several impressive buildings overlooking the Padang. Most prominent are **City Hall** and the **Supreme Court**. These buildings, with Corinthian columns, house the seats of government and justice. City Hall was completed in 1929 and its steps have seen many major events such as the formal surrender of Japanese forces in 1945 to Admiral Lord Louis Mountbatten. The Supreme Court was completed in 1939. Its classical murals were executed by Italian artist Cavaliere Nolli. Inside high vaulted archways and columns support a richly panelled wooden ceiling. It is well worth seeing.

At the end of the Padang, opposite the Singapore Cricket Club, is the **Victoria Memorial Hall** and **Victoria Theatre**. The elegant Victorian Theatre, to the left of the clock tower, was originally completed in 1862 as Singapore's Town Hall. On the right is the Victorian Memorial Hall built as a tribute to Queen Victoria in 1905 and now the permanent home of the Singapore Symphony Orchestra. Outside is a bronze statue of Raffles, founder of modern Singapore. Across the other side of the Padang stands the **Cenotaph**, a solemn sandstone reminder of two World Wars.

Nearby is the **Lim Bo Seng Memorial**, which commemorates the deeds of a young leader of the resistance movement who died a tortured captive in 1944. From here you have an excellent view across the Singapore River to Merlion Park where the 8-meter-high Merlion (half-lion, half-fish) stands as the symbol of the city.

If you now follow the river upstream, you reach what is probably the colonial heart of Singapore. You first come to **Empress Place**, Singapore's first major conservation project to come alive. From a fairly tired old building, the new has re-emerged like a beautiful butterfly. Built in 1854 as a courthouse, on the site where Raffles first stepped ashore, the building accommodated various government departments over the years. Its new life, as a world-class museum and exhibition center, began in 1989 with a series of magnificent exhibitions from China.

I strongly advise you to ask about Empress Place when you visit Singapore. If future exhibitions are to the standard of those that I have seen, this becomes a "must see" on every visitor's itinerary. Apart from the exhibition, Empress Place also houses a Chinese restaurant, a silk shop, Chinese arts and crafts shops, and an Asian antique emporium. The building is open daily from 9:30 A.M. to 9:30 P.M. Admission to the exhibition is around S$6 for adults, S$3 for children.

When you exit Empress Place, head for the river and you will see a copy of the original **Raffles statue** on the river bank. Close by is **Parliament House**, the oldest government building in Singapore. The core of today's structure was originally a magnificent two-story mansion built in 1827 by architect George Coleman. Here you get the chance of some magnificent panoramas—the juxtaposition of ornate colonial facades with glittering glass and chrome high-rise. Singapore, it seems, thrives on the winds of change.

THE CITY

Frankly, the city center of Singapore has little attraction. It is mainly a collection of high-rise office buildings housing banks, insurance companies, airlines, and so forth. New buildings appear all the time like mushrooms after heavy rain. There are, however, a few reasons why visitors will go there. The first is because of the **General Post Office**. This is the first building you see when you cross the Singapore River from Empress Place. It is situated in Fullerton Road (Tel: 532-3753). If you have letters coming c/o *poste restante*, this is where they will be. The office is open from 8:30 A.M. until 5:30 P.M. weekdays and until 1:30 P.M. on Saturday. You can also make international telephone calls from the telecom center within the same building.

Most of the major banks are in the city and if you have complicated transactions to attend to, this is the place to go. Exchange rates vary a little from bank to bank and some make a service charge on exchange transactions, but in my experience it is not worthwhile worrying about this. If getting the highest possible rate is your top priority you may get a better rate for cash at one of the money changers. These are situated along the **Change Alley** shopping arcade or in Raffles Quay.

Change Alley is, or was, Singapore's most famous place for bargains. In the days before Orchard Road, this is where all visitors headed. Time has taken its toll, but it still exists as a shopping center, even if in a different form. The old alley ran between Collyer Quay and Raffles Place. It was narrow, crowded, and dirty. Today's version is called Change Alley Aerial Plaza and it is an elevated, air-conditioned pedestrian walkway. Somehow it is not quite the same.

Heading down Shenton Way parallel to the waterfront, you may wish to stop off for a meal at the 100-year-old **Lau Pa Sat Festival Market**. The cast-iron octagonal structure, originally imported from Scotland, has been nicely restored to provide an entertainment area close to the city's financial heart.

Our ultimate destination now is Chinatown, so if you walk along Cross Street or Boon Tat Street you will be heading in the right direction. Before reaching Chinatown you come to **Telok Ayer** Street. This is important because there are three impressive but widely different religious structures here. This street was once the original seafront where newly arrived immigrants came ashore and offered prayers of thanksgiving for safe passages to their new home. The **Al-Abrar Mosque** was built in 1850-55 by Indian Muslims. It is now a national monument. The present building replaced the original thatched *attap* hut that served as a mosque from 1827.

The **Nagore Durgha Shrine** was built by southern Indian Muslims between 1828 and 1830. It skillfully blends East and West. At street level you see Doric columns and Palladian doors, while above is a traditional, intricate Muslim facade. Most memorable of all are the twin turrets. The **Thian Hock Keng Temple** is the oldest Chinese temple in Singapore. It was completed in 1841, replacing a humble joss house established here in 1821 by grateful Hokkien immigrants. You can see 150-year-old ancestral tablets and stone slabs inscribed with the names of the temple's benefactors. There are granite pillars entwined with dragons, a plaque from the Chinese emperor, rooftop dragons, burning joss sticks, and beautifully painted doors and gold-leafed panels. The temple is open daily from 5:30 A.M. till about 9 P.M.

CHINATOWN

The area straight ahead is Chinatown. It was once one of the most fascinating areas of Singapore but today it is only a shadow of its former glory. Originally, wealthy Chinese built shop houses here—shops on the ground level, homes above them. They constructed them side by side in terraces using elaborate neoclassical architectural details such as ornate pilasters, columns, and decorative molding. This style came to characterize much of Singapore.

A few years ago it looked as if Chinatown would disappear completely—to be replaced by hideous high-rise slab apartment blocks—but fortunately the government realized the international appeal of this area and took action. Hopefully further destruction has been stopped. If you are curious, there are enough things in this area—from medicines, curios, and foodstuffs to household goods, paper money, and calligraphy—to keep you happy for hours.

The most northerly part of Chinatown borders the Singapore River. Here, along Boat Quay, you can still see the old riverside shrines and trading company offices. In nearby Phillip Street, the **Temple of the Calm Seas** was built in 1852-55 with a roof covered with a mass of miniature pagodas and human figures. Phillip Street leads into Telok Ayer Street, but when you reach Cross Street, turn left, then left again into Amoy Street. Follow this to Pekin Street and eventually to China Street.

These streets are all lined with Chinese shop fronts with their covered walkways and streetside activities. Old men still ride by on bicycle rickshaws, you can visit a traditional Chinese medical hall where the pharmacist selects centuries-old remedies from dozens of drawers inscribed with Chinese characters, and you will even find a last remaining darkened Chinese wine shop.

Follow China Street back to Cross Street then find Club Street, which was named for all the trade guilds and self-help groups located here. Gemmill Lane leads off to the left and here a weathered archway leads

An Indian Hindu temple in the heart of Chinese Singapore.

into the Yeung Ching School, an old "free" school established for needy pupils. Club Street leads to Ann Siang Road and eventually to South Bridge Road. During your wanderings you will have seen a street calligrapher who can read your fortune in your hand or your face, shops where idol carvers and temple gods makers are busily at work, and others where you can buy theater masks and lion heads.

When you cross South Bridge Road you enter the real heart of Chinatown. Sago Street is where you can see shops making paper houses and cars to be burned at funerals. In neighboring Trengani Street you can take your pick of local fruits, flowers, and dried foods. In Mosque Street, the old shop houses that were originally built as stables now display the wares of secondhand dealers. In these areas you can see evidence of government action to restore rather than destroy. It is an encouraging sign.

Food opportunities are endless. The Chinese restaurants are for the locals not tourists, but you will be welcome if you stop for a drink or a meal.

Incongruously situated in the heart of Chinatown is the **Sri Mariamman Temple**, the oldest Hindu temple in Singapore. It was originally a wood and *attap* shrine built around 1827, but by 1847 much of today's present building was in existence. With its delightful *gopuram*, or tower over the entrance, it is built in the south Indian style. An amazing collection of colorful Hindu figures gaze out, begging you to take a photograph. You are welcome to enter the temple and you will often find that a noisy and colorful ceremony will start up while you are there. If you happen to be here in October, you may be lucky enough to see devotees walk over a four-meter-long pit of burning coals in the courtyard.

Chinatown is an area for personal discovery. All the streets are full of interest and I strongly recommend that you just wander around. It is quite easy to spend half a day just exploring. The **Tanjong Pagar** area just to the south of here is equally worth some of your time. This represents the new Singapore attitude towards conservation and pres- ervation. It has successfully survived the city's bulldozer period. While you could be critical of the color schemes being used, I am sure few will argue that the reconstructed shop houses are not far better than what existed before and far superior to any modern style development. It is an area that begs the visitor to stop and explore. Applying concrete, plaster, and paint to an old building is easy. Saving the character of the building, the energy and feeling of community—everything that makes a neighborhood an interesting and happy place to work, live, shop, or visit—is much more difficult. At Tanjong Pagar it has been achieved.

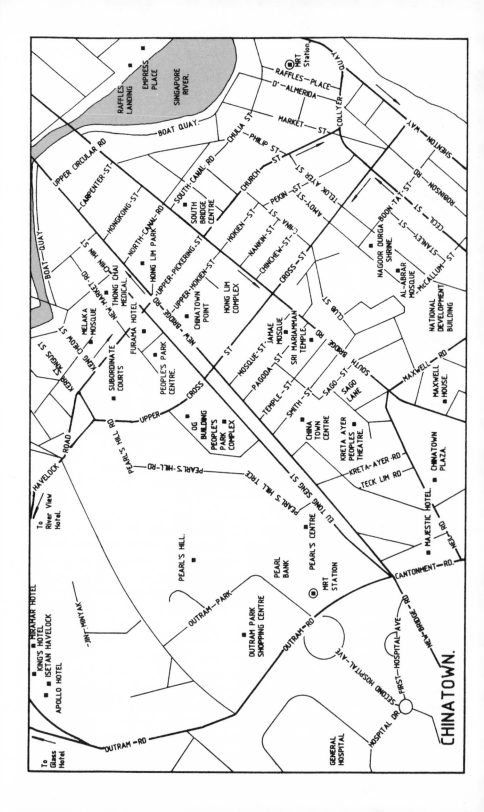

CHINATOWN.

There are discoveries to be made everywhere. One example is the **Tea Chapter** (Tel: 226-1175), which occupies two floors of a shop house at 9A Neil Road. For the serious tea drinker, there is an ancient tea ritual to get that perfect cup of tea. I found that fascinating but even if you are not fanatical about that ancient brew, the atmosphere and old-world charm will still appeal. Tea Chapter is open from 11 A.M. to 11 P.M. daily. There are often Chinese musical performances and poetry recitals at night. Close by there are some fascinating shops like House of Clogs and High Point Kite Shop.

There are also several other innovative, warm tea houses, restaurants, bars, and lounges in this area. Personal discovery is the best bet.

JURONG

I am going to take a very narrow view on Jurong because frankly I think that is what the visitor will do. For Singaporeans, Jurong is the economic miracle that keeps their country prosperous, but for visitors it is simply an industrial area where there are six worthwhile attractions. From Chinatown you reach Jurong by bus or MRT. From the Outram Park MRT station you travel to Jurong East station for the Science Center, to Chinese Garden station for the Chinese and Japanese Gardens, and to Lakeside station for the Jurong Bird Park, the Jurong Crocodile Paradise, and the Singapore Mint.

The Science Center and Omni-Theatre (Tel: 560-3316) on Jurong Town Hall Road is educational fun for all ages. It is one of the best such facilities in Asia. There are over 500 exhibits and push-button demonstrations that cover physical and life sciences from electronics to human birth. There are films to watch and countless opportunities to peer at, touch, and participate in exhibits. The center is open from 10 A.M. to 6 P.M., Tuesdays through Sundays. Admission is S$2 for adults, S$0.50 for children. The adjacent omni-theater has several afternoon screenings covering space journeys and other subjects. Tickets cost S$9 adult and S$4 child. You can book ahead for particular screenings.

The **Japanese Garden** and the **Yu Hwa Yuan Chinese Garden** are both off Yuan Ching Road. Each covers about 13 hectares (32 acres) and the two are linked by a long ornamental bridge. The gardens are modelled on those of the Japanese minimalist landscaping style and the imperial Sung dynasty style. They provide a unique opportunity to contrast the exuberant Chinese style with the calm and reflective Japanese style. Both are open from 9 A.M. to 7 P.M. but there is no admission after 6 p.m. Joint admission is S$2.50 for adults and S$1.20 for children, with a camera charge of S$0.50.

The **Jurong Bird Park** (Tel: 265-0022) on Jalan Ahmad Ibralim is a 20-hectare (50-acre) reserve that houses over 300 species and more than 5000 birds. In the world's largest enclosed walk-in aviary, a 30-meter-high waterfall cascades into a valley filled with tropical rain forest. Exotic waterbirds, lorikeets, ibises, peacocks, and many native southeast Asian birds thrive here. In the nocturnal house, lighting turns day into night so you can observe owls, kiwi, night herons, and other rare species when they are most active. A giant aviary houses the World of Southeast Asian Birds.

You can also see several shows—the King of the Skies birds of prey show at 10 A.M. and 4 P.M., the Free Flight show at 10:30 A.M. and the delightful Parrot Circus at 3 P.M. You can tour the park by foot or by tram car. Admission is S$6 for adults and S$2.50 for children. The park is open from 9 A.M. to 6 P.M. daily and it is probably best early or late in the day when the birds are more active and easier to see. Bus No. 250, 251, or 253 go to the park from the Jurong Interchange. For something different, the park serves Breakfast with the Birds each morning from 9 A.M. to 11 A.M. at the Song Bird Terrace. The cost is S$9.50 for adults, S$8.50 for children.

The **Jurong Crocodile Paradise** (Tel: 261-8866) is right next door to the Bird Park. This is a breeding farm, but the 2500 crocodiles are also a major tourist attraction. The farm contains a large landscaped area complete with running stream and tropical vegetation where hundreds of reptiles enjoy an environment somewhat akin to their natural homes. There is also a crocodilarium where you can view crocodiles from some unusual angles, a nocturnal enclosure for simulated night viewing, and a show that features crocodile wrestling and other performances. The farm is open from 9 A.M. to 6 P.M. daily. Admission is S$4.50 for adults and S$2.50 for children.

The **Singapore Mint Coin Gallery** (Tel: 265-3907) at 249 Jalan Boon Lay is a free attraction admired by many. You can watch an audio-visual show of the minting operations, see a display of coins, medals, and medallions from Singapore and around the world, and shop for coins and souvenirs. It is open from 9:30 A.M. to 4:30 P.M., Monday through Friday.

The **Tang Dynasty City** (Tel: 261-1116) is the latest attraction in Jurong. This S$50-million leisure and entertainment park replicates an ancient Tang city. Attractions include an underground palace, a 15-story pagoda, a summer palace, lodging houses, and a pool. Adults S$15, child S$10, lunch S$20, dinner show S$38.

Paddle-boating and swimming at Sentosa's lagoon.

The 18-hole Sentosa Tanjong course, on the resort island of Sentosa.

SENTOSA ISLAND

Twenty years ago it was a military base, now it is southeast Asia's premier island attraction. That's quite an achievement and it hasn't been done cheaply or easily. Five years ago, Sentosa Island was generally considered to be a flop by international visitors, but not any more. And in the next few years there will be even more attractions to draw visitors here. Many locals go to Sentosa to swim or laze around in the parkland. International visitors will go there primarily for the individual attractions. These are many.

Underwater World is Asia's largest tropical fish oceanarium. You enter by a bridge over a turtle pond then view a six-minute audiovisual show that examines man's relationship with the sea. The heart of the attraction is a moving footway that traverses beneath two gigantic tanks teaming with fish and marine life. There is a touch pool and various other exhibits. It is one of the better attractions of this kind that I have seen. Admission is S$9 for adults, S$4 for children. Opening hours are 9 A.M. to 9 P.M. daily.

Pioneers of Singapore and Surrender Chambers takes you on a journey back in time to a more colorful period of Singapore's past. Life-size tableaux depict the men and women who helped build Singapore. See the humiliation and the joy of victory in two momentous events of World War II, helped by the latest audio-video technology. Admission is S$3 for adults and S$1 for children.

The nearby **Butterfly Park** has over 2500 butterflies from 50 species fluttering around among the visitors. This attraction also has a world insectarium where you can see everything that creeps, crawls, or flies. The Park is open daily from 9:30 A.M. to 5:30 P.M. Admission is S$2.50 for adults and S$1.50 for children.

The **Rare Stone Museum** (Tel: 275-0277) is claimed to be the only collection of its kind in the world. Over 4000 rare and unique stones show you landscapes, famous figures, and other fascinating designs carved by nature. Admission is S$2 for adults and S$1 for children.

Fort Siloso (Tel: 275-0131) is a look at what Sentosa was like in a previous life. You can visit underground tunnels and gun turrets filled with the sounds of men at war. The guns were all pointing in the wrong direction when the Japanese invaded in World War II. While most of the other attractions on the island were made just for visitors, you know that this is the real thing. Somehow it has more impact.

An additional attraction at Fort Siloso is the new permanent exhibition of life as a prisoner of war in Singapore. "Behind Bars" focuses on prison life during the World War II Japanese occupation and includes the reconstruction of two prison cells, reproductions of Changi Prison murals by POW Stanley Warren, and original Changi life sketches by POW "Puggy" Haxworth. There is also a five-minute video.

There are several other components to Sentosa. Visit the Maritime Museum, see the musical fountain, wander down the nature walk, visit the orchid garden, or relax in the fountain gardens. Sporting facilities include a bicycle track, a roller skating rink, two golf courses, a boating lagoon, and swimming facilities. On Friday, Saturday, and Sunday evenings there is a night market with more than 40 stalls. The new Riverboat Restaurant patterned on a Mississippi paddle steamer adds a further dining option.

Normal admission tickets to Sentosa Island cost S$3.50 for adults and S$2 for children. They cover return ferry, unlimited monorail and bus rides, and admission to the many "free" attractions on the island. There is an "after-5 P.M." ticket for S$3.

Getting to Sentosa is relatively easy. You can catch Bus No. 143 or 167 from hotels in the Orchard Road area to the World Trade Center. Ferries leave here every 15 minutes for the five-minute ride to Sentosa Island. Alternatively you can board the cable car from Cable Car Towers next to the World Trade Center and enjoy the spectacular views as you soar across to the island. This is well worth taking at least one way. A causeway link to the mainland opened in 1993.

Accommodation is available on the island at the 220-room **The Beaufort Resort** (Tel: 275-0331), which opened in 1992. It is a fine hotel with a relaxing atmosphere and fine service. There are excellent sporting facilities. Under construction at present is the 450-room **Rasa Sentosa Beach Resort**. Transportation on the island is by monorail to seven stations, by bus, or by rental bicycles. The attractions are too scattered to visit them all on foot but you will find that even when you use the monorail or bus, you will end up doing quite a bit of walking. Sentosa is a place for comfortable shoes.

OTHER ATTRACTIONS

While the areas we have covered to date have been relatively compact, there are a range of attractions scattered throughout the rest of the country. The major ones are these.

Changi Prison Chapel is situated in the Changi Prison on Upper Changi Road, out past the airport. To the 85,000 soldiers and civilians held captive during World War II, Changi Prison remains a stark emotional symbol of their wartime experiences. For many, the prison chapel was a source of strength over those long dark years. The chapel has been rebuilt and today it is a place of pilgrimage by war veterans and visitors alike. A guest book with the inscription "Lest we Forget" allows visitors to pay tribute to the faith, courage, and perseverance of the prisoners.

Visitors may also see the astonishing drawings, sketches, and photographs from those days in the prison museum. Opening hours are from 8:30 A.M. to 12:30 P.M. and from 2 P.M. to 4:45 P.M. on weekdays and from 8:30 A.M. to 12:30 P.M. on Saturdays. The chapel holds a Sunday service from 5:30 P.M. to 6:30 P.M. to which all are welcome.

The Botanic Gardens (Tel: 474-1165), located on the northern edge of the main city, consistently rate among the top five visitor attractions in Singapore. The park features broad sweeping lawns, areas of virtually untouched jungle, a 2500-plant orchid enclosure, and extensive lakes. Virtually every tree has its own story—from the banyan with its massive aerial roots, to the sealing wax and betel nut palms, and the South American cannonball tree with its ball-shaped fruit.

It was here in 1877 that Henry Ridley propagated Brazilian rubber plants that had been sent from London's Kew Gardens. From these saplings sprang the Malaysian rubber industry. The government has commenced work on a S$50-million development plan that will see the gardens expand from 47 to 54 hectares, add a huge cloud forest attraction, expand the orchid enclosure, and establish spice gardens, a rubber tree plantation, cacti and water gardens, a tram system, and visitor and education centers. The gardens are open from 5 A.M. to 11 P.M. and admission is free. It is an ideal place for an early morning jog or a more sedate stroll later in the day.

The **Zoological Gardens** (Tel: 269-3411) are on Mandai Lake Road in a lush 90-hectare (220-acre) setting by the tranquil Seletar Reservoir. Considerable effort has gone into achieving an "open zoo" where moats and rock walls take the place of bars. There are more than 1700 animals of some 172 species including endangered animals such as cheetah, Sumatran tiger, Malaysian tapir, clouded leopard, and rare golden lion tamarins. The zoo is world-renowned for its special orangutan breeding program and boasts the largest colony of any zoo in the world.

On every day except Sundays you can have breakfast with an orangutan and observe some crazy antics at close hand. It is a very popular and recommended adventure. You need to arrive at the zoo by 8:45 A.M., pay your S$7 admission, then go to the Orangutan Terrace where you pay S$11 for breakfast. Don't forget to take your camera and get some great shots of your friends cuddling the furry beast. The breakfast is not exactly a gastronomic sensation but it is a unique experience.

The zoo has daily attractions including polar bear shows at 10 A.M., 1 P.M., and 4:45 P.M.; primate and reptile shows at 10:30 A.M. and 2:30 P.M.; and elephant and sea lion shows at 11:30 A.M. and 3:30 P.M. The zoo is open seven days a week from 8:30 A.M. to 6 P.M. "Zoo express" buses operate to the zoo and back twice daily from many hotels. For transportation, admission to the zoo and the Mandai Orchid Gardens, adults pay S$20 and children S$14. (Tel: 235-3111 for bookings.) No one that I know has come away from the zoo disappointed.

The **Mandai Orchid Garden** on Mandai Lake Road is four hectares (10 acres) of orchids. It is a breathtaking vista for anyone who ever thought an orchid spelled tropical romance. The gardens are open daily from 8:30 A.M. to 5:30 P.M. with admission S$1.50 for adults and S$0.50 for children. Take bus No. 171 from the downtown area.

Another "garden" attraction is the **Bukit Timah Nature Reserve** on the Upper Bukit Tiham Road. This popular parkland on Singapore's highest land point allows you to trek through the type of tropical vegetation that covered Singapore when Raffles arrived. Clearly marked trails show you exotic birds, butterflies, the occasional monkey, and good views over the island. Admission is free. The walk to the top takes about an hour, is best done early in the morning, and requires sensible walking shoes. The air is heavily laden with the musty odor of dampness and decay. Lichens and moss cling to rocks and boulders hidden from the sun. From the branches above, trailing vines and creepers veil the sun, which only penetrates in pencil-thin shafts. Take bus No. 171 or 172 from the downtown area.

A new outdoor attraction is set to open sometime soon. Called the **Williton Flower Center**, the 15-hectare complex at Mandai will boast a staggering 50,000 orchid varieties in addition to other flowers such as roses and carnations all set in landscaped gardens. There will be an orchid information counter, an audiovisual theater, refreshment bars, a restaurant, souvenir shops, and classrooms for flower-arranging courses.

Back in the city, the **Van Kleef Aquarium** (Tel: 337-6271) on River Valley Road is worth seeing if fish are your thing. Built in 1955 with funds donated by Mr. Van Kleef, a Dutch industrialist living in Singapore, the recently renovated aquarium has an impressive collection of more than 6000 specimens of freshwater and marine species of fish, molluses, crustaceans, and amphibians. Opening hours are 10 A.M. to 6 P.M. daily. Admission is S$1 for adults and S$0.50 for children. Feeding time is 12 noon. Take bus No. 123 or 143 from Orchard Road or No. 122 from North Bridge Road and Bencoolen Street.

The **Haw Par Villa** or the **Tiger Balm Gardens** have been around for years but anyone who visited 10 years ago would simply not recognize the gardens today. The original Chinese mythological theme park was financed by the fortune the Aw brothers made from their amazing Tiger Balm cure-all mixture. A few years ago it was considered to be a joke by many foreign visitors but now after extensive restoration and supplementation, and the addition of twenty-first-century technology, it is an excellent attraction.

You can walk or ride through the mysterious world of Chinese legends. Outdoor performances of martial arts, music, dance, and puppetry take place in the amphitheater and in outdoor performance areas. There are numerous food and drink kiosks and souvenir shops. The gardens are open daily. Admission is S$16 for adults, S$10 for children. Bus No. 10, 30, 143, 146, or 192 pass the door.

The **Guinness World of Records Exhibition** at the World Trade Center boasts more than 1000 record-breaking figures, facts, and artifacts. It is the first of its kind in Asia and the fifth in the world. It is open from 10 A.M. to 9 P.M. daily. Admission is S$4 for adults, $3 for children.

There are numerous other sight-seeing attractions that you will enjoy if you have the time to see them but I acknowledge that they perhaps have more limited appeal. The Sunday morning **Bird Concert** is one case in point. Proud owners bring their singing birds in beautiful cages to perform at an informal concert outside a coffee shop at the corner of Tiong Bahru and Seng Poh Roads starting at 8 A.M. A visit to **Mount Faber** will provide scenic views spanning the city and harbor and it is a good place for spectacular sunsets. You can catch cable cars to Sentosa from here.

Tucked away in woodlands on the north of Singapore island, the **Kranji War Memorial** is a peaceful haven away from the city. Here under rows upon rows of headstones, some without names, lie the remains of all the Allied soldiers who died in Singapore in World War II.

In this same area you see small farms and estates partly hidden by dense scrub and undergrowth. One of Singapore's most profitable exports from these small farms is orchids. The larger farms cover many acres and the owners don't seem to mind if you stop to admire their crop. Take the time to visit Sembawang village. It isn't featured in tourist brochures and few visitors ever see it, but it's well worth the drive. So too is the Pandan River, a post of entry for trading boats from Indonesia. This is an entry to another world. The Pandan River is no more than two kilometers long, but it stands in total contrast to the nearby main harbor where container ships and super tankers weigh anchor. The cargo at Pandan is not transistors or oil, it's bundles of rattan from Java, sacks of salt from Thailand, and bags of charcoal. Here, along stone jetties there are no heavy cranes loading and unloading. Here it's muscle power and strong bodies sweating under the tropical sun.

At the other end of the city are a collection of southern islands. **Kusu Island** and **St. John's Island** have a regular ferry service from the World Trade Center (there are two services weekdays and eight on Sundays) but the others can only be reached by chartered boat or sampan. Tranquil, tree-shaded St. John's is a large, hilly island with sandy beaches and safe lagoons. Kusu also has good beaches and you can visit the hilltop shrine where Muslims come to pray, and the colorful Tua Pekong temple to which thousands of Chinese devotees make their annual pilgrimage. Avoid going on Sundays because then there is little difference between city and islands when it comes to crowds.

Seking Island is something else. The years seem to roll back the moment you get off the boat. It's hard not to feel transported back 50 years. Some 500 people live on the small island, mainly old folk and the very young. Young adults are usually lured by the bright lights of the city. You reach here by bumboat from the Jardine Steps or Clifford Pier. The journey takes about an hour.

The **Pewter Museum** (Tel: 221-4436), which occupies three restored shop houses at 49A Duxton Road in historic Tanjong Pagar, is reputed to be the only one of its kind in the world. There are items such as century-old incense burners, lamp stands, Chinese altar pieces, tobacco boxes, and wine chalices. The museum occupies the upper floor while the ground floor is a display room of modern pewter items that are for sale. It is open from 9 A.M. to 5:30 P.M. daily. Admission is free.

It is possible to travel further afield as well. From the Regional Ferry Terminal at the World Trade Center, you can catch a ferry to the Indonesian Islands of Batam and Bintan. A return trip to Batam cost S$26, while Bintan is S$13. From the same terminal you can take a trip to Malaysia's Troman Island. The return cost is S$138.

7. Guided Tours

Singapore is a regulated country so you do not have the proliferation of small tour operators that you do in some other Asian cities. That means that you can get accurate and reliable tour information from your hotel tour desk or from the information centers in Raffles City and Scotts Center. Here is a brief rundown on the most popular tours but you should check the latest information when you arrive in Singapore.

The **City Tour** operates daily in the morning and afternoon. The duration is 3½ hours and the cost is about S$22 for adults, S$11 for children. A typical tour will start with a drive along Orchard Road, passing the Presidential Palace, the Padang, and the colonial buildings, then it crosses the Singapore River, passes the city financial district, and stops for a walk in Chinatown. You will visit a Chinese and Hindu temple then go to Mount Faber for its panoramic view.

You will visit a handicraft center or two before proceeding to the botanic gardens and its orchid enclosure. A few tours include the 45-minute Instant Asia Cultural Show. For first-time visitors this is an excellent orientation tour of the city and I strongly recommend it to everyone. While it is not thrilling, it is very informative and will help you with further sight-seeing.

The **East Coast Tour** is also daily, both morning and afternoon. The tour proceeds to East Coast Park past Katong's charming old residences. Then it is almost country as you pass through coconut palms and fruit trees on the way to Changi Prison and rustic Changi village. You next visit a crocodile breeding farm, a gem factory (with its mandatory shop), and finally visit the Buddhist Temple of a Thousand Lights. This is not my first choice of a tour, but you do see a different side of Singapore compared to the high-rise of downtown. Duration is three hours and the cost is about S$18 for adults, S$9 for children.

The **Sightseeing 1819 Tour** gives you a feel for the history of Singapore. You visit the site where Raffles landed in 1819, see Victoria Memorial Hall and Victoria Theatre, observe the outside of Empress Place, Parliament House, the Supreme Court and City Hall, then visit St. Andrew's Cathedral. From here you have high tea, and go on a guided tour of the National Museum. For history buffs it is 3½ hours packed with interest. The cost is S$22 for adults and S$13 for children. Departures are Monday to Friday in the afternoon.

The **Jurong Bird Park Tour** operates daily both in the morning and afternoon. The tour takes you to the park where you watch one of the bird shows then have time to explore by yourself. On the way back to the city most tours pass by the center of Jurong Town and visit the Chinese Garden. Duration is 3½ hours and the cost is about S$25 for adults and S$18 for children.

There are several tours to the zoo but you should check with your hotel tour desk to see what is actually operating when you are there. One that is being heavily promoted is an afternoon **Zoo Special**, which has "High Tea" with an orangutan. There is always some fun and games with that. You have about 1½ hours at the zoo before or after your meal to look around and see one of the animal shows. The zoo special tour costs around S$35 for adults and S$17.50 for children. There is also a morning **Zoo Tour**, which visits the Mandai Orchid Farm and has a buffet lunch at the zoo. The cost is around S$30 for adults and $18 for children.

The **Contrasting Culture Tour** is great for visitors who would like to see why Singapore is called a multicultural society. The tour first visits Little India where you can breathe the aroma of spices and amble among the small shops. You next visit Arab Street to enjoy the Muslim culture, and finally it is to Peranakan Place for a snack and a look at this unique mixed Chinese and Malay culture. This morning tour operates four days a week and costs about S$30 for adults and S$15 for children.

There are a wide range of harbor and island cruises. One-hour cruises on a bumboat are offered at 10 A.M., 12 noon, 2 P.M., 4 P.M., and 6 P.M. on the Singapore River. Hotel pickups do not operate for these tours but other particulars are available by telephoning 533-3432. Light refreshments are served on board while you cruise past quaint shops and "go downs," skyscrapers, and some fine colonial buildings. Singapore River Cruises (Tel: 227-9678) have half-hour tours, on the hour, from 9 A.M. to 7 P.M. for S$6.

There is also the chance to cruise on a Chinese junk. Daytime cruises depart at 10:30 A.M., 3 P.M., and 4 P.M. Prices are around S$25 for adults and S$10 for children. The 6 P.M. and 6:30 P.M. cruises include dinner and cost from S$40. Contact Watertours (Tel: 533-9811) or Eastwind (Tel: 533-3432) for further details.

A 33-meter air-conditioned pleasure cruiser, the *Singapore Princess* offers a choice of four daily sailings. Morning Glory departs at 9:15 A.M. and offers tea and light refreshments. Afternoon Delight departs at 4 P.M. with tea and cakes. Both cost about S$23 for adults and S$15 for children. Midday Pleasure departs at 12:15 P.M. and has a buffet luncheon. The cost is S$33 for adults and S$22 for children. Starlight Escapade is a three-hour dinner cruise departing at 7:15 P.M. Adults about S$50 and children S$38. Cruises are operated by Island Cruises (Tel: 221-8333).

J and N Cruise (Tel: 223-8217) operates the triple-decker catamaran *Equator Dream*, which cruises around the southern islands. The two-hour luncheon cruise costs S$35 for adults and S$20 for children. The 2½-hour Discovery Cruise with afternoon tea allows for a half-hour stop at Kusu Island. The cost is S$25 for adults and S$15 for children. The Sunset Dinner cruise is priced at S$60 for adults and S$40 for children. It departs at 6:40 P.M. and returns at 9 P.M. The Rendezvous Cruise with a mobile disco operates from 10 P.M. to 1:00 A.M. every Sunday to Thursday for S$20 per person and Friday and Saturday 10 P.M. to 2 A.M. at S$30 per person.

Trishaw tours are a reminder of the past. There are still about 500 registered trishaw riders left in Singapore and you can find some gathered at the fringe of Chinatown, in Little India, in Geylang Serai, and outside Raffles City. If you like the idea of a trishaw tour that will take you to several interesting spots in the city, call Henry at Trishaw Tours (Tel: 828-3133), or Tour East (Tel: 235-5703) for more details. These can be a fun experience.

There is a daily **Sentosa Tour** that departs at 9 A.M. and returns at 6 P.M. The full day includes ferry and cable car rides and entrance to several of Sentosa Island's attractions such as the Pioneers of Singapore and the Surrender Chambers. The cost for adults is about S$34 and for children S$17. I enjoy Sentosa Island and this tour gets you there and back without worry or fuss.

For those readers who are into night tours there are several to choose from. The first takes you to the open-air Newton Circus Food Center. Here, you can try a tempting selection of local food, then go to Chinatown to be introduced to a host of cultural delights. Finally you can dance the night away at the Wharehouse, Singapore's largest disco. Tour departs at 6:30 P.M. The cost (including dinner) is adults S$45 and children S$29. Another takes you to Bugis Street then to Raffles Hotel.

The third tour begins with a peaceful seafood dinner at the East Coast Parkway, then there is a scenic drive to Toa Payoh Town Center— one of Singapore's busiest housing estates—and finally to Newton Circus Food Center. Price is adults S$39 and children S$29. A further alternative begins with an eight-course Chinese seafood dinner at a Chinese restaurant then provides after-dinner entertainment at the Caesar's Palace nightclub. Price is S$45 per person.

Battlefield tours are a relatively new development. One half-day tour visits significant World War II battle sites at Bukit Timah, Kranji, Pasir Panjang, and Opium Hill. It also visits the old Ford Motor factory where the British surrender took place. This tour operates each Wednesday and costs S$32. Details of this and other battlefield tours are available from Malaysia and Singapore Travel Center (Tel: 737-8877) or Singapore Sightseeing (Tel: 737-8778).

If you cannot find a packaged tour that suits your needs but feel you need help with sight-seeing, you can have your own guide to show you around the island at your own time and pace. Some "guides" will offer

A Chinese opera singer. (Courtesy of the Singapore Tourist Promotion Board)

a wide range of services so it is better to stick to official guides recommended by the Singapore Tourist Promotion Board. The Registered Tourist Guide Association of Singapore (Tel: 338-3441) offers licensed guides at a rate of between S$100 to S$150 for a three-hour special interest custom tour. These can be excellent if you have several people travelling together.

Tours also operate to Johore Bahru, Kukup, and Malacca in Malaysia and to Batam Island in Indonesia. Passports are required for these tours. The Johore Bahru tour is for 3½ hours in the morning at a cost of around S$20, while the others are full day tours with a cost of between S$60 and S$75.

8. Culture

We have seen already the cultural diversity of Singapore. This is highlighted in the "**Instant Asia**" cultural show where within 45 minutes you can experience all the Asian cultures of Singapore. The show opens with a bang—a traditional Chinese Lion Dance. To the clash of symbols and gongs, the "lion" leaps, twists, and rolls to bid you welcome. You will see lovely Malay girls deftly twirling lighted candles and performing the traditional dances. Indian dancers, jingling with balls and flashing with jewels, tell stories with their bodies, hands, feet, and eyes. Indian snake charmers blow flutes and coax a python to perform. The show is performed daily at 8 P.M. Monday to Friday at Singa Inn Seafood Restaurant, 920 East Coast Parkway (Tel: 345-1111).

Instant culture on a wider scale is available at the Mandarin Hotel "ASEAN Night" where songs and dances from the Philippines, Malaysia, Thailand, and Indonesia as well as Singapore are performed at the poolside every night except Monday. Dinner starts at 7 P.M. and showtime is 8 P.M. You can attend without dinner. Admission is around S$45 per adult diner, S$24 nondiner (Tel: 737-4411). A somewhat similar event occurs at the Cockpit Hotel every night. Dinner is at 7 P.M. and showtime at 8 P.M. Admission is around S$40 adult diner (Tel: 734-2001).

It is also worth catching the "Life and Times of Singapore" lunchtime show at the Jubilee Hall playhouse at Raffles Hotel. Tickets are S$10.

Another event which western visitors will put into the culture category is Chinese opera. **Wayangs** are Chinese operas performed in the open air. The audience brings their own chairs, or stands and watches. Gongs and drums bang, maidens weep piteously, and fierce warlords stroke their long beards. Vivid costumes, lurid makeup, highly stylized movements, and deafening noise make it a striking spectacle although you will have little idea about the story line. Wayangs are staged all year but are more frequently seen in August and September.

Active participation in a cultural experience is possible by visiting the Havelock Community Center, 45 Merchant Road. Here you can join the international folk dancing sessions every Saturday from 2 P.M.-4:30 P.M. Admission is free and further details can be obtained from Tel: 533-7152. It is also worth checking out the activities at the YMCA in Orchard Road. There are aerobics classes, dancing classes, martial arts classes, and more, which can provide a good opportunity to meet some locals.

Check the daily papers for happenings at "**The Substation**" (Tel: 337-7800), Singapore's first home for the arts. The center in Armenian Street is converted from a power station built in the 1920s. There is a range of activities from arts and crafts exhibitions, plays, films, concerts, to a Sunday flea-market with some unusual bargains. The market is open from 10 A.M. to 5 P.M. at the Kopi Garden, an open-air area designed for outdoor arts activities. Sometimes there is also a food fair operating here.

Traditions and crafts are dying out everywhere as we plunge headlong into a technological life-style but down the side streets and byways of the city you can find a number of people who want their craft to endure despite the odds being stacked against them. Fortunately the visitor-industry will probably be their salvation.

In a community as diverse as Singapore's, it is no surprise to discover that there are a whirl of feasts and festivals throughout the year. Some are small and are confined to one ethnic group while others embrace the whole population in a mass of color and pageantry. Here are some of the more important festivals.

New Year's Day, January 1, is a public holiday but there are no major celebrations. If there was any doubt in your mind whether Singapore was a Western or Asian country, just compare the country's response to the calendar new year with the later Chinese lunar new year.

Chinese New Year in late January or early February is the most important event in the entire Chinese festive calendar. Red paper lanterns and fairy lights adorn the streets of Chinatown, Boat Quay, and the Padang, while shops come alive with a frenzy of people purchasing new year goodies. You see that oranges for good luck and flowers and kumquat trees for beautification are particularly popular. All debts must be settled and the house spotlessly cleaned and redecorated before the new year begins.

You should wander through the streets of Chinatown where calligraphers paint goodwill messages and friends exchange *hong baos*, gifts of money wrapped in red and gold paper packets. These were originally handed to unmarried people but they are more widely distributed now and are a symbol of good luck and prosperity. This is a time for visiting family and friends and, for visitors, there is an opportunity to try the many ethnic delicacies, such as raw fish, a symbol of prosperity prepared specially to usher in the festive season. Chinese new year is a two-day public holiday throughout Singapore.

The Chingay Parade is held in conjunction with the new year celebrations. Originally a Chinese cultural procession, Chingay has now evolved into a colorful spectacle of drama, dance, and music embodying the Republic's racial mix and traditions. The procession is now held along Orchard Road and features floats, dancers in illuminated costumes, stilt walkers, lion and dragon dances, acrobats, and others all amidst the clashing of cymbals and beating of gongs and drums.

Thaipusam, the Hindu festival of penitence held early in February, brings one of the world's most spectacular displays of human endurance and religious devotion to the streets of Singapore. The festival is held in honor of Lord Subramanian, son of Lord Siva, and entranced penitents take part in amazing acts of devotion. Penitents pierce their bodies, foreheads, cheeks, and tongues with sharp skewers and weighted hooks, and walk in a trancelike state from the Perumal Temple in Serangoon Road to the Chettiar Tank Road Temple, accompanied by chanting well-wishers.

The participants appear to feel no pain and there is no trace of blood from the holes in their bodies. Access to both temples is free of charge and there are no objections to photography but remember to remove your shoes within the courtyards and expect huge crowds no matter where you go.

Good Friday is another public holiday. Christians all over Singapore go to church and observe a day of solemnity. A highlight is the special candlelight service held at St. Joseph's Church in the evening. Thousands bearing candles gather in the church grounds with others spilling into the surrounding street. The crucifix and the statue of Mary, dressed in black, is borne in a procession around the church compound.

Hari Raya Puasa marks the end of Ramadan, the Muslim fasting month, and is a day of celebration for Singapore's Muslims. It is a public holiday throughout the city. Muslims dress in new clothes, offer prayers at mosques, and spend the rest of the day visiting friends and relatives, and feasting. In Geylang, huge celebrations take place at night with the fairgrounds teaming with crowds.

In fact Geyland has been bright and colorful right through the fasting month. Lights adorn the streets and peddlers and hawkers are on every street corner. Another area that thrives during Ramadan is Bussorah Street behind the Sultan Mosque. The bazaar atmosphere attracts Muslims from all over Singapore as they come to buy special Malay cakes and delicacies for the breaking of their fast after nightfall.

The fourth major religious group, the Buddhists have a major celebration on **Vesak Day** in May. This public holiday commemorates the birth, enlightenment, and death of the Buddha. Celebrations begin before dawn and by early morning the temples are thronged with crowds. Monks in saffron robes chant *sutras*, free meals are given to the poor, worshippers make donations, and birds are released from cages to gain merit. Many temples hold brilliant candlelit processions and put on vegetarian feasts. Some will also stage special exhibitions and conduct orientation ceremonies and lectures on the Buddha's teachings. Among the most spectacular celebrations are those at the Kong Meng San Phor Kark See Temple complex in Bright Hill Drive, and at the Temple of the Thousand Lights in Race Course Road. Visitors are welcome at the celebrations.

The **Dragon Boat Festival** in late May honors an ancient Chinese poet who drowned himself in protest against the evils of corruption. In an attempt to save him, fishermen raced out to sea beating drums and thrashing the water to try to scare away fish that might attack him. Today participants from all over Asia and around the world take part in Singapore's dragon boat races. The 12-meter-long boats, painted with scales and decorated with an awesome dragon's head and tail, fight for supremacy in a colorful regatta in Marina Bay. An on-shore carnival is held on the promenade of the bay during a week-long period.

The Festival of Arts is held every two years (even years) during June. Besides theater and concert hall shows, there are more than 200 free public performances during the month-long program including street theater, promenade shows, concerts in parks, and performances at shopping centers, art galleries, and hotels. You can see Chinese opera, Indian dance, Peranakan drama, and a host of international companies. The festival opens with a promenade performance at the Padang in a carnival atmosphere.

National Day is August 9. It is a public holiday. Singapore celebrates its emergence as an independent republic with a procession including military contingents, girl pipers, acrobats, folk dancers, and so forth. Admission to the National Stadium or the Padang for this event is by ticket only.

The **Festival of the Hungry Ghosts** is very much a Chinese festival. During the seventh lunar month (August-September period), the

Chinese believe that spirits of the departed wander the earth. In order to honor these spirits, joss sticks and paper money are burned, and food is offered. Market stall holders pool their resources and hold lavish celebrations complete with Chinese opera to appease the spirits and ensure a prosperous year.

The **Navarathi Festival** is equally an Indian festival. Nine nights of classical Indian music, dance, and song recitals are held in September between 7 P.M. and 10 P.M. in the Chettiar Temple hall in Tank Road, in homage to the consorts of the gods making up the Hindu trinity.

The **Mooncake Festival** celebrates the overthrow of the Mongol dynasty in China. On the fifteenth day of the eighth moon (usually late September or early October), the Chinese eat mooncakes while children parade brightly colored paper lanterns, each with a flickering candle inside. Mooncakes are rich, round pastries filled with a mixture of sweet red bean paste, lotus nut paste, and salted egg yolk. According to Chinese legends, secret messages of revolt were carried inside cakes such as these that led to the uprising that ended the Mongol dynasty. You can buy mooncakes from supermarkets or local Chinese stores.

The **Pilgrimage to Kusu Island** is a month-long festival in October when thousands of Chinese Taoists crowd onto ferries for the six-kilometer journey to Kusu Island, where they make offerings at a sacred temple dedicated to Tua Pekong. Fruit, flowers, joss sticks, candles, red-shelled eggs, and chickens are offered, both at the Chinese temple and at a Malay shrine.

Thimithi, the fire walking festival in October or November, is one of those amazing mysterious events that defies rational logic. This Hindu festival draws a big crowd to watch devotees walk over a four-meter-long pit of burning coals in the courtyard of the Sri Mariamman Temple in South Bridge Road. The Temple becomes jam-packed with people hours before the ceremony which commences at 3 P.M.

Deepavali, the joyous Hindu festival of lights, marks the victory of light over dark, good over evil. It is held during October and is a public holiday. In the weeks before Deepavali, Little India is a fairyland of lights and decorations as shops and temples prepare to welcome the festival. Shoppers crowd the area to buy new clothes, gifts, and food. On the eve of Deepavali, hundreds of lamps decorate Indian homes. In Hindu temples, shrines are decorated with flowers, alters piled high with offerings of fruit and flowers, and the presiding deity of each temple is paraded around the grounds. Perhaps the best place to see this spectacle is the Perumal Temple in Serangoon Road.

Festival of the Nine Emperor Gods is held on the ninth day of the ninth lunar month and is regarded by some as one of the most auspicious days of the year. It is devoted to honoring the nine emperor gods who are believed to cure ailments and bring luck and longevity. The highlight of the celebration is a procession of the images of the gods, borne in chairs, followed by crowds of worshippers bearing yellow flags. You will need to contact the Singapore Tourist Promotion Board (Tel: 330-0431) for the location and time of this procession.

Christmas on the equator is a spectacle of brilliant lights and pageantry, although most Singaporeans are not Christians. The pre-Christmas celebrations are centered on Orchard Road where millions of tiny lights decorate the trees and roadsides. The lights appear in late November. The official turn-on is followed by a parade along Orchard Road. On Christmas Eve, Orchard Road becomes one huge stage when dozens of choirs sing carols by candlelight to mark the festive season. The light-up ends on January 2. All churches hold services on Christmas Day and many have other special celebrations.

9. Sports

Singapore's year-round warm climate is ideal for some sports but visitors will find that, for many, the middle of the day is just too hot to enjoy some of the more vigorous land sports. It's at these times that sailing, wind surfing, swimming, or scuba diving can be enjoyed. Singapore has a fine array of sports facilities and most are available to the visitor. Here is a run-down on where to see, participate in, or inquire about the sport that may interest you.

Archery is a minority sport but visitors are welcome to contact the **Archery Club of Singapore** (Tel: 258-1140) at 5 Binchang Walk.

Athletics is amazingly popular. Singaporeans are keen to keep fit and the government encourages this activity. There are jogging, walking, and cycling tracks throughout the city and athletics clubs that welcome visitors. One of the major centers for athletics is the huge **National Stadium at Kallang**, and local, national, and international events are held here on a regular basis. You can call the **Singapore Sports Council** (Tel: 345-7111) for details of upcoming events.

Badminton is a great passion with Singapore sports fans. There are many courts tucked away within the city and your hotel desk is the best guide to which is nearest for you. If you plan to see a top-level game while you are in Singapore, the **Sports Council** (Tel: 345-7111) will be able to help with particulars.

Bowling centers in Singapore are of a good standard and shoes (even large sizes) are available for rent at most centers. For visitors the

Orchard Bowl (Tel: 737-4018) at 8 Grange Road (open 10 A.M.-1 A.M.) and the **Super Bowl** (Tel: 221-1010) at 15 Marina Grove (open 24 hours) are two of the most convenient. It is cheaper to bowl before 6 P.M. on weekdays rather than at other times.

Singapore is ideal for *canoeing*. There are canoe centers located at both ends of the **East Coast beach** that offer canoes and paddles for rent. Opening hours are 9 A.M. to 6 P.M. daily. Single canoes are available at S$3 per hour, while double canoes are S$5. Bus No. 14 operates from Orchard Road to the East Coast beach. Canoes can also be rented on Sentosa Island in the vicinity of the swimming lagoon.

Cricket is played between March and September on the Padang every Saturday from 1:30 P.M. and every Sunday from 10:30 A.M. You're welcome to watch from the Padang but entrance to the **Singapore Cricket Club** (Tel: 338-9271) is restricted to members or visiting overseas members of some major clubs.

For *cycling* enthusiasts bikes can be rented from the **East Coast Bicycle Center** (next to the Food Center) or from the **East Coast Recreation Center** (Tel: 449-0541), next to McDonald's. Rates are about S$2 per hour.

Golf has become a passion in Singapore. The island has 17 lush courses designed by some of the leading names in golf architecture. Standard attire is shorts or slacks with an open-neck golf shirt. Clubs, carts, shoes, balls, and caddies are available for rent. You will need to telephone the clubs to make bookings. Here are a few suggestions.

The **Singapore Island Country Club** (Tel: 459-2222) on Upper Thomson Road is generally considered to be the finest course on the island. There are two 18-hole, par 71 courses available to visitors weekdays only. The cost is S$100 per player with a caddy fee of S$25. The **Keppel Club** (Tel: 273-5522) at Bukit Charmin is an 18-hole, par 72 course close to the city. Costs are S$50 per player weekdays and S$90 for weekends with a caddy fee of S$18.

Then there is the **Sentosa Golf Club** (Tel: 472-2722), which has two 18-hole, par 72 courses. The very scenic Tanjong course is open to the public and this includes the spectacular second-hole green that is placed on a small island. Green fees are S$50 per person on weekdays and S$120 on weekends. For those looking to improve their driving ability the **Parkland golf driving range** (Tel: 440-6726) at the East Coast Parkway has 48 bays, a 200-meter range and is open from 7:30 A.M. to 10 P.M. The cost for 90 balls is S$5 before 3:30 P.M. and S$6 after 3:30 P.M.

Horse racing is held by the **Singapore Turf Club** (Tel: 469-3611) at the lush green Bukit Timah racecourse on Saturday afternoons 32 times a year. Racegoers can see every race, including Malaysian races, on a huge 18m. x 6m. color video screen. The eight-event program starts about 2 P.M. At other times race meetings in Kuala Lumpur, Ipoh, or Penang in Malaysia, are televised live at the club.

For those who like to ride rather than watch, *horseback riding* is available at the **Singapore Polo Club** (Tel: 256-4530) on Thomson Road. The cost is S$50 per one-hour ride. The Saddle Club at the **Singapore Turf Club** (Tel: 466-2782) is normally for members only but visitors are sometimes catered to.

Racquetball is a recent sport and the only public courts are at the **East Coast Recreation Center**. Here three American-standard courts are available from 7:30 A.M. to 11:30 P.M. daily for a cost of S$5 per hour per court before 4:30 P.M. and S$7 after 4:30 P.M.

Rugby Union is organized by the **Singapore Cricket Club** (Tel: 338-9271) during the September to March period. Games are played on the Padang every Saturday with a kickoff time of 4 P.M.

Sailing opportunities are somewhat limited but the **Changi Sailing Club** (Tel: 545-2876) on Netheravon Road welcomes visitors. You need to telephone ahead to determine the best time to visit. If you are a Laser sailor, you can rent a boat from the **East Coast Sailing Center** (Tel: 449-5118).

Scuba diving is popular around the many small islands to the south of Singapore island. You can rent diving gear from the **Sentosa Sports Center** (Tel: 275-0554) at the eastern lagoon on Sentosa Island if you show your qualified Dive Card. For beginners, there is an introduction to scuba diving course lasting one day, available at S$180 per person. The sports center also arranges snorkeling expeditions to the southern islands.

Soccer matches are usually held at night under lights at the National Stadium. Details of games can be found in local newspapers or by calling the **Singapore Sports Council** (Tel: 345-7111).

Squash is a very popular recreational sport in Singapore despite the heat. There are many squash centers all over the country including the **National Stadium** (Tel: 348-1258), the **East Coast Recreational Center** (Tel: 449-0541) and the **Clementi Recreation Center** (Tel: 778-8966) at 12 West Coast Walk. The cost of court rental varies from about S$5 during nonpeak times to about S$8 for evenings and weekends.

Swimming is available at many hotels, at Sentosa Island, the small southern islands, and at the East Coast Beach. There are also several public pools. Before lying in the sun, however, you must appreciate the strength of tropical rays and come well equipped with sunscreen and protective clothing. Apart from these facilities there is the **Big Splash**

(Tel: 345-1211), on the East Coast Parkway, which has slides, a wave pool, a flow pool, and a children's pool. It is open from 12 noon to 5:45 P.M weekdays except Wednesday, and 9:30 A.M. to 6 P.M. on weekends. Admission is S$4 for adults and S$2 for children.

A similar facility is available at the **CN West Leisure Park** (Tel: 261-4771), Japanese Garden Road Jurong. There is a wave pool, and a 50-meter water slide and it opens Tuesdays to Friday from 12 noon to 6 P.M. and weekends from 9:30 A.M. to 6 P.M. Admission is S$4 for adults and S$2 for children.

Tennis courts are found in many hotels and there are also some excellent public facilities. You could try the **Farrer Park Courts** (Tel: 251-4166) on Rutland Road, the **Singapore Tennis Center** (Tel: 442-5966) on East Coast Parkway, or the **Tanglin Tennis Center** (Tel: 473-7236) on Sherwood Road. Most centers have night courts. Costs vary from about S$4 to S$8 an hour depending on the time of day.

Waterskiing is restricted to a few locations off the coast. One of the better facilities is at the **William Water Sports Center** (Tel: 283-3495) at Ponggol. It is a bit difficult to get to (Bus No. 64 or 65 from Orchard Road to Selegie Road then Bus No. 83 to Ponggol End) but the facilities are good. They run skiing courses but also offer speedboats and skis for rent at an hourly rate of S$55.

Windsurfing has boomed in popularity and if you are an enthusiast, head for the **East Coast Sailing Center** (Tel: 449-5118) where windsurf boards are available at S$20 for the first two hours and S$10 for every subsequent hour. The center also offers four-hour crash courses for windsurfing from 10 A.M. to 2 P.M. and 2 P.M. to 6 P.M. daily, priced at S$100.

10. Shopping

Singapore is a shopper's paradise. It is recognized as one of a handful of places that has goods from around the world sold in modern comfortable conditions at prices often lower than those in the country of origin. There are gems from Sri Lanka, silks from China and Thailand, cameras from Japan, sportswear from Korea, computers from the United States, and compact discs from Australia. On top of this, there is the adventure of ethnic shopping. You can shop in air-conditioned shopping malls, in department stores, in bustling bazaars and in tiny cram-packed shop houses. In fact you can shop almost anywhere. Visitors to Singapore often find that they are shopping despite their natural inclinations.

Many visitors initially head for Chinatown Point in the heart of

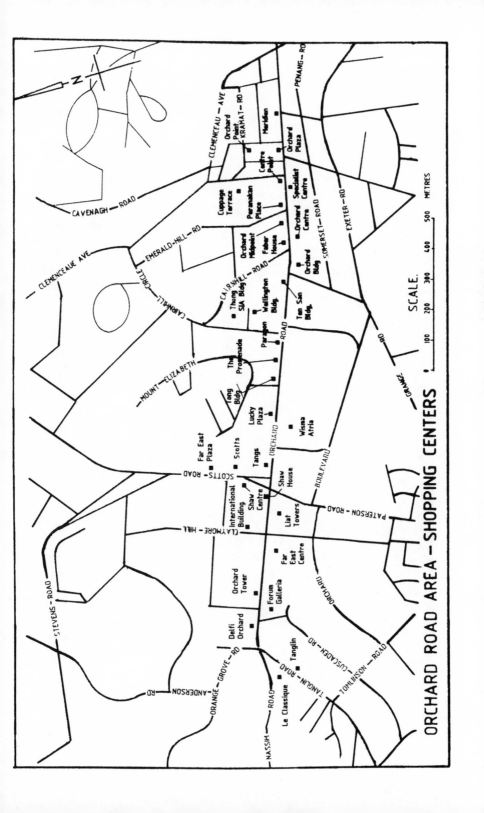

ORCHARD ROAD AREA – SHOPPING CENTERS

Singapore is becoming a fashion center for much of Asia.

Chinatown. Shoppers will find more than 30 shops stocked with jade art pieces, brass and pewter ware, antique porcelains, rosewood furniture, and Persian carpets. The center is open from 10 A.M. to 9:30 P.M. Monday to Saturday.

The most popular buys in Singapore are watches, cameras, *batik*, electronics, and jewelry but these represent just a fraction of the items on sale. These are some of the things you might look for in Singapore.

Antiques. A fascinating collection of Asian antiques awaits the avid collector. Items such as furniture, ancient maps and prints, Korean chests, jade, masks from Indonesia, Straits Chinese silver, and much more can be found in outlets all over Singapore.

Tanglin Shopping Center is one of the best places to buy unusual and rare finds from all over the world. You could try **Antiques of the Orient** (Tel: 734-9351) or **Moongate** (Tel: 737-6771) among many others. Both are members of the Good Retailer Scheme, which should mean that all pieces are genuine and are reasonably priced. Nonya handcrafted silver ornaments are avidly collected and are one of the few antique wares that are unique to southeast Asia. Walk down the row of restored shop houses in Cuppage Street behind Centrepoint in Orchard Road, and visit such antiques shops as **Babazar Design Market** (Tel: 235-7866).

Other areas to try are Smith Street and Temple Street in Chinatown, and Neil Road and South Bridge Road in Tanjong Pagar. At the Holland Road Shopping Center, **Lim's Art and Craft** (Tel: 467-1300) has a wide range of goods at several outlets while **E & E Antique Co.** (Tel: 468-2621) has some most unusual pieces.

Antique Furniture. The best place in Singapore for antique furniture is Upper Paya Labar Road, which is several kilometers northeast from Orchard Road. If you are serious about buying, the distance will not worry you and you can be assured that the goods are genuine—most are still in a rough state waiting to be refurbished. **Chin Yi Antique House** (Tel: 284-2104) and **Mansion Antique House** (Tel: 741-6195) are two places that specialize in Colonial, Peranakan, and coffee house furniture. **Just Anthony** (Tel: 283-4782) is another outlet that has a fine showroom, and a large yard stacked with items awaiting repair. Much closer to Orchard Road is a row of antique and second-hand dealers on River Valley Road near Tank Road. You will find **Ming-Ching** (Tel: 235-6509) and **Tong Mern Sern Antiques and Crafts** (Tel: 734-0761) here. Antiques and second-hand junk tend to be mixed up together, but you may find a bargain.

Art. The works of Singapore's local artists will capture your attention. Traditional Chinese brush painting, academic watercolor, and

Shopping in modern shopping complexes is one of the joys of a Singapore visit.
(Courtesy of the Singapore Tourist Promotion Board)

The "other side" of Singapore shopping.

Paris-school oil paintings have been joined by a host of contemporary works by young artists. Some of the better artists are Ong Kim Seng, Ng Eng Teng, Thomas Yeo, Eng Tow, and James Tan. You will find art galleries primarily along Orchard Road. **Sun Craft** (Tel: 737-1308) in the Tanglin Shopping Center, **Orchard Gallery** (Tel: 732-7032) in Orchard Point, **Della Butcher** (Tel: 235-7107) in Cuppage Terrace, **Gallery Mei** (Tel: 235-3156) in the Far East Shopping Center, and **Art Forum** (Tel: 737-3448) in the Promenade are a selection you could try.

To see an artist at work you should visit **Yong Gallery** in Marina Square where Yong Choong Thye will demonstrate his skill in Chinese calligraphy. **Koh Pu Lim Associates** (Tel: 294-8338) operate a worldwide mail order service for marketing Singapore artists and craftsmen. Some fine textile, lacquerware, and basketware ethnic arts is available from **Tempo Decloe** (Tel: 338-1038) at North Bridge Road. Handcrafted artifacts from throughout the orient are available at **Jiangsu Artefacts** (Tel: 227-9145) in Neil Road.

Artifacts at 19 Duxton Road is all about bronze. There is a good selection of small and large pieces for a range of prices. Gnarled and twisted root carvings reach out of the window of **Resin Co** (Tel: 222-4045) at 15-16 Duxton Road. Made from actual root timber, no two pieces are the same. Here you will also find the time-honored Chinese art of cork sculpture. Three dimensional master pieces are sculptured from cork and oak bark, and encapsulated within glass frames.

Batik. This art form originates from Indonesia and Malaysia and is very popular among the Malay population of Singapore. There are specialist shops on Tanglin Road, on Arab Street, and in almost all department stores (**C.K. Tangs** is excellent), and shopping complexes. Most popular buys are clothing, tablecloths, curtains, handbags, and paintings. Be aware that there are handmade and machine-made varieties. The machine-made fabrics are inexpensive and can be picked by their consistent color and pattern.

Cameras. An almost unrivalled range of camera equipment is available at duty-free prices in Singapore. You can chose between all the famous brands such as Nikon, Minolta, Pentax, Olympus, Hasselblad, and Canon. You will find that Singapore retailers often have new models months before they appear in the United States, Canada, Europe, or Australia. North Bridge Road, Coleman Street, and the major shopping complexes are the places to browse and compare prices. **Cathay Photo Store** (Tel: 339-6188) with several branches, **A & P Photo** (Tel: 734-0201) in Lucky Plaza, and **Albert Photo** (Tel: 235-2815) in Orchard Towers and several other locations, are three places among hundreds that you could try.

Carpets. By definition, an Oriental carpet is handmade of wool and silk by native craftsmen and measures larger than six feet by nine feet. In the past, the term only referred to carpets made in Persia (Iran), but it now includes those from China, India, Pakistan, Turkey, and the small Middle East countries. Authentic pieces are becoming scarce as carpetmaking as a way of life diminishes. The value of a carpet depends on the material, the compactness of the weave, the complexity of the design, the age, size, place of origin, and scarcity. Most people will need to rely on dependable dealers for advice.

For Persian and Pakistan carpets I recommend **Hassan's Carpets** (Tel: 737-5626) in the Tanglin Shopping Center or **Qureshi's Carpets** (Tel: 235-1523) in Centrepoint. **Amir and Sons** (Tel: 734-9112) in Lucky Plaza also deals with these plus a variety of Chinese carpets. **Chinese Carpets** (747-7583) at 72 Eunos Avenue near Paya Lebar MRT station has a spacious showroom draped with a mass of majestic woolen rugs and carpets in a color and design to suit most tastes. They also have a selection of silk carpets.

Computers. Singapore is a good place to pick up a personal computer and there are many specialist shops in which to browse. U.S. original-brand computers are no cheaper here but Asian brands are at bargain prices. The difficulty is to know just what you are buying. Singapore-made Limco, and Taiwan-sourced Multi-tech are two brands that appear to offer reliable quality and are IBM-compatible. The place to go if you're in the market for hardware or software is **Funan Center** on North Bridge Road. There are numerous computer outlets within this complex. Nearby Peninsula Plaza also has several places worth trying. Near Orchard Road, **Datatrend** (Tel: 733-6922) in the Shaw Center has a good reputation.

Electronics. You will find almost every well-known name brand on sale in Singapore at prices that could be considerably less than at home. Your best bet for stereo systems, TVs, and VCRs is Sim Lim Tower on Rochor Canal Road. Row after row of shops on four levels deal in similar items so competition is intense. I have found **Litaron Electronics** (Tel: 294-6410) on level two to be helpful and reliable but I am sure that many of the other dealers are also. Plaza Singapura in Orchard Road is another center for electronics with a branch of **City Chain Stores** (Tel: 336-2805), **Pertama Audio**, **Mach Sound Company**, and others.

Fashion. Both men's and women's clothing are excellent buys. Locally made dresses in up-to-date styles are moderately priced. More exclusive styles are available in local designer's collections. You will find hundreds of locally owned boutiques throughout Singapore with locally made products. Imported clothes from the famous fashion houses of Europe and Japan are also available in hotel shopping arcades and in Orchard Road and Scotts Road shopping complexes.

One of the best collections of fashion is at Style Singapore, a major store at Park Mall in Penang Road opposite Dhoby Ghaut MRT station. More than 60 Singaporean designers and labels are found over three floors in this modern complex.

As well as the individual operators there are some chain boutiques that you will find in many different locations. These include **Bene Fashion Singapore** (Tel: 732-9058) in Scotts, Centrepoint, and Forum Galleria; **Bylines** (Tel: 235-4686) in Scotts, Plaza Singapora, Marina Square, Lucky Plaza, and Parkway Parade; **Pattina Fashions** (Tel: 339-1891) in Plaza Singapura, Centrepoint, and Scotts; **Sunny and Grace** (Tel: 235-0798) in Centrepoint, Parkway Parade, Lucky Plaza, and Marina Square; and **Transmarco Fashions** (Tel: 734-9175) in City House, Centrepoint, Lucky Plaza, Mandarin, and Changi Airport.

For men, superb clothes and accessories at the Paragon Shopping Center can be found in **Chanrai** (Tel: 734-1220), and **Milan's Men's Boutique** (Tel: 732-9022). Other top fashion centers are Wisma Atria, the bright blue building in Orchard Road, and the Promenade Center, which is almost opposite.

Gems. With Sri Lanka, Nepal, and Thailand nearby, Singapore has a good source of precious and semiprecious gemstones. High-grade diamonds, rubies, emeralds, sapphires, and other stones can be bought loose or set into pieces of your own choosing. Most jewelry stores will be able to provide you with a selection of gems and the following specialists, all members of the Good Retailer Scheme, will amaze you with the range available: **A & E Gems** (Tel: 235-0583) on Lucky Plaza, **Pan-Singapore Gem Trading** (Tel: 339-5377) at 11 Beach Road, and **Singapore Gems & Metals Co** (Tel: 475-9733) on Kung Chong Road.

Gold. Chinese goldsmith shops offer an array of glittering chains, rings and earrings in 22k or 24k gold—gold in the West is often 9k or 18k. Such gold is priced according to weight and the prevailing market rate, the design quality, and the workmanship. The greatest concentration of Chinese goldsmith shops is in South Bridge Road at the Pidemco Center. Call in on **Chap Mai Jewellery Manufacturer** (Tel: 532-7605), **Gobin International Jewellery** (Tel: 532-3666), and **Chin May Jewellery** (Tel: 532-4433) all in this dazzling complex.

Other good places to shop are in People's Park Complex in Upper Cross Street (**Golden Watch and Jewellry**; Tel: 523-2662), Arab Street (**Mean Sing Goldsmiths**; Tel: 298-7704), Far East Shopping Center (**Tai Heng Goldsmiths & Jewellery Co**; Tel: 737-0560), and other Orchard

Road complexes. Indian goldsmiths settled in the Serangoon Road area and their intricate designs are quite different from Chinese designs.

Gold-dipped Orchids. An orchid bloom preserved forever by a coating of pure gold is a most original souvenir from Singapore. The blooms are made into pins, earrings, and pendants. Tiny ferns and leaves are treated in the same way. The best-known brand is **RISIS** and carries the seal of approval from the Singapore Institute of Scientific and Industrial Research. Information on RISIS orchids is obtainable from Tel: 278-9393. The orchids, together with gold eggs and small figurines are available in department stores, souvenir shops, and at Changi Airport.

Handicrafts. Two of the best places to see how many handicrafts are made are Tanjong Pagar and Marina Square. Both have daily demonstrations of such arts as Chinese calligraphy, marble seal carving, and painting of Chinese opera masks. Of course, you can also buy at these locations. Try **D'Magdalene** (Tel: 339-4535) and **Good Friends Pottery Arts** (Tel: 339-3547) at Marina Square. Another place to try is **Mei Shop** (Tel: 338-5775). In Tanjong Pager, the **Gu Zhai Art Gallery** at 36A Tangong Pager Road has a particularly fine selection of pictorial and calligraphy Chinese scroll paintings.

Jade. Through the ages, jade has been considered the most precious of all stones by many Chinese. Jade comes mainly from China or Burma. It occurs in many colors and the more distinct the colors, the more prized it is by collectors. Many Chinese believe jade can ward off accidents and illness. Take note of how many older Chinese women wear a jade bangle on one wrist. Modern jewelers combine it with gold or precious stones to made stunning pieces. There is much imitation jade around, so if making purchases, be sure to go to a reputable jeweler. True jade should look almost greasy. The jade being peddled on the streets is almost all imitation. **Kwok Gallery** (Tel: 235-2516) in the Far East Shopping Center specializes in jade and porcelain.

Jewelry. Fine modern jewelry is found in jewelry shops in hotel arcades and shopping complexes on Orchard Road. There are enough jewelry stores scattered throughout this area to make a goldminer's heart beat with joy, including some internationally known names. **Larry Jewelry** (Tel: 732-3222) has outlets in Orchard Towers, Lucky Plaza, and Raffles City. **H. Sena** (Tel: 732-5689) has outlets in the Shangri-La Hotel, and in Raffles City. Made to order pieces can be made in two to four days in some instances.

Leather Goods. From the distinctive red and green stripes of Gucci to the untanned leather products that are a specialty of Indonesia, you will find an enormous range in Singapore. Shopping for quality leather items can be concentrated in the Orchard Road region where exclusive outlets of Cartier, Bally, Givenchy, Dior, Dunhill, and Lanvin can be found in hotels and shopping centers. Many of these are also available in department stores. Cheaper prices can be found at People's Park Complex, where all kinds of accessories from Italy or locally made are available. You will need to be careful of imitations though, in this part of town. Cheap leather goods from India and Indonesian are found in Arab Street. **Nan Hen Leather Goods** (Tel: 338-3702) at 108 Middle Road and **Leather Lodge** (Tel: 235-1026) in Centrepoint are two well-respected outlets.

Optical Goods. If you wear sunglasses, contact lens, or spectacles you should track down some of the bargains in exclusive eye wear. Qualified opticians and retail outlets can be found along North Bridge Road, South Bridge Road, Tanglin Road, and Orchard Road. New lenses can usually be supplied in hours. Try **Federal-Optiek** (Tel: 733-5222), and **Optics Premier** (Tel: 733-1919) in Centrepoint, or the **Tanglin Visionaid Center** (Tel: 235-8250) at 32 Tanglin Road.

Pewter. See how fine modern pewter made from Straits refined tin is shaped into mugs, vases, pitchers, candlesticks, bowls, and more. The **Royal Selanger Museum** and demonstration center is now at Ming Village in Jurong. It is a place to watch as skilled craftsmen and women each work on a different step in the cutting, soldering, hammering, and polishing process. There are other outlets at Delfi Orchard, Paragon, Raffles Hotel, Shangri-La Hotel, Marina Square, Raffles City, and The Plaza.

Porcelain. You can find items dating back from the Ching to the Tang dynasty. Export wares from the Philippines and Indonesia are abundant but the more rare pieces of celadon and Ming blue are becoming difficult to find. There are a few shops on Temple Street in Chinatown where you may still turn up a treasure. Another suggestion is **Katong Antique House** (Tel: 345-8544) at 208 East Coast Road.

Silk. Chinese, Japanese, and Thai silks abound in beautiful flowing colors. Silk is sold by the meter and many shops will tailor-make dresses, blouses, or suits to your own design as well as offer ready-made items. For Chinese silk try **China Silk House** (Tel: 235-5020) in the Tanglin Shopping Center. There are also branches at Scotts, Lucky Plaza, Centrepoint, and Marina Square. An alternative is the **Silk City** (Tel: 227-6789) at 46 Duxton Street.

For world-renowned Thai silk, shop at **Design Thai** (Tel: 235-5439) in the Tanglin Shopping Center, **Jim Thomson Silk** (Tel: 235-4379) in the Orchard Parade Hotel, or **Miss Ming** in Delphi Orchard. Malaysian silk interwoven with gold thread, handmade in the State of Kelantan, can be found in Arab Street. For Indian silk, go to High Street or Serangoon Road.

Sports Equipment. Sports-conscious Singapore offers an infinite variety of sporting equipment. Every shopping center has at least one store stocked full of tennis and squash rackets, hockey sticks, inflatable rafts, billiard cues, scuba tanks, sail boards, and golf equipment. There are international brands such as Adidas, Fila, Puma, Nike, and Reebok. **Royal Sporting House** (Tel: 733-8555) in Centrepoint and several other shopping complexes is a good place to see a wide variety of equipment. **Transview Sports** (Tel: 732-0955) in the Specialists' Center is a good place for golf equipment. **Sports Life** (Tel: 732-4769), at the Far East Plaza, Lucky Plaza, and Midpoint Orchard, has everything.

Tailoring. The 24-hour tailoring of Hong Kong and Bangkok is not quite so popular in Singapore. Here the emphasis is more on quality. Timing can be fast if needed, and prices are reasonable rather than cheap. There appear to be far more men's tailoring shops than women's. The hotel shopping arcades are not a bad place to start. You could try **Coloc House of Fashion** (Tel: 732-6244) in the Dynasty Hotel and Raffles Singapore or Wai Cheong Tailors (Tel: 235-7692) at the Shangri-La Hotel.

Watches. The choice is astonishing. You can buy anything from a gaily colored plastic watch to an exquisite gold and diamond masterpiece. There are watches from Japan, France, Switzerland, and elsewhere. You are also likely to be offered a variety of cheap fake watches from small vendors or sidewalk touts. These are probably illegal, so beware. **The Hourglass** (Tel: 733-1262) in the Palace Renaissance Arcade and branches at Scotts, Lucky Plaza, Centrepoint, Peninsula Plaza, and Changi Airport is one of the most well known watch shops.

The **Rolex Showrooms** (Tel: 737-9033) is in the Tong Building, 302 Orchid Road. The **Seiko Showrooms** (Tel: 737-6122) is in the Thongsia Building, behind the Crown Prince Hotel. The Baume & Mercier range is available at **Piaget** (Tel: 732-8055) in the Hilton Hotel. Cartier watches and other gifts are available at boutiques in Lucky Plaza, Palais Renaissance, and the Hilton Hotel. Bargaining is expected in all the watch show rooms in the major shopping centers and a 25-percent reduction on the initial price is not unusual. Make sure you ask for an international guarantee card.

Department Stores. Singapore has so many small shops and shopping centers that you would think department stores were unnecessary. In fact the opposite appears to be the trend—in recent years there have been several new department stores come onto the scene. For visitors the stores have two huge advantages—you don't have to bargain, and the range is so great that you will be able to make a selection without being harassed. Just remember that you may not get the absolute lowest price for your purchase but at the same time you will not get caught by paying a very high price because you didn't know the market. Several of the department stores are almost legends and should be visited.

Robinson's (Tel: 733-0888) in Centrepoint has been established since 1858 in various locations. The present store is somewhat cramped, particularly when they have a sale, but it is convenient and everyone in Singapore knows where it is. The emphasis is on a high standard of quality goods and services.

Yaohan (Tel: 733-2785) in Plaza Singapura is the oldest Japanese store in Singapore and with reasonable prices and good merchandise, it has gained popularity with locals and visitors. **C.K. Tang** (Tel: 737-5500) in Orchard Road near Scotts Road first opened in 1940 and has since provided fashionware, household goods, electronics, toys, and souvenirs at fair prices. It has a good range of Chinese merchandise.

There are several Japanese department stores. **Daimaru** (Tel: 339-1111), in Orchard Road, Havelock Road, River Valley Road, and Marine Parade, has excellent ladies' fashions and shoes. **Sogo** (Tel: 339-1100) in Raffles City has Japanese fashions and a good range of homewares. **Tokyu** (Tel: 337-0077) in Marina Square has a good range of international fashions, cosmetics, sporting goods, and stationery. **Meitetsu is in the Delfi Orchard shopping center. Isetan is in Wisma Atria and at Shaw House.**

French fashions are very much on show at **Galeries Lafayette** (Tel: 732-9177) in Liat Towers, Orchard Road, and in the OUB Center in the banking district. Then there is **Metro**, Singapore's own homegrown department stores with branches in shopping centers all over town. **Metro Grand** (Tel: 737-6033) at Lucky Plaza and **Metro Paragon** (Tel: 235-2811) at Paragon, Orchard Road, are both good examples of the chain. Other branches are in the Royal Holiday Inn, Far East Plaza, The Plaza Beach Road, and at Marina Square. **O.G.** (Tel: 535-7788) is another chain particularly popular for inexpensive fashions and shoes. Stores are located at People's Park, Orchard Road, and Plaza Singapura. **John Littles** (Tel: 737-2222) in the Specialists' Center is justifiably famous for cute outfits for kids plus other items for the whole family. **Marks and Spencers** from England is in Centrepoint.

Shopping Tips. "Shopperholics" will find Singapore a paradise. Most stores and shopping centers are open between 10 A.M. and 10 P.M., seven days a week. Prices in department stores are fixed but most other shops adopt prices that allow for bargaining. You should bargain at more than one store before you buy, to try to establish what the correct price should be. Credit cards such as American Express, Diners Club, MasterCard, and Visa are widely accepted. Do not agree to pay an extra charge to use these cards. Make sure you are happy with your purchase before you leave the shop. Department stores are helpful with exchange but many smaller shops are not so accommodating. It is a good idea to shop at the stores that display the red and white Good Retailers Scheme sticker on their windows.

On major purchases, international guarantees are obtainable from dealers, however, they may not be automatically offered to you. Check the guarantee to ensure that it has been filled in correctly and endorsed with the shop's stamp. Do not accept photocopied or untidy warranties and beware of pirated goods, which are not protected by guarantee. If you come up against any unethical practices or excessively rude service, immediately contact the complaints department of the Consumers Association of Singapore (Tel: 270-5433).

There is also an excellent small-claims court that is valuable to visitors. The court was set up to ensure that visitors with disputes on purchases have adequate legal recourse, even if they are only staying a few days. Once a visitor has lodged a complaint, a letter of notification is hand-delivered to the opposite party within three hours. The visitor and the defendant will appear before the registrar the next day to try to settle the matter between themselves but if no solution is found, the magistrate will conduct a hearing the same day to settle the matter in court. It is a wonderful system. Visitors can telephone 530-9896 for further details. The only cost is a S$10 administration fee. The court operates daily except Sundays.

11. Entertainment and Nightlife

You can forget the Manila or Bangkok type of nightlife in Singapore. It just does not exist. In fact, many visitors have declared Singapore a disaster after dark and have left with this impression. The truth is that Singapore has quite a deal of nighttime activity but it is just a little hard to find. Apart from dining, there are cocktail lounges, nightclubs, discos, concerts, theaters, and cinemas. There is no sharp distinction between where the visitor goes and where the locals will be, but of course, you will find more visitors in the Orchard Road area establishments than you will in those farther afield.

Unfortunately the pungent smells, sights, and good times of Bugis Street, Singapore's historic night haunt and only internationally known nighttime attraction have been reduced to pleasant, soft-focus memories

The streets of Chinatown are alive at night.

by urban developers who ripped it down. It has recently been rebuilt, but it is doubtful that the atmosphere can ever be recaptured.

Bars, Lounges, and More. Most hotels have a relaxed music lounge where you can chat with friends, have a drink, and listen to the live group or solo artist. Happy hours from 5 P.M. to 7 P.M. substantially reduce drink costs but these are places to drop into at any time during the evening. The equivalent of these outside the major hotels are places like **Bier Keller** in Centrepoint where there are drinks, a live singer, food, and no cover charge. Drinks at the hotel lounges during happy hour are S$2-S$6. They can rise by 100% during the evening. Other places popular with the locals are **5 Emerald Place** (Tel: 732-0818), off Peranaken Place; **Peyton Place** (Tel: 235-3420) in Orchard Towers; and the **Boom Boom Room** (Tel: 339-8187) in Bugis Street. These all stay open until the early hours of the morning.

The last time I went to the **Saxophone Bar** (Tel: 235-8385) in Cuppage Terrace, it was jam-packed with people to the point that you couldn't move. Drinks were being passed over the heads of patrons because waitresses had given up trying to serve those away from the bar. Despite this, or maybe partly because of it, the atmosphere was great and the sounds from the jazz group were superb. The music doesn't start until about 10 P.M.

You can also catch some good music at **Club 392** (Tel: 734-8233) in Orchard Towers. This rock and roll club has beer at S$7 and spirits at S$8 and happy hour between 4 and 9 P.M. A hard-working local group belts out requests and old favorites between 10 P.M. and 2 A.M. **Anywhere** (Tel: 734-8233) in the Tanglin Shopping Center is another place that is well worth a visit. It is closed on Sunday. These places generally do not have a cover charge.

There are a number of more conventional bars where you get a real "pub" atmosphere. By the Singapore River, **Paddles** provides a great venue for a quiet drink after midday, with sandwiches, hamburgers, omelettes, and fish and chips served between noon and 3 P.M. and 6 and 8 P.M. This delightful old shop house with timber beams and posters on the wall has a lovely little area at the back with tables amid palm trees. There is music and videos at night. The **After Five** wine bar at Holland Park is also worth visiting.

In the Tanjong Pagar area there are several options. Check out **The Bermuda Triangle** (Tel: 221-4901), which is tucked away on Duxton Road. It has an air of mystery about it and some quite novel twists that will have more impact if I don't tell you about them. It is open from 3 P.M. till midnight. The **JJ Mahoney Pub** (Tel: 225-6225) is at 58 Duxton Road. It has good drink prices and karaoke in the evening.

Close by at 10 Duxton Hill, the **Flag and Whistle** (Tel: 223-1126) sets out to create an old English pub. It is open from 11 A.M. till midnight with happy hours from 5:30 till 8 P.M. Here also you will find the excellent **Duxton Chicago Bar and Grill** (Tel: 222-4096) with its live jazz each evening, at 6 Duxton Hill and **Elvis' Place** (Tel: 227-8543) at No. 1A. The **Road House** (Tel: 222-7058) at nearby 44 Craig Road has blues each evening, while the **Unchained Melody** pub at 52 Tanjong Pagar Road has a sing-along format.

Out at Holland Village the **Java Jive** (Tel: 468-4155) is popular with the yuppies, trendies, and some others. It is small and cozy and you can't miss it because of the sailboard dumped outside. The Jive opens at 5 P.M. and patrons are entertained by music videos until the live entertainment starts at 9:30. You will be encouraged to sing along with the rest of the crowd. Almost everyone does.

The **Hard Rock Cafe** (Tel: 235-5232) is currently the hottest place in town. You will have to stand in line to get in here most nights although the restaurant/bar/music lounge caters to hundreds of people. It is open from midday to 3 A.M. with the music starting at 11 P.M. Singapore's tough no-smoking in restaurants law has had no effect on the popularity of this place. You will find Hard Rock at 50 Cuscaden Road just off Orchard Road.

Theater Restaurants. These are the Asian version of the Las Vegas glamour show. You can enjoy a cocktail, eat a Chinese feast, and watch a lavish floor show. The largest of these is **The Neptune** (Tel: 224-3922) at Collyer Quay, run by the Mandarin Hotel. The only problem is that it is often booked up for private functions, so you need to inquire about the show and reservations as far in advance as possible.

Nightclubs. Singapore's nightclubs are somewhere between a Western nightclub and an Asian theater-restaurant. They generally do not open till 9 P.M., have singers from Taiwan and Hong Kong, and offer dance hostesses who are hired by the hour. The biggest and most lavish is the **Lido Palace** (Tel: 732-8855) at the Concorde Hotel Shopping Center, Outram Road. There is a spectacular cabaret show, 300 hostesses and prices of: first drink S$35, second drink S$16, hostesses S$25 per hour. Showtime is 9:30 P.M. till 2:45 A.M. It helps if you happen to understand a little Mandarin. Other popular clubs with similar attractions are the **Golden Million** (Tel: 336-6993) at the Peninsular Hotel, the **Grand Palace** (Tel: 737-8922) at the Orchard Building, 1 Grange Road, and **Maxim** (Tel: 338-6555) at Supreme House, Penang Road.

Discos. Two pre-war warehouses by the Singapore River have been converted into Singapore's largest disco, **The Warehouse** (Tel: 732-9922). There is a huge video screen, a dance floor for 500 people, and an upper deck with a dance corner. Charges Sunday to Thursday are S$16 for two standard drinks and on Friday and Saturday it rises to S$24.

Thank God It's Friday (Tel: 235-6181) at the Far East Plaza, Scotts Road, has a lively disco from 10 P.M. to 2 A.M. and a great lunch and dinner menu. During the midday to 7 P.M. happy hour, drinks are at the amazing price of S$3. After this there is a first drink charge of S$7 for nondiners on Sunday to Thursday and S$14 for two drinks on Friday and Saturday. There is a good mixture of people and a happy atmosphere. The **East-West Express** (Tel: 339-1618) in Marina Square has dinner, then after 9:30 P.M. the disco starts. Cover charges are S$10 weekdays, S$14 on Fridays, and S$17 on Saturdays. **Zouk** (Tel: 728-2988) is a yuppie haunt of Jiak Kim Street. Cover charges, including two drinks, are from S$12.

Then there are the hotel discos. I don't claim to be any expert here but the word around town is that there is good action at **Scandals** (Tel: 338-8585) in the Westin Plaza, **Chinoiserie** (Tel: 733-1188) in the Hyatt Regency, **The Music Room** (Tel: 737-2233) at the Hilton Hotel, and **Xanadu** (Tel: 737-3644) at the Shangri-La.

Live Band Dancing. **Top Ten** (Tel: 732-3077) in Orchard Towers is currently the place to be. Imported stars guarantee elbow-to-elbow action on the dance floor. Cover charges are S$15 Sundays to Thursday, S$20 Fridays and Saturdays, inclusive of first drink. The tiered floor provides great viewing of the stage and the dance floor, and two bands play continuous music from 9 P.M. to 3 A.M. In the same building, **Caesar's** offers a combination of bands and recorded music. Charges here are S$12 Sundays to Thursday and S$20 on Friday and Saturday. For your money you get elegant columns, lissome toga-clad maidens, top bands, and a good sound system.

Concert. The 86-member Singapore Symphony Orchestra was only founded in 1979 but already it has made a mark on the world scene. Regular "SSO" concerts are held at the Victoria Concert Hall, starting at 8:15 P.M. Prices range from S$4 to S$15. Program details are in local newspapers or you can telephone the "SSO" office on 338-1230. Tickets are obtained from the concert hall box office, or at Tangs or Centrepoint in Orchard Road.

Theater. The streamlined modern Drama Center at Canning Rise behind the National Museum, and the gracious old Victoria Theatre in Empress Place are both venues for everything from Western plays to Malay drama. The Victoria Theatre is also the venue for ballet, musical comedy, Gilbert and Sullivan, and classical Chinese operas. Your daily newspaper will provide details of events or you can check with the Victoria Theatre Booking Office (Tel: 337-7490).

Cinemas. Singaporeans love movies and there are clean, air-conditioned cinemas all over the island screening English, Chinese, Malay, and Indian language movies. The latest Hollywood releases have their first-run in Orchard Road cinemas. Evening and weekend sessions often sell out before the movie starts. Programs are in daily papers. Action movies are obviously the most popular because there is always a large choice of kung fu and Western cops and robbers movies.

12. The Singapore Address List

Aircraft Flight Information	Tel: 542-4422
Ambulance	Tel: 995
American Express (Lost cards etc.)	Tel: 737-8188
Automobile Association of Singapore	Tel: 737-2444
Banks—Bank of Singapore, 101 Cecil Street	Tel: 223-9266
Bank of America, 78 Shenton Way	Tel: 223-6688
Chase Manhattan Bank, 50 Raffles Place	Tel: 530-4111
Consumers Association of Singapore, Shenton Way	Tel: 222-4165
Diners Club	Tel: 294-4222
Fire Station	Tel: 995
General Post Office, Fullerton Square	Tel: 533-8899
Immigration Department	Tel: 532-2877
Malaysia Airlines	Tel: 336-6777
Police	Tel: 999
Railway Information	Tel: 222-5165
Registered Tourist Guide Association	Tel: 270-7888
Samaritans of Singapore	Tel: 221-4444
Singapore Tourist Promotion Board	Tel: 339-6622
Singapore Airlines, 77 Robinson Road	Tel: 229-7293
Taxi	Tel: 452-5555
Telephone Directory Assistance	Tel: 100
Time of Day	Tel: 1711
Tourist Information Center, Raffles City Tower	Tel: 330-0431
Visa Card	Tel: 345-1010
Weather Report	Tel: 542-7788

PENINSULAR MALAYSIA

6

The Land and Life
of Malaysia

Malaysia consists of the Malay peninsula and Sabah and Sarawak on the island of Borneo. The country is made up of thirteen states and one federal territory. In peninsular Malaysia, a mountain range runs from the Thai border to the state of Johor, effectively separating the eastern part from the west. As a result of this, and the heavy tropical rainfall that blankets the country, there are many rivers in the country that historically formed the main arteries for trade and travel. The importance of these rivers is shown by the fact that most states in peninsular Malaysia take their names from the principal river in each area.

The interior of Sabah is crisscrossed by a series of mountain ranges, the most prominent of which is the Crocker Range with its well-known Mt. Kinabalu being the highest peak in southeast Asia (4100m.). In Sarawak the interior is generally mountainous with the highest range forming the border with Indonesia. The longest river in the country is the Rajang in Sarawak (560 kilometers) and this is navigable by small steamers inland for about 160 kilometers.

About two-thirds of Malaysia is covered by rain forest. Rice cultivation is practiced in all parts of the nonforest area but primarily in the states of Perlis, Kedah, and Pinang, with newer areas in Perak, Selangor, and Kelantan. Most of the larger rubber and oil-palm estates are located on the west coast of the peninsula.

The coastline of eastern peninsular Malaysia consists of long stretches of fine, sandy beaches, while much of the western coast is mangrove. In Sabah and Sarawak there are some stretches of good beach but also large areas of mangrove.

Malaysia lies entirely in the equatorial zone so the climate is hot all year. Rainfall varies considerably from one area to another due primarily to the effect of the northeast and southwest monsoons that blow alternatively. The northeast monsoon from about October to March comes off the open South China Sea and is responsible for the heavy rains that hit the east coast of the peninsula, and Sabah and Sarawak, particularly during the December to February period. April, May, and October are usually the wetter months for the western part of the Malay Peninsula.

The total land area of Malaysia is around 330,000 square kilometers, something similar to Italy. Peninsular Malaysia only represents about 40 percent of this area. The estimated population in 1991 was 18.5 million and this is growing at a rate of about 2.4 percent a year.

The natural vegetation of Malaysia is forest—either mangrove, swamp, dry land, high mountain, or classic rain forest. Apart from the mangrove forests, all others are extremely rich in growth and it is not uncommon to find more than a hundred species of plants in a single acre. Sabah and Sarawak are also known for two very interesting plants—the *Rafflesia*, the world's largest flower; and the family of pitcher plants of which *Nepenthes raja* is the largest.

Malaysia is rich in wildlife but many of the larger animals are rarely seen in the wild. Tigers, panthers, and leopards come into this category but they are known to exist in reasonable numbers. Civets are more often seen because they have fewer inhibitions, but the Malayan wild dog is a rarity. Honey bears are the principal omnivors but are rarely seen outside sanctuaries or zoos. Elephants exist in the deep jungle as do selandangs, the largest member of the wild ox family.

The deer and monkey families are well represented with numerous species, while numerically the fruit-eating and insect-eating bats are the largest species of mammals. Mention must be made of some unusual and totally protected mammals. Unfortunately you are not likely to see them in the wild. One is the tapir—a beast still in the process of evolution. Then there are the Javan and Sumatran species of rhinoceros, which are in great danger of extinction. Finally there are three species of gibbon that are occasionally seen, but often heard.

Malaysia abounds in birds, fish, reptiles, and insects. There are crocodiles, snakes, and 80 species of lizards, but none are of concern to most tourists. You are much more likely to come in contact with beetles, mosquitoes, and butterflies than you are to find the more unpleasant varieties.

There are a number of animals that are unique to Borneo. The most famous is the loveable orangutan, but they also include the proboscis monkey and the tarsier. The Borneo hornbill is a justifiably well known creature but it too is not commonly seen.

The People

Malaysia has a highly variegated ethnic mix that produces a multiracial society. This has come about primarily by immigration in the period from the early 1800s to the mid-1900s. Broadly speaking, there are two main categories: those with cultural affinities indigenous to the region, and those whose traditional cultural affinities lie outside. The first group are classified by the Malaysian government as *bumiputera* and these have a number of privileges denied to the others.

The *bumiputera* groups themselves are highly differentiated. The first group is the **Aborigines** (*orang asli*) who represent the original settlers of the region but who now survive only in small numbers in scattered groups, mainly in peninsular Malaysia. The **Malays** form the predominant group in this category. They consist of Malays who have long settled the east coast of the peninsula and parts of Sarawak and Sabah, Sumatrans who crossed the Straits of Malacca during the last 200 years, Javanese who have arrived within the last 150 years, and the Bajar people in Sabah. The third group are the **ethnic** people found in Sabah and Sarawak. In Sarawak these include the Iban, Bidayah, Melanar, Kenyah, Kayan, and Bisayah people. In Sabah they include the Kadazan, Murat, Kelabit, and Kedayan people.

The non-*bumiputera* groups consist primarily of the Chinese and the Indians, with much smaller communities made up of Arabs, Sinhalese, Eurasians, and Europeans. The Chinese and Indians have had contacts with this region for at least 2000 years but, except for the Chinese Baba community in Malacca, no substantial permanent settlement occurred until the nineteenth century. During the early period of the British colonial time, the Chinese found opportunities for investment and labor in the tin mining industry, and the Indians primarily came as agricultural labor on coffee and rubber estates. World War II effectively stopped further immigration but large numbers have chosen to make Malaysia their home.

The Chinese population of Malaysia is largely derived from South China, with the Cantonese and Hokkien forming the largest dialect groups. Among the Indians, the largest group are the Tamils from South India, with significant Sikh and Malayalee minorities.

While Malays constitute 55 percent of the population of peninsular Malaysia and total *bumiputera* make up 59 percent of the total Malaysian population, there are very significant regional variations. Perak, the Federal Territory, and Negeri Sembilan have non-*bumiputera* majorities, while Kelantan, Terengganu, and Perlis have relatively few non-*bumiputera* people. Generally speaking, the non-*bumiputera* groups tend to concentrate in the urban centers so all the major cities and towns except Johor Bahru, Kuala Terengganu, Kota Bharu, and Kuantan have significant non-*bumiputera* majorities.

The Government

Malaysia is a constitutional monarchy, its head of state being the Yang di-Pertuan Agong, one of the Malay Rulers who is elected by all Malay rulers, for a period of five years.

The country has a bicameral parliament consisting of a Senate comprising 58 members, and a House of Representatives. Elections to the House are held every five years (maximum) on the basis of universal adult suffrage. The Cabinet, which is headed by the prime minister, consists only of members of the legislature and is collectively responsible to parliament. The Senate is made up of two representatives from each state (26) and 32 members appointed by the King.

In Malay states, the rulers retain their pre-independence position except that generally they can no longer act contrary to the advice of the State Executive Council. The nonroyal states are each headed by a Yang di-Portua Negeri, federally appointed for four years. Each state has a unicameral legislative with elections held every five years (maximum).

The Malaysian constitution is derived from the constitution of the Federation of Malaya that was promulgated in 1957. This constitution was the result of a constitutional commission made up of an expert from Australia, India, and Pakistan, and presided over by Lord Reid from the United Kingdom. After detailed discussion in which the three major political parties of the time—UMNO, the MCA, and the MIC—played a major part, the proposals were accepted by the Federal Legislative Council and on the formation of Malaysia in 1963, the existing constitution was retained but amended to permit the admission of Sabah, Sarawak, and Singapore.

Since 1957 there have been many acts of parliament amending the constitution. The general effect of these amendments has been to increase the powers of the executive at the expense of the legislature and the judiciary, to weaken the safeguards to protect the fundamental rights of the individual, and to strengthen the federal government at the expense of the states.

The major political parties in Malaysia are the Alliance Party now called the Barisan Nasional (BN), the Parti Islam Se-Malaysia(PAS), the Democratic Action Party (DAP), and several smaller parties in Sarawak and Sabah. The BN has held power in Malaysia since independence. It was formed by an amalgamation of the old UMNO, MCA, and MIC parties and, in the early 1970s under the leadership of Tun Abdul Razak, efforts were made to get other parties to join so that "politicking" could be reduced. Several parties were induced to join and since then this party has entered into various coalitions to control almost all state parliaments as well. The PAS was briefly a member of BN but its declared aim of establishing an administration run on strict Islamic principles caused some problems. It regularly gains more than 15 percent of the national vote. The DAP is one of the major opposition parties and gains much of its vote from the Chinese community.

The present prime minister is Dr. Mahathir b. Mohamad. He was born in Kedah state in 1925, graduated from the University of Malaya in Singapore as a medical doctor, and was first elected as a MP for Kota Setar in 1964. He was once expelled from UMNO for a "breach of party discipline" but has been prime minister and president of UMNO since 1981.

The Ninth Yang di-Pertuan Agong was elected by the conference of Rulers in 1989. His Majesty was born in Perak state in 1928, and studied law at Nottingham University in the United Kingdom. He served in many legal positions in Malaysia before becoming a High Court Judge in 1965 at the age of 37, which made him the youngest judge in the commonwealth. In 1979 he became Chief Justice Malaya. In the meantime His Majesty was created Raja Kechil Bongsu in Perakin 1962 and subsequently, by a special decision of the Perak State Council, he was appointed Raja Muda in 1983. He succeeded to the throne of Perak in 1984.

The Economy

At independence, peninsular Malaysia was the world's largest producer of tin and the second largest producer of rubber, while Sabah depended largely on its timber and Sarawak on its petroleum, rubber, and pepper for their prosperity. These industries enabled Malaysia to be in the forefront of Third World nations, but at the same time the country was dangerously placed at the mercy of the fluctuations in the world tin and rubber markets.

The main aim of Malaysia since independence has been to end this reliance on a few major commodities by diversifying the economy in the agricultural sector and by promoting industrialization in selected sectors. This trend was particularly marked during the 1980s.

The government has played a leading role in the development of the national economy. The general path has been set by a series of five-year plans. Today the manufacturing sector has by far the largest revenue, with the wholesale and retail sector the next most important. Despite this, agriculture and mining are two very important industries through their contribution to the country's gross domestic product (GDP), employment, and foreign exchange earnings.

Agriculture provides 20 percent of GDP, 30 percent of employment, and 20 percent of Malaysia's export earnings. It also supports the manufacturing sector by providing the resources and the market necessary for it. Malaysia is currently the world's primary exporter of natural rubber and palm oil. These together with cocoa, timber, pepper, and tobacco dominate the growth of this sector. Among food commodities, rice production takes top priority but the country is not yet self-sufficient in rice.

Rubber has had such an enormous influence on the development of peninsular Malaya, that from the start of the industry in the 1890s, it grew to the point that in 1930 it was the most important export crop, and rubber trees covered two-thirds of the cultivated area of the peninsula. In the early 1990s rubber continues to be Malaysia's predominant export crop and it holds fourth place in export earnings. Malaysia accounts for 30 percent of world production.

Palm oil followed along after the rubber industry with the first plantings taking place in 1917. By 1940, peninsular Malaya ranked fourth in the world among producers and in the 1960s it reached number one, a position it has held ever since. Today Malaysia produces 55 percent of the world's palm oil.

Rice cultivation represents the oldest agricultural industry in Malaysia but up until recently, it was also the most backwards and least rewarding. Since World War II, great strides have been taken to reduce dependence on rice imports and to raise the production and living standards of rice farmers. Since 1945, production has increased by 60 percent, reducing the imported rice from 75 percent to 40 percent of the country's needs. Self-sufficiency, however, seems remote, particularly with the government's declared intention to encourage a high birth rate and a large population increase.

Of the other major crops, Malaysia is the third largest producer of cocoa in the world with about 11 percent of the market. It is the fourth largest producer of pepper. And it is a significant producer of timber.

Minerals are dominated by tin and petroleum. Tin has been important for hundreds of years while petroleum has only been significant since 1972. Other minerals of importance or potential include copper, gold, bauxite, iron ore, and coal. The mining sector currently contributes around 10 percent to GDP and employs around 40,000 workers.

Tin has been mined in peninsular Malaysia both for local use and for export to China since the earliest recorded times. The sultan of Malacca used tin ingots for currency, the Dutch tried to control trade by building forts at the river mouths, and from the 1840s tin mining determined the pattern of the peninsula's history and development for the rest of the century.

During the twentieth century the industry has gone through a series of peaks and troughs, and in the 1980s Malaysia's tin production dropped by more than half and many mines closed. Despite this, the country remains the leading world producer.

Petroleum and gas are now Malaysia's most valuable exports. The industry had its beginnings when the first oil well was opened at Miri in Sarawak in 1910. It was not until the 1970s, however, that the industry boomed. In that period, offshore oil fields were discovered in Terengganu, Sabah, and Sarawak waters. Work to exploit these resources commenced immediately and the results can be seen today. Malaysia currently produces more than 600,000 barrels a day.

Natural gas development is also being used to reduce the country's overdependence on oil as an energy source. In Sarawak, the Baram Delta Gas Gathering Scheme is underway in the Miri area. In Terengganu, the Peninsula Gas Utilisation project is being undertaken. Natural gas is piped on land at Kerteh where it is processed then used for domestic consumption or exported. Now a 730-kilometer pipeline is being built to serve other areas including as far south as Singapore.

Manufacturing industry played a minor role in the Malaysian economy until recently. Now it is the government's declared aim to convert Malaysia into a Newly Industrialised Country, and this sector of the economy contributes 25 percent of the GDP. Nearly 20 percent of the labor force is now engaged in manufacturing.

The electronics industry is probably the most well organized and largest industry in the country, making Malaysia the largest exporter of semi-conductor components to the United States. There is a move towards higher value-added products and greater automation, and the government is giving priority to the production of audio and visual components, computer peripherals and parts, and telecommunications equipment. Malaysia is currently the world's second largest producer of room air-conditioners, and a major producer of color television sets.

Malaysia is becoming a leader in the manufacture of rubber-based products. The tire and tube sector is obviously the most important but rubber gloves, balloons, footwear, swimming caps, and so on are also important. There is a growing number of foreign manufacturers producing here for export.

Trade with the rest of the world still has considerable dependence on a small number of industrialized nations but the picture is changing. A small but growing percentage of Malaysia's goods are now being exported to countries which were insignificant five years ago. Malaysia during the late 1980s was able to achieve a positive trade balance with exports exceeding imports in each of the last five years.

The major export products are electrical and electronic products, which represent 30 percent of the total exports; petroleum products (10 percent); palm oil (6 percent); rubber (6 percent); timber (6 percent); and liquid natural gas (3 percent). In the 25 years between 1965 and 1990, agriculture dropped from 55 to 30 percent of the total exports, minerals dropped from 30 to 15 percent, and manufacturing rose from 12 to 55 percent. Clearly a dramatic change took place.

Religion

Fifty-three percent of Malaysians classify themselves as Muslim and, under the constitution, Islam is the religion of the Malaysian federation. All states with the exception of Sarawak have Islam as the state religion.

Islam is primarily identified with the Malays although some non-Malays also adhere to this faith. The first evidence of its presence in Malaysia was from an inscription in Terengganu that has been dated to the fourteenth century.

Although Malacca's first ruler, Parameswara, became a convert to Islam around 1410 A.D., it was not until some forty years later that it became the state religion. From that time onwards, however, Malacca became a vital key to the spread of the religion throughout the Malay peninsula, Sumatra, Java, Borneo, Celebes, and beyond. Malacca also became an important center for Islamic teaching under the patronage of her rulers, until the time of the Portuguese conquest in 1511.

While Islam is enshrined by the constitution, there is also provision that every person has the right to profess and practice his own religion, and also has the right to propagate his faith, although the right to propagate other religions is not permitted by law among people who are Muslims.

The National Mosque in Kuala Lumpur is the most powerful symbol of Islam within the country but there are also state mosques (some of these are extremely grand), and hundreds of smaller local mosques. Many follow the general pattern of Middle East mosques while others have deviated to some extent into modern or other designs.

Muslim courts have been established by state governments and in 1988 the constitution was amended so that secular courts of Malaysia no longer have any jurisdiction over any matter within the jurisdiction of the Muslim courts. The Muslim courts are in the process of being organized into different tiers involving local courts, a High Court, and a Court of Appeal, in parallel with the secular courts. Muslim courts have jurisdiction only over Muslims.

Buddhism is the second largest religion with 17 percent of the population following this faith. It is largely identified with the Chinese but also with the Thai, Sinhalese, and Burmese. While there was Buddhism in Malacca from the fifteenth century, it was only during the great immigration period of the nineteenth century that it became an important faith in Malaysia.

Buddhist temples and associations are to be found in all the major centers of population throughout Malaysia and it is estimated that there are more than 3,500 of them. There are two main streams of Buddhism—the Chinese, and the Therarada—and both are represented here. The latter stream is particularly strong in Kelantan, Kedah, and Perlis because of Thai influence in these areas over the years. Most organizations belong to the Center for the World Fellowship of Buddhists.

Confucianism and Taoism represent the third largest group of adherents. They are entirely identified with the Chinese and are perhaps more a set of moral codes and principles, rather than a religion. Their presence is reflected in household altars, little shrines along the roadsides, and a multitude of temple schools and charitable institutions all over the country. Taoism has undergone attempts at revival and reform in the last 50 years.

Christianity is the religion of about one million people or eight percent of the population. Of these about two-thirds are in Sabah and Sarawak where they constitute about one-third of the total population. The presence of Christianity is obviously a result of the European connection in Malaysian history. It first arrived with the Roman Catholic Portuguese in the sixteenth century, with protestantism introduced by the Dutch a century later. The real missionary period came in the nineteenth century when the churches played a major role in education development. Christmas Day is a public holiday throughout Malaysia with Easter only celebrated as a public holiday in Sarawak.

Hinduism has long had an influence in Malaysia. Brahmanical Hinduism flourished before the coming of Islam and is still reflected in Malay language and literature, and in various traditional ceremonies. The Hinduism practiced in Malaysia today, however, comes from the nineteenth and early twentieth centuries with the big Indian migration to the region. It is estimated that today about 85 percent of Malaysian Indians are practicing Hindus.

Language

The national language, Bahasa Malaysia, is established under the constitution. It must be used for official purposes including those by federal and state governments and, since constitutional amendments, by all authorities including local authorities and statutory bodies. The status of Bahasa Malaysia may not be questioned under a constitutional amendment enacted in 1971. Despite this, the constitution still stipulates that no person can be prevented from using, teaching, or learning any other language (except for official purposes).

In practice the use of Bahasa Malaysia has become much more widespread in recent years and with it has come a reaction against English for road signs, government notices, and information signboards. It appears too, that much less emphasis is being given to the learning of English in schools. The result is that you can find groups of people in Malaysia who can neither understand nor speak English, and this has become a problem to some tourists and other visitors.

Fortunately Bahasa Malaysia in its basic form is a very simple language and visitors can quickly pick up a few words. After a few days you may be able to make yourself understood with a combination of words and sign language. Certainly it is worthwhile making a little effort to do this. The locals will be impressed and will reward you with extra help and courtesy.

Here are a selection of words and phrases that you will find useful in Malaysia.

Numbers

one—*satu*	six—*enam*
two—*dua*	seven—*tujuh*
three—*tiga*	eight—*lapan*
four—*empat*	nine—*sembilan*
five—*lima*	ten—*sepuluh*

eleven—*sebelas*
twelve—*duablas*
twenty—*dua puluh*
twenty-one—*dua puluh satu*
twenty-two—*dua puluh dua*

thirty—*tiga puluh*
one hundred—*seratus*
one thousand—*seribu*
one million—*satu juta*
slow down—*perlahan*

Time

daytime—*siang hari*
nighttime—*waktu malam*
today—*hari ini*
tomorrow—*esok*
yesterday—*semalam*

hour—*jam*
day—*hari*
week—*minggu*
when?—*bila?*
what time—*pukul berapa*

Greetings

good morning—*selamat pagi*
good afternoon—*selamat tengah hari*
good night—*selamat malam*
good-bye—*selamat tinggal*
How are you?—*apa khabar?*
Have a good trip—*selamat jalan*
Please come in—*sila masuk*
You're welcome—*sama sama*

Directions

where—*di mana*
left—*kiri*
right—*kanan*
north—*utara*
south—*selatan*
east—*timur*

turn—*belok*
go straight—*jalan terus*
stop here—*sula berhenti di sini*
go up—*naik*
go down—*turun*
west—*barut*

Useful Words

I—*saya*
we—*kami*
he/she—*dia*
they—*mereka*
you—*anda*
where?—*mana?*

yes—*ya*
no—*tidak*
a little—*sedikit*
a lot—*banyak*
male—*lelaki*
female—*perempuan*

thank you—*terima kasih*

help—*tolong*

stop—*berhenti*

go—*pergi*

what?—*apa?*

money—*wang*

please—*tolong*

wait—*tunggu*

want—*mahu*

Travelling

bus—*bus*

train—*kereta-api*

ship—*kapal*

ticket—*tikit*

trishaw—*beda*

beach—*pantai*

palace—*istana*

river—*sungai*

island—*pulau*

room—*bilik*

bathroom—*bilik mandi*

toilet—*tandas*

street—*leboh*

road—*jalan*

I'm going to—*saya pergi ke*

village—*kampung*

small town—*pekan*

town—*bandar*

city—*negri*

hill—*bukit*

mountain—*gunung*

shop—*kedai*

cave—*gua*

open—*buka*

closed—*tutup*

bed—*tempat tidur*

post office—*peja bat pos*

lake—*tasik*

Food and Drink

fried rice—*nasi goreng*

boiled rice—*nasi putih*

fried noodles—*mee goreng*

soup—*sup*

fried vegetables—*cap cai*

chicken—*ayam*

water—*air*

meat—*daging*

orange juice—*air jeruk*

coffee—*kopi*

hot—*panas*

delicious—*enak*

meat—*makan*

fish—*Ikan*

egg—*telur*

pork—*babi*

crab—*detam*

beef—*daging lembu*

prawns—*udang*

fruit—*buah*

sugar—*gula*

milk—*susu*

tea—*teh-o*

cold—*sejoh*

drink—*minum*

vegetables—*sayur*

Questions and Comments

Can you help me?—*Bolehkah encik tolong saya?*
How do I get there? —*Bagaimanakah saya boleh ke sana?*
How far is it?—*Berapa jauh?*
How long will it take?—*Berapa lama?*
How much is it?—*Berapa harganya?*
What is your name?—*Apa nama anda?*
Where do you come from?—*Anda datang dari mana?*
Can you speak English?—*Boleh anda bercekap dalam Bahasa Inggeris?*

Food

The uninitiated visitor to Malaysia is faced with a bewildering array of food that seems to be available all day and night. Eating out is very much part of the Malaysian life-style and the visitor should make the most of the opportunities to sample new cuisines. There is probably no better way to meet a Malaysian than to ask someone to help you select a restaurant in which to eat.

Malaysia's food is available in open-air stalls, simple basic restaurants, coffee shops and fast-food outlets, and sophisticated air-conditioned restaurants. Do not eat exclusively in any one of these, as all offer different pieces of the giant eating out picture, which you should experience.

The key to enjoying Malaysian food is not only knowing what to eat but where to find the best food. Locals hold long and serious discussions over where to get the best chilli crab, the tastiest *nasi lemak*, or the freshest rice *rebus*. The different chapters in this book will help you make a selection, but don't neglect to ask a local about your choice. Bear in mind, however, that Asian food tastes may be different from our own, and certainly the locals put far less emphasis on atmosphere than we do. While a lovely setting and reasonable food may be great in your view, locals may tell you that the food is terrible so you should not go there for any reason.

The three major ethnic races and the native races in Sabah and Sarawak have each contributed a large variety of dishes to the Malaysian scene. Some are delicate and subtle, while others are hot and spicy. While some may be the same as you find in other countries, others are quite different and uniquely Malaysian. Be a bit adventurous in your eating and you will be rewarded with some taste sensations that you will never find at home.

Malay cuisine is characterized by the coconut cream, chilli, and

Satay—*popular and good anywhere.*

The durian, a new taste (and smell) experience.

indigenous spices that are often used. The most celebrated of Malay food is undoubtedly *satay*—skewers of spice-marinated slices of beef or chicken, barbecued over charcoal, and eaten dipped in a spicy peanut sauce. Another popular dish is *nasi padany*—where you choose between curried chicken, beef, prawns, or fish to go with a bowl of steamed white rice. Sometime during your stay, try a breakfast of *nasi lemak*—rice cooked in coconut milk, served with spicy anchovies and egg, and garnished with peanuts and cucumber.

Sabah cuisine is primarily from the Kadazan people, and popular dishes include marinated raw fish; *sup manuk on hing*, which is a chicken soup enhanced with rice wine; and *hinompula*, a dessert made from tapioca, sugar, coconut, and the juice of screwpine leaves.

Sarawak cuisine reflects the influence of the sea and rivers. The most popular dish is *terubok* fish, either steamed or grilled whole with its scales still on. Other popular dishes are *pansuh manok*—chicken pieces cooked in a bamboo cup and served with rice—and *umai*—a raw fish salad.

Chinese cuisine in Malaysia covers almost all the entire regional variations available in China. It is renowned for its subtle and delicate flavors. There is an amazing choice in dishes and all are prepared and freshly cooked in minutes. Do not judge a restaurant by its decor because in Malaysia it is the food that counts, not the dragons and lanterns that we love in the West. Sizzling prawns, ginger beef, barbecued pork ribs, shark's fin soup, steamed grouper, and sweet-and-sour dishes are among the most popular in hundreds of Chinese restaurants throughout the country.

Indian cuisine covers both north and south Indian food. Visit one of the banana leaf restaurants where you eat with your hands. Often they will specialize in vegetarian food—lentil curries, piquant chutneys, and fresh yogurt. Indian unleavened breads, cooked on griddles in view of diners, are very popular with lentil and meat curries. If you have the chance, try *murtabak*—a cooked dough filled with minced meat, beaten egg, and onions.

Nyonya cuisine is a wonderful blend of Malay and Chinese. Chicken *kapitan*—chicken cooked with coconut milk blended with fresh spices—is a firm favorite. You will find that *orak-otak*—minced fish, coconut milk and spice, steamed in banana leaves—is a snack well worth trying.

Western food is available in all the major hotels and in a few other places. The hotels are OK, but be wary of Western dishes in Malay, Chinese, or Indian restaurants because they often bear little resemblance to their overseas counterparts. Fast-food chains are well established so you can enjoy fried chicken, hamburgers, and donuts while you decide on your next local meal.

Some Malaysian **fruits** will be foreign to many people but most are delicious. While we know pineapple, banana, coconut, and papaya in the West, you will be surprised at the taste and the varieties that you find in Malaysia. Perhaps it is because they are fresher than some we get at home. In rural areas they are often straight off the tree or bush. It is also worth trying the very popular durian, despite its strong smell; the mangosteen, with its sweet, juicy, white flesh; the starfruit, which is an excellent thirst-quencher eaten whole or as a juice; the ram-butan, a sweet juicy fruit with the appearance of a hairy red lychee; the pomelo, an oversized but less tart grapefruit; the chiku, which is soft and sweet and looks a bit like a kiwi fruit; and the mango, which may suddenly become your favorite fruit.

The Social Culture

Malaysia is particularly rich in social and artistic aspects of culture because it has elements of five major cultures—Islamic, Chinese, Indian, Western, and indigenous—within its community. You see the social culture primarily through the festivals, the customs, the games and pastimes, and the arts. Each has an influence on the visitor.

Festivals dot the Malaysian calendar and most have origins in religion. The two most important festivals of the Islamic year are the Hari Raya Haji, which marks the successful conclusion of the annual pilgrimage to Mecca, and Hari Raya Puasa, which marks the end of the fasting month of Ramadan. The birthday of the Prophet Muhammad and the start of the Islamic New Year, known as Maal Hijrah, are two other important occasions.

For Buddhists, the main festival is the birthday of the Buddha or Wesak Day; for Christians it is Christmas. There are many Chinese festivals, but by far the most important is the Chinese New Year. For some Chinese this is the only chance they have all year for a few days' break. Some other important Chinese festivals are the Ching Ming Festival, the Moon Cake Festival, the Festival of the Seven Sisters, and the Birthday of the Jade Emperor.

The Hindu Indians have three major festivals—Deepavali, Thaipusam, and Ponggol—but there are numerous other local events. The Sikhs celebrate the birthday of Buru Nanak, and Vesakhi, the Sikh new year. In Sabah, the Kadazan Harvest Festival is celebrated with gusto, while in Sarawak, the Iban Harvest Festival has come to represent the state's major holiday.

The following is a list of the major public holidays in Malaysia.

NATIONAL PUBLIC HOLIDAYS

Chinese New Year—Movable, late January or early February
Labor Day—May 1
Hari Raya Puasa—Movable, late April or early May
Wesak Day—Movable, May
King's Birthday—June
Hari Raya Haji—Movable, usually July
Awal Muharran—Movable, late July or early August
National Day—August 31
Birthday of Prophet Muhammad—Movable, October
Deepavali—Movable, October
Christmas—December 25

The following are celebrated by four or more states.

New Year's Day—January 1 (Not Johor, Kedah, Kelantan, Perlis, and Terengganu)
Thaipusam—Late January or early February (Negeri Sembilan, Perak, Penang, and Selangor only)
Nuzul Quran—April (Kelantan, Melaka, Perak, Perlis, Selangor, and Terengganu only)

Most of the major state holidays are mentioned in the individual chapters.

GAMES AND PASTIMES

The games and pastimes traditional in Malaysian society are legion. Although primarily identified with particular ethnic groups, many have become more universal in recent years. These are some of the more interesting:

Bird singing contests are held locally and nationally. This is a traditional pastime particularly in the north of peninsular Malaysia where the value of champion birds can rise to over M$50,000 a bird.

Congkak is a traditional Malay indoor board game for women and children. It is slowly being introduced to a wider public.

Kite flying is enjoyed by both the Malays and Chinese but it is only in Terengganu and Kelantan that it is still a major activity.

Lion dances are associated with Chinese festivals when they are performed as entertainment, and to help with the collection of donations.

Self-defense exists in many forms but basically they all represent variations on a theme that emphasizes bodily dexterity combined with

Top spinning. (Courtesy of the Malaysia Tourism Promotion Board)

self-discipline. The Malay forms are often called silat, while kendo, tae kwon do, judo, and tai-chi have Chinese origins.

Sepak Takrau is a court game played with a rattan ball. There are some similarities to netball except here you use all parts of the body except the arms and hands to propel the ball over the five-foot-high net.

Top spinning is centered in Kelantan where men produce beautiful wooden tops that in the hands of a skilled player can be made to spin for over an hour on end.

ARCHITECTURE

Unfortunately there are almost no Malay buildings in Malaysia more than 200 years old. The buildings that are older than this are primarily examples of Chinese, Hindu, or Western architectural styles. Malacca is obviously the city with the most history and style, and fortunately this is now being recognized and attempts are being made to preserve and enhance what is left.

There are, however, some examples of traditional palace architecture elsewhere—almost all have been built this century—with the Astana at Sri Menanti in Negeri Sembilan, and the Istana Lembah at Kuala Kangsar, two of the best examples. Both of these are now museums. British colonial architecture is well represented in places such as Taiping and Batu Gajah, while the neo-Moorish style of the Sultan Abdul Samad Building, and the Kuala Lumur railway station, have appeal to visitors today.

MUSIC AND DANCE

Traditional Malay music is performed on ceremonial occasions, and as accompaniment to dance and drama for entertainment. Perhaps the basic element is the *gendang* (drum) of which there are at least 14 types. Other instruments include the gong, *cerucap* (seashells), *raurau* (coconut shells), *kertuk* (bamboo), *celampang* (wood), flutes, and *gambus* (string instrument). There are also a number of traditional instruments from Sabah and Sarawak.

The **Nobat** is a special royal orchestra consisting of four or five members, using drums, flute, trumpet, and gong, which is only employed for state ceremonial occasions. There are four such orchestras in the peninsula at present, at Kedah, Terengganu, Perak, and Johor.

The number of traditional dance forms throughout the country is quite vast. They range from the *andus* and *berunsai* dances of Sabah, to the *joget*, *mak inang*, and *serampang* of the peninsula. The *ngajat* dancers

Hand painting pottery.

are very popular with the Iban and other ethnic groups in Sarawak. The *tarian lolin* is a popular dance on the tourist circuit because of its attractive play with candles, but this actually originates in Sumatra, Indonesia.

HANDICRAFTS

Various forms of handicraft flourished in the past but they have largely been displaced by modern manufactured items for everyday use. Recently, however, there has been a revival in local handicrafts, especially for the tourist market, and once more they are becoming easier to find.

Silverware manufacture was once widespread but now it is restricted to Kelantan (where it is flourishing), and the Maloh people in Sarawak. Kelantan silver is fine and delicate with intricate patterns.

Brassware manufacture was also widespread but now its production is restricted to Terengganu and Sarawak. Terengganu is the home of the traditional white brass.

Pandan weaving is still popular and there are mats, baskets, dish covers, sun hats, fans, bags, and other goods made from the leaves of the screwpine.

Pottery continues to be a significant industry in Sarawak where it is booming both with the tourist and domestic markets. It has also been revived in Perak, and in a small way elsewhere.

Masks and wood carvings are still produced in Selangor and Sarawak. The Mah Meri people do wonderful wood carvings, while the Iban and other groups produce masks.

Weaponry has long been important to Malays with the *Keris*, the unusual wavy-bladed dagger, being the most well known symbol of the Malay world. Daggers, swords, and spears are all produced, often with loving craftsmanship.

Weaving is still practiced and each district has its characteristic style. The ceremonial cloths of Sabah and Sarawak are outstanding while the woven cloths of Kelantan and Terengganu have a good reputation. The fabulous gold-threaded cloths (*benang mas* and *songket*) are very popular with visitors.

Batik was once the monopoly of the Javanese (Indonesia) but in the last forty years this art has become entrenched in Kelantan and Terengganu. The cloth imprinted by the application of wax and resin by stencils, has become a major industry.

THE MEDIA

There are three television networks broadcasting in Malaysia. TV1 and TV2 are government services and TV3 is a private network. All programs originate in Kuala Lumpur. Much of the programming is in Bahasa Malaysia but there are also Chinese, English, and some other language programs. The government networks "promote national unity, stimulate public interest, develop civic consciousness and provide information and education." There is an aim of 70 percent local content on television. All networks carry advertisements.

Radio Malaysia is a government service that provides six networks throughout Malaysia. One of these services (radio 4) broadcasts in English. It operates 11 hours a day on weekdays and 18 on weekends. English language newspapers have program and frequency details.

Since the original printing press act of 1948, there have been several amendments to give the government greater control of the press. Some of these prevent public discussion or questioning of "sensitive issues" and others involve major penalties for printers, publishers, and editors who fail to "keep to the facts" in their publications.

While the majority of publications are in Bahasa Malaysia, there are significant publications in English. The *New Straits Times*, the *Star*, the *Malay Mail*, and the *Business Times* are all daily English newspapers in peninsular Malaysia. In Sabah the *Sabah Times*, and the *Daily Express* are printed daily in English, while in Sarawak there is the *Borneo Post*, the *People's Mirror*, and the *Sarawak Tribune*. There are a few Malaysian journals and magazines published in English.

7

Who Are the Malaysians?

Malaysia occupies a strategic position at one of the world's major crossroads. It has long served as a land bridge between mainland southeast Asia, the islands of Indonesia, and ultimately the islands of the Pacific beyond. Later it became a natural meeting place for traders from the East and the West.

Early Settlement

The lush tropical forest and the abundance of plant and animal life existing in it, made Malaysia an easy place for the settlement and sustenance of small, self-supporting human communities, without the need for wider contact.

Evidence exists that this was one of the earliest homes of man. Stone implements found at Lenggong in Perak, at Tingkaya in Sabah, and the remarkable finds in the Niah Cave of Sarawak, provide evidence for this conclusion. The discovery of a human skull at Niah, which has been dated at 40,000 years old, caused a sensation. Other finds of stone implements have confirmed man's existence here for that period. At a site in Sabah, a stone tool factory has been discovered that dates from 31,000 years ago. Little is known about these early settlers but it is believed that they were probably a people akin to the present-day Australian aborigine.

The earliest of the present-day inhabitants of Malaysia are the *orang asli* of the peninsula, and the mongoloid inhabitants (Kadazan, Dusan, Iban, etc.) of Sabah and Sarawak. Some of these people still pursue a largely nomadic life, scarcely touched by the twentieth century, but others are willing participants in modern Malaysia. It is estimated that these people reached Malaysia about 5000 years ago.

These early settlers were probably the pioneers of the general movement of people southwards from China and Tibet through mainland southeast Asia and the Malay peninsula to the Indonesian archipelago and beyond.

The Malays Arrive

The early Malay people arrived in two waves but the dates are in some dispute. These people also came from the north and first settled the coastal regions. It is thought that they may have been pushed out of Thailand by waves of new settlers entering that area. The first group (the Proto-Malays) were probably established in Malaysia by 1000 B.C. They were fishermen and sailors and lived on the rich resources of the oceans surrounding peninsular Malaysia.

The second group (the Deutero-Malays) followed a few centuries later. They came with more advanced farming techniques and a new knowledge of metals, and they quickly spread throughout the region. The Malay people today have much in common with the Indonesians and the southern Filipinos, due no doubt to their similar ethnic backgrounds.

There is no evidence that the Malays or the earlier settlers in the region ever shared any common political goals or even had much contact. In fact, although there were elements of a common culture, the groups of self-contained people remained politically fragmented. The ubiquitous thick jungle and mountainous terrain of the interior inhibited communication, while the absence of broad, flood-prone river valleys and deltas, except in parts of Sabah and Sarawak, precluded the development of irrigated agricultural land that elsewhere formed the basis of early civilizations.

Early Trade and Outside Influences

A dramatic change occurred around the first century B.C. with the establishment of regular trade links with the world beyond southeast Asia. The first contacts were made with the Chinese but it was the Hindu and Buddhist elements of Indian culture that had the major impact on the region.

Over a period of a thousand years, these influences gradually left their mark in language, literature, and social custom. The period was marked by a tremendous growth in East-West trade and the establishment of Hindu ministates at the mouths of most major rivers on the peninsula. In Borneo there was no such influence and while there is evidence of trade between Borneo and China prior to the sixth century A.D., there seems to have been little Indian influence.

There were other influences on the region as well. The Funan kingdom of Indo-China exerted some influence over northern Malaysia at one time. The Khmers may have had some control at one time but the evidence for this is fairly sketchy. Certainly the strong Sumatran-based Srivijaya empire held sway for several centuries, but was eventually overtaken by the Java-based Majapahit empire. Just what control these outside civilizations had over the still scattered Malay communities is really not known but it is thought to be general rather than specific.

The Hindu-Buddhist period of Malaysian history came to an abrupt end with the arrival of Islam. This was brought to the region by Arab and Indian traders and after about 1400 A.D. this became the major influence on the region. When a Sumatran prince decided to base himself at Malacca, this center became the most powerful city-state in the region. In the fourteenth century, with the help of the Chinese emperor, Malacca extended its influence over much of peninsular Malaysia, Sumatra, and into Borneo. Islam spread with this influence. It had a profound effect on Malay society and the Malay way of life.

In some ways the Malacca kingdom marks a high point in Malay culture. It grew rich and powerful but this in the end proved to be its undoing. The wealth and influence eventually attracted the Portuguese and in 1511 a fleet of warships arrived to take over the town. After a brief struggle, the Sultan of Malacca fled south in an effort to re-establish his kingdom in Johor while the mantle of Islam was passed to the sultanate of Brunei.

European Influence

The Portuguese take-over of Malacca shattered the Malaccan empire and allowed it to become the center of European power in the region. The natural Malay successor was the newly established state in Johor, but due to the activities of smaller rival groups, it never grew to any level of importance. The vacuum created by all this activity could have been filled by the emerging sultanate of Brunei, but was curtailed by the establishment of the Spanish colony in the Philippines and the Dutch influence in Java.

The Malay peninsula states, which had been controlled by Malacca, failed to take advantage of their newfound freedom. They fought and squabbled among themselves, each becoming more isolated from the others. Eventually there were attacks made on Malacca and after 130 years the Portuguese enclave fell to the Dutch in 1641.

The Portuguese had failed to fully exploit Malacca's advantage as a trade center and the Dutch had even less success. The Dutch tried to keep trade entirely to themselves but the result was that Malacca continued to decline in importance. Meanwhile the rest of the Malay states remained isolated sovereign units, with only minor contact and cooperation.

It was not until the arrival of the British that this situation changed. Captain Francis Light arrived in Penang in 1786 and established a trading post. By adopting a free trade policy, the settlement boomed and by 1800 it had a sizable population. The success of this post, and the British distrust of the Dutch, caused Thomas Stamford Raffles to look for a further area to develop. In 1819 he established Singapore. This caused some problems with the Dutch but it was resolved amicably with the transfer of the British base at Bencoolen in Sumatra to the Dutch, in exchange for Malacca. The die was now cast, with British influence set to spread throughout peninsular Malaysia.

The British brought Penang, Singapore, and Malacca under the one banner as the British Straits Settlement and effectively governed it from Bengal in India. In 1867 it became a Crown Colony and the process of the political integration of the Malay states into a modern nation-state began. The British managed to bring more and more of the country under their influence without a fight, and even without total control. Treaties were entered into with Malay rulers giving them local control but allowing Britain to manage "external" affairs.

The major move in this process was the establishment of the Federated States of Malaya—a joining together of Perak, Selangor, Negri Sembilan, and Pahang.

In Borneo, the situation was somewhat different. The Sultan of Brunei had general sway over the region but was faced with continuous outbreaks of rebellion. In 1838 James Brooke, a British adventurer, arrived in Borneo and decided to help the sultan quell one of these disputes. The sultan, in gratitude, installed Brooke as Rajah over an area of country that is now part of Sarawak. Brooke and his successors ruled an ever-expanding region for more than 100 years as benevolent dictators. In the process they eliminated the dreaded Borneo pirates, suppressed head-hunting and inter-tribal fighting, and put Sarawak on the road to democracy.

In the area that we now know as Sabah, another saga was being played out. The U.S. consul in Brunei obtained a 10-year lease on North Borneo from the Sultan of Brunei. He then sold it to the American Trading Company. The company started a settlement but ran into financial problems and eventually sold out to the Austrian consul in Hong Kong. He in turn managed to get the lease renewed for another 10 years, then obtained the financial support of the Dent Brothers in London for development purposes. In 1882 the British North Borneo Chartered Company took over the right to the lease and in 1888 North Borneo became a British protectorate.

By 1910-20, the political organization of the region was clearly under British control. The Straits Settlements of Singapore, Malacca, Penang, Labuan, the Cocos Isles, and Christmas Isle was a British Crown Colony. The Federated Malay States of Negeri Sembilan, Pahang, Perak, and Selangor were a British protectorate under the tutelage of a British advisor in each state. Sarawak was a British protectorate ruled by the Brooke family, and Sabah was a British protectorate ruled by the Chartered Company of British North Borneo. Brunei had also become a British protectorate.

The British had operated an open immigration policy for 150 years, which had encouraged the arrival of thousands of Chinese who were attracted by the tin mines. When rubber plantations were planted throughout the peninsula, the supply of local labor was not enough so Indians were brought in. Chinese and Indians continued to pour in and by the 1930s these immigrants eventually outnumbered the Malays in peninsular Malaysia and Singapore.

The Japanese

The Japanese invasion of Malaya and British Borneo in 1941 was swift and effective. The entire peninsula and Singapore were overrun within 2½ months. This was the first and only time that the region had been totally controlled by a foreign Asian power. The Japanese ran a brutal administration and received little cooperation from the locals. The Chinese in particular were bitterly opposed to the Japanese because of their previous invasion of China, and an underground resistance army was formed. Remnants of British forces also continued a guerrilla struggle throughout the war so that the Japanese were constantly tormented.

In Sarawak the Japanese invasion nullified the new constitution that was to establish self-government for the country, but in the peninsula, the occupation focused the forces of nationalism. When British rule returned in 1945, the political situation was entirely different from what it had been four years earlier.

Post-War

The British authorities realized this situation, so changes were immediately made. The Straits Settlements were dissolved. Penang and Malacca were joined with the Malay states to form a new Malayan Union. Singapore became a separate colony, as did Sarawak and British North Borneo. Labuan was joined to British North Borneo, while Brunei remained a British protectorate. The Malay Union idea provoked strong opposition from the Malay population and in 1948 it was replaced with the establishment of the Federation of Malaya. At the same time the British committed themselves to working towards independence. Shortly afterwards the Malayan Communist Party decided the time had come to end British rule and so started the 12-year "emergency."

Independence

Under the pressure of the communist rebellion and a strong Malay nationalist movement, the British introduced elections to peninsular Malaysia. The first federal elections were held in 1955 and an alliance of three racially based parties won 51 of the 52 seats contested. Tunku Abdul Rahman was appointed the federation's first Chief Minister. Malaya achieved independence (*merdeka*) in 1957. Local elections were introduced in Sarawak in 1959 and in Sabah in 1962.

Independence for Malaya, however, didn't bring immediate peace to the region. The communist problems continued to smolder and in neighboring Singapore, politics were becoming increasingly more radical. Both Britain and Singapore were keen for Singapore to join with Malaya in a wider federation, but the idea was generally opposed by the Malays in Malaya.

In an attempt to overcome this problem, Tunku Abdul Rahman proposed a wider federation of Malaya, Singapore, Brunei, Sabah, and Sarawak. The idea had mild internal support but met with instant opposition from the Philippines who made a claim over Sabah, and by Indonesia who saw it as a "neo-colonial plot." After a British commission and a United Nations mission went to Borneo to report on public opinion, the go-ahead was given to the formation of Malaysia. On 16

September 1963, Malaysia was formed, without Brunei, which at the last minute declined to join.

Malaysia

The early years of Malaysia saw many problems. Indonesia launched its "confrontation" policy and sent guerrilla forces across the border into Sabah and Sarawak, and made landings in Singapore and peninsular Malaysia. Internally there were problems between Singapore and Malaya over the question of Chinese influence, and the privileged position of Malays in the federation. Lee Kuan Yew, the Chinese leader of Singapore, still had left-wing problems at home so he decided to take drastic action. He conducted a purge of radical elements, undertook some major steps to reform the country, and refused to bow to Malay pressure on some key issues.

The result was that Singapore ceased to be a member of Malaysia in 1965 and became an independent country. Malaysia was now a predominantly *bumiputera* country and for a while the problems diminished. With the fall from power of Indonesia's President Sukarno, confrontation was brought to an end in 1966 and in this same year, the Philippines gave formal recognition to Malaysia. The whole thing came unstuck again in 1969 when violent intercommunal riots broke out, particularly in Kuala Lumpur, and hundreds of people were killed. Parliament was abandoned and an emergency government—the National Operations Council—was established. Parliamentary rule was restored in 1971 but in the interim, many talented and wealthy Chinese left the country.

Since 1971, the political path has been smoother. Tun Abdul Razak succeeded Tunku Abdul Rahman as prime minister, and he was followed by Tun Hussein Onn. All came from the ruling coalition of political parties—formerly called the Alliance but now called the National Front. During the 1970s, Malaysia achieved considerable economic progress and forged an identify for itself in international affairs. It was instrumental in the formation of ASEAN, it recognized Communist China in 1974, and it joined the grouping of nonaligned nations to distance itself from its colonial past.

The 1980s saw a continuation of this movement. Dr. Mahathir Mohamad became prime minister in 1981 and has since encouraged Malaysia to identify closer with the Middle East Islamic world. At the same time he has set out to establish heavy industry in the country. There have been further moves to ensure that Malays have a larger share in the nation's wealth. There has also been a reversal in the policy to encourage a reduction in the birth rate. Now the policy is to achieve a population of 70 million based on a growth rate of 3.2 percent per annum. With the *bumiputera* birth rate already much higher than other groups in the population, this will ensure a growing percentage of *bumiputera* people.

The 1990s are seeing a further development of Malaysian nationalism. With growing economic wealth, the country is set to play a leading part in southeast Asian politics and economics.

8

Kuala Lumpur and the Hill Resorts

1. The General Picture

It was originally virgin tropical forest, then miners found tin and started a small settlement. It grew to become the capital of the state of Selangor and now it is the capital of Malaysia.

Now fondly referred to as K.L., the city is still growing, still building, but it is a city where size does not overwhelm you. The population is just over 1.2 million, small by world standards, but K.L. is still very much the center for the nation's activities in politics, culture, education, sports, and business.

For the visitor, K.L. is a good place to first encounter Malaysia. There are several fascinating places to visit and the city is a better mix of Malay, Indian, Chinese, and Western influence than anywhere else in the country. All major financial institutions and many of the largest private companies have their headquarters in K.L. The three oldest universities in the country are all within a 30-minute drive of the city center. K.L. is a city of fusion and contradiction. The skyscrapers shout for attention, signaling progress and the twentieth century, while the pre-war shop houses and colonial bungalows reach back toward a slower pace of life.

K.L. has become the best place to shop, not only for those authentic products of Malaysia, but also for foreign ones. Shopping is done in ultramodern shopping centers, or adventurously at the street markets

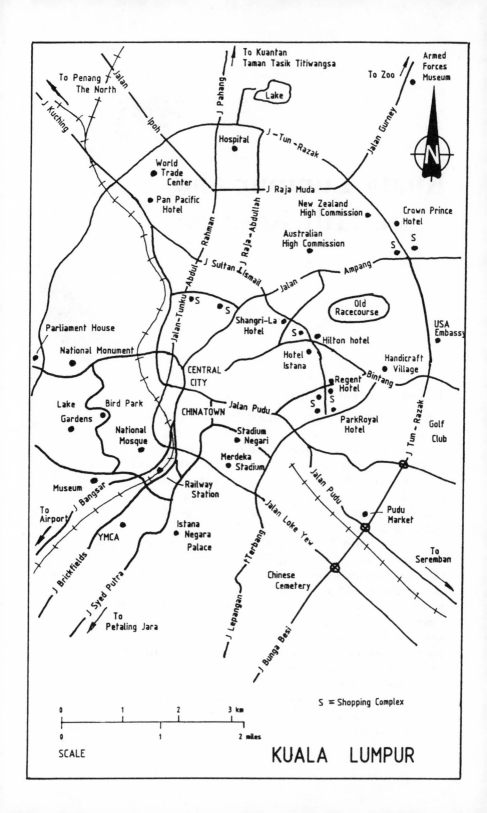

and *pasar malam* (night market). A few years ago K.L. was called a cultural desert but the city matured in the late eighties and early nineties and now there are good eating and entertainment opportunities.

Kuala Lumpur is no replica of Singapore. The two cities are quite different in many respects. Just because you have visited one doesn't mean that you should ignore the other. The pace in K.L. is distinctly slower, the facilities less obvious, but some visitors will find it easier to understand, although not necessarily easier to see. The single-minded zeal which overseas Chinese communities in Singapore, Hong Kong, and Taipei bring to business is tempered here, but nevertheless K.L. is on the same path.

English-speaking visitors will quickly encounter a problem. The British colonial rulers left behind a rich legacy in many areas but the Malaysians have largely turned their backs on the English language and now all road signs, information boards, and names are in Malay. As a result, foreign visitors have difficulty in finding places they wish to visit and even when they do get there, much of the interest is dimmed by lack of English language signs and information. It is no wonder that many visitors leave without seeing all the sights and are disappointed with this aspect of K.L.

Despite this situation, no international visitor should go to Malaysia without spending a few days in K.L. To understand this heart of the nation, you need to get into the streets, to explore, to absorb. You can do this in safety by walking. K.L. is not the city it was last decade. It is alive, constantly changing and adjusting to the new needs and wants of its inhabitants and visitors. It is, I believe, a reflection of the new sophistication that is coming to Malaysia and which will be increasingly seen during the next decade.

2. Getting There

K.L. is served by more than 30 international airlines. Subang Airport, 24 kilometers from the city, is the gateway. The airport is modern and adequate for the present volume of traffic but is not in the league of the major airports in Singapore or Bangkok. There are two independent terminals but if you are arriving on an international flight you will use the facilities of Terminal 1.

Provided your passport is in order you will quickly pass through immigration. Note that the visa in your passport is for entry into peninsular Malaysia only, not for Sabah or Sarawak. After collecting your luggage, you will go to customs where spot checks on baggage are made. If you have to pay any customs duty or deposit on a temporary import, be sure to get an official receipt in English that you can read. Be aware also of the penalties for drug offenses. Under no circumstances should you carry anything of a doubtful nature with you.

The airport has the usual international facilities—restaurant, bank, post office, shops, information counter, hotel reservation facility, car rental agency, and taxi booth. If you are arriving from another country, change some of your money into local currency. You will need it for the bus or taxi to get you to town.

There are three alternatives from the airport to the city, however, wise travellers will only consider the first two. The public bus is the cheapest method. The trip takes 45 minutes when traffic is light, much longer when traffic is heavy. The service operates regularly and is easy to negotiate. The bus travels to the Kelang Bus Station in Jalan Sultan Mohamed and the cost is about M$1.20.

The second alternative is the limousine/taxi service, which operates on a coupon system to eliminate fare cheating from the airport. You state your destination at the ticket counter and will be told a price depending on the fare zone. There are 13 different zones with prices from about M$13 to M$30. A trip to the center of the city will cost about M$18. You use the ticket to pay the driver. There should be no other charge.

The third alternative is to deal with the taxi touts who will try and get you into a taxi without your buying a coupon. The driver will pay the tout for his trouble, then will try to extract whatever he can from you. It is just what you don't need when you first arrive in a new country.

Visitors can also arrive in K.L. by rail and road. There are good **train** services from Singapore and Thailand that arrive at the marvelous old Kuala Lumpur railway station. There is an information counter at the station for new arrivals, and taxis are available to any part of town. **Long-distance buses** also operate these routes, arriving at the multistory Pudu Raya Bus Station in Jalan Pudu. Buses tend to be cheaper than the train but given the choice I would pay the extra to get the additional space, safety, and comfort of the train. There are also **long-distance taxis** from Johor Bahru (for Singapore), Butterworth, and Penang (for Thailand), and most major peninsular Malaysian towns. Most of these also arrive at the Pudu Raya Bus Station.

3. Local Transportation

The only practical way of getting around K.L. is to walk or to take a taxi or bus. The city is well spread out and streets are not on a grid pattern so it can be difficult to find your way by yourself. Most visitors will be less keen to walk during the day because temperatures can be high and the sun very strong.

I find K.L. **buses** difficult to understand and frustrating to use, yet despite this the Tourism Promotion Board keeps advising me that seeing K.L. by bus is a "delight." Maybe it is just me. There are two types of city buses—those using fare stages, and minibuses, which operate on a fixed fare.

There are numerous bus stands around the city but it seems almost impossible to get a bus map. Certainly the major information centers around the city do not have them. What they do have is a book that details the various routes, but this is almost useless for a visitor who knows few district or street names. For short trips it's probably best just to hop on any bus going in the general direction you want. The minibus fare will be M$0.50, the regular bus about M$0.30. The driver or conductor will probably not speak English but at the same time will not hassle you if you overstay your fare. To get to specific places in the suburbs it is best to ask at your hotel then walk to the bus station that serves the area to which you are going.

Fortunately **taxis** are easier. They can be hired from taxi stands, from outside hotels, or hailed by the roadside. All taxis have meters and most drivers will turn the meter on once you board. You should check, however, that the driver can speak some English, knows the destination, and will activate the meter, before you climb inside. It's also a good idea to check that the meter starts at the basic flag fall (about M$0.80 for a non-air-conditioned taxi and M$1 for an air-conditioned cab).

As well as the basic fare there are a number of extras which may apply. These include a 50-percent surcharge on the fare between midnight and 6 A.M., a charge for each passenger in excess of two, and a charge for every piece of luggage. You will find that taxi drivers are not keen to go to the airport for just the meter charge. I am told it is because they do not know if they will get a fare back to the city. No such excuse exists for those drivers who refuse to operate by meter from the main railway station. This appears to be just a blatant attempt to exploit the visitor. In this case I strongly recommend that you jot down the taxi number, then telephone the complaints service (Tel: 255-1045). It will not help you, but it could improve the situation for everyone in the future.

Rental cars are available but unless you are planning some travel outside K.L., I don't believe this is a good choice of transportation around the city. For countryside travel, however, it can be excellent. Major rental companies in K.L. include:

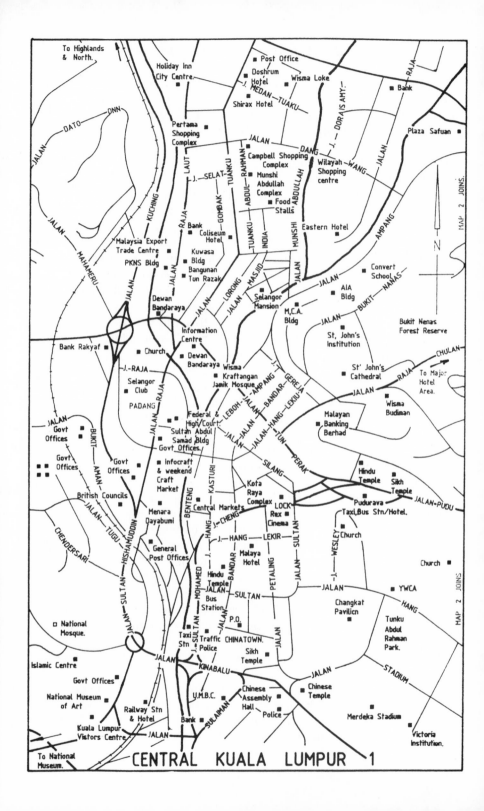

CENTRAL KUALA LUMPUR 1

Avis Rent-a-Car—40 Jalan Sultan Ismail, Tel: 241-7144; Subang Airport, 746-2994

Budget Rent-a-Car—29 Jalan Yap Kwan Seng, Tel: 242-5166; Subang Airport, 746-4658

Hertz Rent-a-Car—214A Komplex Antarabayia Jalan Sultan Ismail, Tel: 243-3433; Subang Airport, 746-2091

SMAS Rent-a-Car—UBN Tower, Tel: 230-7788

Thrifty Car Rental—LPPKN Building, Tel: 230-1588

4. The Hotel Scene

Luxury, homeliness, and economy are all available in K.L. hotels. A room in a top hotel will cost M$300 and up, while at the bottom end you can still find a few self-contained rooms for M$30. In between the choice is vast, and getting a room is usually not too difficult except when major events are taking place.

The following is a personal selection of accommodations in three different categories. It is by no means exhaustive. I am sure there are some wonderful bargains out there that I have never heard of. When you find one, please let me know. In the meantime I hope you can find something suitable from the following.

EXPENSIVE HOTELS

The **Shangri-La Hotel** (Tel: 232-2388) is my favorite in this category. The lobby has space, gleaming glass, and expanses of polished marble. The 659 rooms and 35 suites are luxurious with prices starting at about M$350. There is impressive service from a well-trained staff. Outside there is greenery, a landscaped pool, and a superturf tennis court. Health club amenities—sauna, jacuzzi, massage, and gymnasium—are available for the energetic. Inside, an English pub, the Club Oz nightclub, and a choice of four restaurants ensures that your evening needs are easily met. A business center and a squash court are there for those who need them.

I enjoy the atmosphere at the Shangri-La. It is professional but never intrusive. The decor is subdued but the furnishings are elegant. Then there is the option of the exclusive Horizon Floor with its butler and lounge for complimentary breakfast and cocktails. With the twenty-first floor providing a panoramic view over K.L., it's a hard place to leave. Rooms are around M$400. (Book with the Shangri-La International offices; United States and Canada 800-457-5050, Australia 008-222-448, United Kingdom 441-581-4217, or with the hotel direct at 11 Jalan Sultan Ismail, 50250, K.L., Malaysia; Fax: 603-230-1514.)

The **Regent of Kuala Lumpur** (Tel: 241-8000) is another fine hotel in the Regent tradition located in the heart of the business and shopping district. All 469 luxurious rooms and suites enjoy panoramic views of the city, and the personalized service is synonymous with the name Regent. Recreational facilities include a beautiful landscaped outdoor pool, and a splendid health club with two air-conditioned squash courts, a gymnasium, an aerobics room, saunas, a steambath, a whirlpool, spas, massage services, and a beauty salon and barber shop. Rooms are available from around M\$430.

You enter a huge multilevel lobby with a soaring roofline. Terraces are dripping with greenery and bright flowers. It's a real voyage of discovery as you move from lounge to bar to restaurant all set amid waterfalls and gardens. In the evening the whole atmosphere is enhanced by strings playing popular tunes and classics. Your dining choices are the informal Brasserie, the classic Grill Room, the authentic Edo Kivin Japanese restaurant, and the very popular Lai Ching Yuen Cantonese restaurant. (Book with the Regent organization or direct with the hotel at 160 Jalan Bukit Bintang, 55100 Kuala Lumpur, Malaysia; Fax: 603-242-1441.)

Situated along Jalan Sultan Ismail in the same general area as the Shangri-La and the Regent, are two other excellent hotels—the very popular Kuala Lumpur Hilton, and the Parkroyal Kuala Lumpur. The **Kuala Lumpur Hilton** (Tel: 242-2122), 581 rooms, long held the distinction of being the city's finest hotel. Despite the newer arrivals, it is still able to lay claim to the title of "one of the best" and probably "the most popular." The Hilton enjoys a fine location overlooking the Selangor Turf Club racetrack, and its restaurants, bars, and discotheque are justifiably famous. Malay and European gourmet food is available in the rooftop Paddock Restaurant, while nightly entertainment is featured in the Aviary Lounge. There are several other restaurants, the very English Club Bar, a swimming pool, a health center, tennis and squash courts, a medical center, the Tin Mine discotheque, two shopping floors, and a business center. Room rates start at about M\$350. (Book with the Hilton organization or direct with the hotel at P.O. Box 10577, 50718 K.L., Malaysia; Fax: 603-242-9064.)

The **Parkroyal Kuala Lumpur Hotel** (Tel: 242-5588) is situated about a kilometer down the road. It has a wide range of five-star accommodations, restaurants, bars, and sporting facilities. It has the largest hotel swimming pool in K.L., and there are tennis and squash courts. Room prices start at around M\$330.

The lobby is decked out in beautifully carved timber and it has four huge chandeliers. The Garden Bar off the lobby is a popular retreat, while the Grill, and the Parkroyal Court offer Chinese and Western fare. A steamboat dinner is often available and there are regular poolside BBQs on Saturday and Sunday. Casual dining is available downstairs at the Payang Coffee Lounge. (Book with Southern Pacific Hotels or direct on Jalan Sultan Ismail, 50250 K.L., Malaysia; Fax: 603-241-5524.)

Two new hotels have opened in this area in the past two years. The **Hotel Istana** (Tel: 241-9988) is aiming at the top of the market. The 516-room hotel is at the corner of Jalan Raja Chulan and Jalan Sultan Ismail in the heart of downtown. There are Japanese, Chinese, Malay, and European restaurants, two lounges, a garden bar, and a music-theque—a dreadful name for a lounge, bar, disco, and karaoke entertainment area. Rooms are stylish and come complete with minisafe, two telephones, and coffee- and tea-making facilities. Bathrooms have baths and separate shower and toilet compartments plus full-length mirror, hair dryer, and scales. Room rates start at M$350. (Book with the hotel at P.O. Box 1291, Kuala Lumpur; Fax: 603-244-1245.)

The **Concorde Hotel** (Tel: 244-2200) has emerged from the shell of the old Merlin Hotel. It has been extensively reworked and the result is appealing. There are 630 rooms and suites, five business floors, a selection of bars and restaurants, and some shopping facilities. The location is excellent. Room rates start at M$230. (Book with the hotel at 2 Jalan Sultan Ismail, 50250 Kuala Lumpur; Fax: 603-244-1628.)

All the hotels mentioned to date are along, or close to, a one-kilometer stretch of Jalan Sultan Ismail. The **Pan Pacific Hotel** (Tel: 442-5555) is several kilometers from here in an area next to the Putra World Trade Center.

This is also the location for the Malaysia Tourism Promotion Board's (MTPB) tourist information counter. For delegates to a meeting in the trade center, this is an ideal location and it provides a good base for exploring north-central K.L. The hotel is a striking modern building with a spectacular atrium-style lobby complete with bubble elevators. Each of the 571 rooms is furnished in attractive modern style, complete with lounge chairs, coffee table, and writing desk. The marble-lined bathrooms have bathtub and separate shower. There are Chinese, Japanese, and European restaurants as well as a 24-hour coffee shop. The hotel also has a music room and several bars. For recreation there's a health club, tennis and squash courts, and a swimming pool.

Rooms at the Pan Pacific start at about M$360 and go up to M$4000. Rooms are available with either two single beds or one double. (Book through the Pan Pacific organization—U.S. Tel: 714-957-1300, Australia Tel: 02-264-1122, or with the hotel direct at Jalan Putru, Kuala Lumpur, Malaysia; Fax: 603-441-7236.)

There are several more hotels in this category that can be recommended. Of the two Holiday Inns, I prefer the atmosphere of the older and smaller **Holiday Inn on the Park** (Tel: 248-1066). The **Melia Hotel** (Tel: 242-8333) on Jalan Imbi, 309 rooms, has its regular clients as do the ultramodern but somewhat out of the way **Ming Court Hotel** (Tel: 261-8888), the 576-room **Crown Princess** (Tel: 262-5522) out on Jalan Tun Razak, and the more central **Equatorial Hotel** (Tel: 261-7777). The large **Federal Hotel** (Tel: 248-9166) with its revolving restaurant and good location continues to attract people looking for good accommodations at a reasonable price.

The **Carcosa Seri Negara** (Tel: 282-1888) is in a class apart. This complex lies in 15 hectares of landscaped gardens just five minutes from the city center. Both the Carcosa and the Seri Negara mansions were built in traditional style at the turn of the century for the governor of the Malay States and his guests. They have been open to the public since 1990. A butler meets each guest at the airport and is on personal duty throughout his or her stay. In all there are 13 suites. The Mahsuri Restaurant serves classical Continental dishes and original recipes using Malaysian herbs and spices. The adjoining bar is furnished in its original colonial style. Curry tiffen and lawnside BBQs are prepared each week. The sports center includes two tennis courts, a swimming pool, two saunas, and a gym. The 24-hour business center is equipped with computers, pagers, and secretarial services. Rates start at M$850 and rise to M$2500. (Book by telephoning—United States: 800-223-1588, Canada: 800-531-6767, Australia: 008-818-328, United Kingdom: 0800-282-684, or by contacting the hotel direct at Taman Tasik Pendana, 50480 K.L. Malaysia; Fax: 603-230-6959.)

MEDIUM-PRICE HOTELS

This category includes some of the older "international" type hotels, the more expensive Chinese-run hotels, some modern small hotels, and a few others.

The **Mandarin Hotel Kuala Lumpur** (Tel: 230-3000) is typical of the first category. This Chinatown area of the city is fascinating, quite safe, and close to many sight-seeing attractions. It is, however, very crowded and car access can be a problem. The hotel is close to the Kelang Bus Station (for airport transfers), and within walking distance of the railway station. Room rates start at about M$120 and rise to M$450 for

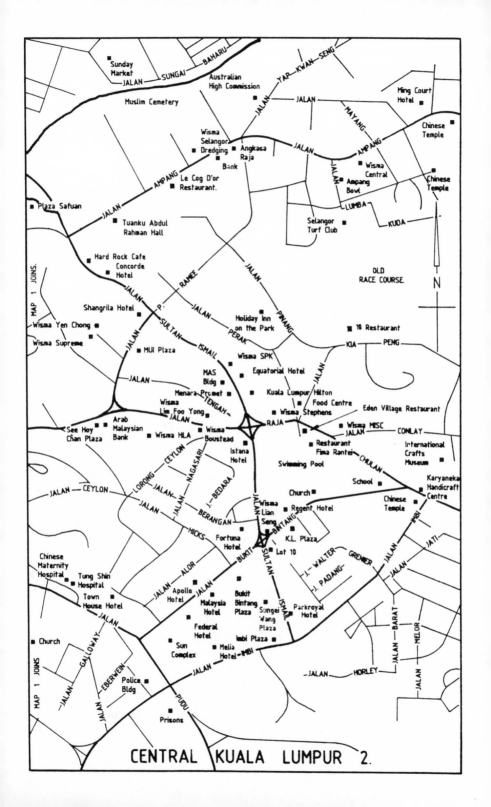

CENTRAL KUALA LUMPUR 2.

the suites. (Book with the hotel at 2 Jalan Sultan, 50000, Kuala Lumpur, Malaysia; Fax: 603-230-4363.)

The **Asia Hotel** (Tel: 292-6077) at 69 Jalan Hussein is another longtime favorite. It is not in an area that I particularly like but I admit that could be simply a lack of knowledge. There are shops, markets, cinemas, and so forth in the surrounding area but it is too far to walk to the central city. The Asia has adequate facilities and about 200 rooms that are somewhat tired, but for M$110 and up it is reasonable value.

Those visitors with their own transportation might like to try **Shah's Village Hotel** (Tel: 756-9322), a modern motel some 20 kilometers from the city in Petaling Jaya. Good clean accommodations are available in 44 rooms at a cost of about M$120. (Book by writing to the hotel at 3 Larong Sultan, 46710, Petaling Jaya, Malaysia.)

Not too far from here, the **Subang Airport Hotel** (Tel: 746-2122) is convenient for those who are leaving or arriving at an hour when normal people are asleep. The 160 rooms are right by the terminal but the rooms are soundproofed and the hotel has a restaurant, bar, swimming pool, and shuttle bus service to the city. The lobby is rather dark but the smallish rooms are clean and bright. (Book with the hotel at Kompleks Airtel Fima, 47200, Subang, Malaysia; Fax: 603-746-1097.) Room prices are around M$200, with day use about M$80.

Back in the city you will find the modern **Hotel Pudu Raya** (Tel: 232-1000) with its 200 rooms built above the Pudu Raya bus terminal. If you plan to venture to the country regions by bus, this location is perfect. The rooms are clean, quiet, and air-conditioned and prices start at about M$110. (Book through the hotel at Pudu Raya Bus Station, Jalan Pudu, 56100, Kuala Lumpur.)

The **Apollo Hotel** (Tel: 242-8133) is an older-style hotel in busy Jalan Bukit Bintang. All rooms are air-conditioned and have carpet, telephone, TV, piped music, and attached bathrooms. There are shopping and eating opportunities all around the hotel. (Book on Fax: 603-342-7813.) Room rates start at around M$70.

The **Malaysia Hotel** (Tel: 242-8033) is almost directly across the road. The 58 rooms are bright and cheerful and the hotel has a restaurant and bar, 24-hour room service, a spa, karaoke, aand car parking. Rooms start at M$100. (Book at 67 Jalan Bukit Bintang, 55100 Kuala Lumpur; Fax: 603-242-8579.)

Here also is the **Cardogan Hotel** (Tel: 344-4883), housed in an old building that has been nicely renovated. The 70 rooms have facsimile machines, video players, and minibars. There is a business center, a sauna, art gallery, coffee house, club, and room service. The room price of M$160 includes breakfast and access to the club. (Book at 64 Jalan Bukit Bintang, 55100 Kuala Lumpur; Fax: 603-244-4865.)

BUDGET ACCOMMODATIONS

Budget accommodations are available in several hostels and a large selection of cheap hotels scattered around town. You should be aware that many of the small, cheap hotels are unsuitable for visitors because of their extensive "short-time" trade. The ones listed here are considered suitable for both men and women, even those travelling solo.

The cheapest accommodation is available in the hostels. The most centrally situated is the **Meridian International Youth Hostel** (Tel: 232-5819) on Jalan Hang Kasturi, to the side of the central market. A dormitory bed is available for less than M$10 with a hostel card, and little more without a card. It's not a wonderful place, but it's an excellent value for the money.

The **YMCA** (Tel: 274-1439) is not so well located but when you find it, you will discover that it is clean, the staff is friendly, and there is a variety of accommodations. Dormitory beds are about M$12, while rooms without private baths are M$30, and with private bath, air conditioning, and TV they cost M$50-60. There is a M$1 temporary membership charge. Men, couples, and women are all accepted. There is a good restaurant. The YMCA is located on Jalan Tun Sambanthan about a kilometer south of the railway station. Buses No. 5, 33, 40, and 49 all go close by.

The government-run **Wisma Belia** (Tel: 274-4833) is on Jalan Syed Putra about two kilometers south of the central city. The 115 rooms are fairly basic but are air-conditioned. Those without baths are M$25-35 and those with baths are M$60 and up.

The Chinatown area is one of the best places for cheap hotels but look before you leap. Two recommendations here are the **Nanyang Hotel** (Tel: 238-7477) with 32 rooms from about M$40, and the **Lok Ann** (Tel: 238-9544) with 21 rooms, some with air conditioning and telephone, from about M$45. The Nanyang is at 113 Jalan Sultan, and the Lok Ann just around the corner is on Jalan Petaling. For something cheaper but still tolerable, try the friendly **Lee Mun Hotel** on Jalan Sultan. You should be able to get a room for around M$20.

Another popular cheap area is Jalan Tuanku Abdul Rahman and the parallel Jalan Raja Laut. It was here that I found the excellent **Transit Villa** (Tel: 441-0443) run by a charming friendly couple who speak great English. They offer dormitory accommodation in either mixed or female rooms for M$10. As well, they have individual fan rooms for

M$20-26, and one air-conditioned room for M$32. All rooms are carpeted. There is a TV lounge, a luggage room, lockers, and an outdoor terrace. The door is locked so that nonguests are kept at bay. They serve Malay and Continental breakfasts. The surrounding area is fascinating. This place is good value. Somewhat different is the nearby **Shiraz Hotel** (Tel: 292-2625), on Jalan Meln Tuanku, which has 60 rooms ranging in price from M$45. Further north and over on Jalan Raja Laut, the **City Hotel** (Tel: 441-4466) has similar facilities and prices.

There are many cheaper hotels in this area but again you need to be a bit selective. In fact you will find that some hotels here will not be interested in you because the short-time market is more lucrative. In this lower-price range, the **Hotel Rome** (Tel: 441-1241) provides 21 large, clean rooms from about M$30; the **Kowloon Hotel** (Tel: 293-4246) has 80 rooms, most with air conditioning from M$40; and the ancient **Coliseum** (Tel: 292-6270) at 99 Jalan T. A. Raman may still have some rooms without bath for around M$20.

In other areas, the **K.L. City Lodge** (Tel: 230-1584) on Jalan Pudu opposite the bus terminal has a range of air-conditioned and non-air-conditioned rooms and dormitories. Food is available at the restaurant. The **Malaysian Youth Hostels Association** (Tel: 230-6870) has facilities on Jalan Kg Attap for about M$15 a night. **Permata Guest House** (Tel: 441-8766) on Jalan Ipoh has dormitories and rooms for about the same price. I would like some comment on these last three suggestions because I haven't personally inspected them myself.

5. Dining and Restaurants

Multiracial Kuala Lumpur offers a mouth-watering array of food—spicy Malay dishes, a variety of Chinese food, exotic cuisine from North and South India, as well as Nyonya and Western food. The range of eating options runs from open-air makeshift stalls to exclusive luxury restaurants. Prices go from ridiculously cheap to call-the-bank-manager. Let's consider some of the eating options.

The *open-air restaurants* and *food bazaars* provide great opportunities to try a variety of food at rock-bottom prices. The food is usually very good, although often you will have to point to what you want because it is difficult to tell exactly what it is. A good place to start is the upper floor of the Central Market. The choice here is vast. You will find Malay, Chinese, Indian, Western fast food, and more. There is no need to give particular recommendations—you can walk around and choose for yourself. Some outlets have their own seating area but many ask you to use the large communal space. Select your food, pay for it, then find a table. It is open during the day and early evening.

You will also find hawker food centers in many of the large modern shopping malls. These are the modern face of Malaysian food. More traditional are the open-air food stalls at places like Munshi Abdullah, close to Jalan Tuanku Abdul Rahman and the Campbell shopping center; the food plaza, behind the Hilton Hotel; and the food center, close to Jalan Raja Muda Stadium in the north part of the city.

Then there are the *night markets*. These provide opportunities to combine eating with shopping. The most famous and biggest is the Saturday Pasar Malam in Jalan Tuanku Abdul Rahman. It is held every Saturday evening on a sealed-off stretch of the road not far from the central city. The food stalls here are mainly of the take-away variety but there are also many permanent restaurants lining this length of road, so if you want something more substantial, your needs are easily met.

The other alternative is the Sunday market, which is actually held Saturday night in Kampong Bahru in the northeast part of the city. This is a food, produce, and handicraft market that appears to be rarely visited by Western visitors but there are also opportunities to try genuine Malay food at very low prices.

Malay restaurants are naturally very popular and easy to find. There are hundreds along Jalan Tuanku Abdul Rahman. **Satay Ria** (Tel: 291-1648) along here, has a good reputation for cheap take-outs but there are many more you could try. Elsewhere in the city there are several restaurants that are worth tracking down. **Satay Express** is on the ground floor of Central Square, next to the Central Market. The *satay* is excellent and they serve other Malay favorites. You can dine on the outdoor terrace or in the air-conditioned section. **Bunga Raya** (Tel: 293-3888) in the Putra World Trade Center, near the Pan Pacific Hotel, has established a dedicated clientele by offering prices around M$65 for two. At the other end of town, near the Regent Hotel, the **Rasa Utara** (Tel: 243-83224), in the Bukit Bintang Plaza, likewise has a loyal following. Both serve *satay*, *nasi lemak*, and *soto ayam* as well as a wide range of other dishes. The nearby **Satay Anika** (Tel: 248-3113) is also worth a visit.

Back on Jalan Pinang Kia Peng, near the old racetrack, and within walking distance of the Equatorial Hotel, the Hilton Hotel, and the Holiday Inn on the Park, is the **Yazmin Restaurant** (Tel: 241-5655). This is aimed firmly at the visitor and is very popular. The restaurant advises that customers should make a reservation and when you do, you will be convinced by the staff to have dinner and see the cultural show. This will cost on the order of M$45 for each person but the food and the performance are both good.

Another experience worth considering is the **Titiwangsa Seafood Floating Restaurant** (Tel: 422-8400) at Titiwangsa Lake Gardens. The restaurant is built out over the lake and the atmosphere in the evening is delightful. The menu is constantly changing but the variety is always extensive and the quality remains high. You will need to go by taxi and it's a reasonable drive from most hotels, but there is no other experience like this in Kuala Lumpur.

Another popular venue for seafood, especially for locals, is by the fringe of the Subang Airport. There are a number of fine seafood restaurants located here. The specialty dish is Sri Lankan crab, cooked with chillies. To get there, head for the airport and follow the road beside Terminal 2 to the Subang village. The distance from the city does not seem to worry the locals and they say the experience is worthwhile for everyone. Closer to town, the **Putra Laut Seafood** restaurant is situated in a big covered area next to the Pan Pacific Hotel. It has good food at popular prices.

Chinese restaurants can be found in all areas of the city but many are concentrated in Chinatown. Most of the Chinatown restaurants are cheap, basic, and easy to deal with, even though most people may not speak English. I have learned to be comfortable just walking into one of these places, wandering around to see what is offered, then pointing to what I want. I am usually happy with the food and the price. You should try this too.

There are, however, some more up-market Chinese restaurants that you could consider. My experience with these is very limited but my friends in K.L. recommend the following. The **Dynasty Garden Chinese Restaurant** (Tel: 262-1411) is in Plaza Yow Chuan, on Jalan Tun Razak, the major ring road around Kuala Lumpur city. You will have to decide for yourself if the drive here is worthwhile. An alternative that is much closer is the **Hakka Restaurant** (Tel: 985-8492) in Jalan Bukit Bintang. This specializes in Hakka cuisine and I recommend that you make a reservation to ensure a table. A meal for two can cost up to M$80. The **Marco Polo Restaurant** (Tel: 242-5595) is even closer to many of the luxury hotels. This is situated in the Wisma Lim Foo Yong complex and is justifiably popular with locals and visitors alike.

Restoran 123 (Tel: 261-4746) on Jalan Ampang, offers ethnic village atmosphere through the use of wood, *attap*, and local flora. This is far more cozy than most Chinese restaurants and they have a fine selection of seafood and other dishes. It is open all day until midnight. **Yook Woo Hin** restaurant on Jalan Petaling is a place famous for Cantonese *dim sum*. Try the prawn rolls and the barbecued pork dumplings. They are delicious. Vegetarians could head for the **Restoran Vegetarian** (Tel:

248-7606) near the Regent Hotel, behind the Pizza Hut on Jalan Sultan Ismail. It advertises itself simply as "the best Chinese vegetarian restaurant in K.L." **Restoran Rainbow Palace** (Tel: 292-6408) in the Campbell Complex has good food and luxurious decor.

Indian and Pakistani restaurants are concentrated in the Jalan Masjid India area. As with Chinese restaurants you will find plenty of small, cheap eateries that will give you a taste of this food style for little cost. Then there are the up-market restaurants that specialize in more exotic dishes.

I'm not an Indian-food fanatic so perhaps I am not the best person to make judgments about these restaurants but **Bangles** (Tel: 298-3780) meets my taste at a reasonable price. Further north, the **Shiraz** (Tel: 291-0035) has excellent Pakistani food, and I am told that the adjacent **Omar Khayam** (Tel: 291-1016) is equally good. You will find several **Bilal Restaurants** around this area. The one at 33 Jalan Ampang (Tel: 238-0804) is one that I enjoy. It has great *Beriyani*.

Finally, the renowned **Devi Annapoorna** (Tel: 282-3799), in the same Medan Tuanku area, is a "must" for vegetarians. This restaurant has considerable ties to the Indian community and has an authentic feel about it that some more commercial restaurants lack.

Western restaurants are concentrated in the major hotels but there are some outside. You could try **The Ship** (Tel: 241-8805) in Jalan Sultan Ismail near the Regent Hotel for good steaks. Prices are reasonable. For a top location **Le Coq d'Or** (Tel: 242-9732) on Jalan Ampang would be difficult to beat. The fine old mansion is a delightful setting for a first-class restaurant. Prices are expensive but not outlandish. Something more down-market but nevertheless very nice is **Caleo's Italian Restaurant** (Tel: 241-0882) on Jalan Pinang. There is a pizza menu and a more extensive à-la-carte dinner menu with main dishes around M$30. Also worth trying is the **New Copper Grill Restaurant** (Tel: 248-5912) in the shopping center opposite the Hilton Hotel. The staff here is helpful and friendly, and the food is great. Steaks cost M$25-30. Many visitors will enjoy a meal at the flashy **Eden Village Restaurant** on Jalan Raja Chulan. The seafood is particularly good.

Then there are the Western fast-food outlets. You will find Kentucky Fried Chicken at many locations and there are also outlets for McDonald's, A & W, Shakey's Pizza, Dunkin' Donuts, and so forth. Fanatics of this food may be a little disappointed in some of the fare. It looks almost the same as what you are used to, but the flavor is certainly not identical. Also worth trying is the amazingly popular **Deli France** on the second level terrace in the Lot 10 shopping complex next to the Isetan department store.

Other *Asian cuisines* are available. The **Koryo-won Restaurant** (Tel: 242-7655) in the Antarabangsa Complex on Jalan Sultan Ismail is good for Korean food. **Chikuyo-tei** (Tel: 230-0729) in Plaza See Hoy Chan on Jalan Raja Chulan has a good reputation for Japanese food, and **Restoran Seri Chiangmai** (Tel: 248-2927) on Jalan Perak behind the Equitorial Hotel, and **Sri Thai** (Tel: 756-3535) in Wisma Selangor on Jalan University in Petaling Jaya, both have hot and spicy Thai food. For Nonya food I recommend the **Nonya Heritage Restaurant** on Jalan Sultan Ismail.

It is also worth mentioning **10 Kia Peng** (Tel: 242-4269), which doesn't quite fit into any of the above categories. This used to be a large colonial bungalow but it is now a hawker center, restaurant, arts and crafts center, and night spot all rolled into one. I have had a delightful meal under the stars trying bits and pieces from a variety of stalls, but there is a more formal dining room as well. Afterwards you can stay on for the disco or relax in the lounge with a beer or cocktail.

Finally there are the *hotel restaurants.* These offer some of the best cuisine in K.L. and should not be ignored. Few hotels have Malay restaurants but most have excellent Chinese food and many also offer Western cuisine. Almost all the hotels mentioned in the budget accommodations section have basic Chinese restaurants where the food is sometimes excellent and always cheap. But the luxury hotels also have their Chinese restaurants and these can be the location for a memorable feast. The best of these are the **Shang Palace** (Tel: 232-2388) at the Shangri-La, the **Inn of Happiness** (Tel: 242-2222) at the Hilton, **Ming Place** (Tel: 261-8888) at the Ming Court Hotel, the **Hai-Ten-Lo** (Tel: 442-5555) at the Pan Pacific, and the **Golden Phoenix** (Tel: 261-7777) at the Equatorial. Dinner at any of these will cost M$60-M$100 for two.

For Western food you can choose between good set menus at the dining room of the **Station Hotel** (Tel: 274-7433) for under M$15 each; steak, roast chicken, or fish at the restaurant in the **Coliseum Hotel** (Tel: 292-6270) for about the same price; or go right up-market to the **Lafitte** restaurant (Tel: 232-2388) in the Shangri-La Hotel for an excellent selection of top-quality European cuisine. Here you can expect to pay M$100 and higher for two. **Melaka Grill** (Tel: 242-2222) in the Hilton Hotel is another excellent place for steak.

Then there are the Asian-food hotel restaurants. You will be delighted with the Thai food at the **Sawasdee Thai Restaurant** (Tel: 248-1066) at the Holiday Inn on the Park. At the **Nadaman Restaurant** (Tel: 232-2388) in the Shangri-La you will be introduced to a 150-year-old tradition in Japanese dining. This is a true culinary art form.

Sultan Abdul Samad Building, Kuala Lumpur. (Courtesy of the Malaysia Tourism Promotion Board)

National Museum, Kuala Lumpur.

6. Sight-seeing

Let me make one thing clear right now. Kuala Lumpur is not in the same league as Singapore, Bangkok, or even Penang when it comes to sight-seeing attractions. The Tourist Development Corporation produces some excellent general literature but there is a decided lack of good specific literature about the city, so the visitor starts off severely disadvantaged compared to some other places. I stayed in a major Kuala Lumpur hotel for three days in the middle of Visit Malaysia Year (1990) and, despite going to the tour desk every day, I was unable to obtain any information on tours that were supposedly operating so I decided to sight-see by car. This turned out to be an extremely frustrating exercise because my map was in English but every road sign and direction indicator was in Malay so it was almost impossible to find some of the attractions.

While this is something you can laugh about afterwards, it is a major problem for visitors and will severely handicap K.L. tourism in the future as more people give up and go some other place where it is easier. If you find yourself in doubt or difficulty, do not be afraid to ask the locals for directions. The people are friendly and will go out of their way to help. English is widely understood so spoken language is not a major problem in most parts of the city.

Despite these problems, if you are in Kuala Lumpur you should try to see some of the highlights. The central area is best explored on foot. The place to start is at the **Padang** now renamed **Dataran Merdeka**, a grassy square where Malaysia's independence (actually at that time it was Malaya) from the British was proclaimed in 1957. Today it is the site of what is called the world's largest freestanding flagpole, and it is a very popular meeting and mixing center for K.L.'s young brigade. There is an underground shopping center beneath the grass.

The area surrounding here is great for building watchers. Across the road is the old Secretariat Building now known as the **Sultan Abdul Samad Building**. It was built in the 1890s and its Moorish architecture with curving arches, domes, and a 41-meter-high clock tower make it one of the city's most photographed buildings.

Nearby is the **Infokraf building** in similar architectural style. This is the Information Center for Malaysian Handicrafts and there is a permanent exhibition of the more innovative designs as well as handicraft items to buy. It opens Saturday to Thursday from 9 A.M. to 6 P.M.

The **Royal Selangor Club** with its splendidly incongruous mock-Tudor facade is a wonderful contrast as it looks across from the other side of the green swathe of lawn and garden.

Also close by is the **Masjid Jame**, a mosque built at the birthplace of Kuala Lumpur at the confluence of the Klang and Gombak Rivers. It is a picturesque structure of domes, minarets, and small towers. You can walk south from here along the river to the **Central Market**, an arts and crafts bazaar with a wide variety of works on sale by local artists and craftsmen as well as a comprehensive array of souvenirs and food outlets. It is an excellent place to visit even if you do not plan to buy.

The area to the southeast of here is known as **Chinatown**. It is a colorful, noisy area that is often crowded with people, vehicles, and street stalls. You can visit traditional Chinese shop houses that sell herbs and medicines, flowers, food, and household goods. The **Sri Mahamariaman Hindu Temple** on Jalan Bandar is one of K.L.'s more interesting religious buildings. It was built in 1873 and is decorated by intricate carvings, gold embellishments, precious stones, and exquisite Spanish and Italian tiles.

At the other end of Chinatown on Jalan Stadium, is the **Chan See Shu Yuen Temple**. This typical Chinese temple with open courtyards and symmetrical pavilions is ornately decorated with glazed tiles and sculptures on the outside, and wood carvings and paintings inside. It serves as a religious and cultural meeting place.

By walking west along Jalan Kinabalu you cross the river and reach the very modern **National Mosque** (*Masjid Negara*). This is an imposing building in extensive grounds with pools, pathways, and various buildings. Visitors may visit Saturdays to Thursdays from 9 A.M. to 6 P.M. and on Friday from 2:45 P.M. to 6 P.M. You will have to remove your shoes before entering the main hall and you must be attired in conservative dress. You can wear a borrowed robe if your own clothing is not suitable.

Close to the mosque, the **Malayan Railway Headquarters** building is another attractive Moorish building that is often photographed. It is connected to the **Kuala Lumpur Railway Station** by a subway. Someone said that the British architect must have been "high" when he designed this building. Certainly the mix of arches, minarets, towers, and spires makes this one of the most distinctive and easily recognized railway stations in the world.

Back across the road from here, the old colonial Majestic Hotel has been transformed into the **National Art Gallery**. There is a collection of works by Malaysian artists, and exhibitions of local and international artists are held throughout the year. Opening hours are 10 A.M.-6 P.M. daily except noon to 3 P.M. on Friday when it closes. Admission is free. The Kuala Lumpur Visitors Center is right next door but the amount of available literature it has to give visitors is quite small.

It is now about a half-kilometer walk along Jalan Damansara to the **National Museum** (*Muzium Negara*). Some interesting displays are housed within a large Malay-style building. There are sections on Malay history, arts and crafts, weapons, birds and mammals, entomological specimens, and major economic activities. It is open daily from 9 A.M. to 6 P.M. except Fridays when it closes between 12:15 and 2:45 P.M. Admission is free.

You really need your own transportation or a taxi to see the remaining attractions of the city. It would be a pity to miss the **National Monument** in the Lake Gardens. This huge bronze sculpture is surrounded by pools, fountains, and water lilies. The monument was constructed in 1966 and commemorates those who fought against Communist insurgents in the 1950s.

In a landscaped area just below the National Monument is the **Asean Garden**. This is a collection of prize-winning sculptures from some of the finest artists in the Asean region. It is well worth seeing. The main **Lake Gardens** is across Jalan Parliament from here. This is a 60-hectare green belt built over some old tin workings. There is a small lake with boats for rent, well-trimmed lawns, tropical flowers and trees, and play areas for children. It really is a delightful spot. Further "attractions" have been built in the gardens such as an orchid garden, an expanded lake club, and an aviary. I'm not completely sure that these are improvements to the gardens, but they add to the attractions for the active visitor. The walk-in aviary, which spreads over three hectares of valley, is the largest in the region. Admission is M$3. A good view of some of the birds is available from the restaurant.

Parliament House is also in this general area. The imposing building stands on a small hill and can be seen from several vantage points. When parliament is sitting, visitors who are keen enough can make arrangements with the authorities for a visit. I have never managed to get past the gate.

Some kilometers south of here, the **International Buddhist Pagoda** is worth seeing. This reflects the contemporary architectural design of pagodas, and it houses Buddha images and replicas of pagodas from various countries. It is situated in Jalan Berhala off Jalan Tun Sambathan. Farther out still is the **Thean Hou Temple** built on a hilltop overlooking Jalan Syed Putra. This is one of the largest and most ornate Chinese temples in the region.

The **Malaysian Tourist Information Complex** at Jalan Ampang offers several facilities for visitors. Besides information counters, it contains facilities where visitors can change their currency; book flights, package tours, and trips to the National Park; and make

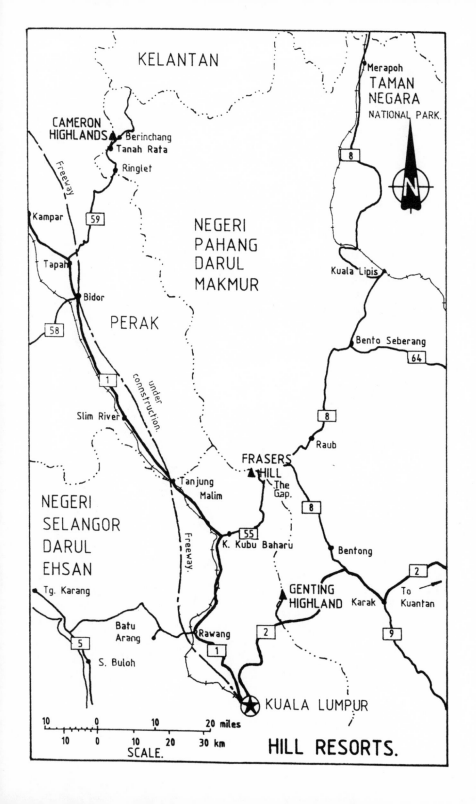

HILL RESORTS.

Thousands of devotees ascend the 272 steps to the Batu Caves during the annual Hindu festival of Thaipusam.

international and local telephone calls. Souvenirs and handicrafts are also available.

Until recently Kuala Lumpur recalled the old adage about Los Angeles as a cluster of suburbs in search of a city. K.L. is much smaller but its major hotels, shopping malls, government, and commercial tower blocks have been similarly dispersed and linked by spaghetti trails of looping freeways. Now at last K.L. is developing a "heart" and it's a much more attractive city because of it.

NORTH FROM KUALA LUMPUR

The trick to finding your way out of Kuala Lumpur is not to look for Highway 1 signs, or signs to Ipoh, Thailand, Hill Resorts, or anything else that a visitor might think of. The only clue is a sign that says UTARA. You won't find it on any map because this is not a place, it is the Malay word for North. Unless you know this, you could be in K.L. forever.

The highway department is working on the new freeway that will eventually link to the Thai border, but close to Kuala Lumpur there are only some sections of the new road opened. The old road (Highway 1) is narrow, winding, and heavily trafficked. Be careful.

The first major point of interest is only about 13 kilometers from the city. Here in a massive limestone outcrop, you find the **Batu Caves**. These are many things to many people. To Hindus, this is a holy sanctuary and the scene of the annual Thaipusam festival. To scientists, it is home to species of rare flora and fauna. To visitors, it is a place to visit and enjoy. Once a year, half a million Hindu devotees and sightseers converge on Batu Caves for the festival. For the rest of the year Batu reverts to the all-encompassing serenity that has been its hallmark for more than 400 million years. You can reach here on Len Buses No. 69 and 70.

Access to the caves is via a flight of 272 steps. The Temple Cave is a huge airy cavern with various shrines lining its walls. Next to the Temple Cave is the Dark Cave, with its stalactites, stalagmites, and limestone columns. Down on ground level there is the Art Gallery and Poets Cave.

Just north of here you can visit a batik factory to see the process and perhaps buy a souvenir, then about nine kilometers farther on, **Templer Park** is a tract of jungle originally preserved by the British High Commissioner, Sir Gerald Templer. Now the 1200-hectare park has marked jungle trails, swimming lagoons, and waterfalls. It is extremely popular on weekends so its probably better to visit on a weekday.

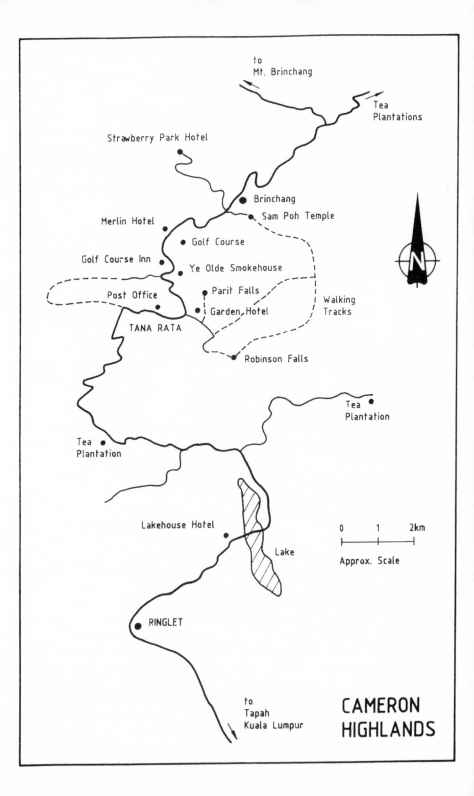

Most interest now lies in the hill resorts farther north. It's about 150 kilometers from here along Highway 1 to Tapah. There is nothing particularly remarkable about this town but for visitors it is important as the gateway to the Cameron Highlands. You can reach it by bus or train from Kuala Lumpur and Butterworth on a variety of services every day. Tapah has a government-run rest house at **Bukit Rumah Rehat** (Tel: 05-641-199).

CAMERON HIGHLANDS

Strawberries and cream, crackling log fires, and cool air are not things that you normally associate with the tropics. But these are just what are offered on the Cameron Highlands, a delightful area about 60 kilometers from Tapah.

Just over a hundred years ago, a British surveyor named William Cameron was on a mapping expedition when he found "a fine plateau with gentle slopes shut in by lofty mountains." It was not long before tea planters moved in and opened up a vast area for tea cultivation. They were followed by Chinese market gardeners and, once a road was established, the expatriate population found a new and cool getaway for their vacations.

Today the Cameron Highlands still has all three. Tea and vegetables are still grown here, and the tourism industry continues to grow. Fortunately it hasn't grown to the point where the highlands are under major visitor pressure. It is just one of those delightful places where you can relax and enjoy life as it should be. The Tudor-styled bungalows are still there, dotting the hills with colonial grandeur. Years ago these were holiday homes for planters and miners, now they are rented by the locals and foreign tourists for weekend retreats.

The drive to the highlands from the Kuala Lumpur-Ipoh road is one long, winding climb. The road is good but this is not a fast drive. There are several points of interest on the way so allow two-three hours to do the 60 kilometers.

The **Kuala Woh Jungle Park** is a recreational park surrounded by lush jungle. There is a hot-water natural pool and several waterfalls with crystal-clear cold water. Restrooms, camping sites, and rest huts are available and there is a canteen. Close by you will find an aboriginal settlement but the jungle inhabitants here are hardly in their traditional state.

Some 10 kilometers farther on, the **Lata Iskandar Waterfall** is a popular tourist stopover. The air is noticeably cooler now and if you try the water below the waterfall, you will find that it is positively cold.

There are restrooms, picnic areas, fruit stalls, and small restaurants. Trekkers and nature lovers will find the surrounding jungle irresistible. Paths lead through the forest and many of the trees are named.

The road finally reaches the 1300-meter-high plateau and the first of the highland towns—Ringlet. The soil is rich and the climate conducive to growing temperate and sub-temperate fruits and vegetables. Ringlet is probably the least interesting of the towns but there is some cheap accommodation in town, and, a few kilometers farther on, the **Lake House** (Tel: 05-996-152) is a magnificent "old-world" hotel in a great position overlooking a lake. This would be a excellent location for fishermen, and there are some interesting walks in the area. Room prices are from about M$220.

The road climbs another 300 meters to the main center of Tanah Rata, passing tea plantations, market gardens, and some jungle on the way. It's here that the scenery really starts to take off. The air is cool and clean. There are jungle streams, lakes and waterfalls, rolling green hills, and a slower pace that breathes tranquility. At times the road and rolling hills are covered with a thin blanket of mist. The wind can be cool and invigorating, so unlike the tropics.

Tanah Rata has plenty of appeal. There are shops, food stalls, hotels, restaurants, gardens, a series of signposted walks, waterfalls, and the ever-present highland peaks. Camera-toting tourists can be seen strolling along taking in the sights, sounds, and scents. The town has a good collection of budget and midmarket accommodations for those who would like to base themselves here. In the budget category, the **Town House Hotel** (Tel: 05-901-666) has rooms from around M$18, while the **Hollywood Hotel** (Tel: 05-941-633) near the post office, has rooms from around M$20.

The government **Rest House** (Tel: 05-901-254) is one step up with rooms with attached baths going for about M$30. The **Federal** (Tel: 05-901-777) has some budget rooms but also some low midrange ones at around M$30-40. Up another step, the **Garden Hotel** (Tel: 05-901-911) is in a lovely location just out of town but with space and greenery all around. Rooms here start at about M$70.

Tanah Rata has a good choice of restaurants. I had breakfast one morning at the Malay food stalls next to the bus terminal. There was a choice of toast, sausage and egg, or rice with a variety of dishes. Nothing costs more than M$3. Across the road from here there are two good Indian restaurants—the Thanam and the Kumar—and an equally good Chinese place called the Hong Kong. The Garden Hotel restaurant has a renowned steamboat, which is where you blend your own meat, vegetables, and eggs into soup on a burner at the table. It really is great fun.

Even if you are not big on walking, there are two short walks around Tanah Rata that you should try. Both lead to waterfalls. The walk to Parit Falls (Walk 4) is flat and easy, and the path is well marked. The falls are not great but you see some jungle, can learn some of the tree names from the labels, and generally enjoy the outdoors. Walk 9 to Robinson Waterfall is slightly more strenuous but it is still manageable by almost anyone. On this walk you are likely to see some of the famous butterflies that abound in the highlands. You will also see bougainvillea exploding in a symphony of color like you have never seen before.

It's about three kilometers from here to the golf course, and some of the best accommodations in the highlands. Undoubtedly my favorite place is **Ye Olde Smokehouse** (Tel: 05-901-214), 20 rooms, from around M$150. I am a sucker for the atmosphere of this place. It reminds me of the country inns in Europe with its latticed windows, wooden beams, comfortable velvet upholstered furniture, roaring open fires, a grandfather's clock, rich carpets, and friendly service. Some of the rooms are small but who cares, they all have so much wonderful nostalgia and character. It epitomizes an English, upper-class life-style that is like an outpost of the British Empire.

I remember an evening here, sitting around the lounge fire with pre-dinner cocktails, talking with other guests from Kuala Lumpur, Austria, the United States. and Canada, then dining on roast beef and fruit pies in the charming dining room. The evening cost about M$50 but it was one of the most memorable I have spent in southeast Asia.

Close by is the **Golf Course Inn** (Tel: 05-901-411), a modern place with motel-style rooms. The front rooms look out over the golf course and are quite attractive. There is also a good Chinese restaurant. Rooms are from M$90. Go a little farther and you come to the modern but attractive **Merlin Inn Resort** (Tel: 05-901-205). This well-located hotel has panoramic views across the golf course and is justly popular. Room prices start at about M$160.

The golf course itself is a good 18-hole layout with full and half-day rates. All golf equipment can be rented from the club house. The 6,178-yard layout was formerly one of the top courses in the country but it has suffered at times from lack of adequate maintenance. Some of the fairways and greens are verdant and lush but other parts of the course are surprisingly bare.

The final center of population is the town of Brinchang, a popular place for Malaysians and Singaporeans. There are a number of reasonable hotels here but most have little character. The best rooms are probably in the **Kowloon Hotel** (Tel: 05-901-366) at about M$45. The largest hotel is the **Highlands Hotel** (Tel: 05-901-588) and this is acceptable at about the same rate. There are a number of small, cheaper places.

Brinchang also has some reasonable restaurants. The Kowloon has good Chinese food, while the Sri Sentosa has Indian fare. A few kilometers out from Brinchang is the largest hotel in the Cameron Highlands, the **Strawberry Park Motel** (Tel: 05-901-166), with 180 rooms. Potentially this is a lovely resort but when I visited last, it was not all together. At rates of M$200-400 a room, you expect facilities to be in working order. Some were not. It is also a place where you need your own transportation because you are quite a distance from anywhere else. I hope to see an improvement when I return.

The Highlands at most times are a riot of color; the greens of the golf course, the deep jungle, the vegetable patches, and the tea plantations; the reds of the strawberries and the roses; the violet of the morning glory and bougainvillea; and the black and white of mock-Tudor cottages.

Beyond Brinchang the road continues to other small villages and tea plantations, and there is a branch that takes you to the top of Gunung Brinchang (2032 meters), the highest point on the Malaysian peninsula that can be reached by car. Near Brinchang there is the colorful Sam Poh Temple with Buddha statues, stone lions, and all the usual paraphernalia. Also nearby is a settlement of the *orang asli* aboriginal people. You will occasionally see these people, complete with blowpipes, on the side of the roads.

If you are an insect person, the newly opened Cameron Highlands Butterfly Garden is a must. There are creepy-crawlers of all types on display—beetles, giant spiders, stick insects, moths and butterflies, and scorpions. After taking in the view and the insects, you can drop by at the Yue Yong Lou Traditional Chinese Tea House, situated in the basement of the garden's souvenir center.

FRASER'S HILL

To reach Fraser's Hill from the Cameron Highlands you have to retrace your path to the main highway then travel back towards Kuala Lumpur until you reach Kuala Kubu Baharu. From here it is a pleasant 45-minute drive through lovely mountains to a place known as the Gap. The final eight kilometers from here are spectacular and this section operates as a one-way road between 7 A.M. and 7 P.M.—one hour up, one hour down, throughout the day.

Fraser's Hill (1500 meters) is named after an adventurer—Louis James Fraser—who built himself a shack, operated a mule train, and

Golf course at Fraser's Hill.

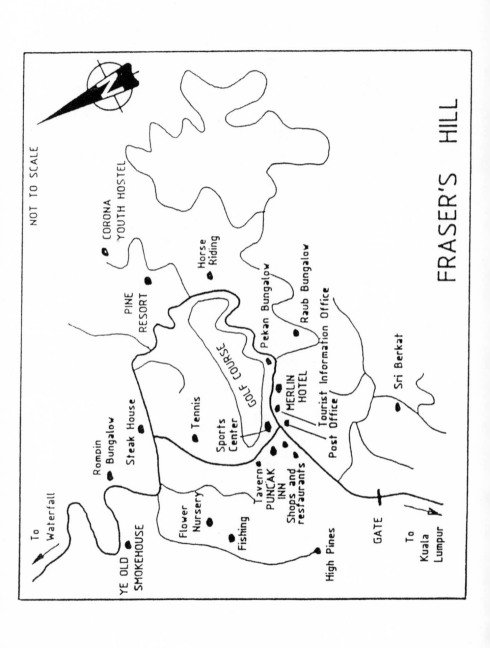

NOT TO SCALE

FRASER'S HILL

To Waterfall

YE OLD SMOKEHOUSE

Rompin Bungalow

Steak House

Flower Nursery

Fishing

Tennis

Sports Center

Tavern

PUNCAK INN

Shops and restaurants

High Pines

GOLF COURSE

MERLIN HOTEL

Post Office

Tourist Information Office

GATE

To Kuala Lumpur

PINE RESORT

CORONA YOUTH HOSTEL

Horse Riding

Pekan Bungalow

Raub Bungalow

Sri Berkat

perhaps ran an illegal gambling and opium den in the late nineteenth century. Respectability came to Fraser's Hill in 1919 when it was surveyed, and development started soon afterwards.

Where the Cameron Highlands are large, Fraser's Hill is small. You can almost walk to everything of interest, and the lovely town center is a real drawing card for everyone. It is an enclave far removed from the hustle and bustle of the cities, yet it is anything but boring. The crisp mountain air and the luxuriant green growth are a tonic to the body and the spirit.

Fraser's Hill is a vacation spot. There are no huge plantations or other development. What you have is a small town, a 9-hole golf course, a good range of accommodations, a lake for fishing, an area for horseback riding, and lots and lots of jungle.

On first appearances, Fraser's Hill is a well-maintained place. This is due to the Fraser's Hill Development Corporation—a semi-government body that controls much of the accommodations and other facilities. Unfortunately after staying a short while, you realize that things are not what they seem. The sports complex is supposed to be the social center of town but the last time I was there, the swimming pool was closed, one of the two squash courts was out of action, the saunas were not working, the restaurant was closed, and the whole place was very run-down. It is such a shame. I've been told recently that things are improving again so I hope this is correct.

Fortunately you can enjoy Fraser's Hill without the sports center. Some of the private accommodation is good, there are other restaurants, and frankly it's better to be outdoors than inside. The walking trails are generally well marked and the lovely flowers, temperate trees, and panoramic views provide an environment that is to be enjoyed.

The best accommodations come down to a choice of three places. The **Merlin Inn Resort** (Tel: 09-382-300), 109 rooms, is a modern hotel with nice rooms and good facilities overlooking the golf course in the center of town. For location, it is *the* place to be. Everything is within walking distance and you will probably spend little time actually at the hotel. Room rates are M$140-350. **Ye Old Smokehouse** (Tel: 09-382-226), 12 rooms, is almost the opposite. It is about a kilometer from town, with its own bar, restaurant, and lovely garden. This is a place to be alone with a favorite friend where you can enjoy the peace and tranquility of a lovely setting. Room rates are M$150-250.

Then there is the **Fraser's Pine Resort** (Tel: 09-783-2810), 96 modern condo-style apartments, which is situated at the other end of the development about two kilometers from the town. Each condo has a kitchen and bathroom and within the complex there are tennis and

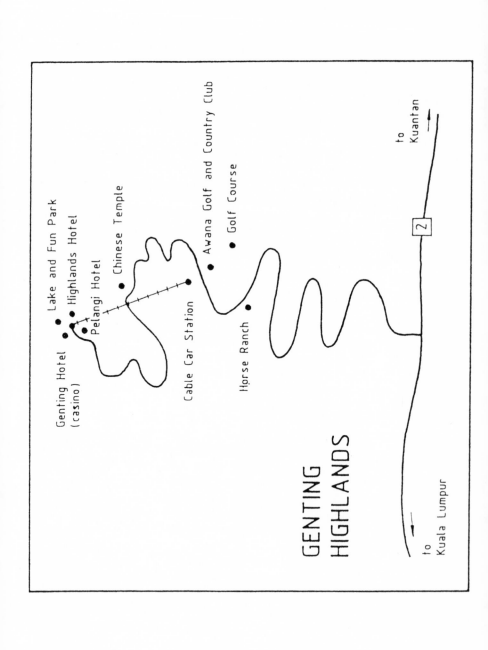

GENTING
HIGHLANDS

Genting Hotel
(casino)

Lake and Fun Park

Highlands Hotel

Pelangi Hotel

Chinese Temple

Cable Car Station

Awana Golf and Country Club

Golf Course

Horse Ranch

to
Kuantan

2

to
Kuala Lumpur

squash courts, a children's playground, saunas, a BBQ pit, indoor game facilities, and a bar and restaurant. Daily room rates are from M$150 for a one-room unit to M$400 for three rooms.

Other options are the **Puncak Inn** (Tel: 09-382-055), 20 rooms, run by the Fraser's Hill Development Corporation, right in the town center with small rooms from M$80 upwards, or the government-run **Seri Berkat Rest House** (Tel: 09-341-026), nine rooms, about three-fourths of a kilometer from town, with similar prices.

Then there are the Fraser's Hill Development Corporation bungalows. These only open when demand warrants so it's not always possible to get the one you want. You book all of these at the information center (Tel: 09-382-044) near the Merlin Hotel. The bungalows have full catering facilities or you can arrange to have meals cooked for you. Unfortunately most of these bungalows have seen better days. The contrast between these and some of the company and privately owned bungalows that are used for employees or time-share owners is quite striking.

Most visitors will want to eat out. You have a choice of olde English at the Smokehouse, sizzling steaks at the Steakhouse, à-la-carte meals at the Merlin Restaurant and the Pine Restaurant at the Pine Resort, and cheaper offerings at the Arzed, Hillview, and Puncak restaurants in the village. Before and afterwards you can sit around a roaring log fire in Ye Olde Tavern, or listen to some music at the Merlin Inn.

GENTING HIGHLANDS

You can reach the Genting Highlands in about an hour from Kuala Lumpur by bus or car. There are eight daily bus services from the Pudu Raya Bus Terminal in Kuala Lumpur, adults M$4.50 one way. A taxi for 4 people from K.L. will cost around M$35. It takes at least twice that long if you are travelling from Fraser's Hill. After returning to the Gap, you turn left and eventually reach Route 8 at Teranum. Turn right and travel through Bentong until you reach Route 2. Head towards Kuala Lumpur and after about 25 kilometers you come to the turn off to the Genting Highlands.

The approach road should have warned me that the Genting Highlands is not another Fraser's Hill. The road to Fraser's is single-lane, that to the Genting Highlands is four-lane. The development at Fraser's is low-rise amid beautiful greenery. That at Genting is concrete high-rise set amid huge parking lots. On a clear night, the flashing neon lights of the Genting Highlands can be seen from Kuala Lumpur as if they were a lighthouse.

I guess you conclude that the Genting Highlands is not my kind of place. Well, that's true, but I have to admit that this is by far the most popular place with the affluent citizens of Kuala Lumpur. If casinos appeal more than jungle walks, artificial lakes and cable cars more than waterfalls and jungle-clad mountains, and concrete more than green grass, then Genting is the place for you. Just why anyone would destroy a perfectly good mountain for this, however, is a mystery to me.

The best accommodations on the hilltop are at the **Genting Hotel** (Tel: 211-1118), 700 rooms, from M$200. The hotel has several restaurants, a bowling alley, squash courts, an indoor swimming pool, a casino, a discotheque, and a huge showroom for visiting performers. Down-market from here, the **Highlands Hotel** (Tel: 211-2812), 262 rooms, is connected to the Genting Hotel by an elevated walkway and guests can use the facilities of either hotel. Room prices here start at around M$130.

The **Pelangi Hotel** (Tel: 211-2812), 150 rooms, has the cheapest hotel accommodations at M$75 a room. You don't get anything wonderful for that price. If you have more than two in your party, you could consider staying at the **Ria Apartments** (Tel: 211-1828) or the **Kayangan Apartments** (Tel: 211-1818). A two-bedroom Ria apartment will cost around M$100 in the off-season and M$200 in the peak season, while a three-bedroom Kayangan apartment will cost M$150 in the off-season and M$300 in the peak season. You can sleep up to eight people in the three-bedroom units.

The peak has an artificial lake with rowboats for rent, a car-railway to ride, a fairly basic fun park, and concrete caves. But there is another side to the Genting Highlands. You find this 700 meters down the hill at the base of the cable car. Here is the attractive **Awana Golf and Country Club** (Tel: 211-3015), 200 rooms, which overlooks the golf course and green valley. It is a world apart from the concrete jungle above. Rates start at around M$260.

Rooms at the Awana are huge. Each has a separate lounge area and balcony. There is a coffee terrace and a poolside restaurant, an outdoor heated swimming pool, a scenic jogging track, tennis and squash courts, and a well-equipped gymnasium. The 18-hole golf course is challenging and well maintained, and hotel guests receive a discount on the normal M$40 green fees weekdays and M$80 on weekends. If you plan to stay at Genting, this could be the best choice.

On the drive back to Kuala Lumpur you should watch out for signs to the **National Zoo and Aquarium**, close to the city, and off to the left. The zoo has 200 species of Malaysian and exotic mammals, birds and reptiles, on a large site. There are a number of educational displays, camel and elephant rides, an aquarium, a restaurant, and picnic areas. It is open daily from 9 A.M. to 6 P.M. and admission is M$4.

7. Guided Tours

Several different companies operate half-day, one-day, and extended tours from Kuala Lumpur. The hotel where you are staying will have some arrangement with one particular company so you will be steered in that direction by the hotel. Some of the major hotels have tour desks that are operated by the various tour companies. In some cities this arrangement can be a disadvantage to passengers but in Kuala Lumpur it doesn't seem to matter much because in my experience there is little to distinguish one operator from another. If you wish to make some local inquiries you could contact Tour Fifty One (Tel: 261-8830), Amshild (Tel: 238-3317), or Asian Overland Services Tours (Tel: 292-5622) as well as the agency in your hotel.

The **City Tour** is the standard half-day tour in central Kuala Lumpur. It lasts about three hours and is available both in the morning and afternoon. A typical tour makes stops at the Karyaneka Handicraft Center, the War Memorial, the National Museum, and the National Mosque. It will also drive past the city stadiums, the Jame Mosque, Chinatown, the House of Parliament, the King's palace, the railway station, and the Dataran Merdeka area.

This tour is not wildly exciting but I strongly recommend that you take it if you want to see the main points of interest in a short time. To do the same thing by public transport, taxi, or rental car is quite a hassle. The cost is around M$26 and I consider this a reasonable value.

There is also a **Countryside** half-day tour that includes some of the points of interest on the edge of the city. Different companies have different names for this tour, but all follow a fairly similar itinerary. You will usually visit a rubber plantation, the Selangor Pewter Demonstration Center, a batik factory, and the Batu Caves. If you take both tours, you will go away with a reasonable idea about Kuala Lumpur. They can both be done in one day if your time is short.

There are two more half-day tours that are more specific. The first is the **Templer's Park Tour**, which lasts about three hours and departs both morning and afternoon. Templer's Park is a tropical rain forest about 22 kilometers north of the city. It offers fresh air and rugged beauty in a setting of peace and quietness. You can take a swim in the clear mountain waters or simply stroll around and enjoy the setting. The tour costs around M$35.

The second tour is to the **National Zoo**. Some companies also include a visit to Mimaland, a recreational parkland with a huge swimming pool, a lake, a giant maze, a children's playground, and a prehistoric animal kingdom. The National Zoo is spread through 55 hectares of bushland and has a good collection of African and Asian animals. It is heavily promoted by the Malaysian Zoological Society but many visitors will decide they can see something similar back home. The three-hour zoo tour costs around M$34, while the one that also includes Mimaland takes an extra half-hour and costs an additional M$4.

The **Cultural Night Tour** is another that is worth considering. It shows you some of the different cultural elements that make up the Malaysian potpourri. The tour first takes you to the Sri Mahamariaman temple, the oldest and largest Hindu temple in the city. You will smell the burning of jasmine and hear the chanting of Hindu priests as you inspect the carvings and other features of this very interesting place. From here you take a short walk to the open-air bazaar of Chinatown to experience the hustle and bustle of this thriving street market. The last part of the evening is more relaxed at a Malay buffet dinner and cultural show. The tour lasts about three hours and costs around M$60.

There are several one-day tours that visit various parts of Malaysia from Kuala Lumpur. The most popular is the tour to **Malacca**. The nine-hour tour departs daily and covers all the most well known places in this historic city. You see the Porta de Santiago, built in 1511; St. Paul's church, where St. Francis Xavier was once buried; the pink-colored Dutch Stadhuys; various Chinese temples; the Malacca Museum; the Portuguese Square; and so on. On the way back to K.L., you drive through plantations and Malay villages to see a side of modern rural Malaysia. The cost is around M$80.

Another popular trip is to **Port Dickson**. The two-hour drive takes you through typical Malaysian countryside before you reach this popular beach area. Most tours give you a brief look around the area before taking you to one of the major resorts for lunch and a few hours on the beach or in the pool. The cost is around M$75.

The tour to **Fraser's Hill** is quite different. Here you have the chance to experience the virgin tropical jungles and cool air of this great mountain resort. You are taken on a short tour of Fraser's Hill before lunch then you visit the Jeriau Waterfall for jungle walking or swimming in the cool mountain pool. The eight-hour trip costs around M$80.

Another option is the **Pulau Ketam Adventure**. This is an "off the beaten track" excursion to Pulau Ketam—the island of crabs. You travel to Port Klang by coach then take the ferry to Pulau Ketam. On arrival you take a leisurely stroll to see how an entire fishing community lives

National Day parade in front of Federal Secretariat (Sultan Abdul Samad) Building, Kuala Lumpur. (Courtesy of the Malaysia Tourism Promotion Board)

Night market, Kuala Lumpur.

in a village built entirely on stilts out over the water. You have lunch at a local restaurant then return to the mainland for a coach ride to see the fabulous palace of the Selangor Sultan, then go on to Kuala Selangor. There is time to visit Fort Melawati and the adjacent nature reserve before travelling back to Kuala Lumpur. The nine-hour trip costs around M$90.

The Genting Highlands Resort has a day trip to the **Genting Highlands** that travels via the Lake Garden, and the Batu Caves. It provides lunch at the Genting Highland Resort and gives you several hours to visit the casino (a long-sleeved shirt with tie is required for men), or enjoy some of the other facilities that are available. Obtain further details from Tel: 241-3555.

As well as the conventional tours there are several other special-interest tours available. I suggest you contact Asian Overland Services Tours (Tel: 292-5622) if any of the following have appeal:

- Basic rock climbing, which includes jungle trekking and the learning of simple rock climbing techniques.
- Cave exploration in an unspoiled limestone cave.
- River rafting on a jungle stream.
- Bird watching on a 600-acre reserve.
- Cycling and camping using mountain bikes as transportation.

8. Culture

The Malaysians are extremely fond of festivals and other community activities so the calendar is jammed with these events. They are a good way for visitors to see another side of the culture and customs of a country and can add an extra dash of color and excitement to a visit. The Kuala Lumpur region celebrates all the national events and some special ones of its own. Here is a rundown:

New Year's Day is a public holiday and one of the quieter days in the city. Malaysia's urban population follows the Western tradition and ushers in the new year with lively parties that start on New Year's Eve. Most people need time to recover.

Federal Territory Day is February 1. Malaysia has two Federal Territories; Kuala Lumpur and the island of Labuan, in Sabah. Each has a public holiday and parades, exhibitions, sports contests, and cultural shows are organized.

Thaipusam is a Hindu festival celebrated with great zeal in early February. Devotees pay homage to Lord Murugan by piercing their bodies with sharp objects and carrying the *Karadi*, an elaborate edifice. In Kuala Lumpur a grand procession makes its way from the Sri Mahamariaman Temple in the central city to the Batu Caves some 13 kilometers north of the city. It is weird, exciting, and difficult to explain, even when you have seen it.

Chinese New Year is late January or early to mid-February. This is probably the only time of the year that Chinese businesses are closed. It is essentially a family and friends event with lots of visiting and feasting but visitors will see lion dances and hear huge firecrackers in major shopping complexes and hotels. Chinese New Year is celebrated over 15 days but shops seldom close for more than two or three.

Awal Ramadan is the beginning of the fasting month for Muslims. Every evening before the breaking of the fast, colorful roadside stalls are set up offering traditional cakes, pastries, and dates.

Cheng Beng Day in April is important to the Chinese. On this day families visit and worship the graves of ancestors by burning joss sticks, candles, and joss paper, and by bringing food offerings.

Hari Raya Puasa (usually late April or early May) is a joyous occasion for Muslims after fulfilling a month of fasting. People usher in the day by attending prayers at mosques then have open-house celebrations throughout the day. Malay cultural performances and exhibitions are held in conjunction with this day.

Wesak Day in May is the most important day for Malaysia's Buddhists. This recalls three significant events in Buddha's life—his birthday, his day of enlightenment, and his attainment of Nirvana. Temples are thronged with people offering incense, joss sticks, and prayers.

The Birthday of H.M. The Yang Dipertuan Agong, the king, is celebrated on the first Wednesday in June. Kuala Lumpur is gaily decorated with lights and pennants and there are celebrations at the Royal Palace, Lake Gardens, and Merdeka Stadium. There are cultural and modern entertainment shows, and traditional games.

Hari Raya Haji is a national holiday. This celebration is an important day in the Muslim calendar. In the morning, Muslims offer prayers of thanksgiving in mosques, and later in the day hold "open house."

Maal Hijrah is another national holiday. It is the New Year's Day of the Islamic calendar. Religious discussions and lectures are held in many places.

National Day (August 31) completes the series of mid-year holidays. This is a public holiday celebrated with fervor. There are street parades, stage shows, sporting events, and a whole host of other activities to celebrate the birthday of independence.

Malaysia Fest in late September is celebrated in all the leading hotels and shopping centers. Food from each of the 13 states is featured on special menus, and cultural shows and handicraft exhibitions are part of the celebration.

The **Moon Cake Festival** in late September or early October is celebrated nationwide but the best place to see the celebrations is in Chinatown. The festival marks the overthrow of the Mongol overlords in ancient China and is celebrated with the exchange and eating of moon cakes. In the evening children light colorful lanterns in all shapes and sizes.

The Birthday of Prophet Muhammad is a national holiday. Muslims gather for processions, religious lectures, and the recitation of holy verses from the Koran.

Deepavali in October or November is another public holiday. It is one of the prettiest of the Hindu festivals as every Hindu home will be brightly decorated with lights, a practice which symbolizes the ultimate triumph of good over evil. It is a time of feasting and celebration. Indian cultural performances and exhibitions are held in various venues.

Christmas on December 25 is the final public holiday for the year. On Christmas Eve, midnight services are held at all churches while carollers bring joy to shopping centers, hotels, and old folks' homes. Most Christians hold open-house on Christmas Day for relatives and friends.

Apart from these special events, there are regular cultural events in Kuala Lumpur that you may like to see. The Malaysian Handicraft Village on Jalan Bukit Bintang has weekly events that include music, dance, theater, costume parades, and so forth. The center is open from 9 A.M. to 6 P.M. daily.

In a traditional Malay-styled building on Jalan Conlay, the Malay Theater Restaurant provides authentic Malay cuisine and Malay cultural dances in an interior richly decorated with intricate wood carvings.

Yazmin Restaurant has been renowned for years for its home-style Malay cuisine and its cultural experience. In the evenings a cultural troupe entertains with dances, a martial arts display, and a re-enactment of a traditional Malay wedding ceremony.

On most Saturday nights and Sunday afternoons, at the Anniversary Theater in the Lake Gardens, established and upcoming Malaysian talents take to the stage. The shows are a mixture of traditional and modern song and dance, hosted by well-known Malaysian personalities. Sometimes you can hear the current popular rock bands or solo artists.

For anyone interested in recent history, the National Archives of Malaysia on Jalan Duta screens historical documentary films every

Saturday from 10 A.M. till noon. The building also has permanent exhibitions of interest to visitors.

9. Sports

Malaysians are enthusiastic sportsmen and women, so facilities for international sports such as golf, tennis, horse racing, soccer, cricket, and squash are good. In complete contrast you can also enjoy some local sports such as giant top spinning and kite flying.

Golf is obviously one of the sports that has most appeal to visitors. Courses in or near K.L. are excellent and in comparison with some countries, the course fees are very reasonable. The **Royal Selangor Golf Club** is Malaysia's second oldest golf club. It is now one of the leading clubs in Asia with two 18-hole courses and a 9-hole, par 3 course. The course is close to central K.L. and has an arrangement with several leading hotels for guests to play on a first-come, first-served basis. Green fees for visitors are M$150. Tel: 984-8433.

The **Sentil Golf Club** (Tel: 442-4278) has a challenging 9-hole layout close to central K.L. The course is flat but it is not easy. The atmosphere is friendly and the club also has a pool, a restaurant, and a driving range. Green fees are M$30 weekdays for visitors.

The **Armed Forces Club** (Tel: 241-1113), also known as Kelab Angkatan Tentera, has a 9-hole hilly layout with tricky greens. There is also a pool, a dining room, and a driving range. Green fees for visitors are M$20 weekdays.

The **Saujana Golf and Country Club** (Tel: 746-1466) is just outside the city, close to the airport. With its two 18-hole championship courses, it is Malaysia's most prestigious golf resort. The club house is enormous and has four indoor squash courts, four tennis courts, an olympic-size swimming pool, a gymnasium, a theater-restaurant, bar, lounge, and coffee terrace. Green fees are M$100 for visitors on weekdays.

The nearby **Kelab Golf Negara Subang** (Tel: 776-0388) is another club with two 18-hole courses and great facilities, which extend to tennis and squash courts, swimming pools, sauna, restaurant, lounge, bar, video library, and driving range. Visitors are welcome during the week with green fees M$50 in the morning and M$80 in the afternoon.

There are several other courses that visitors can play, provided arrangements are made through their hotel or travel agent.

10. Shopping

Kuala Lumpur's shopping has improved dramatically in recent years to the point that it now is the best place to shop in the whole of

Malaysia. No other place can offer the same great variety of local and imported goods and, because of strong competition, prices have become quite attractive.

Shopping can be done adventurously at the street markets and *pasar malam*, leisurely at shopping complexes, or seriously in specialty stores. Designer products by Gucci, Calvin Klein, Christian Dior, and others can now be found close to shops selling *batik*, pewter, pottery, and Malaysian handicrafts.

The place to visit for an introduction to Malaysian handicrafts is the Information Center in the Infokraf building in Jalan Raja. You will see contemporary designs of age-old arts and crafts together with their more traditional forbears. Then head to the Karyaneka Handicraft Center on Jalan Raja Chulan. Here goods are displayed according to where they are made. If you visited all 13 state houses you would have a complete picture of the enormous variety on offer.

Pewter is one of Malaysia's prime exports. The product, made of 97 percent tin, is exhibited at the Selangor Pewter Showroom at 231 Jalan Tuanku Abdul Rahman. You can buy ready-make products or order something to your specific taste and design. It is also possible to visit the factory in Setapak Jaya just north of the city, but it would be wise to telephone the public relations office (Tel: 422-1000) to obtain details.

Selberan, the jewelry arm of Selangor Pewter has won several international jewelry competitions. It has over 5000 designs in rings, earrings, pendants, necklaces, and so on. The jewelry is now exported to Europe, Australia, and throughout Asia.

Malaysian-made Bonia's wide range of products include leather key chains, handbags, belts, and luggage, as well as accessories such as scarves and ties. Pelco leather bags, shoes, and wallets are also widely available.

Batik items can be found all over the city but some exclusive designs on high-quality cloth can be found at the **Batik Malaysia Berhad** showroom (Tel: 291-8608) in Wisma Batik on Jalan Tun Perak. Visits to the factory where the *batik* is made can be arranged by telephoning 984-0205.

The **Central Market**—also known as Pasar Seni—houses a wide range of activities and products in a cavernous building that was once a wet market. Now Malaysian artists can be seen painting portraits, printing T-shirts, or weaving designed-to-order towels. Other shops specialize in souvenirs, jewelry, stationery, and ready-to-wear clothes. In my experience this is not a particularly cheap place to shop but there is plenty of action and people-watching to compensate.

Jalan Tuanku Abdul Rahman and offshoots is a great area for shopping. The variety is amazing and you should practice your bargaining skills before venturing out, but the experience will be long remembered. When you get tired of walking, the **Pertama Shopping Complex** is a good place to shop. There is a large Metro department store and you will find good bargains in clothes and shoes. On Saturday night a stretch of Jalan Tuanku Abdul Rahman is closed off to traffic and turned into a weekend market. There are some great bargains and much junk. The problem is, it is hard to tell the difference between them. It is also worth visiting **Globe Silk Store**, one of the oldest department stores in K.L. There is a wide range of fabrics, luggage, lingerie, and cosmetics. Check out Jalan Masjid India for Indian handicraft.

Chinatown is probably more a looking area than a shopping area for most visitors. Jalan Petaling is the place to go here to take in the color and excitement. It is particularly attractive early evening when the street stalls light up and the area is thronged with shoppers, families, and others.

Then there are the major shopping complexes. It is here that you will find the luxury imported goods and the up-market local clothes and handicrafts. These complexes also stock a wide range of household goods, furniture, and products used by the local population so there are plenty of locals buying as well as visitors. Here are some of the more popular complexes.

Ampang Park (Tel: 261-4311) was one of the earliest shopping complexes in the city but it is still very popular with the locals and is sought out by visitors in the know who are looking for good handicraft and souvenir shops. The complex is on the corner of Jalan Ampang and Jalan Tun Razak, a few kilometers east of the central city. It is anchored by the Hankyu Jaya store and there are also some excellent small boutiques, as well as a wonderful range of cozy restaurants, food stalls, and dimly lit coffee houses.

Plaza Yow Chuan (Tel: 248-6912) is across Jalan Tun Razak from Ampang Park and the two are connected by an overhead bridge. This is an up-market center with top-quality jewelry, fashion wear, duty-free items, and dining. There is also a post office, a money changer, discos, and a recreation club.

City Square is the newest one-stop shopping center in Jalan Ampang. It has Metro Jaya as its main tenant and there is a nine-level shopping bonanza of 200 shops. Among these is the largest Christian Dior boutique in Asia. City Square is linked with Plaza Yow Chuan by a high-roofed, glass-covered promenade.

Sungai Wang and **Bukit Bintang** plazas (Tel: 243-0411) are adjacent shopping centers located in the so-called golden triangle on Jalan Sultan Ismail close to many of the major hotels. They are probably the busiest shopping centers in the city with well-known stores such as Parkson Grand, Metro Jaya, MPH Guardian, and St. Michael's being some of the tenants. You can spend many a pleasant hour strolling through the tasteful and tacky shops, not really knowing or caring whether you are in one center or the other. The two plazas have a host of fast-food outlets and some good restaurants.

K.L. Plaza (Tel: 241-7315) on Jalan Bukit Bintang, opposite the Regent Hotel, is the home of the Mun Loong department store that spreads over five floors. There are frequent promotions and sales, so it's well worth dropping by to see if you can pick up a bargain.

The Mall (Tel: 442-7122) on Jalan Putra opposite the Pan Pacific Hotel has a large selection of goods—fashion, household items, souvenirs, electronic goods, and food. The four-story atrium is sheathed with azure glass, which conceals a lighting system that synchronizes with music. The Mall houses a branch of the huge Japanese department store, Yaohan. Cheap snacks are available in the basement, while Medan Hang Tuah—a hawkers' emporium—is a food square on the fourth floor where replicas of pre-war facades provide an interesting historic ambience.

Lot 10 is the newest and undisputedly hottest shopping center in town. It is located at the heart of Kuala Lumpur's Golden Triangle and premier shopping belt. It hopes to fill the twin needs of a rapidly growing retail industry and the increasing demands of the discerning consumers of today. From the outside the initial indications of the dynamism of Lot 10 are the natural curvature of the building and the unusual choice of color combination. Elements of mother nature play an important role in Lot 10, both interior as well as exterior. The main tenant here is Isetan, the Japanese department store. Up-market smaller outlets provide a good contrast.

Three other complexes are worth mentioning but there are many more to be found throughout the city. The **Campbell Shopping Complex** on Jalan Dang Wangi is extremely popular with the locals, and visitors will find it is a good place to shop for bargains in clothes and shoes. **Imbi Plaza** on Jalan Imbi across from the Park Royal Hotel is almost exclusively up-market with plenty of brand-name designer goods including watches, computers, and leather products. **Wisma Stephens** near the Hilton Hotel is a center for good tailors, salons, and boutiques.

Shopping hours vary somewhat from area to area but in general major complexes are open from 10 A.M. to 10 P.M. daily, while smaller shops will operate from 9:30 A.M. to 7 P.M. every day except Sunday.

Banking hours are Monday to Friday 10 A.M.-3 P.M., Saturday 9:30 A.M. to 11:30 A.M.

Kuala Lumpur has developed into a good duty-free shopping center. At Subang Airport there are excellent facilities in the 30-store Duty Free Plaza. Some of the items offered are liquor, cigarettes, perfume, cosmetics, chocolates, pewter, clocks, watches, electronic goods, fashion *batik*, handicrafts, sports goods, and jewelry. The prices are competitive with other international airports in the region. The Metropolitan Duty Free Shop (Tel: 261-6500) in Permas International, between the Hilton and Equatorial hotels, is a popular outlet in the central city. This has a free pick-up service between 10 A.M. and 8 P.M. each day.

11. Entertainment and Nightlife

Kuala Lumpur was once known as a cultural desert and the city shut down at 9 P.M., but that has all changed. Now there is a range of entertainment and nightlife to suit everyone.

The Malaysia Tourist Information Complex (Tel: 243-4929) on Jalan Ampang has cultural shows performed nightly. The building, which saw the installation of the first King of Malaysia and the first sitting of Parliament, now holds an exhibition on Malaysia, and hosts daily performances of traditional pastimes.

The City Hall Auditorium (Tel: 291-6011) at Jalan Raja Laut is another place to check on. It often holds weekend musical performances by the Kuala Lumpur Symphony Orchestra where music by Mozart and Bach is played alongside Malaysian classics, and the occasional contemporary Malaysian song. The hall also stages theater and music by various other groups.

Cinemas are extremely popular and you will have no trouble finding a movie in English. The first show usually starts at 1 P.M. with the last show about 9 P.M. Ticket prices are about M$5.

Most of the major hotels have lounges where you can listen to live or recorded music while you have a quiet drink or a cup of coffee. The Shangri-La, Pan Pacific, and Ming Court hotels all serve good coffee in a nice atmosphere. Blue Moon at the Equatorial Hotel has a disc jockey who spins songs of yesteryear. Japanese lounges have sprouted everywhere but, unlike in places such as Bangkok, locals and visitors are welcome to share the scene.

Jazz lovers are reasonably well catered to. Contemporary jazz is played regularly at the Hilton Hotel, and **Cee Jays** (Tel: 232-5734) near the Shangri-La Hotel has an interesting and adventurous band that is dragging a regular crowd. Petaling Jaya, a modern suburb to the southwest of K.L. city, is another good place for jazz. The **Hard Rock Cafe** (Tel: 244-4152) next to the Concorde Hotel in Jalan Sultan Ismail opens 11 A.M. to 2 A.M. It is very big on beverages and has a live band from 10:30 P.M.

Discotheques have sprouted all over Kuala Lumpur in recent years. The **Tin Mine** at the Hilton Hotel and **Club Oz** at the Shangri-La are considered to be the best of the hotel discos. There is a cover charge and fairly strict dress rules at both, so the crowd is rather up-market. Outside the hotels there is a range of options from great to fair. You will find more locals and a more casual atmosphere at these outlets.

Monroe's Place, in the building opposite the Hilton Hotel, has many supporters. Beer during happy hours is only M$3.45, and there is a set lunch and dinner at reasonable prices. A DJ operates the disco after 9:30 P.M. every day of the week. This has a M$10 cover charge.

Then there is **Phase Two** (Tel: 248-2063) also on Jalan Tun Razak, with particularly good acoustics and a variety of patrons. **Faces** (Tel: 248-8055) on Jalan Ampang is currently one of the hottest places in town.

Studio Thirty (Tel: 241-9475) provides an excellent view of K.L. city from its 30th-floor location in the Menara Promet building opposite the Hilton Hotel. **The Turf** (Tel: 242-4319) at 10 Jalan Kia Peng provides facilities for diners at this complex to kick up their heels later in the evening. **Eleven LA** (Tel: 232-6907) at Leboh Ampang has a disco on the ground floor and live jazz and R & B on the first floor. If you just feel like walking and discovering, a good area is Jalan Pinang, Jalan Perak, and Jalan Ramlee, between the luxury hotels and the racetrack. Here you will find numerous pubs, local discos, restaurants with live music, and lounges. You should be comfortable in any of them and the prices will be a pleasant surprise. One of the most popular of these is **Betelnut** (Tel: 241-6455), a music lounge/restaurant on Jalan Pinang, but you could also try **La Bamba pub and lounge, and the Tin Pan Alley** BBQ corner.

Nightclubs are not quite as easy to find. The **Pertama Cabaret and Night Club** (Tel: 298-2533) at the Pertama Complex, the **Campbell Nightclub** (Tel: 292-9655) in the Campbell Complex, and the **Flory Nightclub** (Tel: 241-0288), are all situated within shopping complexes, all aim at the local market, and are all suitable for visitors. The **Copacabana** (Tel: 241-8006) at the Federal Hotel will have more visitors among its patrons.

12. The Kuala Lumpur Address List

Airlines
—British Airways   Tel: 232-5797
—Northwest Orient Airlines   241-5303
—Qantas Airways   238-9133
—Singapore Airlines   292-3122
—Thai Airways International   293-7100
Airport
—MAS Information   746-3000
—DCA Information   746-1235
Bus services
—Hentian Bas Putra (East Coast)   442-9530
—Klang Bus Station (around K.L.)   230-7694
—Pudu Raya Bus Station (North and South)   230-0145
Diplomatic Missions
—Australia   242-3122
—Canada   261-2000
—New Zealand   248-6422
—Singapore   261-6277
—Thailand   248-8222
—British High Commission   248-8222
—U.S.A.   248-9011
Kuala Lumpur Tourist Association
—Jalan Sultan Hishamuddin   238-1832
Malaysia Tourist Information Complex (MATIC)
—109 Jalan Ampang   242-3929
Malaysia Airlines
—Jalan Sultan Ismail K.L.   261-0555
Railway Station   274-7435
Taxi
—Comfort Taxi Service   733-0507
—Fed. Territory & Selangor Taxi Assoc.   293-6211
Malaysia Tourism Promotion Board
—Putra World Trade Center   293-5188
Tourist Police   243-5522
Telephone Service
—Emergency   999
—Inquiries   102
—International calls   108

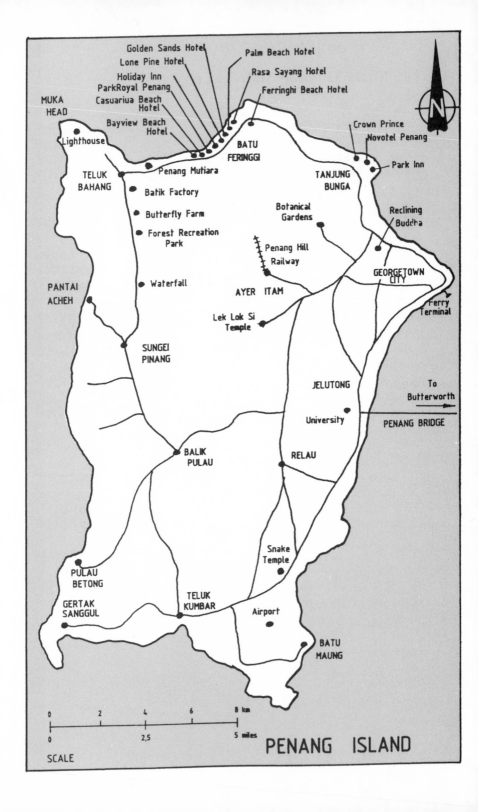

PENANG ISLAND

9

Penang and the North

1. The General Picture

The northwest states of Malaysia—Perlis, Kedah, Perak, and Penang—
are the nation's rice bowl and tin-producing heartland. Three of these
states border Thailand, while all have a coastline to the Straits of
Malacca.

This region has also been the traditional center of Malaysian tourism.
There are lovely near shore islands, excellent beaches, and rugged
mountains. Visitors will be attracted to the resort hotels on Pulau
Langkawi and Pular Pangkor, but undoubtedly the most popular
destination of all is the island of Penang.

Penang, a 285-square-kilometer island, with a thriving, cosmopolitan
city, busy port, international airport, lovely beaches and backing rain
forest, and a huge selection of luxury beach hotels, is a place that every
visitor should visit.

This was the oldest British settlement in the Far East. It was established by Francis Light of the British East India Company in 1786.
Nearly 50 years later, Penang, Malacca, and Singapore were joined by
the British to form the Straits Settlements and Penang's golden age had
begun. Much of what you see today can be traced back to those early
days.

Penang is an easygoing, colorful place that is perfect for visitors. The
main city is called Georgetown and, although it has a population

The beach is a big attraction at the resort hotels.

approaching 500,000, most visitor interest is centered in an area that can be explored on foot, or with a bicycle rickshaw. It is the best city in Malaysia in which to wander around. No matter where you walk, you will find plenty of interest.

Elsewhere on the island, there are nice beaches, luxury resorts, jungle walks, a mountain railway, intriguing temples, and more. Penang offers almost all of Malaysia's attractions in a compact form that is unavailable anywhere else in the country.

The Langkawi islands are 100 kilometers north of Penang and are linked by ship and plane. These islands are being heavily promoted by the Malaysian government and there is some resentment to this in Penang where the population perceives that the central government is giving preference to Langkawi. While both islands offer beaches and a good holiday experience, no visitor should substitute Langkawi for Penang. They are just not comparable. Visit both or just visit Penang.

The same can be said of Pangkor, some 150 kilometers to the south. I particularly like this island for a relaxing holiday experience but you should still not miss Penang. Elsewhere south of Penang, the cities and towns of Ipoh, Sungai Siput, Kuala Kangsar, and Taiping are all worth a visit while the mountain resort of Maxwell's Hill (Bukit Larut) is a delight.

2. Getting There

The Penang International Airport is at the southern end of the island, about 20 kilometers from the center of Georgetown. It is about 35 kilometers from the major beach resorts. There are direct air links with many parts of Malaysia; Singapore; Bangkok, Hat Yai, and Phuket in Thailand; Medan in Indonesia; Hong Kong; and many other parts of Asia. There is a huge number of daily flights to Kuala Lumpur, which then link to most major cities in the world.

Taxis operate from the airport using a coupon system. You buy the ticket inside the terminal and give it to the driver. Typical fares are M$15 by ordinary taxi to Georgetown; M$18 by air-conditioned taxi to Georgetown, and M$25-30 to the major beach resorts. Taxis take about 30 minutes from the airport to the city.

There is also a public bus from the airport to Georgetown (No. 83). It operates all day and until about 10 P.M.. The fare is about M$2 and it takes about an hour to reach the central city.

You can also reach Penang by train from Singapore, Kuala Lumpur, and Thailand. The journey from Kuala Lumpur to Butterworth (on the mainland opposite Penang) takes about six hours and there are air-conditioned carriages available for first- and second-class passengers. From Butterworth you take the ferry to Penang Island. It is a 24-hour service for both passengers and motor vehicles.

Long-distance coaches operate between Kuala Lumpur and Penang or Kuala Lumpur and Butterworth. Despite the existence of a bridge linking Penang to the mainland, most coaches appear to prefer to operate to Butterworth with passengers making the last leg by ferry. Certainly when you are leaving Penang it is better to travel to Butterworth to pick up a coach. From Butterworth there are services to Ipoh, Kuala Lumpur, Singapore, Kota Bahru (on the east coast), Hat Yai in Thailand, and to Kuala Perlis for the Langkawi ferry and to Lumut for the Pangkor Island ferry.

Long-distance taxis also operate from a depot beside the ferry terminal in Butterworth. You can, however, also book them from your hotel in Penang and this is more convenient. Taxis operate to Ipoh, Kuala Lumpur, the Cameron Highlands (a hill resort), and to some other destinations. Fares are often about 50 percent more than the bus. Thai taxis operate to Hat Yai, and my experience with this service is that it is fairly comfortable and reliable.

Since the completion of the Penang Bridge in the mid-1980s, you can drive to Penang. The bridge is claimed to be the longest in southeast Asia (about 13.5 kilometers) and the fourth longest in the world. You pay a toll when driving from the mainland to the island (M$8) but there is no charge for the reverse journey.

3. Local Transportation

When you are in Georgetown, before worrying about public transportation, you should walk. This is by far the most interesting of all Malaysian city centers and you should take the time to absorb the atmosphere before it disappears as it has from other major centers in Asia.

Set off in any direction and you will discover beautiful old Chinese houses, gracious colonial buildings, temples, crowded narrow lanes, street stalls, markets, and the sights, smells, and sounds of an Asian Chinese city.

Trishaws are three-wheeled, one-man-powered vehicles perfect for those trips that are just too long for a comfortable walk, or for a slow-paced tour around the city. This is a great form of transportation in Georgetown's relatively uncrowded streets, and late at night the trishaw can be a perfect slow, quiet, romantic vehicle. There are supposed to be set fares for trishaws in Penang but as a visitor you will

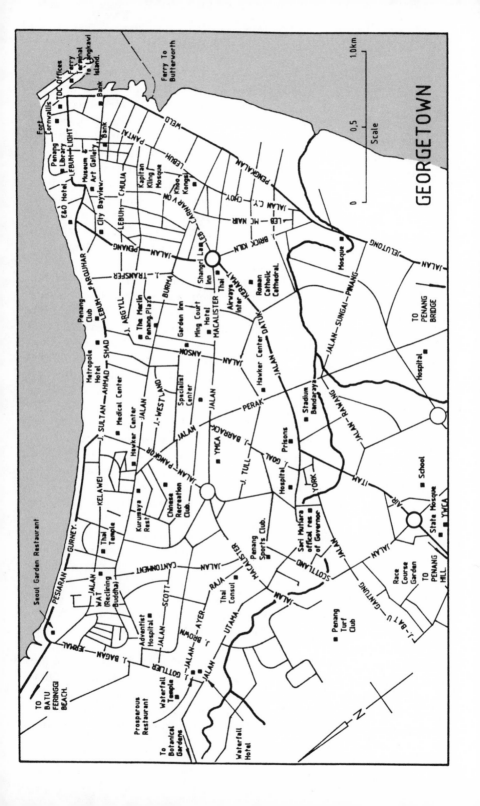

GEORGETOWN

have to negotiate a fare before you board. You should base your offer on about M$3 for a two-kilometer journey. If you want to hire the trishaw by the hour, a reasonable rate is M$10. Most of the drivers speak some English. Visitors should not feel self-conscious as they might in other Asian cities, for this is one of the most common forms of transportation here and not a mere tourist gimmick.

City buses are operated by the municipal council and several private companies. The council buses operate from the main terminal at Lebuh Victoria, close to the ferry terminal. There are 13 routes and each bus is distinguished by a number. For visitors the most important routes are No. 1, which goes to Ayer Itam (for the Kok Lok Si Temple); No. 7 to the Botanical Gardens; and No. 8, which operates from Ayer Itam to the Penang Hill Railway.

Green, blue, and yellow buses operate from a terminal at Pengkalan Weld near the ferry terminal and also from a new terminal that is part of the KOMTAR project (that tall monstrosity in the center of the city). Green buses service Air Itam; blue buses serve the northern coast of the island, passing all the major beach resorts to Teluk Bahang; yellow buses serve the southern and western parts of the island including the international airport, the Snake Temple, and eventually all the way around to Teluk Bahang where you can take a blue bus back to Georgetown.

Taxis are equipped with meters but drivers are very reluctant to use them. You can insist that the meter be turned on or you can agree to a price before you board. For short distances within the city, you should offer M$3-6. Penang Hill will cost at least M$10, the Botanical Gardens about M$8, the Snake Temple M$15, and the beach resorts M$12. If you manage to get a taxi driver to use the meter, he can charge an extra 50 percent between 1 A.M. and 6 A.M.

Bicycles are not a bad way of seeing Georgetown and the immediate vicinity. They can be rented from some of the budget hotels in Lebuh Leith and Lebuh Chulia and from some of the bicycle repair shops around town. You will pay M$5-10 per day.

Motorcycles can also be rented in both Georgetown and at the beach areas. You will pay about M$25 for a 100cc. bike in reasonable condition. You should contact the Penang Development Corporation (Tel: 832-111) for advice.

Rental cars are an excellent way to explore the island and some of the adjacent mainland. Most of the major international and local car rental companies offer a choice of vehicles and packages. Some companies will accept your current home license while others will insist on a valid international driver's license. Some of the major car rental companies include:

Avis Rent-A-Car—E & O Hotel (Tel: 373-964), Rasa Sayang Hotel (Tel: 811-522), and Penang International Airport (Tel: 839-633)

Hertz Rent-A-Car—Penang Bowl Building (Tel: 375-914), Golden Sands Hotel (Tel: 811-662), and Penang International Airport (Tel: 830-208)

Budget Rent-A-Car—Penang Road (Tel: 631-240), and Penang International Airport (Tel: 838-891)

National Rent-A-Car—Penang Plaza (Tel: 367-196)

Sintat Rent-A-Car—Penang International Airport (Tel: 830-958)

4. The Hotel Scene

Many of Penang's luxury hotels are on the northern beaches and almost all the budget hotels are in central Georgetown. Between these two extremes you will find midrange hotels in central Georgetown, on the outskirts of the city, and at some at the beaches.

EXPENSIVE HOTELS

Georgetown only has two hotels that really qualify in this category, and two others that offer good accommodations at reasonable prices. The two luxury hotels are a complete contrast, and which one you choose depends on whether you like modern style or character.

The **Eastern and Oriental Hotel** (the E & O) (Tel: 635-322) is my kind of hotel. I guess I am in good company because Somerset Maugham and Noel Coward, among others, have counted it among their personal favorites. The hotel has recently been restored and refurbished but it has retained its distinct old-world charm and atmosphere while keeping abreast of the needs of the modern traveller.

The hotel is situated in an absolute seafront site close to the shopping, commercial, and entertainment areas of Georgetown. The lobby is spectacular with a huge dome covering the reception area, the Palm Court, and other facilities. The 1885 Grill is a place to pamper yourself in the splendor of Victorian times with a selection of local and Continental dishes and a variety of fine wines. The intimate, candle-lit atmosphere with the views to the flood-lit garden is quite delightful. Afterwards try your favorite drink in the Anchor Bar Lounge, which is reminiscent of the 1920s and the planter's era, with its stained-glass arches and tiles.

The E & O has 100 rooms with prices from about M$120. My personal choice is a junior suite (about M$200) overlooking the garden and the swimming pool. All rooms are carpeted and have private bathroom, telephone, music, TV, video, and refrigerator. (Book with the hotel at 10 Farquhar Street, 10200 Penang; Fax: 604-634-833.) There is no beach in Georgetown.

The **Shangri-La Hotel** (Tel: 622-622) is Georgetown's largest and most modern hotel. It is built adjacent to the 65-story KOMTAR Tower, which is the central point of the city's commercial district. The 442-room hotel has been built on a grand scale with a huge lobby and spacious bedrooms. There are three restaurants, a bar, a lounge, a swimming pool, a disco, a gymnasium, and more. The hotel has all the features you would expect from a modern international hotel. Prices start at about M$260 for a room. (Book with the hotel at Jalan Magazine, 10300 Penang; Fax: 604-626-526.)

The **Merlin Penang** (Tel: 376-166) is 295-room modern hotel offering excellent facilities for most attractive prices. The rooms have all the usual facilities while the hotel has two restaurants, a lounge, a coffee house, a disco, shops, a health club, and a swimming pool. The hotel is situated in an area about a kilometer from many of the city's main attractions, so if you are not a walker you need to consider this fact. There are, however, excellent shopping and restaurant options close to the hotel. Rooms are available for a very reasonable M$160. (Book with the hotel at 3 Jalan Laut, 10050 Penang; Fax: 604-376-615.)

The **City Bayview** (Tel: 633-161) has rooms at about the same price. This is an older hotel than the Merlin (in fact it was managed by the Merlin group some 20 years ago), but in my opinion it is in a much better location. The 160-room hotel has good, well equipped rooms, a revolving restaurant, a lounge with a live band, a Continental cuisine restaurant, and a coffee house. A swimming pool is located on a sundeck. Room rates are from M$160. (Book with the hotel at 25 Farquhar Street, 10200 Penang; Fax: 604-634-124.)

Out on the northern beaches there are some excellent resorts adjacent to average-to-good beaches. The water close to Georgetown suffers from pollution and some of the beaches farther out have not been well looked after, so they come as a disappointment to some who have believed the full-color promotional brochures they have seen. Nevertheless, the luxury resorts along these beaches provide great facilities for relaxing and recharging the batteries, and in fact some people can stay for days without actually swimming in the sea.

The first three hotels are located at Tanjung Bunga, which is midway between the city and the main tourist beach of Batu Feringgi. The **Park Inn International** (Tel: 808-808), 200 rooms, is a nice property with a mixture of business and tourist guests. The rooms have the usual facilities and there is a pool, a lounge, a terrace, a restaurant, a pub with live bands, and a karaoke room. Room rates are from M$200.

(Book with the hotel at 33 Jalan Tanjung Bungah, 11200 Penang; Fax: 604-808-333.)

The **Novotel Penang** (Tel: 803-333), 318 rooms, caters primarily to tourists. There are tennis and squash courts, a large pool, a health club, children's facilities, and a small private beach with water sport equipment. Rooms are undramatic, but are well equipped and there are bars, restaurants, and a discotheque. Room rates start at M$200. (Book with the hotel at Jalan Tanjung Bungah, 11200 Penang; Fax: 604-803-303.)

The **Crown Prince Hotel** (Tel: 804-111), 280 rooms, is a new high-rise hotel close-by. Rooms and public areas are well presented and the hotel has all the facilities most travelers will need. There is a 24-hour coffee shop, a lounge, a restaurant, a pool, a squash court, minigolf, and a gymnasium. Room rates are from M$210. (Book with the hotel at Jalan Tanjung Bungah, 11200 Penang; Fax: 604-804-111. U.S.A. toll-free Tel: 800-223-2094.)

The **Rasa Sayang Hotel** (Tel: 811-811) has been the largest and most expensive resort at Batu Feringgi for several years. It has a beachfront location, and the hotel consists of several low-rise buildings that form a crescent shape overlooking a large pool, spacious gardens, and the beach. It has style and character and is built as this type of hotel should be. Half the hotel rooms have lovely views of the pool, gardens, and beach while the other rooms look outwards and have views that could be missed. Naturally these latter rooms are cheaper. The lobby is large and runs into an open lounge and bar—it's all quite delightful.

A new 211-room wing was opened in late 1993 with its own swimming pool, spa, bar, health center, and Chinese restaurant. The accommodation is deluxe. This is a hotel that one can enjoy. (Book with Shangri-La International or direct with the hotel at Batu Feringgi Beach, 11100, Penang; Fax: 604-811-984.) Room prices now start at about M$350.

The **Penang Mutiara** (Tel: 812-828) is a luxury hotel of a different kind on Teluk Bahang beach. This is five-star luxury of the crystal chandeliers, bow ties, and caviar type. I do not like concrete high-rise beach hotels yet I have been seduced by the design and the sheer luxury of this hotel. The huge lobby that spills down through several levels to the pool and the beach is sheathed in glass that brings the beach and the deep blue sea right in among the marble and polished brass.

This is the only major hotel at Teluk Bahang so the hotel has had to provide everything to keep guests happy. It has done this with three major restaurants, several bars, a garden terrace, a discotheque, a recreation club, and a fitness center. There is a choice of rooms from about M$350 to M$450 and suites from M$650 to M$6000. (Book with Mandarin Singapore International, United States 212-838-7874 or 213-627-0185, Australia 02-276-677, with the Leading Hotels of the World organization, or with the hotel direct on fax: 604-812-829.) The nearby fishing village is quite attractive and there are several small local restaurants.

The **Penang Parkroyal** (Tel: 811-133), 333 rooms, is a similar development, this time on Batu Feringgi beach, which opened in 1991. The facilities are excellent, the location is good, and the hotel has developed into a fine property. There are several themed bars, restaurants offering Western, Malay, Chinese, Indian, and Japanese cuisine, strolling musicians, and a discotheque. Children have their own play area and a games and video room. There is a tennis court, gymnasium, and a host of water sports. Room prices start at M$300. (Book with the hotel at Batu Feringgi, 11100 Penang; Fax: 604-812-233.)

The Bayview Pacific (Tel: 812-158), 366 rooms, also opened in 1991 and has all the usual facilities in a medium-rise concrete tower. There are nice gardens that contain some low-rise accommodation units, a large pool, and water sport facilities. While this is a nice property, I feel it is really a city-style hotel that happens to be built on the beach. Room rates start from M$160 for the low-rise units and M$240 for the tower block. (Book with the hotel at Batu Feringgi, 11100 Penang; Fax: 604-812-140.)

There are four more resorts at Batu Feringgi that should be mentioned. Starting from the east then moving west is the 350-room **Feringgi Beach Hotel** (Tel: 805-999), which is operated by Federal Hotels International. It is across the main road from the beach but an overhead bridge does much to solve that problem. The building is concrete high-rise, but many of the rooms do have nice water views and there are good restaurant, bar, and pool facilities. (Book with Utell International worldwide, United States 800-223-9868, Canada 800-663-9582, Australia 008-221-176, or direct with the hotel at Batu Feringgi, 11100 Penang; Fax: 604-805-999.)

Next is the **Golden Sands Hotel** (Tel: 811-911), which is another Shangri-La International property. This hotel was extended and refurbished in the late 1980s and is very attractive. The medium-rise, crescent-shaped hotel has many rooms with attractive sea views, but others (hill view) effectively have no view. The lobby gently rolls into the garden and its several pools, palms, lawns, bar, and so forth. It is very effective. The beach looks nice but there is limited shade and the whole thing is spoiled somewhat by the very aggressive beach boys who try to sell you whatever they think will appeal. It's interesting to note that rooms have hair dryers and tea- and coffee-making facilities. Room rates start at about M$280 and move upwards to M$800 for suites. (Book with the hotel on fax: 604-811-800.)

There is a gap then to the **Holiday Inn** (Tel: 811-601). The hotel is in two parts: a nondescript building of 160 rooms adjacent to the beach, and a new tower across the road from the beach. They are joined by a footbridge. Rooms are large and the atmosphere is pleasant. The pool and gardens are less spectacular than many hotels but the restaurants and bars are attractive and well run. (Book with the Holiday Inn network or direct with the hotel on Fax: 604-811-389.) Room rates are around M$250.

The **Casuarina Beach Hotel** (Tel: 811-711) is slightly less expensive than most of the above, yet it is probably one of the best integrations of hotel lobby, restaurants, garden, pool, and beach that I have seen. The rooms are large but not as luxurious as some but the whole property has a nice atmosphere. (Book direct with the hotel at Batu Feringgi, 11100 Penang; Fax: 4-812-155.)

Finally there is the **Equatorial Penang** (Tel: 838-111), a large, modern international hotel built on its own hill out towards the airport. The facilities are excellent but I am not sure why, when you are on an island, you would choose a location neither in the city nor on the beach. (Book with the hotel by writing 1 Jalan Bukit Jambull, 11900 Penang; Fax: 604-848-000.)

MEDIUM-PRICE HOTELS

The **Bellevue Penang Hill Hotel** (Tel: 892-256) is my favorite hotel in this category but its location on the top of Penang Hill will be a problem to many visitors. It is a place to relax in quiet comfort rather than be a base for busy sight-seeing. The 12-room hotel is tastefully decorated and has some great artworks and a delightful garden. The hotel once belonged to Mr. Halliburton during the early days of the East India Company. He was known then as the Sheriff of Penang. Room rates are around M$100. (Book with the hotel at Penang Hill, 11300 Penang.)

You will pay around the same for a room at the **The Oriental** (Tel: 242-111), will get no garden, but you will be in the center of the city. The hotel is pleasant and each of the 94 rooms is quite adequate. This area of Penang Road has hotels, restaurants, shops, nightlife, markets, and more, so there is plenty to see and do all day and night. (Book with the hotel at 105 Penang Road, 10200 Penang.)

The **Hotel Waterfall** (Tel: 370-887), 35 rooms, is some three kilometers from the central city on the road to the botanical gardens. The area is very pleasant, the staff is helpful, and public transportation to the city is frequent. Room rates start at around M$100. (Book with the hotel at 160 Jalan Utama, 10450 Penang; Fax: 372-324.)

The **Hotel Waldorf** (Tel: 26-141) is down-market from the hotels previously mentioned but it represents a good value for the money. The 57-room hotel is on Lebuh Leith, not far from the Oriental and City Bayview hotels. Rooms are clean, though sparsely furnished; there is a restaurant with good food at reasonable prices; and I found the staff very courteous and helpful. Because I had arrived without any Malay money, the hotel receptionist gave me M$20 so I could buy a few necessities I needed before the shops closed at 10 P.M. It is that kind of hotel. (Book direct at 13 Leith Street, 10200 Penang.) Room rates are about M$40-$60.

There are several more hotels in Penang Road that fall into this midrange category but I have no experience with any of them. The **Town House Hotel** (Tel: 368-722), 45 rooms from M$80; the **Continental** (Tel: 26-381), 116 rooms from M$95; the **Hotel Malaysia** (Tel: 363-311), 126 rooms from M$95; and the cheaper **Hotel Central** (Tel: 21-432), 140 rooms from M$75, are all on Penang Road between the E & O Hotel and the KOMTAR building.

If you are still not satisfied with any of these, the 64-room **Gallent Hotel** (Tel: 379-584) at 6 Transfer Road, or the 124-room **Golden City Hotel** (Tel: 27281), both have rooms from around M$60 a night. The **Mingood Hotel** (Tel: 373-375) at 164 Argyle Road has 52 rooms of a similar standard.

Out at Batu Feringgi Beach, the **Palm Beach Hotel** (Tel: 811-621) just scrapes into this category with rooms from M$150. This hotel is operated by the Shangri-La group, so you have the use of the facilities of the Rasa Sayang and Golden Sands hotels without their price tag. The hotel has its own pool, two restaurants, and tennis and squash courts so there is plenty to do. The rooms are nothing special, but it is a good value when you compare it with other beach prices. (Book with the hotel at 105A Batu Feringgi, 11100 Penang.)

Just a few hundred meters farther on is the **Lone Pine Hotel** (Tel: 811-511) with 54 rooms from M$90. This is the cheapest of the beach hotels and the last time I saw it, it was somewhat run-down. If your need is the beach rather than expensive accommodations, this may suit you. The hotel has a small pool. (Book direct at 97 Batu Feringgi, 11100 Penang; Fax: 604-811-282.)

BUDGET ACCOMMODATIONS

Penang is probably the best place in Malaysia for budget accommodations. There is a large collection of budget hotels along Lebuh Chulia and Lebuh Leith.

At the top end of the range is the **Cathay Hotel** (Tel: 626-271), 37 rooms, almost next to the Hotel Waldorf in Lebuh Leith. This has more exterior and lobby style than all the other budget hotels put together but at M$46 for the cheapest room it is also more expensive than most. Nevertheless, if appearances are important to you, the Cathay will make you happy. Air-conditioned rooms are from M$60.

Across the road from here, the **New China Hotel** (Tel: 631-601) remains popular. Rooms cost from about M$18 and there are dormitory beds for about M$8. There is a restaurant with fair food, and a noisy bar. The place looks quite clean and it is a meeting point for backpackers so you can pick up some interesting information. The **Lum Fong Hotel** next to the New China Hotel has a very popular Tiger Bar and a small restaurant, and rooms from about M$19.50. Directly opposite here is the **Modern Hotel** (Tel: 635-424) with large rooms from about M$25. Both of these hotels are clean but noisy.

The **Eng Aun Hotel** (Tel: 372-333) on Lebuh Chulia is another favorite, although I am not quite sure why it is so popular. It has a parking lot that puts the hotel back from the road noise but the rooms are just adequate. I guess the M$15 price tag is a help. The **Eastern Hotel** (Tel: 614-597) is another recommended establishment that has clean rooms and a friendly staff. Farther down, the **Yeng Keng Hotel** (Tel: 610-610) has large, quiet rooms from M$14. The **Plaza Hotel** on Ah Quee Street near The Kapitan King Mosque has rooms and dormitories on three floors with prices from M$7 to M$30.

Apart from these you will discover many more budget hotels around Georgetown. Don't be afraid to walk in and ask to see a room. If you don't like what you see, or can't negotiate an agreeable price, it is no problem to leave.

Bed-and-breakfast facilities have recently become available on Penang. Some of these are purpose-built and offer clean and comfortable rooms. Try **Anggerick Villa** (Tel: 883-760) on Jalan Hilir Pemancer at Bandar Geluger or **Sinar Suria Lodge** (Tel: 889-660) at 15 Lorong Batu Uban 1, Taman Century.

A final alternative is the **YMCA** (Tel: 362-211) on Jalan Macalister about two kilometers from the central city. It is on the bus No. 1 route. Some of the 35 rooms have air conditioning and all have attached showers. There is no need to be a YMCA member and they accept men, women, and couples of the same family. Unmarried couples cannot stay together here. There is a cafeteria and TV lounge so you can meet your fellow guests. Rooms start at about M$35.

5. Dining and Restaurants

Penang is famous for its seafood, its *laksa* (soup), and its hawker food. Try them all before you leave the island.

Penang's hawkers are found on almost every corner of the city, and they offer an amazing range of dishes. One dish that you should try is *Laksa Assam*, thick rice noodles served in a distinctive tangy soup made of fish stock spiced with onions, chilli, fresh turmeric, lemon grass, tamarind juice, and more. For dessert have *Goreng Pisang*, a banana dipped in a specially prepared batter and deep-fried till it is golden brown.

The best places to sample hawker food in an attractive outdoor setting, is along Gurney Drive (you need your own transportation or take a trishaw), or right in the city on the Esplanade. A meal will cost less than M$10 for two. Other popular hawker spots are in Campbell Street, on Penang Road, at the Golden Eagle Center on Jalan Burmah, at the corner of Jalan Anson and Jalan Perak, and at the KOMTAR Food Court. The **Green Planet** on Cintra Street is the place to go for vegetarian and "healthy" food. The yogurt shakes are excellent.

Good *Chinese restaurants* can be found all over Penang. *Dim sum* is popular here and it would be hard to beat the **Shang Palace** at the Shangri-La Hotel. Another popular venue is the **Haloman Restaurant** on Jalan Anson, a little west of the city center. Hainanese restaurants are mainly concentrated in Lebuh Campbell and Lebuh Cintra. The **Sim Kuan Hiwa Cafe** is a good example with excellent chicken rice.

For Hokkien food you could try the **Chuan Lock Hooi Restaurant** on Jalan Macalister, and typical Hakka cuisine is available at the **Dragon Inn** on Jalan Gottlieb (on the way to the botanical gardens). Jalan Gottlieb is also the location of the **Prosperous Restaurant** (Tel: 378-787), which has excellent Cantonese and Hainanese dishes. All these restaurants will run at M$20-$40 for two.

A good choice for *Malay* food is the **Rasa Sayong** in the KOMTAR complex. Malay haute cuisine dining is available at the **Eliza Restaurant** in the City Bayview Hotel. The adventurous can sit cross-legged on a rattan mat.

For *Nyonya food* (a Chinese/Malay mix), it is hard to go past the **Dragon King Restaurant** on Lebuh Bishop near St. George's Church. Also in this area, the **Sun Hoe Peng** on Lebuh Light has a good reputation. Back near Penang Road, there are a couple of extremely popular outdoor Chinese restaurants in Jalan Argll and Jalan Chowrasta. Neither has an English sign. The **Wing Lok** on Penang Road is more up-market and has one of the best steamboat dinners around.

There is a strong Indian presence in Penang and consequently there are some excellent *Indian restaurants*. These fall into three categories— southern Indian, which features spicy curry, *tosai*, and sweet cakes; northern Indian, which features food cooked in a clay oven such as *tandoori* chicken; and Indian Muslim restaurants, which are best-known for their *nasi kandar*, a rice served with chicken, mutton, or fish curry, and an assortment of vegetables.

There are two main areas for Indian restaurants. You will find dozens in the area bounded by Lebuh Chulia, Penang, Pitt, and Bishop. Most are very cheap and the food is good, although you should watch out for some of the curries as they are very hot to the Western palate. **Darwood Restaurant** (Tel: 611-633) on Lebuh Queen is one of the favorites. The other area is bounded by Jalan Penang and Lebuh Chulia, Cintra, and Campbell. These restaurants are more well known to visitors but the food is still quite authentic. Prices here tend to be a little higher but you can still get a good meal for two for around M$10. The **Meeva Restaurant** and the **Hameediyah** (Tel: 611-095), both on Lebuh Campbell, and the **Tap Mahal Restaurant** near the corner of Jalan Penang and Lebuh Chulia, all have a reputation for excellent food. None of these places has "romantic" atmosphere—they are working restaurants serving the needs of the local community.

If you want atmosphere you could try the **Kashmir Restaurant** (Tel: 637-411) in the basement of the Oriental Hotel. It is air-conditioned and has live Indian music. A meal here will cost M$30-40 for two.

There are *Japanese restaurants* in several hotels, and a few around town. All serve a variety of dishes including *sushi*, *sashimi*, and *tempura*. **Myabi Restaurant** (Tel: 375-329) on Jalan Macalister and **Kurumaya** on Jalan Burmah past Jalan Pangkor are considered to be two of the best of the nonhotel Japanese restaurants. *Thai restaurants* can also be found at several locations and some Chinese restaurants also serve some Thai food. There is a good *Korean restaurant*, the **Seoul Garden** (Tel: 366-834) at the corner of Jalan Kelawei and Pesiaran Gurney. Prices are on the high side. *Western restaurants* are mainly in hotels but there are several fast-food outlets in the KOMTAR Complex (McDonald's, Kentucky Fried Chicken, etc.), and elsewhere along Jalan Burma and Jalan Penang. The world's most classy Kentucky Fried Chicken restaurant is probably the one opposite the Merlin Hotel. It's worth a look.

Seafood is available at all hotels and many restaurants in Georgetown and on the beaches. Outside of the hotels try **Restoran Maple** on Jalan

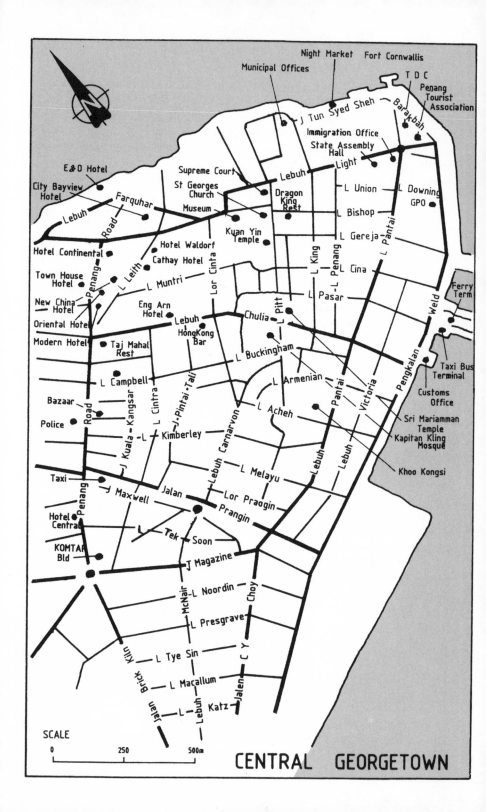

CENTRAL GEORGETOWN

Penang where you can select your fish from a tank, or go out to Pesiaran Gurney and try any of a dozen or so alternatives. If you are staying at the beach, **Eden Seafood Village**, between the Lone Pine Hotel and the Holiday Inn, or the **Sea Pavilion** (Tel: 811-911) at the beach front of the Golden Sands Hotel, is where you should head. A cheaper alternative is the **Happy Garden Restoran** with its nice outdoor setting. In this same area **The Ship**, next to Eden Seafood, has plenty of atmosphere and excellent steaks, while the **Penang Village Restoran** opposite the Parkroyal hotel has good Malay and Western food in a modern, pricey atmosphere. If you would like to go a little farther afield, **The Catch** (Tel: 812-828) at Telok Bahang has seafood of all descriptions in an "environmentally friendly setting." While in this area, the **End of the World** restaurant at the end of the road near the jetty is also recommended for fresh produce at a good price.

6. Sight-seeing

There is more tourist information available on Penang than on most places in Malaysia so it is worth checking out the Penang Tourist Association (Tel: 616-663) near Fort Cornwallis, the Tourist Information Center (Tel: 614-461) at the third level KOMTAR building, or the Penang Development Corporation (Tel: 832-111). There is also a branch of the Tourism Promotion Board (TPB) close to the Penang Tourist Association if you wish to pick up some information on other areas of the country.

Because there are no good free maps of Penang available anywhere, I bought the "new edition" of the Penang Island and City Map from the Tourist Information Center. Unfortunately the map is well out-of-date and less than accurate. It is, however, better than nothing.

Your sight-seeing should start in **Georgetown**. The city was founded when the British first settled the island. It has relics from that early colonial era, it has much from the last century when Chinese entrepreneurs made Penang their home, and there is plenty from this century— all mixed together in a melting pot of cultures, smells, sights, and sounds.

Much of Georgetown remains as it was built. Little has been razed to make way for more modern buildings except for the incredible KOMTAR development in the center of town. Most areas are characterized by low-rise Chinese shop houses and the stately old homes of Penang's elite. It is quite picturesque.

The visitor should start sight-seeing at **Fort Cornwallis**, one of the oldest structures on the island. This is the site where Captain Francis

Light first landed on the island in 1786. Originally the fort was built from timber but in 1805-1810 it was rebuilt in stone. Today the imposing outside walls hide grassy lawns, and the cannons that were once placed strategically for defense have children climbing over them. It may not be the most spectacular place in the world but it's well worthwhile seeing where Penang really began.

At the western end of Fort Cornwallis, the **Municipal Offices** building is one of the most photographed in Georgetown. Attractive lawns let you try different angles on this delightful colonial building that all visitors see on the outside but almost never enter. In fact this whole area is a delight. Lovely shade trees frame views of the impressive **Supreme Court** building and a compulsory stop should be made at the nearby **Penang Museum and Art Gallery** on Lebuh Farquhar.

This delightful old building was build in 1820 as a school but today it houses a fine collection of old photographs, maps, charts, and other relics that provide an insight into Penang's history. Outside the museum is a statue of Francis Light, and an old Penang Hill tram. The art gallery is on the upper floor and there is a permanent display of local work. Opening hours are from 9 A.M. to 5 P.M. daily except Friday when it is closed from 12:15 to 2:45 P.M. Admission is free.

While you are at the museum, take the time to visit the adjacent **St. George's Church**. It is believed that this is the oldest Anglican church in southeast Asia. Since it was built by convict labor in 1818, very little has changed. The lovely building has a marble floor, an attractive spire, and a canopy in remembrance of Captain Light. Services in English are held on Sundays at 8:30 A.M. and 6:30 P.M.

I now suggest that you head south down Lebuh Pitt because there is much to see in this area. The narrow streets of old Georgetown bustle with activity. They are not meant for vehicular traffic and are crowded with pedestrians, trishaws, and vendors. Incense and flowers perfume the air. Shop fronts spill their spices, fruit and vegetables, cloth, and general merchandise out onto the sidewalks and roadsides, adding to the clutter and chaos.

Among all this commercialism you will find temples for all the different religions and races. As you move down Lebuh Pitt, you first come to the **Kuan Yin Temple**. This temple for the Goddess of Mercy is the oldest in Penang and it is believed it was built in 1800. Devotees burn joss sticks and offer prayers for health, wealth, longevity, and fertility. The temple is thronged with people during the birthday of the goddess, which is celebrated three times a year on the 19th day of the Chinese second, sixth, and ninth moon. Normal opening hours are from early morning to late evening. There is always something happening in the front courtyard no matter what time you visit.

The next temple is **Sri Mariamman**, which is on Lebuh Queen, parallel to Lebuh Pitt. Built in 1883, this is the oldest Hindu temple in Georgetown and indicates the strong Indian influence in this mostly Chinese city. The temple has an elaborate *gopuram* above its entrance and inside it is filled with statues of Hindu deities. Among the priceless possessions is a statue of Lord Subramaanian richly decorated with gold, silver, diamonds, and emeralds. The temple is open most of the day but permission to enter should be obtained from temple officials.

Back on Lebuh Pitt, the **Kapitan Kling Mosque** was built in the early nineteenth century by an Indian Muslim merchant. Its ochre-yellow facade and dome-shaped minaret reflect Islamic architecture of Moorish influence. Permission to enter should be sought from mosque officials.

It's just another two blocks to **Khoo Kongsi** on Lebuh Cannon. The Leong San Tong (Dragon Mountain Hall) is the most picturesque in Georgetown. The Kongsi or clan temple is a combined temple and meeting hall for members of the same Chinese clan. This is a magnificent building with intricate carvings on its walls, pillars, and roof, all created by master craftsmen from China. Take particular note of the superb beams that hold the massive roof. Opening hours are from 9 A.M. to 5 P.M. Mondays to Fridays and 9 A.M. to 1 P.M. on Saturdays. If this type of architecture interests you, there are several more clan temples (somewhat less elaborate) along Jalan Burmah.

From Khoo Kongsi it is possible to walk to the bus station near the ferry terminal, or even farther along Pengaklan Weld to the General Post Office. If you reach this far, wander down to Lebuh Pantai and admire the old government offices now used by the Survey and Immigration departments, and the beautiful old bank buildings that were built from 1889 through to just before World War II. Let us hope that the plans put forward to conserve and beautify this street are quickly put into action.

Walk to the **clock tower** at Pesara Raja Edward and you are back to your starting point. The clock tower was presented to the city by a Chinese millionaire in 1897 to commemorate the diamond jubilee of Queen Victoria. It is still a landmark in Georgetown today.

Mention must also be made of another landmark—the **KOMTAR building**. Georgetown is very proud of this building and loudly proclaims it is the tallest building in southeast Asia (65 stories). I think it is a tragedy. It is totally out of scale with the rest of the city and the complex itself is as sterile, cold, and lifeless as similar buildings in the heart of concrete jungles around the world. The rest of Georgetown is vibrant, alive, and chaotic, but always fun. Despite all the glitter and tinsel, the KOMTAR complex is just the opposite.

AROUND PENANG ISLAND

Before heading away from Georgetown, there are one or two more things to see. On a hilltop at Ayer Itam (about 10 kilometers from the center of the city), stands **Kek Lok Si Temple**, the largest Buddhist temple in Malaysia. Construction commenced in 1890 and is still underway.

The whole complex seems more like a tourist attraction than an operating temple, as you have to battle your way through arcades of shops as you climb to the temple proper. Every time I have been there, the closed-in approach has been breathlessly hot so the cold drink seller at the top is probably making a fortune. Struggle up past the turtle ponds and various halls until you reach the base of the pagoda. Now the climb seems worthwhile as there is plenty to see and the 30-meter-high tower can be climbed for the price of a small donation. Towering above everything is a huge white modern statue of the Goddess of Mercy.

You can reach Ayer Itam by public bus, Route No. 1 for government buses or any green bus. The fare is about M$0.75. From Ayer Itam it is a short bus ride to the **Penang Hill** railway station. Any Route No. 8 bus will take you there for about M$0.30.

Penang Hill rises about 820 meters above Georgetown and it provides a great viewpoint and a break from the lowland heat. Access to the top is provided by a funicular railway. The trip takes 30 minutes and involves a change of train at the halfway point. The service starts at 6:30 A.M. and runs every half-hour until about 9:30 P.M. At the top there is the Bellevue Penang Hotel, a cafe, a mosque, a Hindu temple and some nice gardens. Architecture-lovers will find a number of old, historic buildings, the most impressive being Bel Retiro, only a few minutes from the railway terminus. It commands a beautiful all-round view and, in the early days, it served as the residence of the governor. Today it is a favorite resort of high government officials.

From here we will head back towards Georgetown along Jalan Ayer Itam until we come to Jalan Utama. Turn left and head towards the Botanical Gardens. Before reaching them, it is worthwhile stopping at the **Nattukkotia Temple**, the largest Hindu temple in Penang. This is one of the most important centers of rites and ceremonies during the annual Thaipusam Festival. This is a very attractive area and the temple is interesting. You should, however, seek permission to enter from the temple officials.

The **Botanical Gardens** are a 30-hectare (75-acre) haven of peace. There are green lawns, huge rain trees, and a stream that cascades down from the hills. If you are there in the early morning or late afternoon, you will see many monkeys that come to be fed. They are tame enough to be fed by hand.

Wat Chayamangkalaram on Lorong Burmah, off Jalan Burmah, can be visited en route to the northern beaches. This Buddhist temple of Thai architectural style houses what is claimed to be the third-largest reclining Buddha in the world, measuring 33 meters. While the claim may be dubious, the temple itself is colorful and well worth a visit. It is open from early morning until late in the evening.

The road to the northern beaches starts out as Jalan Kelavis then becomes Jalan Bunjung Bungah. It is a thoroughly delightful drive with nice sea views, an occasional small cove, and green vegetation. Fortunately this part of Penang is not plagued by heavy traffic so you can enjoy the drive, or ride. From Georgetown, blue bus No. 93 is the one to take if you are hoping to go right around the island. This goes as far as Teluk Bahang and from here you catch a series of yellow buses around the west, south, and east coasts. The whole journey is about 70 kilometers but it can easily take all day with a number of stops.

It's not really until you get to Batu Feringgi that the better beaches start. This beach has a succession of large resort hotels (see "The Hotel Scene"), restaurants, shops, and even a few night spots. Most of the hotels are situated between the road and the beach so public access is somewhat restricted, but you shouldn't hesitate to enter any of the hotel properties if you would like to take a look.

The road eventually leads around to Teluk Bahang where major hotel development is only just starting. Fortunately the small fishing village remains partially undisturbed, and there are a few small local restaurants where you can grab a snack.

The round-island road now leaves the coast and heads inland. There are a couple of batik factories here where you can see the manufacturing process. Designs are stamped on to white fabric using wax and dye. The factories have large showrooms where the guide shows much more interest in you than she did in the factory. Don't expect many bargains.

About two kilometers down this road, you come to the **Butterfly Farm**. You can find about 100 species of butterflies and local insects in their natural habitat. It is said there are up to 5,000 live butterflies at any one time. The gardens feature waterfalls, ponds, bridges, a mud spring, and a rock garden. Naturally there is a souvenir shop. Opening hours are from 9 A.M. to 5 P.M. on weekdays and from 9 A.M. to

6 P.M. on weekends and public holidays. Admission charges are M$2 for adults and M$1 for children.

Close by is the **Forest Recreation Park** and **Forest Museum**. The 100-hectare reserve has countless species of flowering plants, trees, and ferns, and a good selection of birds, insects, and reptiles. There are paths and freshwater streams. The museum features timber and forest products from all over Malaysia. Opening hours are from 9 A.M. to 5 P.M. Tuesdays to Sundays except between noon and 2:45 P.M. on Fridays when it is closed. Admission is free.

The road now starts to climb and twist and the durian trees, with their accompanying nets to catch the precious fruit, appear. During the fruit season many stalls set up along this road and the traffic multiplies manifold. The Titi Kerawang waterfall is a convenient place to stop but it's difficult to get a complete view of the falls. There is some more jungle and many curves before you reach Sungei Pinang.

There are various roads heading off to the right that lead to little villages on the coast. It's worth seeing Kuala Sungei Pinang, a Chinese village built beside a mangrove swamp, if only to see how awful it is. By contrast some of the Malay villages before you reach Balik Pulau are quite picturesque.

Balik Palau is the main town on the western side of the island. It is quite attractive with many large trees and a few nice buildings. There are several good restaurants and cafes so it is a good place to have a meal break. There are several alternative roads from here but it's worth twisting and turning through the ranges to Teluk Kumbar. Again various roads lead off to the right to some of the south and west coast bays and beaches but none have facilities for visitors.

It's not too far from here to the international airport then on to the **Snake Temple**. This temple, built in 1850, was erected to the memory of a Buddhist priest who was believed to have possessed amazing healing powers. The temple is famous, however, for its many pit vipers that are coiled around the altars and other parts of the temple, in a dazed manner as if intoxicated by the burning incense. The temple is open from early morning to late evening and admission is free.

The road back to Georgetown passes through new industrial developments that show a completely different side to Penang. Off to the left is the **Equatorial Penang Hotel** with its adjacent 18-hole championship golf course, while straight ahead is the **Universiti Sains Malaysia** with its interesting museum/gallery that has items on Malay and Nyonya cultures, the performing arts, and an exhibition of paintings. To the right is the 13.5-kilometer-long Penang Bridge, which links Penang Island to mainland Malaysia.

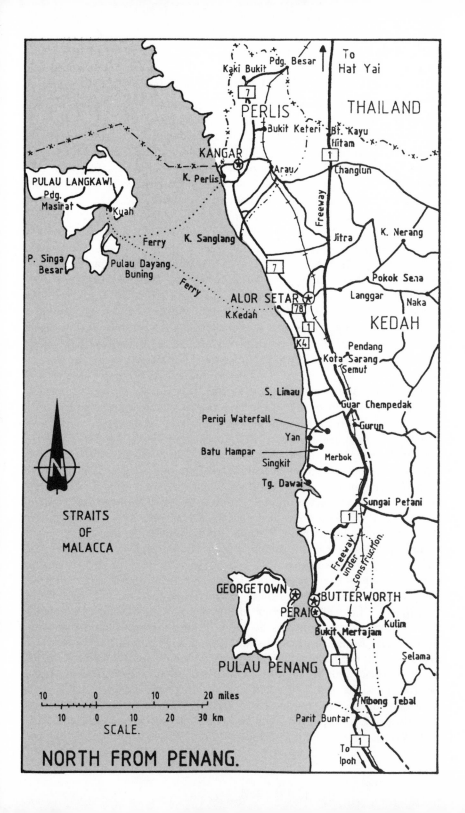

NORTH FROM PENANG.

NORTH FROM PENANG

The Penang Bridge takes you to **Butterworth**, a nondescript sort of place that probably has little interest to visitors. The ferry terminal, railway station, and bus station form a large complex just to the south of the main commercial area. There are several midrange hotels and some restaurants. The 50-room **Travelodge** (Tel: 348-899) and the **Hotel Berlin** are probably the best hotels, while the very basic **Capital Hotel** (Tel: 344-822) has 10 rooms from around M$12.

Highway 1 heads north and eventually reaches the Thai border. On the way it passes through the mainland part of the state of Penang then through Kedah and Perlis. Kedah has a population of about one million people and is known as the rice bowl of Malaysia. You don't have to travel far along the road to see why. Green, swaying rice paddies stretch in all directions. Women, with their heads under conical straw hats, transplant seedlings, while water buffalo wallow contentedly in the mud. The old Route 1 is heavily trafficked and is very slow. There also seems to be slow progress on the construction of the new freeway, which will eventually link the Thai border with the Johor Straits.

The first major town is **Sungei Petani**. It is worth stopping to have a quick look around and to see the modern electronic manufacturing plants that have appeared recently, but the major interest is in the **Lembah Bujang** area to the west. This is regarded as Malaysia's richest archaeological area and findings indicate that it is one of the earliest centers of civilized settlement and development on the Malay peninsula. The ruins, such as Candi Batu Pahat, believed to have been built in the seventh century A.D., are mainly remains of temples and statues of Indian gods. Some have been partially restored. The Bujang Valley Archaeological Museum in **Merbok** houses numerous items.

The best way to see all this is to turn off the highway and head for Merbok, then continue to the coast, visit the nice beach at Pantai Merdeka where there are some chalets to rent at about M$25 a night (Tel: 04-411-963), then continue north along the coast to **Yan**. Batu Hampar is a favorite picnic spot in this region with its built-in waterfall and swimming opportunities. So too is Sungai Perigi, which drops over 100 meters. Both are worth a short stop. Each is about five kilometers from town at the base of **Gunong Jerai**, a massive limestone outcrop, at 1200 meters, Kedah's highest peak. Perched on top are seven two-bedroom chalets and a 12-room unit, making this the latest hill resort in Malaysia. The 12 rooms are rented out at M$50 per room for a maximum of four people. The two-room chalets are M$90 each and are equipped with cooking facilities. The 11-kilometer drive to the top

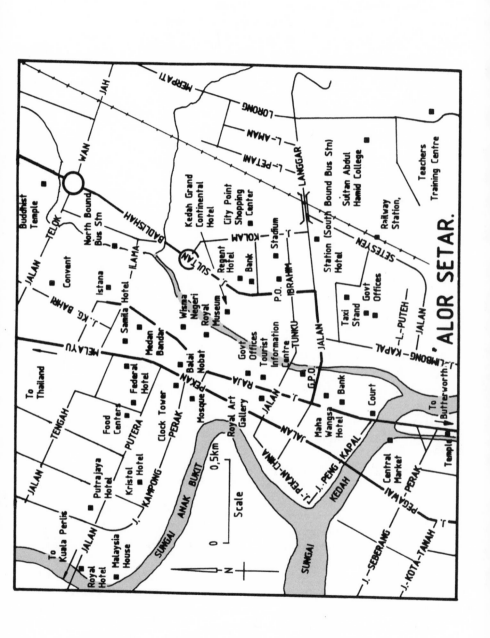

ALOR SETAR.

is very pleasant. If you are not driving you can take the hill resort's regular van service at M\$5 for a return trip. There is a restaurant and cafeteria at the peak. Book accommodations at Tel: 04-413-411. The Sugnai Teroi Forest Recreation Park, halfway up the hill, has a museum of forestry, jungle paths, waterfalls, and camping areas.

Alor Setar is the capital of Kedah. The city has several worthwhile buildings, many are around the *Padang*, or town square. The Balai Besar is an impressive wooden hall built in 1898 with noticeable Thai architectural influences. It is still used frequently for royal and state occasions. Across the square is the Masjid Zahir (mosque), which was completed in 1912 and is one of the largest in Malaysia. Nearby is the strange octagonal Balai Nobat, which houses the instruments of the Royal Orchestra. The instruments are revered and covered in yellow (royal) cloth when not in use.

The Balai Seri Negri (open daily) is the state art gallery, which has a collection of paintings, antiques, and historic relics. Best shopping is found at the Pekan Rabu, an open-air bazaar near the center of town. It operates daily until midnight. Some of the special products to look out for are the items made from bull horn. They include knife handles, ornaments, necklaces, and earrings. For more conventional shopping you could try the Hankya Jaya department store in Jalan Langgar, or Citypoint in the MPKS Complex. Arts and crafts goods are found in Pretty Homes Decor and Gifts in Jalan Kota. On the road north from the city, the very attractive State Museum has some interesting material including artifacts from the Bujang Valley. Next door is the royal boathouse.

If you plan to stay in Alor Setar, you have several options. The largest and most expensive hotel is the **Kedah Grand Continental** (Tel: 735-917), 130 rooms from M\$130 a night. A bit down-market from this is the **Kristol Hotel** on Jalan Kampong Perak. A good midmarket hotel is the **Samila** (Tel: 722-344), 52 rooms, over near the Padang. It has a popular disco lounge that is worth a visit. Room rates start at about M\$70. Budget air-conditioned rooms are available at the **Hotel Regent** (Tel: 711-291) opposite the Kedah Grand Continental from M\$38. There is also a government rest house with rooms from M\$30 (Tel: 722-422).

There are also some reasonable restaurants, coffee shops, and hawkers' centers along Jalan Putera, Jalan Tunku Ibrahim, and Jalan Langgar. You could try Sri Pumpong on Jalan Pumpong for a delicious meal of barbecue fish cooked over a charcoal fire, served with *air assam*. Restoran Bunga Tanjong on Jalan Seberang Perak is a good place for Indian Muslim fare, while Cafe de Siam on Jalan Kota has some

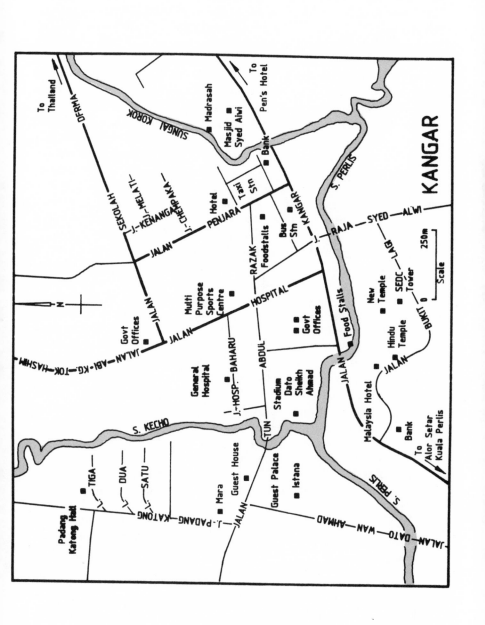

brilliant Thai food as well as some Chinese dishes. The Garden on Jalan Stadium is a glutton's-square-type area set amid lush greenery. It's cheap, it's friendly, and it's recommended.

There is an information center and a general post office, both on Jalan Raja. You can reach Alor Setar from Butterworth by train, bus, or taxi. It's then easy to reach the Thai border at either Changlun Bukit Kayu Hitam for the usual road crossing, or at Padang Besar in Perlis where the railway crosses into Thailand.

Immediately west of Alor Setar is the fishing village of **Kuala Kedah**, one of the departure points for Langkawi island. The trip from Kuala Kedah takes 80 minutes and the fare is M$30. The ferry is of reasonable standard but there are only six trips a day and the published timetable is loosely followed. The terminal at Kuala Kedah was a disgrace the last time I saw it. The facilities are poor, dusty, and dirty, and the surrounding area is a shambles. It makes a very poor impression with most international visitors.

The better approach to Langkawi is from Kuala Perlis in the state of Perlis. You reach it on Highway 7 from Alor Setar. Perlis is the smallest state of Malaysia and it has had a checkered history. It was once part of the Sultanate of Kadah but was occupied in 1821 by the Thais. Following the Anglo-Siamese treaty it came under British rule, then during Japanese occupation during World War II it was handed back to Thailand. In 1945 Perlis again came under British control and it became part of Malaya when it achieved independence in 1957.

Kangar is the capital of Perlis and the only city of any size, but it has little interest to foreign visitors. The city must receive some visitors, however, because the midmarket **Pens Hotel** (Tel: 760-487), 50 rooms, will open an up-market 150-room wing late 1993. Current room rates start at M$100. (Book on Fax: 604-760-472.) The **Sri Perlis Inn** (Tel: 767-266) is a reasonable alternative. Room prices here start at about M$65. The **Malaysia Hotel** (Tel: 761-366) has rooms from M$38, while the **Ban Cheong Hotel** (Tel: 761-184) has budget accommodations from M$22. Malay food is available at food stalls near the GPO, Chinese food at **Soo Guan (Tel: 766-288), Western food at the Sri Perlis Bakery** (Tel: 763-518), and Thai food at **Ramlah Restaurant** (Tel: 762-952).

In some ways the royal town of **Arau**, 10 kilometers south, is more interesting. This is a simple, well-planned town with a Royal Palace, a Royal Mosque, and the Royal Mausoleum interspersed between quaint-looking houses and clusters of fruit trees and coconut palms. There are no accommodations.

Padang Besar is the border town where Perlis merges with Thailand.

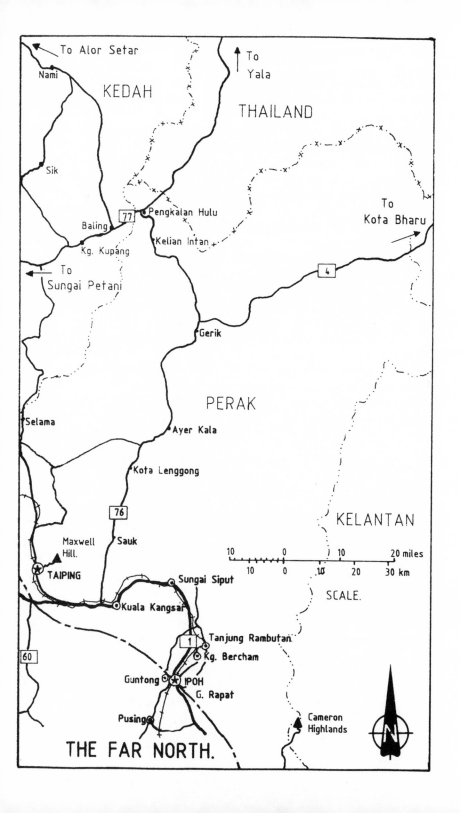

THE FAR NORTH.

The elongated railway station is partly manned by Thai immigration and customs officers while the other half is manned by their Malaysian counterparts. Padang Besar has a duty-free shop and the adjacent Thai town, called Pekan Siam, has textiles, clothes, footwear, handicrafts, and souvenirs much prized by many Malaysians.

Kuala Perlis is at the mouth of the Sungai Perlis, 14 kilometers from Kangar. About 10,000 people live in this muddled but quaintly attractive town where fishing is the main industry but where tourism is rapidly growing. Kuala Perlis has only one hotel worth mentioning, the **Pens Hotel** (Tel: 754-122), 30 rooms, from M$70, a bank, some shops, and a growing number of restaurants. *Laksa*, noodles in a spicy fish soup, is very popular and available everywhere. Taxis and buses link Kuala Perlis with Kangar, Alor Setar, Butterworth, and Padang Besar.

Ferry boats and hydrofoils provide scheduled crossings between Kuala Perlis and Langkawi island. Fares vary from M$10-15 one way and the fast services only take about 45 minutes. Ferry times change depending on demand so it would be wise to contact one of the operators before you arrive in Kuala Perlis. I suggest either **Kuala Perlis-Langkawi Ferry Service** (Tel: 754-491) or **Water Tour Development Company** (Tel: 755-255) as two good alternatives.

LANGKAWI ISLAND

To many in the Malaysian tourist industry, Langkawi is the jewel in the crown. The island is being heavily promoted and the government has spent large amounts to improve the infrastructure and to add appeal to the place. I am in two minds about the result.

The Langkawi islands (there are 104 of them) are beautiful. There are some lovely beaches; the water in many parts is clean and clear; there are waterfalls, jungle-clad mountains, and wonderful legends to hear about. On the other hand I have reservations about some of the things that are happening on the island. Kuah town is being heavily promoted as a duty-free shopping center and there is a great deal of new development taking place. The early buildings were little better than tin sheds but now some substantial concrete structures are appearing. There is plenty of traffic, dust, and activity. It is certainly not my idea of a tropical village. Likewise some of the beaches run the risk of being overwhelmed by cheap "chalets" that have little sanitation and certainly contribute nothing to the local environment.

Langkawi should be one of those getaway places where you can enjoy the beauty and serenity of nature in all its splendor, yet have good facilities for the full enjoyment of the vacation experience. That is not a

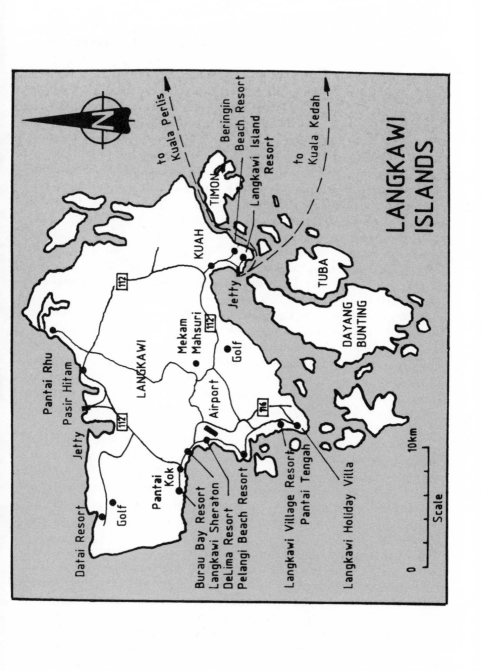

LANGKAWI
ISLANDS

wishful romantic notion impossible to achieve. Some places do it successfully. In my mind Langkawi, with a few exceptions, does not. But that's not to say you shouldn't go to Langkawi. Many people like it. Some love it.

The main island jetty is about 1½ kilometers from **Kuah**, a town of about 2,500 people. The town stretches along the shallow bay and the only real "sight" is the waterside mosque. The Golden Dragon Restaurant, hidden away two streets back from the main road, has good Chinese food at reasonable prices. The big new Hajjah Restaurant on the main road serves seafood and Thai food, while the Orkid Restaurant in the center of town is a good place for seafood in an outdoor setting. The Top Ten Disco is the place for some late action. Unless you are doing business in Kuah or are a shopping freak, this would not be the best place to stay. If you arrive late in the afternoon and are low on cash, you may have no other alternative. In town the accommodations choice lies between the **Region Hotel** (Tel: 04-927-719), 75 rooms, from M$70; the Hotel Langkasuka (above a big, duty-free store); the **Asia Hotel** (Tel: 04-916-216), 15 rooms, from M$35; or the nearby **Langkawi Hotel** (Tel: 04-916-248), 13 rooms, from M$30.

Back past the jetty, the **Langkawi Island Resort** (Tel: 04-916-209) has struggled for several years to survive. The up-market hotel was built well before there were enough well-heeled tourists to fill its rooms, so although it occupies a nice waterfront location and has good facilities, it still struggles to throw off its "white-elephant" tag. Visitors who know little of this situation will enjoy it here. The Mahsuri Terrace, which overlooks the ocean and pool, has good local food and a range of international favorites; the air-conditioned Ports of Call serves Chinese cuisine; and the Eagles Nest cocktail lounge is just the spot for a drink, a chat, and some smooth music. Room rates start at around M$160. (Book with the hotel at Pulau Langkawi, 0700 Kedah; Fax: 604-916-414.) You could also consider the nearby **Benringin Beach Resort** (Tel: 04-916-572). Accommodation here is in chalets. It is not luxurious, but the location and price is attractive. Rooms are from M$85.

You can explore Langkawi by bus, taxi, rental car, jeep, motorcycle, or bicycle. The choice will depend on your time and fitness level. The main interest lies in the beaches and the small *kampongs*, but there are a few other sights. The Durian Perangin Waterfall gets a good amount of publicity but it is only spectacular during and immediately after the monsoon season, and of course this is when Langkawi receives its least number of tourists. The falls are a two-kilometer walk from the Kuah-Tanjong Rhu road at about the 14-kilometer mark. A bit farther along this same road you come to the Telaga Air Panas (hot springs) and the modern Air Hangat handicraft/souvenir village.

Past here, there is a road to the right that leads to Pantai Rhu (Casuarina Beach). This was once considered to be one of Langkawi's best beaches but fashions change. The beach is lined by tall trees and the water is shallow. This is the site of another struggling resort—the **Mutiara Beach Resort** (Tel: 04-916-488), 68 rooms, from M$100—and the adjacent **Mutiara Court** serviced apartments (Tel: 04-917-091), 134 units from M$330. As tourism grows, this may develop with it, but it will be a struggle.

Back on the main road, Pasir Hitam is noted for its so-called black sand but I don't think most visitors will be too impressed. It's a long drive from here to Telaga Tujuh Waterfall but it is worth it. These falls are the most popular on the island and are quite lovely. Water cascades 90 meters down the mountain through a series of seven pools. It's a good place for a swim and a picnic. On the way you will have passed the turnoff to Datai Bay. This isolated area is being developed into a luxury resort complex. There is already a top-quality 18-hole golf course and clubhouse (M$100 a round) and a super-luxury 120-room resort is set to open at the end of 1993. Other planned facilities include a 250-room five-star hotel, a beach club, and golf villas. It's worth a look (further information from Tel: 04-911-600 or Fax: 04-911-216). You will also see Temurun Waterfall, which crosses the road, and nearby Pasir Tengkorak Beach.

Pantai Koh is the first popular beach you come to. There is a collection of midmarket and budget resorts including the **Burau Bay Resort** (Tel: 04-911-061) with nice facilities and room prices from M$200; the **Resort Southern Cross** (Tel: 04-911-352); the **Last Resort** (Tel: 04-911-046); the **Coral Beach Resort** (Tel: 04-911-000); the **Country Beach Motel** (Tel: 04-911-212); the Kok Beach Motel (Tel: 04-911-048); and others. Typical prices for this group are M$30 fan-room, M$50 for air conditioning. At the far end of Pantai Koh is the **Sheraton Langkwai Resort** (Tel: 04-911-901), 220 rooms, which sprawls over a rocky headland between two beaches. This aims to be the best resort on the island and it has the potential to do that. It didn't fully open until mid-1993, so it's still a little soon to judge its success. It's a farther few kilometers to the huge **De Lima Resort** (Tel: 04-911-801), 1500 rooms. Rooms here start at M$100 and there are swimming pools, restaurants, and a shopping mall.

Close by is the modern airport. Flights arrive in from Kuala Lumpur, Penang, and Singapore. South of here on **Pantai Cenang** lies the future for Langkawi tourism. The two-kilometer-long beach is very attractive but the **Pelangi Beach Resort** (Tel: 04-911001), 300 rooms, is the *pièce-de-résistance*.

The imposing open-ended foyer leads to an enormous pool complete with swim-up bar and acres of village-style accommodations linked by a network of paved and colorfully landscaped walkways. The standard rooms have all the five-star facilities you would expect, including a price tag of about M$300, while there are marina club rooms that include complimentary breakfasts and evening cocktails at around M$400, and suites that go up from there. There are sporting facilities to make the most active guest exhausted, and excellent food and drink outlets for those of us who prefer to laze.

Pantai Cenang offers a number of accommodations choices—in fact, this stretch is becoming so popular that on weekends it can almost feel crowded. The **Samarak Langkawi Resort** (Tel: 04-911-377), 28 rooms from M$65, has some well-designed chalets that are a good value, while the nearby **Sandy Beach Motel** has 20 chalets from M$45, a popular restaurant, and friendly owners. Farther south, the **AB Motel**, 26 chalets from M$30, and the **Delta Motel**, 10 chalets from M$18, are probably the best value. Farther south still, around a rocky promontory, lies Pantai Tengah. This is rapidly developing and the beach and surroundings have similarities to Panai Cenang. The best accommodation here is at the **Langkawi Holiday Villa Beach Resort** (Tel: 04-911-701), 258 rooms, with its pools, tennis courts, squash courts, and other facilities. I don't rank it in the same class as the Sheraton or Pelangi Beach Resort, however. Room prices start at M$200. A cheaper alternative is the nearby **Langkawi Village Resort** (Tel: 04-911-511), 99 rooms, from M$135. The cheap accommodation that was once along this beach is rapidly disappearing.

You have to retrace your track to the airport, then turn right to head back to Kuah. On the way it's worth stopping at Kampung Tembikav, the pottery village where you can participate in pottery-making. Then you pass Mahsuri's Tomb, the resting place of a Malay princess who, according to legend, was unjustly accused of adultery, and proved her innocence when white blood streamed from her body at her execution. Nearby you pass the 18-hole Langkawi Golf Course, with its happy combination of challenging and easy holes, for vacationers to enjoy. Green fees are a low M$10 for nine holes.

The other 103 islands have limited interest for visitors except for their isolated beaches and sometime dramatic cliffs. They are interesting from the water and, when the seas are smooth, a yacht cruise in these waters reveals some delightful landscape that should not be missed. If time permits, a trip to Tasek Dayang Bunting, a freshwater lake on an adjacent island, is worth the effort. The nearby Langsir cave is probably not.

SOUTH FROM PENANG

If you cross the bridge from Penang to Butterworth, then turn right, you are on Highway 1 heading south towards Kuala Lumpur. You soon pass into the state of Perak, which contains the richest tin deposits in the world. The state has a population of more than two million. Its capital is Ipoh, an attractive city of wide streets and busy commerce, while Taiping and Kuala Kangsar are two other centers with considerable interest.

Perak has at least two other attractions for international visitors—Maxwell Hill resort (now renamed Bukit Larut) near Taiping, and the island of Pangkor off the coast from Lumut.

As you head south, **Taiping** is the first point of major interest. It is about 80 kilometers from Penang. This is the old capital of Perak and the oldest tin-mining area in the country. It is a lovely low-key town that I thoroughly enjoy and the Malaysians must agree because this is a favorite retirement center. It has the added bonus that there are very few tourists. Taiping central city has some attraction particularly in its older sections but a kilometer or so from the central city there is great appeal. I had been told that the city was renowned for its Lake Garden but I was unprepared for what a delightful spot this is. It is an ideal picnic spot and a great place for a leisurely walk. There are a number of lakes that were once tin-mining excavations, a floating restaurant, water recreation facilities, amazing drooping trees, extensive lawns, a zoo, and a 9-hole golf course. There are public roads through the park that take you to all the points of interest. Don't miss it.

The Taiping State Museum is close to the gardens and is well worth a visit. Built in 1883, it is the oldest museum in the country and its unusual architecture is a further attraction. There are collections of ancient weapons, aboriginal implements, and archaeological treasures. It is open from 9:30 A.M. to 5 P.M. daily. Back towards town, the Pandang is a delightful area that could almost be part of England.

Taiping has two good hotels—the **Meridien** (Tel: 831-133), 88 rooms, and the **Panorama** (Tel: 834-192), 70 rooms. Both have rooms from about M$80. Midmarket rooms are provided in the **Oriental Hotel** (Tel: 825-322) in the central city, or at the new **Rest House** (Tel: 822-571) overlooking the Lake Garden. Rooms here start at about M$40. Budget rooms from about M$28 are available at the **Lake View Hotel** (Tel: 824-941), the **Old Rest House** (Tel: 822-571), and several

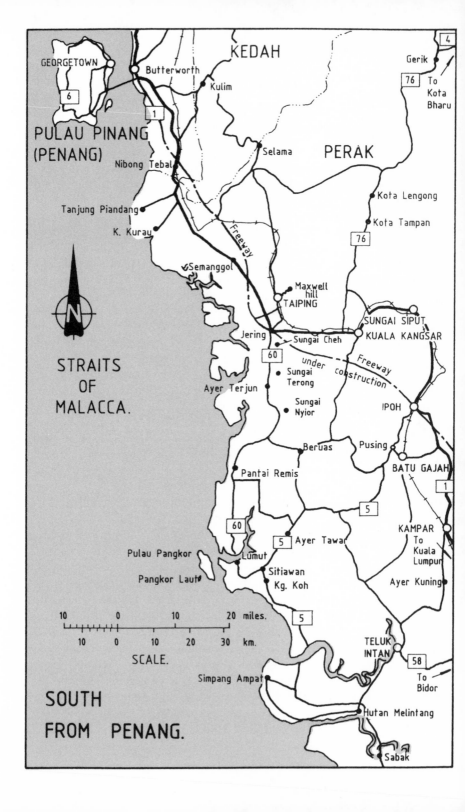

Chinese hotels in the central city. The cheapest rooms I could find were at the **Peace Hotel** (Tel: 823-379) for M$15.

The area surrounding Taiping is very attractive and if you have time it is worth doing a bit of exploring. If you head south you can find several waterfalls. The most spectacular is Sungai Nyior Waterfall, a majestic fall of about 120 meters. This is about 30 kilometers from Taiping near Terong. Also near here is the Sungai Terong Falls where rock terraces produce a broad attractive fall that is bound to impress. The third fall worth seeing is the small and serene Sungai Cheh Waterfall, 20 kilometers from Taiping.

Maxwell Hill (*Bukit Larut*), the oldest hill station in Malaysia, is 12 kilometers from Taiping at an elevation of about 1000 meters. This was originally a tea estate but it is now a delightful, quiet, cool getaway. You don't go to Maxwell Hill for excitement, you go to relax in the clean air and to do some walking.

Access to the resort is by government Land Rovers that run an hourly service from the bottom station near Lake Garden every hour from 8 A.M. to 6 P.M. The road is narrow and extremely winding so traffic is strictly one-way. The up and down vehicles meet at the midway point of the 40-minute trip. The trip costs about M$3.50 each way.

Accommodations on the hill are in two rest houses and several bungalows. The rest houses (**Maxwell** and **Speedy**) provide meals, while at the bungalows you can either make arrangements with the caretaker, or cook your own food. My choice would be to stay at Maxwell guesthouse because I think it is in a better location than Speedy. A room in either will cost about M$25. Most people will find that one or two nights are sufficient. Reservations can be made by telephoning 05-886-241.

Back at Taiping, you should now follow Highway 1 to the royal town of **Kuala Kangsar**. The center of this small town is quite attractive, but you need to cross the small bridge and follow the river downstream for a few kilometers to find the major points of interest. You first come to Ubudiah Mosque, one of the most beautiful religious buildings in Malaysia. A few kilometers farther you can drive right around the imposing Iskandariah Palace, but it is not open to the public.

Perhaps even more impressive than either of these two edifices is the amazing Royal Museum at the end of this road. The building was constructed in 1931 as a temporary residence for the late Sultan. It is preserved for its fine craftsmanship and because it was built without any architectural plans and without a single nail. Today it houses many royal exhibits and is open from 9 A.M. to 6 P.M. daily.

The Ubudiah Mosque, Kuala Kangsar. (Courtesy of the Malaysia Tourism Promotion Board)

Old palace at Kuala Kangsar. Now a museum. (Courtesy of the Malaysia Tourism Promotion Board)

Kuala Kangsar was home to Malaysia's rubber industry. The British administrator, Hugh Low, planted the nine trees that had been brought from Kew Gardens in London. After the invention of the pneumatic tire in the late 1880s, rubber plantations spread to many parts of Malaysia. One of the original trees still stands today in the grounds of the district office near the town center.

The best accommodations in Kuala Kangsar are at the **Rest House** (Tel: 852-811) overlooking the river on the road towards the Ubudiah Mosque. Rooms are about M$25. There are two hotels in town with very basic rooms—the **Tin Heong Hotel** (Tel: 862-066) M$18, and the **Double Lion Hotel** (Tel: 862-020) M$12.

From Kuala Kangsar, it is about 40 kilometers to Ipoh. Six kilometers before the city you will find the Perak Tong temple within the huge limestone caves of Gunung Tasek. This was built in 1926 by a Buddhist priest from China and today it houses more than 40 Buddha statues including one 12.8 meters high. A little way closer to town you will see the Thai Temple with a 24-meter-long reclining Buddha.

In **Ipoh city**, most visitor interest lies in the old town area west of the Kinta River. Here there are some very attractive buildings such as the railway station, town hall, St. Michael's School, and so on. The Padang is also appealing with its adjoining Ipoh Club, a reminder of years past. There is a large tourist information center near the clock tower but be careful because it closes for some long lunches.

Ipoh is a large city by Malaysian standards so shopping is better here than in most smaller places. You could visit complexes like Super Kinta, Yik Foong, and Perak Emporium, which are all in the same vicinity, or go to others along Jalan Sultan Idris and Jalan Laksamana. All these places open from 10 A.M. till 10 P.M.

Ipoh has the best accommodations and restaurants in northern Malaysia, outside Penang. Top of the range is the **Casuarina** (Tel: 505-555), a 200-room resort hotel on the Kuala Lumpur road near the racetrack. It has a large swimming pool, a shopping arcade, a health club, a business center, several restaurants, and a disco operated by Juliana's. Room rates are from about M$230.

Also top of the range is the **Excelsior Hotel** (Tel: 536-666), a 133-room central city hotel with rooms priced from M$190. Somewhat cheaper is the **Tambun Inn** (Tel: 552-211), 100 rooms with prices from M$90; the **Station Hotel** (Tel: 512-588) with 34 rooms from M$80; and the **French Hotel** (Tel: 513-455) with 40 rooms from M$75.

In the budget range, the **Winner Hotel** (Tel: 515-177) has rooms from M$35, while the **Hollywood Hotel** (Tel: 515-322) and the **Embassy** (Tel: 549-496) both have rooms for under M$30. The **YMCA** (Tel:

540-809) has dormitory beds from around M$10 and rooms from M$30. The **Rex Hotel** (Tel: 540-093) has the cheapest rooms in town from M$10.

Ipoh has many good restaurants. For Malay food there is **Serneranjung Restaurant** in Jalan Sultan Idris Shah. For Chinese food try **Restoran Kawan**, or **Restoran Kok Kee**, both in the same street, or **Restoran Szechuan** in Jalan Fair Park. For Indian food I recommend the well-known **Restoran Pakeeza** at 15 Persiaran Green or the **No. 1 Restaurant** in Clark Street.

Top Thai food is found at **Restoran Chao Phraya** (Tel: 542-871) at 2 Jalan Green while vegetarian lovers should head for **Restoran Krishna Bawan** (Tel: 544-457) on Jalan Lahat, or the **Ipoh Vegetarian Food Center** (Tel: 544-223) at 75 Clare Street. The **Rainbow Disco and Night Club** (Tel: 508-960) is an after-hours spot that is very popular with locals and visitors. There are some food stalls near the railway station that are worth trying for a cheap snack or meal. Similar places are in front of Stadium Perak, and behind Ipoh Garden Plaza. **Restoran Foh San** in Jalan Osbourne is the most popular place for breakfast in town.

If you need more sight-seeing you could visit the **Geological Museum** on Jalan Harimar. More than 600 specimens of minerals are on display together with fossils, precious stones, and rock specimens. Hours are from 8 A.M. to 4:15 P.M. weekdays, except it closes from noon to 3:00 P.M. on Friday. Admission is free.

The **Japanese Garden** on Jalan Tambun near the Perak Turf Club is a public park that recreates the aesthetics of a Japanese garden. It opens 4-8 P.M. weekdays and 9 A.M.-8 P.M. weekends. If you travel for a further 10 minutes along this road, you come to the **Tambun Hotel Springs** (Tel: 554-407) a natural spa located at the foot of a limestone hill. There are restrooms, hot swimming pools, saunas, a restaurant, and a lounge. It is open from 3 P.M. to midnight and admission is M$5.

About 30 minutes south of Ipoh, near Batu Gajah, stand the ruins of **Kellie's Castle**. This enormous, mysterious building is a reflection of the prosperity, romanticism, and good life of an older time. The mansion was to have been the second home of William Kellie Smith, a Scottish millionaire who made his fortune from rubber. In 1926, while construction was still in progress, Smith left for England and fell ill and died in Lisbon. His family never returned and the castle was never completed. The castle is a little hard to find, but it's not far from the Ipoh-Lumut road and is well worth the search.

Lumut is a small town 100 kilometers southwest of Ipoh and 200 kilometers from Butterworth. It is a major base for the Malaysian navy but it is important for visitors as a gateway to Pangkor Island. Lumut itself has nothing special going for it but it is far more attractive than many Malaysian waterfront towns. There are some reasonable shops, several restaurants, small parks, a clock tower, two hotel reception areas, and several parking lots for people visiting Pangkor.

The Wa Rong Pak Din restaurant is good and very popular, while if you need to stay overnight the **Lumit Country Resort** (Tel: 935-109) on the waterfront about a kilometer from the ferry terminal has nice rooms and other facilities. Rooms are about M$130. The **Lumit Hotel** is on the waterfront nearer town, with rooms from M$25. Cheaper still is the **Rest House** (Tel: 935-938) at about M$18, and the old, but clean and friendly **Phi Lu Hooi Hotel** (Tel: 935-641) with 10 rooms from M$15.

You can reach Lumut by bus from Ipoh for about M$4 (hourly service) and there are also services from Kuala Lumpur and Butterworth. Long-distance taxis are also usually available on these routes at prices about twice the bus fare. From Lumut you take a ferry to Pangkor. There are regular public ferries that go to the east coast villages of Sungai Pinang Kecil and Pangkor. If you decide to stay on the two luxury resorts, special ferries service these locations.

Lumut is popular for its corals and sea shells that are made into flowers, ships, birds, and other forms. Look around while you are waiting for the ferry and you may pick up a bargain.

PANGKOR ISLAND

Pangkor is an island I enjoy, but parts of it are suffering from overuse and underplanning. You basically have two options—go to one of the luxury resorts and pay high prices to escape the local problems, or mix it with the locals and take the good with the bad.

It you go with the locals, the good is that Pangkor has a string of interesting villages, bicycles to rent, and a choice of midmarket to ultra budget accommodation. The bad is that Pangkor can get very crowded, particularly during school vacations and public holidays, and litter has become a big problem in the villages, along the island road, and on the beaches. This island is naturally a very attractive place but man has added very little to its appeal.

If your budget doesn't stretch to the resorts, head for Pangkor Village. There are shops and restaurants here but I suggest you look for accommodations at Pasir Bogak, three kilometers away on the other side of the island. A taxi will cost you about M$5, you can wait for the

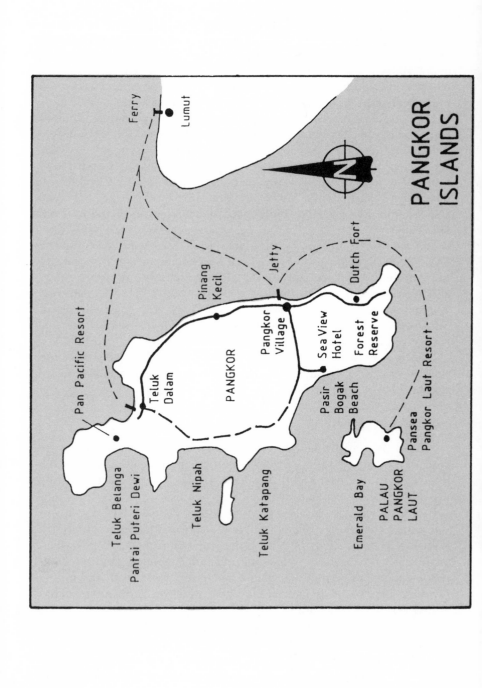

PANGKOR
ISLANDS

Ferry

Lumut

N

Pan Pacific Resort

Pinang
Kecil

Jetty

Dutch Fort

Teluk Belanga
Pantai Puteri Dewi

Teluk Dalam

PANGKOR

Pangkor
Village

Sea View
Hotel

Forest
Reserve

Teluk Nipah

Teluk Katapang

Pasir
Bogak
Beach

Emerald Bay

PALAU
PANGKOR
LAUT

Pansea
Pangkor Laut Resort

island bus, or you can walk it in about 30 minutes. Pasir Bogak is good for swimming most of the year but it would be so much better with more control on buildings and litter.

The best accommodations here are at the **Sri Baya Beach Resort** (Tel: 951-929), 55 rooms and villas, with swimming pools, Thai restaurant, coffee house, and bar, and the **Sea View Hotel** (Tel: 951-605) at the south end of the beach. You can rent an air-conditioned room or a chalet from around M$95. There are restaurant, bar, and sporting facilities and a ferry service to small Pangkor Laut island. Two bonuses are the nice seaside garden and the friendly staff. North from here is the **Beach Huts Hotel** (Tel: 951-159) with rooms and chalets in the M$50-M$120 range. This also has restaurant and bar facilities.

From here, the standard of accommodations falls away. There is the poorly run government **Rest House** (Tel: 951-236), which has cheap but depressing accommodations from about M$16 for a bed to about M$30 for a chalet. A much better value is the **Pangkor Anchor** (Tel: 951-878), which is neat, clean, and well managed. There are mainly young guests here but the rules are sufficiently strict to guarantee privacy and peace while flexible enough to encourage people to mix and meet. Breakfasts are served while other meals can be taken in nearby restaurants or stalls. A mattress costs about M$9 per night; a private hut about M$30. The **Mini Camp** (Tel: 951-164) has many small A-frame huts that provide basic shelter at a very low price.

You will find several seafood restaurants at Pasir Bogak and there are good Chinese restaurants in all the villages on the east coast. Pankor Village has several Indian restaurants as well.

Apart from the village and beaches, the only other places of interest are at the south end of the island. In the village of Teluk Gedung you can see the ruins of a Dutch fort built by the Dutch East India Company more than 300 years ago. It was built to store tin ore and gold that was extracted on the mainland. It underwent a series of attacks from pirates and local Malays and was finally abandoned about 1750. Restoration work was undertaken in 1973.

The other Pangkor option is to stay at one of the luxury resorts. The choice is the Pan Pacific Resort on the main island or the Pansea Resort on Pankor Laut. Both resorts offer excellent accommodations, good sporting facilities, lovely clean beaches, and isolation from the resident population of the island. They are both designed as self-contained capsules needing only the beach and the jungle to add appeal.

The **Pan Pacific Resort** (Tel: 951-091) is a delight. It sprawls along beautiful Golden Sands Beach while preserving much of the natural landscape. Some rooms overlook the large pool with its island bar, then past that to the beach and the clear emerald-green water. When you make reservations, ask for one of these rooms.

There are tennis courts, a 9-hole golf course, hiking trails, jogging paths, and aqua-sports facilities such as windsurfing, hobbie-cats, and fishing, but the atmosphere is one of warmth and tranquility rather than frantic action. Many people come just to lie around the pool, take a quiet walk along the beach, and enjoy the selection of bars and restaurants. Who said there was anything wrong with that? Room rates start at M$280.

Most guests at the resort stay about three days, so the temptation is to relax at the resort rather than see some more of the island. If, however, exploring is your thing, taxis are available to take you the six or so kilometers to the villages on the east coast. Despite the relatively high cost, you should do this to see the "other" Pankor. (Book with the Pan Pacific Group or contact the hotel direct at Teluk Belanga, Pulau Pangkor, 32300 Perak; Fax: 605-951-852.)

The **Pansea Resort** (Tel: 951-395) is on a small island southwest of Pulau Pangkor called Pangkor Laut. It is reached by ferry from Lumut on the mainland or from Pangkor Island. The 94 cottages with thatched roofs, a swimming pool, a sports complex, bars, and restaurants form a complex that is comfortable but not too pretentious.

The calm waters of the beach are ideal for sailing, swimming, or windsurfing, while picturesque Emerald Bay about 20 minutes away has clear blue-green waters, clean sand, and superb jungle. Room rates are from about M$150. (Book with the hotel through its Kuala Lumpur office at 55 Jalan Bukit Bintank, 55100 Kuala Lumpur; Fax: 603-241-2703.)

7. Guided Tours

There are four main tours offered by tour operators in Penang. All have a duration of about four hours and you need to take all of them if you want to get a good picture of Penang.

The **City Tour** visits the tranquil Botanical Gardens, the reclining Buddha at Wat Chayamangkalaram, the Kapitan Kling Mosque, the waterfront, the Penang Museum, and picturesque Khoo Kongsi.

The **Hill and Temple Tour** includes a visit to the Kek Lok Si Temple with its magnificent Pagoda of Ten Thousand Buddhas, and a train ride up Penang Hill.

The **Round Island Tour** covers Batu Feringgi and its fishing villages, a *batik* factory, Balik Pulaur, the Snake Temple, and Fort Cornwallis.

The **Night Tour** includes a dinner, a visit to the *pasar malam* (night market), and a trishaw ride.

The information desk at your hotel will have details of these tours or you can telephone **Newsia Tours and Travel** (Tel: 610-551), or **Cosmos Tours** (Tel: 361-131). You can also do the same tours by private limousine (Tel: 372-942). You will see sidewalk notices outside travel agents, money changers, and other places advertising local tours. Tours seem to be fairly well controlled so I think you will be safe and get reasonable treatment on any of them.

There are day and extended tours from Penang to Langkawi. The Kuala Perlis-Langkawi Ferry Service has a day trip (7:30 A.M. to 8:30 P.M.) that includes a four-hour tour of Langkawi at M$99 per person. Telephone 625-630 for details. Langkawi Holidays has a two-day package from M$140 twin share and a three-day package from M$172 twin share.

8. Culture

Visitors to Penang will find that the easygoing life-style makes people friendly and easy to speak to. Thus, you are more likely to come into contact with local customs and practices here than you are in some other areas of the country. This is an extra attraction for most visitors but it also means that you should be aware of local customs and what is acceptable behavior from a foreigner.

The other thing to remember is that Malaysia is a multiracial society, so what is acceptable by one group may not be acceptable by others. This can be quite bewildering to a visitor but fortunately Malaysians realize that foreigners are not aware of all their customs and are prepared to make allowances.

With all the communities, if you shake hands when saying hello or good-bye, don't use a finger-crunching handshake or vigorously pump the arm. Shake hands with a quick, slight pressure and do this with both men and women. You should be aware that few older Malays or Indians shake hands with members of the opposite sex in their own community, but they will usually do so with a foreigner.

When entering a room, greet everyone in it, even if you do so in English. Do not use the person's name, however, unless you know the individual well, as this is considered too familiar for people who are only casual acquaintances.

If you are visiting an urban home or a rural community, please dress modestly. You should avoid wearing shorts, miniskirts, swim wear, or dresses without bras. Most Asian people are more conservative than many Westerners.

These few tips will smooth social contact and help you understand a little more of the culture. Everywhere you go, speak slowly, softly, and in a pleasant tone. If you do this with a smile, you will find that people will respond in kind.

As with other areas of the country, the North celebrates with a variety of feasts and festivals. These are a great opportunity to see more of the culture of this region.

All the northern states observe national holidays (see Chapter 6), but each also has some special holidays, festivals, and sporting events of its own. The most important of these are:

HRH Sultan of Kedah's Birthday (mid-January) is a public holiday in Kedah. Festivities include traditional boat races, cultural shows, and kite-flying exhibitions.

Thaipusam (February) is celebrated by Hindus as a festival of repentance. It is a public holiday in Penang and Perak. In Penang there is a grand procession of the silver chariot bearing the jewel-studded statue of Lord Subramaniam from the Sri Marimman Temple in Lebuh Queen to the Nattukkotai Temple on Waterfall Road. In Ipoh there is a special procession at Gunung Ceroh Temple.

The **Langkawi Festival** (March) consists of sailing and water ski championships in the waters surrounding these 99 islands, while on land there is a fair, a beauty contest, and a parade.

The **Penang Fun Run** (first Sunday in April) is the largest running event in Malaysia. The 21.2-kilometer run attracts an interesting mix of more than 10,000 local and international enthusiasts. It is open to participants aged 12 and up.

Birthday of Sultan Perak (April 19) is a public holiday in Perak. Celebrations are biggest in Ipoh, Taiping, and Kuala Kangsar.

Nuzul Quran (May) is a Muslim religious day. It is a public holiday in Perlis, Kedah, and Perak.

The **Penang International Boat Festival** (June) is held at Persiaran Gurney in Georgetown. Local and international teams of rowers participate in this dragon boat festival.

The **Penang Grand Prix** (July) features both car and motorcycle races around a street circuit in Georgetown.

Birthday of HRH Raja Perlis (early September) is a public holiday in Perlis. Cultural shows, exhibitions, and sporting events take place in Kangar.

The **Penang International Marathon** (September) attracts a crowd of more than 3000 runners each year including some of the top international names.

The **Festival of the Nine Emperor Gods** (October) is celebrated in Penang by devotees making a pilgrimage to the Kew Ong Yeah Temple at Paya Terubong Hill, Air Itam, and climbing its 1,200 steps. Equally exciting for visitors is the spectacular firewalking ceremony held outside the Chinese temples in Jalan Magazine and Jalan Noordin, and the procession that conveys the spirit of the Emperor God to the waterfront.

The **Lumut Sea Festival** (late October) is held at Lumut in Perak. There are water sports programs and special shows and exhibitions.

The **Penang Festival** (December) is a month-long event that includes a trade and industrial fair, beauty contests, water carnivals, sporting events, and a colorful procession.

9. Sports

Penang is a beach resort, so naturally water sports facilities are excellent. The beaches of Batu Feringgi and Teluk Bahang are suitable for swimming and sunbathing. You can't avoid the water sports. At Batu Feringgi in particular, there are some very aggressive beach boys who will hound you the moment you set foot on the sand. My worst experience has been outside the Golden Sands but others have complained about other areas as well.

The options offered include water skiing, parasailing, and windsurfing. Some of the hotels rent Hobiecats for sailing, and for many this can be as exciting as anything else.

If *sailing* on something larger has more appeal, you can enjoy the luxury of yachting and explore the waters off Penang on various cruise tours. There is a yacht charter operator with a fleet of GibSea yachts that come equipped with medical kits, ship-to-shore communications, and other safety gear. Contact **Pelangi Cruises** (Tel: 812-828).

Similar sporting opportunities are available at Pangkor and Langkawi islands.

Golf is another sport where facilities are good. On Penang, two clubs are open to visitors. The **Bukit Jambul Country Club** offers an 18-hole international standard course. Visitors are charged green fees of M$70 for 18 holes on weekdays and M$150 on weekends. Caddy fees are M$15. The **Penang Turf Club** charges M$30 for 18 holes on weekdays and $50 on weekends. Contact Bukit Jambul (Tel: 842-255) or Penang Turf Club (Tel: 376-701).

Elsewhere the **Royal Perak Golf Club** at Ipoh has a nice 18-hole layout and superb clubhouse facilities (Tel: 05-573-266) M$30 on weekdays, and there is a delightful 9-hole course at Taiping called the **New Club** (Tel: 05-823-935). There is a course at the **Pan Pacific Resort** on Pulau Pangkor and the superb **Datai Bay Gulf Club** course on Palau Langkawi (Tel: 04-911-600). The course fee is M$100 and buggy hire

M$40. The 18-hole **Cinta Sayang Country Club** at Sungai Petani in Perak (Tel: 04-419-550) is a lovely course with many well placed hazards. Visitors are welcome weekdays when green fees are M$50. There is an excellent club house.

Tennis, *squash*, and *badminton* are available at many of the major hotels throughout the region and public facilities for these sports are available in Georgetown and Ipoh.

10. Shopping

Penang has long been a shopping paradise. Up until the 1970s the whole island was a duty-free zone, but this has now been cancelled by the central government. Duty-free goods are still obtainable at selected outlets, however, on a similar basis to most other gateway cities. There are duty-free shops at the international airport and along Jalan Penang and Lebuh Campbell. The Malaysia Tourism Promotion Board has a duty-free shop at the 64th level of KOMTAR. Department stores are located in KOMTAR (Yaohan and Super Department Store) and in Burmah Road and Jalan Dato Keramat. Selangor pewter is available from outlets in KOMTAR and the E & O Hotel.

A few years ago Langkawi was given duty-free status and now there are a collection of shops in Kuah that thrive on this trade. Duty-free shops are also located in the Pelangi Beach Hotel (Calan), and the Langkawi Island Resort (Cergasjaya). In my experience neither Penang or Langkawi can rival the variety available in Singapore or Kuala Lumpur.

Penang shops generally open seven days a week from around 10 A.M. to 9 P.M. or later. The nightly *pasar malam* operates from 7-11 P.M. As well as duty-free items, Penang has some good buys in *batik*, jewelry, pottery, and caneware.

Batik is available direct from factories in Teluk Bahang, specialty shops in Jalan Penang, every shopping complex, and the *pasar malam*. Quality and price vary considerably so you should look around before you buy. When you do buy, don't forget to bargain. *Batik* paintings make an attractive souvenir and these can be found in galleries in Jalan Penang, Lebuh Leith, and at Batu Feringgi.

Jewelry is a favorite item for the Chinese so Penang has a wide range available in jewelry shops and shopping complexes. Jade, pearl, gold, and diamonds in attractive designs are available along Jalan Penang, Lebuh Campbell, and Lebuh Pitt. If you buy at the regular shops, the stones will be genuine. Do not be tempted to buy on the streets unless you know a lot more about precious stones than I do.

Pottery items include terra-cotta pots, glazed coffee and tea sets, vases, ash trays, figurines, and lamp bases. The best range is available at the larger department stores and at Asian Pottery in Tanjung Bungah.

Caneware furniture is available in the shop houses along Lebuh Chulia. You can buy ready-made articles, or custom order a complete furniture set. Small wickerware items are found in shops along Jalan Penang.

Traditional handicrafts are not particularly big in Penang. If you want gold embroidery, bamboo carvings, and seashell designs, you will do best to travel to Kuala Kangsar in Perak where these are prominent cottage industries. The products are sold in the Kuala Kangsar MATA Bazaar and at the Ipoh railway station. The State Tourist Information Center in Ipoh displays a wide range of handicrafts that visitors can buy.

Pasar Malams (night markets) are available in many centers. The one in Penang is rather unique because it moves around Georgetown to a new location each two weeks. You need to ask the tourist office (Tel: 616-663) for the current location. There are several in Ipoh but the largest and most interesting is in People's Park, Jalan Sultan Iskandar. In Taiping, there is a nightly market on Julan Kwasu. In Alor Setar the Pekan Rabu market opens till midnight.

11. Entertainment and Nightlife

Despite what some tourist literature will tell you, Penang does not have a "throbbing, hustling, bustling, exciting" nightlife. Sure there are places to go, but you have to search them out.

For a visitor most action will revolve around the hotels. Most have lounges where you can chat with friends over drinks to background music supplied by a group or solo artist. Some also have discotheques with a cover charge of about M$15, which includes the first drink. Some of the better discos are the Cinta at the Rasa Sayang Hotel (Tel: 811-811), Street One at Shangri-La (Tel: 622-622), the Cinnamon Tree at Orchid Hotel (Tel: 803-333), and the Study at the Mutiara Beach Resort (Tel: 812-828). There is a good local disco and pub at 20 Lebuh Leith without a cover charge. The Polar Cafe off Penang Road is noted for its nightly sing-alongs.

Some cinemas in Penang screen English-language movies. Prices are cheap (M$3-4) and programs change frequently. Screenings are advertized in local newspapers or you can call the major cinemas and inquire: **Cathy** (Tel: 367-762), **Rex** (Tel: 26-270), **Capital** (Tel: 62-196), **Odeon** (Tel: 23-320).

There is a cultural show held most evenings at the Eden Seafood Village at Batu Feringgi. You can see lovely Malay girls deftly twirling lighted candles; Chinese performers with the excitement and noise of the Lion dance; and Indian dancers, jingling with bells telling poetic stories with their hands and bodies. Get further details by telephoning 811-852.

There are a number of bars around Georgetown but most of them are rather down-market. Perhaps the Tiger Bar in Lebuh Muntri and the Hong Kong bar in Lebuh Chulia are worth a visit but frankly, none of them are family spots.

12. The Penang and the North Address List

Airlines
  —Malaysia Airlines, KOMTAR Bld.   Tel: 620-011
  —Qantas   364-428
  —Singapore Airlines, Wisma Penang Gardens   363-201
  —Thai Airways   366-233
Ambulance   999
Bank
  —Citibank, 42 Jalan Sultan Ahmad Shah   363-222
  —Malayan Banking, 9 Lebuh Union   612-067
  —Standard Chartered, 2 Lebuh Pantai   633-000
Churches
  —St. George's Church, Lebuh Farquhar
  —Latter-Day Saints, 16 Jalan Scotland   362-914
  —Wesley Methodist Church, Jalan Burmah
  —Cathedral of the Assumption, Lebuh Farquhar
Clubs
  —Alliance Française, 32 Jalan Kelawei   366-008
  —British Council, Wisma Esplanade, 43 Green Hall   630-332
  —Malaysian German Society, 250-B Jalan Air Itan   366-853
Fire Station   999
Foreign Missions
  —British Representative, Standard Chartered Bank Bld.   625-333
  —Indonesian Consulate, 467 Jalan Burmah   25-162
  —Royal Thai Consulate, 1 Jalan Lebuh Downing   378-029
General Post Office   619-222
Hospitals
  —General Jalan Residensi   373-333
  —Adventist 465 Jalan Burma   373-344

Information
—Penang Development Corporation 832-111
—Penang Tourist Association 616-663
—Tourism Promotion Board 619-067
Medical
—Gleneagles Medical Center 376-111
—Penang Medical Center, 1 Jalan Pankor 20-731
Police 999
Sports
—Bukit Jambul Country Club, Jalan Relau 842-255
—Penang Flying Club, Penang Airport 843-367
—Penang Turf Club, Jalan Batu Gantung 21-463
Transportation
—International Airport 830-811
—Georgetown taxi service 617-098
—Railway station (Butterworth) 610-290

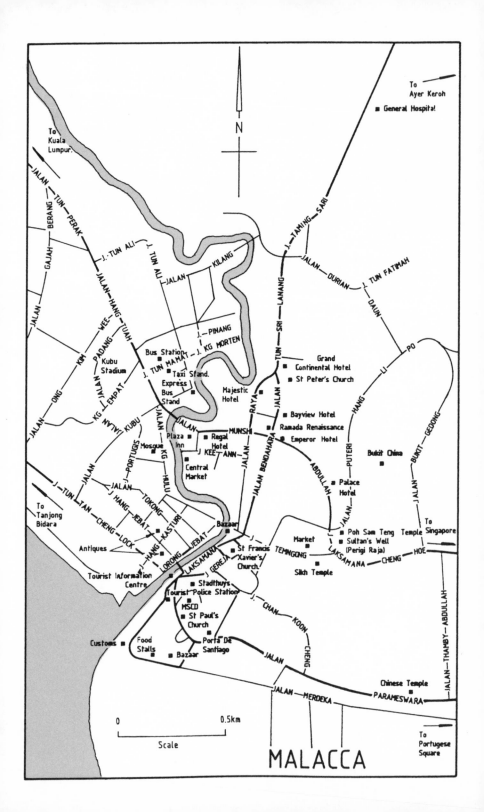

MALACCA

10

Malacca and the South

1. The General Picture

Five hundred years ago, before Singapore, Hong Kong, or Bangkok existed, Malacca was a thriving port. It rose to become a prosperous and powerful center for trade between the East and the West and eventually it became an empire.

It was a Sumatran prince named Parameswara who founded the small port at the mouth of the Malacca River. It had a good harbor, plenty of land and water, and was midway along the shortest route between India and China. Naturally it flourished. Within a short span of a few decades, it became the greatest center for sea commerce in the East.

Such prosperity attracted the attention of the Chinese and then the European colonial powers. The Chinese cemented their relations with the Malaccans when the Sultan married the Chinese princess Hang Li Po. Her retinue was given land east of the town at a place that today is called Bukit China (China Hill).

The Portuguese had no time for such niceties. After the Malaccans attacked some Portuguese traders, the Portuguese had the pretext that they wanted. They just took the town by force and held it for 130 years. Their key to success was the construction of A Famosa Fortress, a citadel so massive that it was never breached in 20 sieges.

The Dutch finally ousted the Portuguese in 1641 and rebuilt the city along European lines. It prospered for nearly 200 years until Sir Stamford Raffles established Singapore as a rival. Then it went into a sharp decline. The British took over control in 1824 and put it into the Federated Malay States in 1896. The Japanese occupied it during the Second World War and finally in 1957 it became independent with the rest of peninsular Malaysia.

Today, Malacca takes on many faces for the visitor. The historic aspects are still important for local and international visitors, but travellers are also discovering the leisure facilities that are available in Malacca and throughout the south. At the same time there has been a dramatic improvement in accommodation facilities in several areas, and the freeway links with Kuala Lumpur have suddenly made this region much more accessible to all.

2. Getting There

Malacca is accessible from both Kuala Lumpur and Singapore. The best connections are by inter-city bus—about 1½ hours from K.L. to Malacca, and 3½ hours from Singapore. Long-distance taxis are also available at fares about 100 percent higher than the buses.

Malacca has a small airport with commuter flights. Train travellers alight at Tampin (some 38 kilometers from the city) and then take a bus or taxi. There is a weekly boat service to Dumai in Indonesia (4 hours).

Johor Bahru, the city in the south of peninsular Malaysia, has a causeway connection to Singapore and road, rail, and air links with Kuala Lumpur.

3. Local Transportation

Central Malacca is small enough to see on foot. This is the ideal way to explore the city. The second preference is to go around by **trishaw**. These were once a common form of transportation but now they are used almost exclusively by tourists. You can rent a trishaw and driver for about M$15 an hour and be taken on a tour of sorts, to the main historic sites or anywhere else you choose. You must bargain for the fare before boarding.

Local **buses** provide a cheap way of moving around. There is a city service (Town Bus Service, Tel: 222-588) with fares less than M$1, and there are local services to all other centers within Melaka State (Syarikat Kenderaan Aziz, Tel: 229-837; Tai Lye Omnibus Co., Tel: 223-812; Melaka Omnibus Service, Tel: 224-387; Bas Tuah Omnibus, Tel: 223-011; and Patt Hup, Tel: 222-890).

Boatrides are available on the Malacca River and along the coast. Departures are from Quayside Jetty in front of the Majestic Hotel. Reservations are made on site.

Taxis are available in Malacca and Johor Bahru at reasonable rates. They have meters but drivers are reluctant to use them. Insist that the meter be used, or be prepared to pay an inflated price. Taxis are available at hotels, hailed on the street, or booked by telephone (Tel: 223-630) in Malacca and (Tel: 234-494) in Johor Bahru.

Travel within the south is best done by bus, long-distance taxi, or rental car. The bus fare between Malacca and Johor Bahru is around M\$12 and the taxi fare around M\$25. By bus from Johor Bahru to Mersing is around M\$6 non-air-conditioned, M\$10 air-conditioned, and M\$20 by taxi.

Trips to several islands are possible. From Malacca a boat service operates from Pengkalan Pernu (Umbai) Jetty to Pulau Besar. The cost is M\$5 per person. From Mersing, the boat to Pulau Rawa costs around M\$20 return, while the trip to Pulau Tioman is around M\$30.

Rental cars are available in Malacca from Sintat Rent-A-Car (Tel: 06-248-888) at the Ramada Renaissance Hotel, or from Avis Rent-A-Car (Tel: 06-235-626) at 27 Jalan Laksamana. There are even more options in Johor Bahru. There you could try Avis Rent-A-Car (Tel: 07-244-824), Budget Rent-A-Car (Tel: 07-243-951), Hertz Rent-A-Car (Tel: 07-237-520), Calio Car Rentals (Tel: 07-233-325), or National Car Rental (Tel: 07-223-432).

4. The Hotel Scene

Malacca has a good range of accommodations in the budget and midmarket price but there is more limited choice in the expensive category. Here is a selection of properties that will meet most needs.

EXPENSIVE HOTELS

The **Ramada Renaissance Hotel** (Tel: 06-248-888), 295 rooms, provides the best accommodations in Malacca. This international hotel offers deluxe facilities and friendly service. It has much to recommend it. The guest rooms are spacious and well appointed, and many have excellent views over the old city and port area. A Renaissance floor provides extra luxury and prestige with a special elevator, 24-hour maid service, and complimentary Continental breakfast and evening cocktails in a private club room.

The approach to the hotel is a little disappointing because it is often

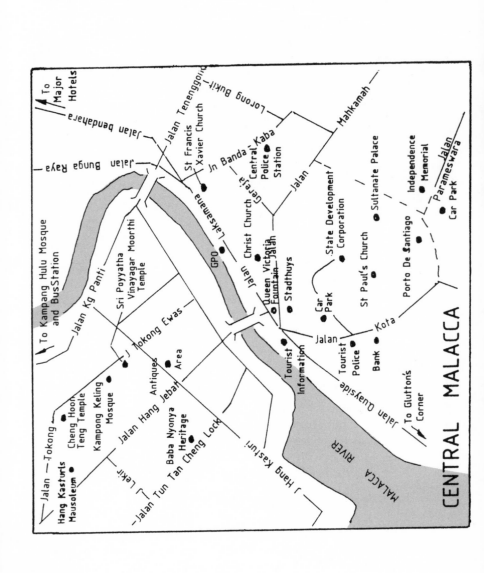

CENTRAL MALACCA

To Major Hotels

Jalan bendahara

Jalan Bunga Raya

Jalan Tenenggoing

St Francis Xavier Church

Jn Banda

Lorong Bukit

Central Kaba Police Station

Mahkamah

Gereja Jalan

Jalan

State Development Corporation

Sultanate Palace

Independence Memorial

Jalan Parameswara Car Park

To Kampang Hulu Mosque and BusStation

Laksamana

GPO

Christ Church

Queen Victoria Fountain

Jalan Jalan

Stadthuys

St Paul's Church

Porto De Santiago

Jalan Kg Panti

Sri Poyyatha Vinayagar Moorthi Temple

Car Park

Tokong Ewas

Kota

Jalan

Police

Bank

Tourist

Hang Antiques Area

Tourist Information

Jalan

To Glutton's Corner

To Kampang Hulu Mosque and BusStation

Cheng Hoon Teng Temple

Kampong Keling Mosque

Jalan Hang Jebah

Jalan Quayside

Jalan Tokong

Hang Kasturis Mausoleum

Jalan Tun Tan Cheng Lock

Baba Nyonya Heritage

Lekir

J Hang Kasturi

MALACCA RIVER

crowded by vehicles and signage is poor, but once inside the doors, the true nature of the hotel is revealed. The spacious two-level lobby is alive with water, music, and people at all hours. A resident band provides live entertainment in the Famosa Lounge while you relax over a refreshing drink. Elsewhere, Malaysian and Western cuisine is available in the 24-hour coffee shop, fine Western dining is offered in the Taming Sari Grill Room, and Cantonese fare is available in the Long Feng Restaurant.

A pool and bar is situated on the ninth floor terrace and this is a delightful spot for a light seafood lunch. After dark the Stardust Discotheque swings into life, while a business center provides facilities for those who need typing, fax services, and so on. Health is not forgotten. There are nonsmoking floors, a health center with a gymnasium, squash courts, and free transportation to the local 18-hole golf course.

All in all, you will find a stay here very pleasant. The hotel is situated within walking distance of the main historic sites in the city. (Book with the Ramada Group, United States Tel: 800-228-9898, Canada Tel: 800-268-8998, Australia Tel: 008-222-431 or direct with the hotel at P.O. Box 105, 75720 Melaka, Malaysia; Fax: 606-249-269.) Room rates start at around M$260.

The **City Bayview Hotel** (Tel: 06-239-888), 182 rooms, provides a good alternative. In fact the two hotels are situated close together and provide many similar facilities. The modern 14-story hotel has good rooms, a nice choice of bars and restaurants, and a friendly staff.

The Heritage Lounge is a cozy spot with bubbling fountains and warm hand-carvings, ideal for conversation and your favorite cocktail. Elegant dining, including flambé specials, are available in the Carnation Restaurant, while the Southern Court Restaurant offers specialties from the Szechuan Province of China. If you are looking for local dishes, the Baidura Cafe overlooking the swimming pool, is the place to go.

The hotel has a health club, a nightclub with Japanese decor, a business center, and a hairdressing salon. Prices start at around M$160. (Book with the hotel at Jalan Bendahara, 75100 Melaka. Fax: 606-236-699.)

The third hotel to quality for this category is the **Emperor Hotel** (Tel: 06-240-777), 244 rooms. Like the other two hotels, this is a modern high-rise building with all the necessary facilities for a pleasant stay. There are several bars and restaurants and other amenities. I have never stayed here so I cannot comment on the rooms or the service. Room rates start at M$175. (Book with the hotel at Jalan Munshi Abdullah, 75100 Melaka; Fax: 606-238-989.)

Two other properties should be included here. One is the **Malacca Village Park Plaza Resort** (Tel: 06-323-600) at Air Keroh, about 14 kilometers from Malacca. This is not the place for an overnight stop, if you plan to see Malacca in just a few hours. Its strength lies in its recreational facilities, and the opportunity to relax in a country resort atmosphere. You can play golf on the 18-hole course adjacent to the hotel, take a stroll to the lake at the front of the resort, have a game of tennis or squash, take a ride on the hotel's horses, or relax in the sauna, steam bath, or swimming pool.

Restaurant choices are the Traders Coffee Shop for Asian and Western food, the Shang San Chinese Restaurant, and the Kiraku Japanese Restaurant. Close by, you can visit the Malacca Zoo, the Recreational Forest, Mini Malaysia, a snake farm, and a crocodile farm. (Book with the hotel at Air Keroh, 754 Melaka; Fax: 606-325-955.) Room rates start at around M$220.

The other is the **Tapa-Nyai Island Resort** on Palau Besar, a 30-minute boat ride from Malacca. Room rates start at M$240. There are extensive facilities. (Book with P.O. Box 356, 75760, Melaka; Fax: 606-243-588.)

MEDIUM-PRICE HOTELS

The choice becomes wider in this category and you can now pick from among three locations—the city, Air Keroh, or the beach.

In the city, my choice would be one of the following four hotels. Two are reasonably close to the Ramada while the other is about a mile away. The **Grand Continental Hotel** (Tel: 06-240-088) is the largest and best of the three. The 63-room hotel has become popular with local business travellers and standards are being kept up. Room prices are M$90-100. (Book with the hotel at 20 Jalan Tun Sri Lawang, 75100 Melaka.) The **Tan Kim Hock Hotel** (Tel: 06-235-322), 38 rooms, is a cheaper alternative for those visitors with their own transportation. This Chinese-style hotel has rooms from M$75 and at this price they are a reasonable value. (Book with the hotel at 153 Jalan Laksamana Cheng Ho, 75000 Melaka.) The third alternative is the 48-room **Palace Hotel** (Tel: 06-225-115), which also has rooms from M$60. (Book with the hotel at 201 Jalan Munshi Abdullah, 75100 Melaka.) The **Plaza Inn** (Tel: 06-240-881) is up-market from the previous three. It has 140 rooms from M$100. (Book at 2 Jalan Munshi Abdullah, 75100 Melaka; Fax: 606-246-063.)

The option, if you enjoy the country, is the **Air Keroh Country Resort** (Tel: 06-325-211). This resort is about 15 kilometers from Malacca, adjacent to the Mini Malaysia attraction, and close to the

Malacca Village Resort. Accommodations are available in motel-style units or in chalets. There is a restaurant on hand offering a variety of local and Western food, and there is often live entertainment in the lounge. The resort has its own swimming pool, and other sporting facilities are close by. Room rates start at around M$100. (Book on Fax: 606-320-422.)

For beach lovers, there are two alternatives. The first is **Shah's Beach Hotel** (Tel: 06-511-120), 49 rooms, about 10 kilometers north of the city. The chalets are built around a central swimming pool. Those closest to the pool are the most expensive. There's an open-air bar and restaurant that is attractive when the weather is calm. Unfortunately the beach is not very good nor the water particularly clean, but the hotel provides a relaxing atmosphere. Chalets start from around M$80 and rise to about M$120.

The other alternative is found another 20 kilometers farther on. The **Tanjung Bidara Beach Resort** (Tel: 06-542-990) consists of 50 motel units and 15 chalets. The beach here is better and it is very popular with locals on weekends when numerous food stalls are set up. The resort has a swimming pool, lounge, and restaurant. Weekday prices start at about M$100 but these rise to over M$130 on weekends. Chalets start at M$160. (Book on Fax: 606-542-995.)

BUDGET ACCOMMODATIONS

Two places stand out at the top of this category. The **Majestic Hotel** (Tel: 06-222-455), 22 rooms, at 188 Jalan Bunga Raya, has a choice of air-conditioned and non-air-conditioned rooms, some with attached bathrooms. The hotel is reasonably quiet and well looked after. Room rates start at about M$25 but the best value are those around M$35.

The **Malacca Hotel** (Tel: 06-222-252), 20 rooms, at 27A Jalan Munshi Abdullah, opposite the Plaza Inn, has similar accommodations and a friendly staff. Fanned rooms with attached bathrooms are about M$30, while air-conditioned rooms start at about M$35. The **Comfort Hotel** (Tel: 249-718) is one of the many small fairly basic, modern hotels in the commercial area south of Jalan Merdeka. Rooms do not have attached bathrooms; fanned rooms are M$24 and air-conditioned ones more than M$35. There are some larger family rooms for M$45. Telephone before trying to find it. Another is **RB Rest House** (Tel: 240-540). Some rooms are air-conditioned (M$40) and some are fanned (M$25). In the dormitory rooms, beds are M$10. The **Melasca Town Holiday Lodge** (Tel: 246-905) has air-conditioned doubles with attached bathroom for M$35 a night.

Out of town there are several alternatives. On the road to Tanjung Kling beach, the old colonial-style **Westerhay Hotel** (Tel: 06-223-196), 10 rooms, offers something different. Large fan-cooled rooms start at around M$20, some have attached bathrooms. This is a good place for peace and quiet, but you are not isolated as buses to town and to Tanjung Kling Beach pass the front door.

At the Ayer Keroh Recreational Forest there are small huts available for overnight stays (Tel: 06-328-401) for less than M$10. Cabins with kitchenettes are also available for those wishing to stay longer at around M$40 a night.

Out at Tanjung Kling Beach there are several budget places with basic facilities. They seem to come and go with regularity so it's best to take a bus to the area then walk along the beach and see what is offered. It would be rare not to be able to find a room or bed space.

At Tanjund Bidara you could try **Bidara Beach Lodge** (Tel: 543-340). Rooms in the old wing go for M$33 a night.

5. Dining and Restaurants

Malacca has a good range of restaurants, street stalls, and coffee shops. Malay, Chinese, Indian, and Western foods are all available, but in addition Malacca offers the opportunity to sample Portuguese and Nonya cuisines.

Nonya is a delicious blend of Malay and Chinese ingredients and techniques developed four centuries ago when Chinese traders married local Malay girls and began this mixed-race culture.

Nonya food is not cheap but it is worth visiting the **Ole Sayany Restoran** (Tel: 06-231-966) at 192 Taman Melaka Jaya to try the best available in an air-conditioned dining room. Some of the favorite dishes are *enche kobin*, *itik tim*, and *mee siam*. All are nicely spiced. A meal here will cost around M$30-40 for two. An alternative is the **Nyonya Makko Restaurant** (Tel: 06-240-737) at 123 Taman Melaka Jaya. Both open for lunch and dinner. Then there is **Jonkers** (Tel: 235-578) at 17 Jalan Hang Jebat. Time has stood still in this charming little place and the food is superb. This is highly recommended. A set meal will cost M$16.

Malay restaurants are scattered throughout the city and you will find Malay food available in most of the hotel coffee shops, and at the major food stall areas and the hawkers' centers. Two conventional restaurants worth trying are **Restoran Anda** (Tel: 311-984) on Jalan Hang Tuah and **Mata Kacing Restaurant** (Tel: 226-184) on Jalan Taming Sari. Both offer Malay delicacies such as *cincalok*, *sambul belacan*, and *sambal tumis udang*. At Glutton's Corner on Jalan Taman, **Restoran No. 35**, and **Mini**

Restoran (Tel: 229-413) are considered by the locals to be two of the best.

Portuguese food is available at Portuguese Square and the adjacent Portuguese Settlement. I have some doubts about this area because it is orientated heavily towards the tourist but I have to admit that on a soft, clear night, when the tide is in and the lights are reflecting off the water, there is heaps of atmosphere. The two major restaurants here are the **Restoran De Lisbon** (Tel: 248-067) and the **Restoran De Portuguese** (Tel: 243-156).

It is a good idea to call ahead to find out if there is any entertainment (and to check that they will be open). Some nights there is a cultural performance of fair quality. Some of the better dishes are the baked fish with a tangy sauce, sambal crab, asam prawns, and devil curry. There are also some other small restaurants in an adjacent area that would be more intimate if you are planning a dinner for two. A good example is **San Pedro** (Tel: 245-734), which has much warmth and friendliness and an excellent baked fish.

Some of the best *Chinese* food is available in the major hotels. The **Long Feng Restaurant** (Tel: 248-888) at the Ramada Renaissance serves fine Cantonese cuisine, while the **Southern Court Restaurant** (Tel: 239-888) at the City Bayview Hotel specializes in food from the Szechuan Province. The **Golden Dragon Restaurant** (Tel: 240-777) at the Emperor Hotel has long held a reputation for good food and service.

Outside the hotels, the **Lim Tian Puan Restaurant** (Tel: 222-727) at 251 Jalan Tun Sri Lamang has perhaps the best reputation in town. The other alternative is to go to Taman Melaka Jaya and try one of the many Chinese restaurants in this area. My recommendations are the **Hiking Restaurant** (Tel: 233-292) at No. 112, **New Good World** (Tel: 222-952), **Lucky Famous Restaurant** (Tel: 240-301), or **King Don Restaurant** (Tel: 226-401). In the central city there are many small local Chinese restaurants that will cost you less than M$10 for two. The food is basic but you will get plenty of local color and have a great experience. If you are staying at one of the expensive hotels, try one of the restaurants just down the road. You will not be disappointed.

Indian food remains the province of small family restaurants. Try leaving the knife and fork behind one evening and tackle the banana leaf food experience to be found at several South Indian restaurants. The **Banana Leaf Restaurant** on Jalan Munshi Adbullah (Tel: 231-607) leaves no doubt as to what it sells. Two adjacent restaurants on Jalan Bendahara also specialize in this style of eating. They are **Sri Lakshmi** (Tel: 224-926) at No. 2, and **Sri Krishna Bavan Restaurant** (Tel: 229-206) at No. 4. The food at each of these places is extremely cheap

(M$3 a plate and up) and abundant, and the experience of eating with the fingers is novel.

If North Indian food is your choice, the **Shibnaam Exclusive Restaurant** (Tel: 238-292) at 252 Taman Melaka Raya would be a good choice.

Thai food lovers have at least two good choices. **My Place** (Tel: 243-848) on Jalan Melaka has a good variety at reasonable prices. The steamed fish cooked in lemon juice is particularly good. The alternative is **Tom Yam Restaurant** on Jalan Batu Berendam. As well as the *tom yum* with seafood, try the *nasi pattaya*, a combination of omelette and rice. It is very unusual.

The best *Western* food is available in the hotels. All the major hotels have Western food outlets while even the midmarket and budget accommodations often serve Western breakfasts and other basic dishes. For those addicts who need a shot of Kentucky Fried Chicken to keep going, there are outlets on Jalan Taming Sari and Jalan Hang Tuah. The **Restoran Pandan** behind the TPB office in Jalan Merdeka serves some good Western dishes as well as a variety of local fare.

Open-air dining is an experience you shouldn't miss. At Glutton's Corner along Jalan Taman, in fact it is not quite open-air because most of the stalls and restaurants have covered areas with laminated tables and timber chairs, but the experience is good nevertheless. This used to be the waterfront but the city has undertaken a big reclamation project that now places this area inland. Because of this change, it has lost much of its atmosphere but most of the stalls and restaurants remain.

The other popular area is Klebang Besar Beach about six kilometers north of the central city. This is not as extensive as Glutton's Corner but the variety of food is similar. While here you should consider a Nonya meal at the charming **Restoran Peranakan** (Tel: 354-436), which is set in a stately mansion with much opulence. You can eat inside or in the garden. There is a "cultural show" most evenings. A branch called **Restoran Peranakan Town House** (Tel: 245-001) has recently been opened at 107 Jalan Tun Tan in central Malacca. Farther out still, there is an area at Long Beach, Pantai Kundor, Tg. Keling, which is good for seafood, and the prices are rock-bottom because they cater to Malays from the nearby *kampungs*.

Back in town, there are several hawkers' centers that appear at night. The ones that have most appeal to the locals are those at Padang Corner, Jalan Parameswara; Banda Hilir, Jalan Thamby Abdullah out towards Bukit St. John; and one in Jalan Kilang, north of the central city.

6. Sight-seeing

History is the main attraction in central Malacca and once a visitor understands the various influences that have held sway on the city over the years, it is quite fascinating. Legacies of these occupations are dotted all over the city but there are two areas of special interest.

1. **East downtown** is the area of Old Malacca, east of the Malacca River. Your first encounter with this is likely to be Dutch Square, which comprises the Stadthuys, Christ Church, Malacca Clock Tower, and the Queen Victoria Fountain.

The **Stadthuys** is believed to be the oldest Dutch building in the Far East and it is the most imposing relic of the Dutch period in Malacca. The building that was completed in the late 1650s, once housed the Dutch governors and their retinue. The building has thick walls, heavy wooden doors, and windows with wrought-iron hinges. It now houses the **Melaka Historical and Literary Museums** (Tel: 220-769). There are authentic relics of the Portuguese and the Dutch, and traditional costumes of the early Chinese and Malays are on display. The museum is open from 9 A.M. to 6 P.M. daily, and there is a small admission charge.

Christ Church is an exquisite piece of Dutch architecture completed in 1753. Take a look at the massive ceiling beams, each cut from a single tree, which are without any joints. The handmade pews are the originals dating back more than 200 years. Above the altar you will notice a beautiful frieze of the "Last Supper" in glazed tiles. Note also the old tombstones in the floor. This is a place to spend a few quiet moments with your private thoughts.

Queen Victoria's Fountain was erected by the residents of Malacca to commemorate Her Majesty's Diamond Jubilee in 1904. It is one of the few British intrusions into the Dutch domain. Next to the fountain stands the **Malacca Clock Tower**. It was built in 1886 with the clock imported from England by the philanthropist Tan Jiak Kim.

St. Paul's Church was a small chapel built by the Portuguese at the top of Malacca Hill in 1521. It was used by Fr. Francis Xavier when he first visited Malacca in 1545 and his body was buried there for nine months in 1553 before it was transferred to Goa in India. In 1548 the Jesuit Society took over the chapel, enlarged it, added gun and cannon emplacements, and in 1596 added a tower. The church was named St. Paul's by the Dutch when they took over Malacca and it was converted into a reformist chapel. It was used until 1753 when Christ Church took over as the main center. After that, St. Paul's hill was used as a burial ground for nobles.

Other changes have occurred over the years. The lighthouse was

The Stadthuys—believed to be the oldest Dutch building in the Far East. (Courtesy of the Malaysia Tourism Promotion Board)

A typical Malay house in Malacca. (Courtesy of the Malaysia Tourism Promotion Board)

once attached to the church but became a separate building this century. The British also demolished the tower and briefly used the building as a powder magazine. The church has been in ruins now for 150 years but the site is a "must" for every visitor to Malacca.

Porta De Santiago, or Gateway of St. James, is the last remaining ruin of the once impenetrable fortress, A Famosa, built by the Portuguese in 1511. During the Dutch takeover of Malacca, the fortress was badly destroyed but the Dutch repaired much of it, including what is seen today. The British planned to totally demolish the fort in the early 1800s, but this last gateway was saved by the intervention of Sir Stamford Raffles in 1808. A path leads from here to St. Paul's.

The **Malacca Sultanate Palace** is a wooden replica of the Sultanate Palace described in the Malay Annals. The building is quite interesting and it now houses the **Malacca Cultural Museum** (Tel: 220-769), which is open from 9 A.M. to 6 P.M. daily except from 12:15 to 2:45 P.M. on Friday. The exhibits include photographic displays, weaponry, musical instruments, and clothes. The highlight is the replica of a Melaka court. There is a small admission charge.

The **Proclamation of Independence Memorial** is the last of the interesting buildings in this area. There are historical documents, maps, treaties, and other items relating to the struggle for and attainment of Malaysia's independence. It opens Tuesday through Sunday from 9 A.M. to 6 P.M. except noon to 3 P.M. Friday. Admission is free.

2. *West downtown* is the area of old Malacca, west of the Malacca River. This is the oldest residential and commercial area, and the narrow streets, prettily decorated shop houses, and ancient temples are most appealing. This is an area to walk in and explore. Here are a few things to look for.

The **Baba Nyonya Heritage Museum** (Tel: 220-777) is a private museum showing something of the culture of the Straits-born Chinese known as the Babas or Peranakans. The museum on Jalan Tun Tan Cheng Lock is housed in three old neoclassical European homes. Floral and pictorial motifs grace the front of the houses while the interiors are adorned with intricately carved fittings finished in gold leaf. The houses are built around open courtyards in a style popular 150 years ago. The interior is displayed so that it looks like a 19th-century Baba Nyonya house.

There is some magnificent furniture including some amazing inlaid mother-of-pearl designs. The costumes and embroidered materials are also spectacular. Other worthwhile items are the ceramics and tilework. The museum is open from 10 A.M. to 12:30 P.M. and from 2 to 4:30

Porta de Santiago, Malacca. (Courtesy of the Malaysia Tourism Promotion Board)

P.M. daily. The admission charge is M$7 but this includes an excellent 45-minute tour.

Hang Kasturi's Mausoleum is something that you will come across in Jalan Hang Jebat. This is the burial place of Hang Kasturi, a famous warrior and one of the Hang Tuah blood-brothers who served the Sultans of Malacca. It's not worth going out of your way to see, but it does fill in another piece of history.

The **Cheng Hoon Teng Temple** on Jalan Tokong is the oldest Chinese temple in Southeast Asia (1650s). The building itself is a wonderful example of South Chinese architecture. It has gabled roofs with ridges and eaves decorated with figures of mythology and animation made from broken glass and porcelain that glitter and sparkle in the sun. Inside, the wood carvings and lacquer work are spectacular. The temple is a combination of Buddhism, Confusianism, and Taoism. Two Chinese lions guard the entrance to the temple's main hall.

The **Kampong Keling Mosque** on Jalan Tukang Emes was built by the Muslim community in 1748 on land given by the Dutch. It has Sumatran-style architecture. There is a three-tiered roof rising like a pyramid and inside there is a beautiful carved wooden ceiling. Beside the mosque is an old minaret structured like a pagoda.

The **Sri Payyatha Vinayagar Moorthi Temple**, on Jalan Tukang Emas close to the Kampong Keling Mosque, was built in 1781. The temple is dedicated to the god, Vinayagar, who is believed to be capable of removing obstacles that stand in the way of businessmen in pursuit of wealth, and couples who want to marry.

The **Kampong Ulu Mosque** is the most popular mosque in the city and the oldest in Malaysia. It was built in 1728 in an architectural style that can only be found in Malacca. It is a little distance from the other points of interest in west downtown but is worth the walk along Jalan Kg Ulu.

The **antique area** is centered on Jalan Hang Jebat, formerly known as Jonkers Street. Authentic artifacts dating back nearly 300 years can be found here. This area is world-famous for such things as Chinese Ming porcelain bowls, Indian brassware, English wall mirrors, Dutch sideboards, old clocks, and so on. You can browse through these shops without being pressured. You may just find a bargain or a fascinating reminder of wonderful historic Malacca.

3. *Elsewhere in Malacca* there are other reminders of the past. All these points of interest can be visited by car or by bus.

The Sultan's Well is located at the foot of Bukit China and dates back to the 15th century. It is believed that it was constructed for the use of Princess Hang Li Poh, the daughter of the Chinese emperor, who married the Sultan of Malacca. The Dutch enclosed the well in 1677 and at one time it supplied much of the town with water. It has now been converted into a wishing well because anyone seeing the state of the water is unlikely to want to drink from it.

The adjacent **Sam Po Kong Temple** was built in 1795 by a Chinese who was grateful that the British had captured Malacca from the Dutch. It acted as a burial chapel for the Chinese community for some years then was dedicated to Admiral Cheng Ho of the Chinese Ming dynasty, who visited Malacca in 1409. There was once a statue of the admiral on the altar but this was stolen years ago. Today it is replaced by a photograph of the statue.

Bukit China was given to Princess Hang Li Poh and her 500 maidens as a residential area when she married the Sultan in 1459. Later the Portuguese built a Franciscan monastery and chapel on the hill but this was eventually destroyed. In the 17th century, the hill was bought from the Dutch and donated to the Cheng Hoon Teng Temple as a burial ground. Today it is the largest Chinese cemetery outside China with 12,000 graves taking up 25 hectares. A walking track allows you to see some of the graves that are now more than 300 years old.

St. John's Fort is a Dutch fort built on the site of an old Portuguese chapel. It was built as a defense against attack from a Malay chief and you will see that the guns face the land rather than the sea. A supposed secret tunnel connecting St. John's Fort with Porta De Santiago has never been found. Today it is a pleasant place but frankly it is not a great attraction.

A little farther on, you turn off to **Portuguese Square**, a tourist spot built in the early 1980s. The design of the square resembles that of Lisbon, but I have an idea that the attraction has not been completely successful as it is rather untidy. At night this is almost hidden so the restaurants and occasional cultural performance can be very pleasant. The adjacent Portuguese settlement houses about 1,500 Eurasians of Portuguese descent.

St. Peter's Church is back in central Malacca, near the major hotels. The generally unexceptional church built in 1710 has some interesting stained-glass windows, a lifesize alabaster statue of the dead Christ, and Iberian influence in its curved ceiling.

The **Tranquerah Mosque** adds a different architectural style to the Malaccan scene. The present mosque on the road to Tanjung Keling was built in the 1850s and is pyramid-shaped instead of the more common dome-shaped Moorish mosque. The pagoda-shaped minaret stands beside the main building. Within the grounds lies the tomb of

Sultan Hussain of Johor, who, in 1819, signed the cessation of Singapore to Sir Stamford Raffles.

4. *Country-side Malacca* is a totally different attraction for visitors. The main area for visitors is the Air Keroh region about 15 kilometers north of Malacca. Here there are several places that are worth visiting, if you are planning to stay in Malacca for several days. You can reach all of them by rental car, bus, or taxi.

The **Mini Malaysia Cultural Village** (Tel: 323-176) is something that will appeal to many visitors. There are 13 attractively crafted Malay traditional houses each representing a different part of Malaysia. Each house contains works of art and culture, and there are regular displays of traditional games, and culture shows. The village is open Monday to Friday from 10 A.M. to 6 P.M. and Saturday and Sunday from 9:30 A.M. to 6:30 P.M. Admission fee is M$3.

The **Ayer Keroh Recreational Forest** (Tel: 328-401) is close by. Here you can walk in a tropical forest, along trails fringed by trees labelled with their names. There are hiking and picnic opportunities and you can even visit a tree house. There are barbecue facilities and a children's playground. The forest is open from 7 A.M. to 6 P.M. daily and admission is free. A little farther on is the **Butterfly Park and Museum Melaka** (Tel: 320-033). It opens 8:30 A.M.-5:30 P.M. daily.

Malacca Zoo (Tel: 324-054) is about two kilometers back towards the city. It covers 22 hectares (about 55 acres) and has many species of animals from Asia and Africa, including the almost extinct Sumatran rhinoceros. The zoo is built on the "open" concept and rates as the second-best in Malaysia. Opening hours are from 10 A.M. to 6 P.M. daily. There is a small admission fee.

The **Ayer Keroh Recreational Lake** (Tel: 221-144), beside the zoo, offers boating, canoeing, and aquabiking as well as a children's playground and walking paths. This is a good spot for families wanting a break from sight-seeing. The lake is open from 8 A.M. to 6 P.M. daily and admission is free. There are charges for water activities.

The **Ayer Keroh Country Club** (Tel: 324-351) has one of the best 18-hole golf courses in Asia with a challenging terrain. You will need to get an introduction from the hotel where you are staying because the guards are very reluctant to let visitors past the gate. After much talking I was allowed to leave my car outside and walk to the clubhouse. There is a pleasant bar and restaurant and other sporting facilities.

The **Malacca Crocodile Farm** (Tel: 322-349) is the largest such park in Malaysia. Visitors can view a range of crocodiles of various species. It is open from 9 A.M. to 6 P.M. daily and admission is M$3.

NORTH FROM MALACCA

There are several roads between Malacca and Kuala Lumpur. The fastest is the new expressway that allows you to cover the 140 kilometers in about 1½ hours. The most interesting though, is probably the route via Port Dickson, Banting, and Shah Alam. By rental car, this can easily take all day when you stop and take in some of the sights. It is also possible to do this by bus (you need to change several times), but you should probably plan to stay overnight in Port Dickson if you choose this method of transportation.

The road from Malacca (Route 5) heads almost west along the coast. You initially pass the development along Tanjung Keling then head inland. Don't miss the turnoff to **Tunjung Bidara** because this is one of the west coast's better beaches and a world apart from the poor beaches close to Malacca. Lush vegetation comes down to the sandy beach and there are toilet and shower facilities. The beach can be quiet on weekdays but on weekends there are opportunities for waterskiing, canoeing, and boating, and food stalls under the trees offer snacks and meals to visitors.

If you continue along the coast road for another 20 kilometers you eventually come to an old Dutch fort that was built in 1757. The main road to Port Dickson, however, runs inland and enters the state of Negeri Sembilan at Lubok China. After passing through rubber plantations you come back to the coast at **Pasir Panjong**. From here, there are nice beaches for eight kilometers to Cape Rachado. Turn off the main road and explore some of the side roads to the coast. You will find a variety of accommodations here that may just tempt you to stay for a while. The beaches at some of these locations are very attractive. A walk on the sand to watch the deep blue sea turn frothy white as each wave splashes on the beach will be the highlight of a stop here.

Cape Rachado is mainly headland forest that forms an important area for migratory birds, and a home for many monkeys. The lighthouse, which was built by the Portuguese in the 16th century, can be reached by a rough road through the forest. The Indonesian island of Sumatra can be seen across the water. The road from here closely follows the coast for the 16 kilometers to Port Dickson. It is an interesting drive.

If you plan to stay in the Port Dickson area, the beach should be the only location you consider. Good accommodations are available at the **Taman Perangman Mutiara** (Tel: 06-405-473), which has 200 bungalows from around M$200 a night. (Book with the hotel at Batu 12 Jalan Pantai, 71050 Port Dickson.) A little closer to town is the midrange **Pantai Hotel** (Tel: 06-405-130), which has a range of rooms from

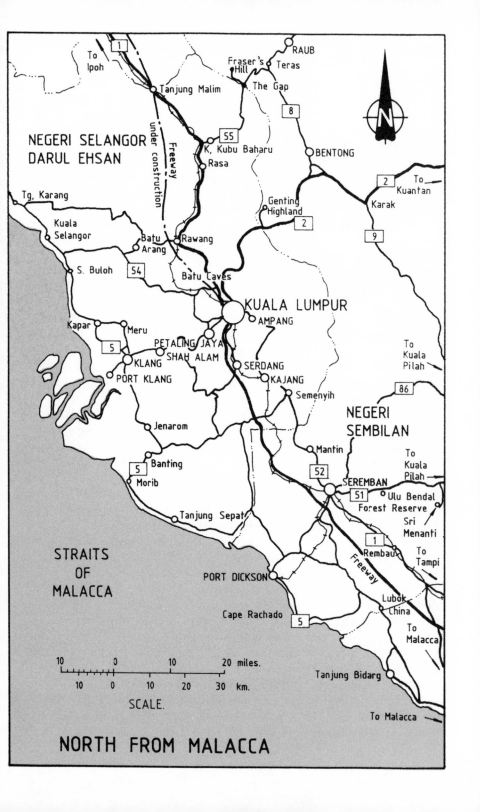

NORTH FROM MALACCA

around M$65. This is a quiet place, a little off the road, and the beach is less popular than farther on. Reasonable accommodations are available at the nearby **Halcyon Guest House** (Tel: 06-405-323), 10 rooms, from around M$60. There is a pool and boathouse.

The three largest hotels are on the next stretch of beach towards Port Dickson. The **Ming Court Beach Hotel** (Tel: 06-405-244), has 164 rooms from M$170-450, while the older **Si Rusa Beach Resort** (Tel: 06-405-233), offers 200 rooms at M$80-120. The large **Regency Hotel** (Tel: 474-100), 217 rooms, opened in 1992. There are ample facilities and rooms from M$180. These hotels are popular with K.L. residents seeking some time by the water. Most of the other high-rise buildings you see along this stretch of beach are condos, which serve the same "escape" purpose. One of the best is the **Tanjung Tuan Beach Resort** (Tel: 473-013) where self-contained apartments rent from M$220-520 a day.

There is very little to see in Port Dickson although it is a reasonably pleasant small town. There are, however, good water sport facilities including the hire of fishing boats and deep sea fishing gear, waterskiing, sail boarding and para-sailing. You will find a couple of good seafood restaurants near the wharf area of town. It is a great place to watch the brilliant orange sun slowly set on a steely-blue sea.

From Port Dickson, continue along Route 5. For the next 35 kilometers or so, you travel an inland route but you finally come back to the coast at a stretch of beach villages which end at **Morib**. This is a popular weekend and holiday beach for K.L. residents. Morib was written into the history books when Allied forces landed on this small stretch of beach in September 1945, marking the end of the Japanese occupation of Malaya. Today the area inland is quiet countryside and the town midweek can be a good place for a relaxing game of golf and a walk along the beach. The only company on the beach is likely to be the whispering casuarinas, the stately palms, the foaming waves at high tide, and the scurrying crabs. At low tide the deserted beach stretches far out to the distant horizon. If you want to stay, the **Hotel Sri Morib** (Tel: 03-858-1732), 20 rooms, a very attractive place at the Kelab Golf Course, is about your only real choice. Rooms are around M$65.

There are no more beaches on this coast for about 75 kilometers but it's worth continuing on the near coastal road (Route 5) until you reach the town of **Klang**. This city was the previous capital of the state of Selangor and, from its strategic position overlooking the Klang River, it guarded the entry to the rich Klang valley. There is a fine Royal Mosque and the old Royal Palace—the Istana Alam Shah. Eight kilometers away **Port Klang** is the major seaport for Kuala Lumpur. For visitors, however, the major attraction is the many seafood restaurants that offer excellent fare including great chilli crab. **Wahyon Grill House** (Tel: 368-8981) is relatively new but it is working hard to create a reputation for top seafood and other dishes. The **Bagan Seafood Village** (Tel: 367-4546) is another.

Public ferries leave the jetty for several offshore islands but these are not particularly attractive and will have limited interest to international tourists. Klang's fort is worth seeing. It was built by the Raja Mahdi, one of the main figures in the 19th-century Selangor civil war. The Klang museum is housed in a former storehouse belonging to Raja Abdullah, one of Raja Mahdi's main opponents.

Most travellers will now head for Kuala Lumpur via the direct route through Shah Alam and Petaling Jaya, but nature lovers and history freaks will continue another 50 kilometers along Route 5 to **Kuala Selangor**. Even before Klang became the capital, Kuala Selangor was the home of the Selangor Sultanate, and two fortresses were built on the hills overlooking the estuary of the Selangor River to guard the city. The larger of the two, on Bukit Melawati, is now the royal mausoleum containing the remains of Selangor's early Bugis rulers.

Bukit Melavati overlooks the **Kuala Selangor Nature Park**, which has been developed by the state government and the Malayan Nature Society. The park consists of 250 hectares of coastal land that is mainly mangrove swamp. Artificial lakes have been created to attract some of these birds and observation sites created. Leaf monkeys can also be seen. A visitor's center has been built on Bukit Melawati and a path leads down from there to the park.

Nearby **Angsa Island** is quite picturesque and there is a four-room rest house available if you want to spend a night in island solitude. Reservations are made at Tel: 03-889-1010. There are no regular ferry services to the island, but the local fishermen are happy to ferry you across for a reasonable sum.

Shah Alam is the new capital city of Selangor, located about 30 kilometers west of Kuala Lumpur. There is still considerable construction going on here but there are several interesting things to see. Top of the list perhaps is the state mosque with its huge, blue aluminum dome. Then there is the busy campus of the Mara Institute of Technology, the still-developing Taman Pertanian agricultural park, and the impressive State Secretariat Building. The Civic Center comprising the museum, town hall, library, and conference center is worth a visit. Take a look at Islama Bukit Kayanyan, the palace of the DYMAL Sultan of Selangor.

A few miles closer to Kuala Lumpur you come to **Petaling Jaya** and

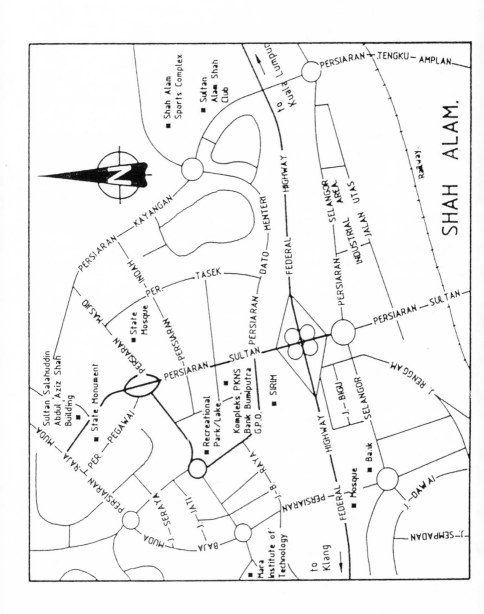

SHAH ALAM.

the nearby international airport. Petaling Jaya is a modern city that has grown to become part of the Kuala Lumpur urban complex. It has a high percentage of modern industry and commerce, so the per capita income is probably higher than anywhere else in Malaysia. This is reflected in the up-market residential areas and in an active nightlife and restaurant scene. The **Petaling Jaya Hilton** (Tel: 03-755-9122), 398 rooms, and the **Holiday Villa Hotel** (Tel: 03-733-8788), 370 rooms, are the best hotels in town. Room rates start at around M$200 a night. Also worth considering is the **Hyatt Saujana Hotel and Country Club** (Tel: 03-746-1188), 230 rooms, just two kilometers from the airport. This has two 18-hole golf courses, a fitness center, and tennis, squash, and swimming facilities. Room rates start at around M$180.

Petaling Jaya has some of the best shopping facilities in Malaysia. Perhaps Subang Parade, which is claimed to be southeast Asia's longest shopping mall, is a good example. Here you will find Parkson Grand, the world's biggest toy store, and a huge seafood center. Some of the interesting smaller shops include Dynasty Art and Crafts, Unique Decorators (crafts and souvenirs), Image Wear (fashion), Femme Wardrobe (fashion), and Jinjing Goldsmiths.

It is appropriate now that we return to Malacca. We will do this by way of Seremban. The fastest way is via the freeway but the more interesting is to take Route 50, then wander along some of the hilly picturesque roads in the vicinity of Broga and Kenggeng. Road N34 is a good example. It winds through forest and small settlements and is quite charming. To be less than 50 kilometers from Kuala Lumpur and find such natural country is quite refreshing.

Seremban is a delightful town. The Lake Gardens are a lovely green area in the center of town with a floating stage as a venue for cultural performances that are held some weekends. Adjacent to the lake is the large, modern state mosque and close by is the classic State Executive Council Building that houses the state library. You could easily spend an hour or two wandering around this area.

Another worthwhile stop is the Taman Seni Budaya handicraft complex about two kilometers west of town. Here local handicrafts are produced and sold, but equally interesting are the old Minangkabar-style houses and palace that have been recreated here. It is believed the Minangkabar people originated in Sumatra and their architecture is distinctive by always having the roof line sweep up at each end like buffalo horns.

The best accommodations in town are at the **Allson Klana Resort** (Tel: 06-729-600), 300 rooms, pool and tennis and at the **Tasik Hotel** (Tel: 06-730-994), 42 rooms, with rates around M$140. The **Carlton**

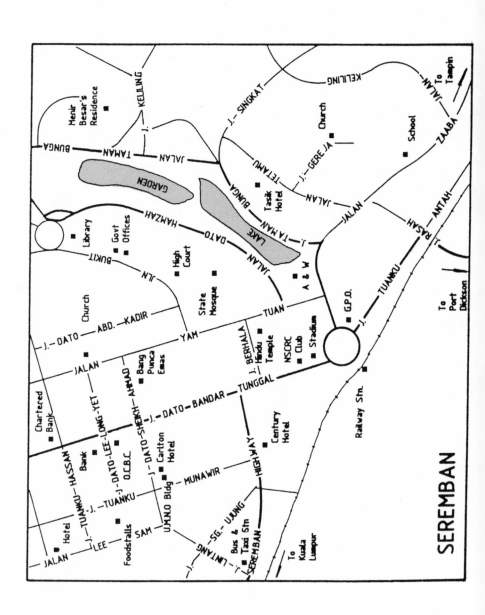

SEREMBAN

Hotel (Tel: 06-725-336) has cheaper accommodations closer to the bus station. The best Malay restaurant in town is probably the **Falmingo Inn**. The **Suntori Restaurant** has good Chinese food and the **Samy Restaurant** has banana leaf Indian food. The most popular shopping areas are Jalan Dato Bandot Tunggul and Wisma Pinca Emas. There is a Parkson department store in both locations.

If you wish to keep off the freeway and enjoy nice countryside, I suggest that you leave town on Route 51 heading east towards Kuala Pilah. About 18 kilometers along this road you come to the Ulu Bendol Forest Reserve. There is a waterfall, a swimming pool, and a restaurant; and this is a great picnic spot. If you don't have your own transportation, you can reach this point by United bus lines from Seremban. You will notice many traditional houses in this area.

Now continue along this road and turn off to the royal town of **Sri Menanti**. Here you will find a 1902 palace built entirely of wood, containing many fine examples of intricate carving. There is also a royal mosque and a newer palace. When you reach Kuala Pilah, turn south onto Route 9 and reach Malacca via Tampin and Alor Gajah.

SOUTHEAST FROM MALACCA

Our aim will first be to visit the east coast of Malaysia, travel south to Johor Bahru at the end of the causeway to Singapore, then travel back to Malacca on the west coast.

There are many alternatives out of Malacca but I suggest the route via Josin, Tangkak, and Jemantah, to Segamat. This takes you past Mt. Ophir (*Gunung Ledang*) where there are a series of waterfalls and swimming holes. It is quite an attractive spot that has become very popular on weekends as a getaway resort.

Segamat is a prosperous town on the railway and old main highway, but now with the construction of the freeway, much of the road traffic to Kuala Lumpur has been diverted elsewhere. This, however, is a junction for Route 12, which takes you to the mideast coast city of Kuantan (see Chapter 11).

If you have taken longer than expected to explore the interesting country between Malacca and Segamat, you will find adequate accommodations at the **Mercury Hotel** (Tel: 07-912-101), 74 rooms, from M$70 a night; or the **Silver Merlin** (Tel: 07-919-913), 70 rooms, from M$130 a night. Good midrange accommodations can be found at the **Mandarin Inn** (Tel: 07-917-966) at M$50 a night, while **The Silver Inn** (Tel: 07-912-211) has rooms from M$40.

You should now follow Route 1 to Chaah, then take the back roads to

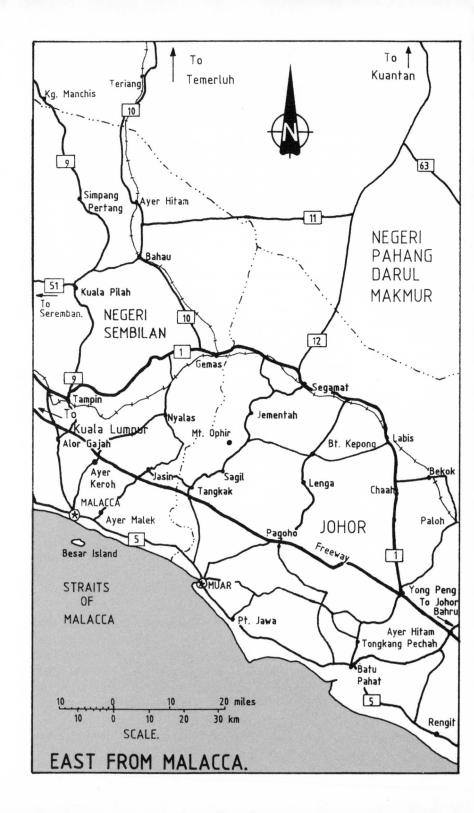

EAST FROM MALACCA.

Keluang. This is another railway center, and it's on Route 50, which leads to the east coast. There is nothing much of interest in this large town but if you need to stay, the **Anika Hotel** (Tel: 07-724-977), 33 rooms, from M$80 has quite good accommodations.

Your destination now is **Mersing**, about 110 kilometers away. This is an interesting fishing village but its main interest lies in its situation as a departure point for several beautiful islands off the coast in the South China Sea. The town itself has an interesting mosque, a few reasonable restaurants, a choice of accommodations, and some excellent beaches both to the north and south. The beach in town is poor. A walk along the beach will reveal sleek, slim fishing boats parked on the sand, their insides filled with nets, which in the half-light look like huge translucent cobwebs. The best accommodations in town are at the **Mersing Merlin Inn** (Tel: 07-791-311), 31 rooms, about 1½ kilometers north of town. Air-conditioned rooms in a garden setting are about M$75 a night. There is a nice swimming pool.

Best midmarket accommodations are at the **Rumah Persinggahan** (Tel: 07-792-102), 18 rooms, near a small golf course, or the **Embassy Hotel** (Tel: 07-791-301) in the center of town. You will find reasonable rooms at these two places for M$35. There are several small cheap Chinese hotels such as the **East West Hotel** with rooms from around M$12. A better alternative perhaps is **Kali's Guest House** (Tel: 07-793-613) where there are accommodation options from M$15-50.

Mersing is the southernmost beach resort on the east coast highway so it is a popular stop for Johor Bahru to Kuantan buses. Express buses to Johor Bahru cost about M$8 and to Kuantan it is about M$12. There are many buses each day but you cannot always get seats on the one you want, particularly on weekends or during school holidays. Long-distance taxis are also available at about double the bus fare.

Some of the off-shore islands are big attractions. The largest, most popular, and most attractive is *Tioman Island*, about 45 kilometers from Mersing. Tioman makes much of the fact that Hollywood chose it to be the mythical Bali Hai in the film production of *South Pacific*. With spectacular mountains, huge boulders, lush forest, white beaches, clear water, and happy brown-skinned inhabitants, it fits the role perfectly. The twin peaks of Batu Sirau and Nenek Semukut, which so prominently featured in the film, tower majestically over the coastline. Today it is accessible by sea from Mersing and by air from Singapore and Kuala Lumpur.

Tioman is about 20 kilometers long and up to 12 kilometers wide but most of it is inaccessible because of the thick jungle and rugged terrain. The major development is on the west coast facing the mainland. Here,

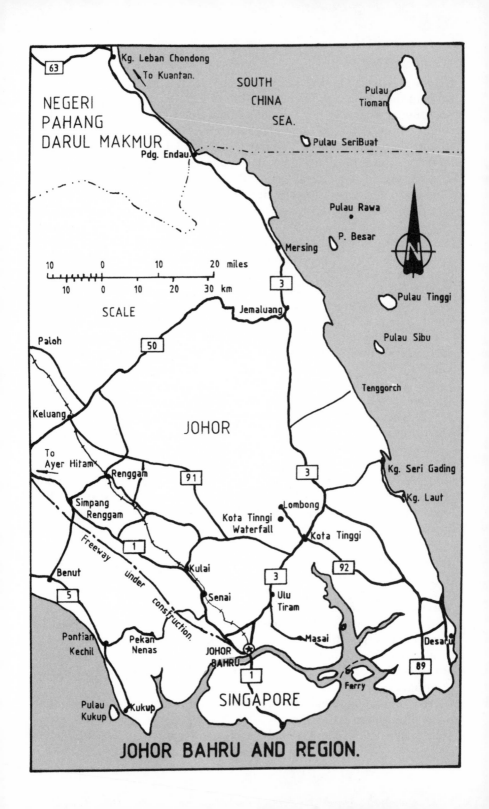

JOHOR BAHRU AND REGION.

there are many budget huts, a few midmarket chalets, and the up-market Imperial Beach Resort. Getting to Tioman from Mersing can be quite confusing. The first problem is the tide. No boats can use Mersing wharf at low tide so there are often groups of people wasting hours at the wharf waiting for something to happen.

The second problem is the proliferation of small boats that operate to Tioman. I visited the **Tourist Boats Association** (Tel: 07-792-501) at 1 Jalan Abu Bakar, the **Tioman Reservations Center** (Tel: 07-791-771) at the old Custom Office, and several other booking agencies in the wharf area and was given a different story by each of them. After sifting through the information it appears that there is a fast boat service (1½ hours) at around $30 one way, and many slow boats (up to 3 hours) at around $20 one way.

The **Berjaya Imperial Beach Resort** (Tel: 09-445-445) on Tioman Island offers 185 air-conditioned rooms, good restaurant, entertainment, and sporting facilities, and a magical location right on the beach. Prices start at M$150 for a standard room in the off-season (November-February) and rise to more than M$350 for rooms and M$1200 for suites in the normal season. Two restaurants serve a variety of Western and local cuisine. The Seri Nelayan specializes in Tioman clay pot, a delicious noodle meal with bean curd, shrimp, mushrooms, and cabbage. The hotel has a nice swimming pool, a 9-hole golf course, TV, telephones, tennis, and so forth. If you are planning to stay here, you should contact the hotel for reservations and transfer information at the time you wish to travel. (Book through P.O. Box 4, 86807, Mersing, Johor; Fax: 609-445-718.)

South of here at Genting Village the **Genting Damai Holiday Resort** (Tel: 07-793-048) has chalets on a nice beach. There is also the **Paya Beach Resort** (Tel: 07-791-432), which has three-day/two-night packages for M$190 per person.

Just a little north of the Berjaya Imperial Beach Resort, is the 20-room **Swiss Cottages** (Tel: 07-248-728). This chalet-style midrange accommodation is on another beautiful stretch of beach near Kampong Lalang. Prices are around M$35-50 per night. As you go north from here towards the airstrip, wharf, and town of Tekek, many more places appear. Most are fairly basic budget huts but some are becoming more sophisticated. It is difficult to prebook any of these although **Tioman Accommodation and Boat Services** in Mersing (Tel: 07-793-048) does have some sort of record of availability. At most times it is better to go to the island, disembark at the Tekek jetty, and wander along the beach till you find something you like. There is no taxi or bus service on the island. Restaurants at Kampong Tekek offer a varied menu of both local and Western dishes, and there are some shops to buy essential provisions. This center also has a health clinic, a police station, and a public telephone.

Farther north from Tekek is **Kampong Ayer Batang** and a large collection of budget huts on a superb beach. Many of these have been built in the last two years and have been kept quite clean, but the facilities are basic. You can still find a bed space here for under M$10 and some backpackers have extended their stays in this area to several weeks. Two further areas are opening up, but access except by water is difficult. **Kampung Salang** is the best place for diving and there is some budget accommodation and a diving center here, while **Juara** on the east coast is an isolated community that has some long, deserted beaches and some basic accommodations and food stalls run by simple, happy locals. The best coral grounds are the waters off *Tulai*, an island to the northwest of Tioman.

The reason for going to Tioman is the peace, tranquility, and beaches but there are also opportunities to hike mountain trails, see some wildlife, and visit the beautiful Mukut Waterfall at the south of the island. During school holiday time, Tioman can be quite busy so many international visitors would prefer to avoid that. The November-February monsoon season is much less crowded but seas can be rough and boats cancelled at times during this period.

Pulau Rawa is another popular island off the coast from Mersing. It is operated by members of Johor's royal family and has been popular for 20 years. *Rawa* is a lovely island with a fine beach, one restaurant called the Cafe de Rawa, and some water sports facilities. The accommodations in bungalows and chalets look fairly basic, but they are quite comfortable. Food at the restaurant is surprisingly good. Reservations have to be made at **Rawa Safaris** (Tel: 07-791-204) in Mersing. Room rates are from around M$65.

Pulau Besar is a larger island about one hour from Mersing. It has a choice of accommodations but the **Hillside Chalet** (Tel: 07-236-603) would be my choice. The resort has 13 large, simple chalets, 30 rooms with private facilities, and a restaurant serving local and Western cuisine. Most of the units have a lovely view of the white beach, the blue sea, and the hazy green of Pulau Tengah in the distance. There are bright green lawns, a very long jetty to get out to deep water, and good fishing, snorkeling, and shell collecting opportunities. Room rates are from around M$85. The **Whitesand Beach Resort** (Tel: 07-334-669) has rooms from M$50, while **Radin Island Resort** (Tel: 07-791-413) has a choice of A-frame huts or air-conditioned bungalows, a restaurant with Malay and Chinese food, and a swimming pool. Room rates are from M$100.

There are still further options. **Pirate Bay** (Tel: 011-762-042) on *Pulau Tengah* is being heavily promoted at present. The resort has water and electricity and wooden chalets with attached bathrooms. It is a place to do nothing except be a beachcomber or sea lover. The cottages are not particularly attractive or well sited but there is a pleasant feel to the resort due to the hospitality and friendliness of the managers and the discretion of the staff.

Pulau Sibu and *Pulau Sibu Tengah* are two islands growing in popularity. They are about 2½ hours from Mersing but it is closer to the mainland village of Tg Sedili. Transportation is much less frequent here so you should arrange something with the resort where you wish to stay. The options are the **Sibu Island Cabanas** (Tel: 07-317-216 in Johor Bahru), 24 units; **The Sea Gypsy Village Resort** (Tel: 07-791-101), 25 rooms; or the **Sibu Island Resort** (Tel: 07-231-188), which is actually on Sibu Tengah Island. There are some beautiful, deserted beaches on the islands. The Sibu Island Cabanas has concrete and timber chalets fronting a lovely beach. There is jungle trekking, snorkeling, and scuba diving, a nearby fishing village to visit, a games room, a souvenir shop, and 24-hour bar and restaurant services. Prices range from M$30-60 per person including breakfast.

Pulau Tinggi is 32 kilometers south of Mersing. For centuries the island was a stopover point for traders plying the East-West trade route. Apart from a small fishing village, Tinggi is largely uninhabited. It has white sand beaches, clear water, and good coral reefs. The 120-room **Smailing Island Resort** (Tel: 07-246-290) consists of wooden chalets with *attap* roofs. Each room is air-conditioned, and has TV, IDD telephone, and attached bathroom. There is a restaurant with local and Western cuisine, a pool, a gymnasium, and water sports facilities. Rates start at around M$360 (Book at No. 17, Tingkat 2, Komplex Tun Abdul Razak, Jalan Wong Ah Fook, 80000 Johor Bahru, Malaysia; Fax: 607-246-491.) The nearby **Tinggi Island Resort** (Tel: 07-791-606) has rooms from M$150 a night. The ferry is M$30 round-trip.

After you visit one or more of the island resorts, you will want to go to Johor Bahru. Route 3 to the south takes you 100 kilometers to **Kota Tinggi**. The town has little interest but it is an important junction for roads to the Kota Tinggi waterfall and the Desaru beach area, and for river trips down to Johor Lama (old Johor). The Sengat Seafood Restaurant has good food at reasonable prices. There are some inexpensive accommodations on the restaurant fish farm, for keen anglers.

At about 635 meters, Gunung Muntahak forms the southern end of the backbone of mountains down peninsular Malaysia. In its lower reaches the waters of the Johor River thunder past huge boulders,

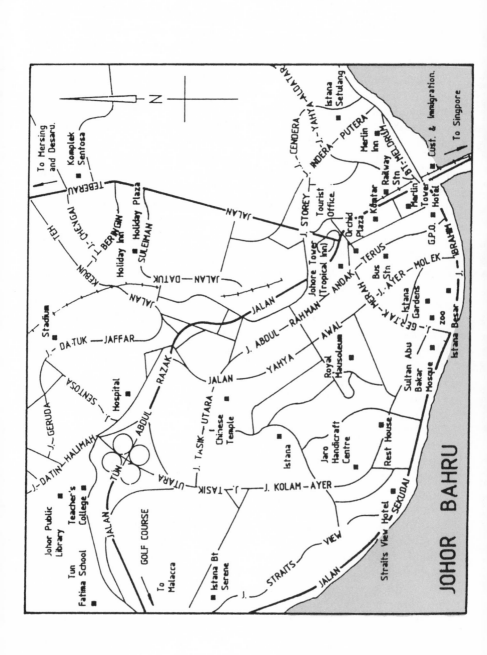

ferns, and hanging vines to finally fall down a 24-meter slope of rocks into two natural pools. The pools and falls have been developed into a popular picnic, bathing, and vacation spot. From here you can climb to the top of the mountain or stay overnight in chalets that cling to the side of the hill on the fringe of the forest, near the falls. Each chalet has a bedroom, a sitting room, and a kitchen equipped with cooking utensils, crockery, cutlery, gas, and a refrigerator. There is a restaurant that serves European, Muslim, and Chinese dishes. A camping site is also available. Book through 07-241-957, extension 30.

The village of **Johor Lama** has considerable historic interest. Until 1587, this was the royal seat of the Johor Kingdom and a thriving trading post. In that year, a three-year quarrel broke out with the Portuguese, culminating in an attack on the town. When the fort was destroyed, the town was sacked and a large booty of precious metals and other treasures was carried away. The town has never recovered. Archaeological excavations have uncovered interesting relics and the old fort has been restored, so now the village is an interesting point to visit. There are no real roads to the village; however, there is a new road to Telok Sengat fishing village, which is three kilometers upriver. There is a nice walk along the river to Johor Lama. Alternatively you can arrange to go downriver by boat.

The other main road from Kota Tinggi goes to **Desaru**. This is a much-publicized but overrated beach resort on the extreme southeast point of peninsular Malaysia. It is popular for weekend visits by Singaporeans but has not yet attracted any great international following. At present there are two hotels, a cluster of chalets, a camping ground, an 18-hole golf course, and some other recreational facilities.

The best accommodations are at the **Desaru View Hotel** (Tel: 07-821-221), 134 rooms, from around M$200 a night. This low-rise hotel has a good swimming pool, four restaurants, and a casuarina-fringed beach. The nearby **Desaru Hotel** (Tel: 07-821-101), 100 rooms, has an attractive restaurant, a bar, a karaoke lounge, and a lounge pool. There is good sporting opportunities, including an 18-hole golf course designed by Robert Trent Jones II. Room rates start at around M$150 on weekdays and M$250 on weekends. For families the **Desaru Chalet** (Tel: 07-821-240) is an option. A standard chalet for two costs M$140. Family units are available. Huts at M$50 and camping sites at M$10 per person can also be rented. The nearby Tanjung Balan fishing village has some local flavor. Rooms are available from M$30 for two.

It's now 1½ hours by road to **Johor Bahru**, the southern gateway to Malaysia. This capital of Johor state is connected to Singapore by a causeway and it suffers greatly in comparison to its southern neighbor.

The city has some historic significance and points of interest, however, but few travellers stop long enough to find out. The city was established in 1866 when Sultan Abu Bakar moved his capital to this location. It has since grown into one of the most progressive cities in Malaysia.

Away from the congested streets, the majestic Istana Besar (Principal Palace) is a treasure house of the state's history. The palace on Jalan Tun Dr Ishmail was built in 1866 by His Royal Highness Sultan Abu Bakar. Since 1992 the palace has also been a museum. Surrounding the palace is a 50-hectare landscaped garden containing a Japanese teahouse and other items of interest. In the evening a stroll along the multicolored lit promenade is a pleasant experience. You will hear the *muezzin*, from the Sultan Abu Bakar mosque, calling Muslims to prayers.

The mosque, set on a hill, is considered to be one of the finest in Malaysia. It took eight years to complete and can hold 2,000 worshippers. The chief landmark of Johor Bahru is the eye-catching Sultan Ibrahim Building with its square tower rising 65 meters into the air. The building houses the State Council Chamber and the state government offices. The Istana Bukit Serene is the current residence of the Sultan of Johor. The building was completed in 1933.

Johor Bahru is becoming a good place for shopping. The modern Kotaraya Plaza next to the Pan Pacific Hotel is very popular as is the Tun Abdul Razak Complex on Jalan Wong Ah Fook. The other major complex is the Holiday Plaza next to the Holiday Inn. This has almost everything you could want.

Another place worth visiting is the Malaysian Craft Center known as Kraftangan Malaysia on Jalan Sungai Chat. The center is open from 8 A.M. to 4:15 P.M. daily and is a show place for Malaysian crafts, fashions, furnishings, arts, jewelry, and so on. Just opposite here is the Johor Area Rehabilitation Organisation where gifts are made by physically handicapped artists and craftspeople. There are original designs of top-quality bedspreads, cushions, table mats, and soft toys.

There are plenty of places to stay in Johor Bahru. Top of the heap is the 500-room **Puteri Pan Pacific Hotel** (Tel: 07-233-333), which opened in 1992. This is both a business and holiday hotel. There are several restaurants, bars, and entertainment outlets. The sports center is excellent. The Pacific Floors caters specifically for busy executives. Room rates are from M$260. (Fax: 607-236-622) Then there is the **Holiday Inn** (Tel: 07-323-800), 190 rooms, on Jalan Dato Sultaiman, with rates from M$180 a night. It has a 24-hour coffee house, a Chinese restaurant with Szechuan cuisine, and a popular disco. There is a fitness room and a business center, and the hotel is adjacent to the large

Holiday Plaza Shopping Center. (Fax: 607-218-884). Next is the **Merlin Tower Hotel** (Tel: 07-225-811), 104 rooms, right in the center of town. Room rates here start at around M$120. This is not to be confused with the nearby, but cheaper **Merlin Inn** (Tel: 07-227-400). Another up-market choice is the **Tropical Inn Hotel** (Tel: 07-247-888) with 167 rooms from M$105. You could also try the new **Crystal Crown Hotel** (Tel: 07-334-422), 122 rooms with pool, restaurants, fitness center, and shops.

The **Straits View Hotel** (Tel: 07-241-402), 30 rooms, on the prome-nade about 1½ kilometers from the center of town, has some old-world charm while there are some fair rooms for M$55 at the **Regent Elite Hotel** (Tel: 07-243-812), 62 rooms, at 1 Jalan Siew Nam. Further down-market, the **Hotel Malaya** (Tel: 07-221-691) has 35 reasonable rooms from M$40 and the **Fortuna Hotel** (Tel: 07-228-671), 23 rooms from M$40, is right in the middle of everything. The old **Century Hotel** (Tel: 07-320-238) has 25 rooms starting at around M$20. Don't expect too much for that price. You can get a similarly priced room at **Budget Lodge** (Tel: 07-242-551) on Jalan Ah Siang, but you really need a vehicle for this location.

Johor Bahru has a good food reputation. You could try one of the hawkers' centers—opposite the railway station during the day, or near the Kompleks Tun Razak at night. The *laksa Johor* is a very popular dish. If seafood is your choice, **Jaw's 5 Seafood Restaurant** (Tel: 07-236-062) on Jalan Scudai is the place to go. Chose between *attap*-roofed Malay-style huts or an air-conditioned building, but enjoy the Cantonese, Hainanese, and Shanghai seafood specialties. On this same road you could also try the **Lido Seafood** restaurant (Tel: 07-221-429).

Good Malay food is found at the **Medina Restaurant** (Tel: 07-226-703) on Jalan Meldrum, while **Granee's Banana Leaf and Pub** (Tel: 07-223-573), and the **Kerala Restaurant** (Tel: 07-224-283) are good places for Indian food. There are many good Chinese restaurants. **Ming Dragon** at the Holiday Plaza (Tel: 07-332-252) is very popular as is **Tong Ah** (Tel: 07-222-472) on Jalan Ibrahim.

There are other entertainment options. **Christine's Place** (Tel: 231-628) on Jalan Tebrau claims it is a one-stop entertainment spot. They have seafood, Chinese cuisine, an outdoor waterfall garden, a bakery, a hair salon, a fitness center, a Japanese nightclub, and charming waitresses. The **Zodiac Lounge** (Tel: 311-901) at the Holiday Plaza has continuous entertainment until late, as does the **Red Baron** at the Holiday Inn. Finally don't miss the **Mecinta Restaurant and Nightclub** behind the Straits View Gardens which has become synonymous with Johor Bahru nightlife.

When you decide to leave Johor Bahru to go to Malacca, if time is not pressing, head for Pontian Kechi on the coast and follow Route 5 all the way to Malacca. If you do this, you should make a detour to the village of Kukup.

Kukup is about 80 kilometers from Johor Bahru but that doesn't stop hundreds of people from travelling there to enjoy the famous seafood. You pass through oil palms and rubber plantations and a few coffee farms on a pleasant 1½ hour drive. At Kukup there are a number of seafood restaurants built out over the water and a stop for a meal is highly recommended. If you have the time, take the boat trip to a fish farm then on to the fishing village that is home to several thousand Hokkien Chinese. This was once a smugglers' hideout but those days are finished. Money today comes from fishing and from tourists.

It's about one hundred kilometers from here to **Batu Pahat**, a riverside town with several hotels, some good restaurants, and a small nightlife scene. There is really no reason to stop here but it could be worth trying one of the Chinese restaurants that have a good reputation in this region.

Batu Pahat, like Malacca, has a Glutton's Corner and here at this open-air market different varieties of food are served nightly from stalls, until well after midnight. It is a fascinating scene. The **Futuna Restaurant** (Tel: 07-449-175) is the best Chinese restaurant in town.

Beyond Batu Pahat, the road is again flanked by tidy rows of rubber trees and small Malay *kampungs* under coconut palms. The next main town is **Muar**, in a riverside setting close to the sea. This is a placid place with an unhurried pace. While the town itself is cosmopolitan with cloth merchants and others spilling their waves onto the sidewalks, the area surrounding the town is steeped in Malay culture. This is a good place to hear the haunting sounds of traditional *ghazal* music or watch an exhibition of *silat*, the Malay art of self-defense.

The best hotels in town are the **Hotel Sri Pelangi** (Tel: 06-918-088) with 80 rooms from M$60 and the **Park View Hotel** (Tel: 06-916-655) with 90 air-conditioned rooms from M$55. There is a pleasant rest house at 2222 Jalan Sultanah with 18 rooms from around M$40.

As you leave Muar, you cross the river and soon enter the state of Melaka. A few kilometers farther on, you pass a colorful intricate wood-carved chieftain's house built in 1894. It is worth a stop to see the verandah columns, the front steps covered with brilliant red, yellow, and blue art nouveau tiles, and the rainbow colors that adorn the building. Between here and Malacca there are several beachside restaurants that specialize in fresh grilled fish with an assortment of local dishes. It is a fitting end to an extensive tour through southern Malaysia.

7. Guided Tours

I have been unable to find out anything about tours in or from Malacca or Johor Bahru. I suggest you talk to the information offices in each place when you get there.

8. Culture

Malacca and the South celebrate all the national festivals and there are some others that are celebrated statewide or just in one district.

In Malacca these extra celebrations add to the festival calendar. The **Malacca Hotel Week** is a week-long celebration in March that features food festivals, decoration competitions, and so on. All the major hotels take part.

The **Mariamman Festival** is a day-long celebration at this temple in Gajah Berong (just west of central Malacca). There is a round the city procession at night. It is held in May.

Wesak Day is celebrated by Buddhists at the Sek Kiah Eerih Temple in Gajah Berand in May. A Mardi Gras-style procession including decorated floats, bands, and acrobatic performances is held at night through the main street.

Sant Sohan Singh's Prayer Anniversary draws thousands of Sikhs from all over Malaysia and Singapore to the Malacca Sikh Temple in May. They join in memorial prayers, singing, and reciting the Sikh holy book over a three-day period.

The **Birthday of TYT Yang Di Pertua Negeri**, the head of the state of Malacca, is celebrated with a parade of uniformed units at the Padang in central Malacca. Government buildings and commercial establishments are decorated for this event in June.

The **Feast of St. Peter** is celebrated in June at the Portuguese Settlement by fishermen. The fishing boats, which are colorfully decorated for the festival, are blessed and prayers offered for a better season.

The **Malacca Sea Carnival** is held at Klebang Besar Beach in August. It includes windsurfing and boat competitions between local and international teams.

The **Malacca Carnival** is a month-long celebration in August that includes traditional cultural performances, an industrial exhibition, a tourism expo, local games, and other shows. It is held at the Ayer Keroh Expo Center.

9. Sports

Malacca is well supplied with sports facilities and visitors are welcome to use most of them. Here is a quick rundown:

Badminton is a very popular sport and there are facilities in almost every center. In Malacca you should go to the **Melaka Badminton Association Hall** on Jalan Tengkera.

Bowling alleys are found at the **Asia Bowling Center** in the Emperor Hotel (Tel: 227-588), and at the **Plaza Inn Bowling Center** in Jalan Munshi Abdullah.

Golf is played at the exclusive **Ayer Keroh Country Club** (Tel: 06-322947) at Ayer Keroh. You need an introduction from your hotel or home golf club. It's much more relaxed at the nine-hole **Jasin Golf Club** (Tel: 06-987-234) at Jasin about 20 kilometers northeast of Malacca.

It's also worth listing some of the other fine courses that exist in the southern part of peninsular Malaysia, away from Malacca. Top of the list would be the **Royal Johor Country Club** (Tel: 07-228-882) near Johor Bahru. This is considered by many professional golfers to be the best in Malaysia. The 72 par course is beautifully maintained and the clubhouse provides a range of sporting and entertainment options. The **Desaru Resort Golf Club** (Tel: 07-838-187) is a fine seaside course with weekday green fees of M$60. The **Seremban International Golf Club** (Tel: 06-775-787) is not so well promoted but it is a very fine course with nine water holes, plenty of sand traps, and sweeping greens. The clubhouse has all the usual fine facilities. Green fees are M$30 on weekdays. The **Port Dickson Golf and Country Club** is currently upgrading and expanding its fine 9-hole course. When finished it will be one of the finest courses in the country. The clubhouse is already in that category.

Health Centers are located at many of the major hotels—Ramada Renaissance, Malacca Village Resort, Emperor, and Ashoka—and there is a public facility at the **Executive Health Center Downtown** on Jalan Tun Sri Lanang.

Jogging can be done almost anywhere but the Ayer Keroh Recreational Forest, Bukit China, and the Padang are where you will find many locals early morning or late afternoon.

Roller skating is available at **Disco Roller Skating Rink** at the Emperor Hotel (Tel: 240-777), or the **Larger Roller Skating Center** in the Soon Seng Plaza, Jalan Kilang.

Snooker tables are available at the **Ramada Club** (Tel: 240-000), the **Broadway Snooker Saloon** at the Emperor Hotel (Tel: 240-777), and at the **Plaza Snooker Center** on Jalan Munshi Abdullah.

Squash facilities are located at the Ramada and Emperor hotels, at the Malacca Village Resort, at **De Yonnex-Ascot Squash Center** on Jalan Tun Perak (6 courts), and at Taman Muhibbah, Klebang Besar.

Swimming pools are a feature of many hotels—Ramada, Emperor,

Malacca Village Resort, Ayer Keroh Country Resort, Tanjung Bidara Beach Resort, Shah's Beach Resort, and City Bayview. As well as these there is a public pool in Jalan Kota, the Melaka Club swimming pool at Tanjung Keling, and a pool at the Ayer Keroh Country Club.

Tennis is another popular sport. No city hotel has courts but there are public facilities at the **Government Services Club** at Bukit Baru. Out of town, courts are available at the Malacca Village Resort, the Ayer Keroh Country Resort, the Tanjung Bidara Beach Resort, and Shah's Beach Resort.

Volleyball courts are available at three district resorts—Malacca Village, Tanjong Bidara Beach, and Ayer Keroh country.

Windsurfing can be enjoyed at Klebang Beach and Tanjung Bidara Beach on weekends and during busy tourist periods.

10. Shopping

Shopping in Malacca ranges from large department stores to colorful bazaars with unbeatable prices (for the locals). Prices are fixed at major shopping complexes but bargaining is welcomed and expected at smaller retail shops and roadside stalls. The bigger shopping centers are found in Jalan Raya, Jalan Hang Tuah, and Jalan Kilang.

Malacca is a great center for **antique** hunters but be aware that you will need the permission of the Director General of the Malaysia Museum before you can export any valuable piece. Even if you don't plan on buying, a visit in and around Jalan Hang Jebat (Jonkers Street) will provide hours of fun as you browse through relics of yesterday—brass bedsteads, porcelain artifacts, and other delightful articles. Two particular recommendations are Fatimah Antik Store at 46 Jalan Hang Jebat and K & S Antiques House at 25 Jalan Hang Jebat.

Handicrafts and souvenirs are found all over but there are some excellent items made from rattan and pandanus at stalls along Jalan Taman, and other items of good quality are at the Malacca Handicrafts Exhibition Center along Jalin Laksamana. There is also a good handicraft center at Mini Malaysia at Ayer Keroh. Two specific shops worth trying are Malacca Souvenir House at 22 Jalan Tokong, and Portobella at 7 Jalan Lakisamana. Malacca Woodwork Art at Kiebang Basar has some interesting items.

The **Night Bazaar** (*Pasar Malam*) can be a good place to shop for basic needs, but it is more like a fiesta bustling with activities from about 5:30 P.M. Malays get groceries, kitchenware, and other household goods here but visitors will be attracted mainly by the atmosphere and food opportunities. The Pasar Malam operates in different places on different nights. A schedule is available from the tourist information office.

Visitors will also be interested in seeing the **Farmers Market** (*Pasar Tani*) which operates from 8 A.M. till noon on Saturdays at Jalan Hang Tuah, and at Masjid Tanah in the district of Alor Gajah. Farmers bring fish, meat, vegetables, fruits, and groceries to town and sell it directly to consumers.

11. Entertainment and Nightlife

When the sun sets, Malacca has a surprisingly good range of nightlife. There are cinemas, discos, pubs, and nightclubs, and the occasional cultural performance. Much of the light entertainment is centered on the hotels or on Jalan Taman Melaka Raya near the old waterfront.

The best place to catch a cultural show is Mini Malaysia out at Ayer Kerok, where traditional games such as top spinning and martial arts are held from about 10:30 A.M. on Sundays and a cultural show is performed from about 4:30 P.M.

The alternative is the Saturday evening show at Portuguese Square, which you can enjoy over dinner or separately beginning at about 8:30 P.M. For nondiners an entrance fee is charged.

There are four major cinemas in Malacca that screen English as well as Malay and Chinese films daily. Shows are normally at 3 P.M., 6:30 P.M., and 9:15 P.M.: The **Federal** (Tel: 223-632), the **Cathay** (Tel: 224-922), or the **Capital** (Tel: 223-632) should be contacted if you have the urge to see a movie.

There are a few discotheques around town, but the only two that are likely to appeal to visitors are the **Stardust Disco** (Tel: 248-888) at the Ramada Renaissance Hotel, and the **Camelot Disco** (Tel: 240-777) at the Emperor Hotel.

The only true nightclub in town is the **Old City Night Club** on Jalan Taman Melaka Raya. It's here too that you will find the **Art Fusion Lounge**, the **Elysium Lounge**, and the **Country Ranch**, all drinking spots with music in the evening. Malacca, incidently, has a good local reputation for Portuguese-descent Country and Western singers and musicians. You can hear some of these in the hotel lounges, although it seems more fashionable at the moment to have a Filipino group. All the major hotels—Ramada, Emperor, City Bayview, Ayer Keroh Country Resort, and Malacca Village Resort—have a lounge with at least some music most evenings.

12. The Malacca and the South Address List

Malacca

Airport—	Tel: 06-222-648
Bank—Bumiputra Malaysia, Jalan Kota	225-253
—Hong Kong & Shanghai, Jalan Kota	222-399
Bus Service—City. Town Bus Service	224-966
—Local. Syerikat Kenderaan Aziz	229-837
Tai Lye Omnibus Co.	220-259
—Long-distance. Singapore Express	224-470
K.L. Express	222-503
Hospital—Malacca General (24 hours)	222-344
Immigration—	224-958
M.A.S.—	235-722
Malacca Tourist Info. Center—Jalan Kota	236-538
Malacca State Devel. Corp.—Peti Surat	220-643
Money changer—Sultan Enterprise, J. Laksamana	241-958
Police—Central station, Jalen Banda Kaba	222-222
Postal Service—G.P.O. Jalan Melaka	323-846
Radio—Radio Malaysia Melaka	242-277
Railways—Malacca Office, Taman Pringgit Jaya	223-091
Taxi—Jalan Tun Mamat	223-630
Telephone—Kedai Telekom, Jalon Hang Tuah	239-929
—Trunk call assistance	101
—International call	108
—Emergency	999
Travel Agent—Malacca Oriental Travel	224-877

Johor Bahru

Airport—	Tel: 07-241-985
Bus Services—National Express, Bangunan Mara	227-220
Johor Tourist Association—	241-122
Johor T.P.B. Office—	223-590
M.A.S.—Orchard Plaza	220-888
Police—	232-222
Railways—	233-040
Taxi—	234-494

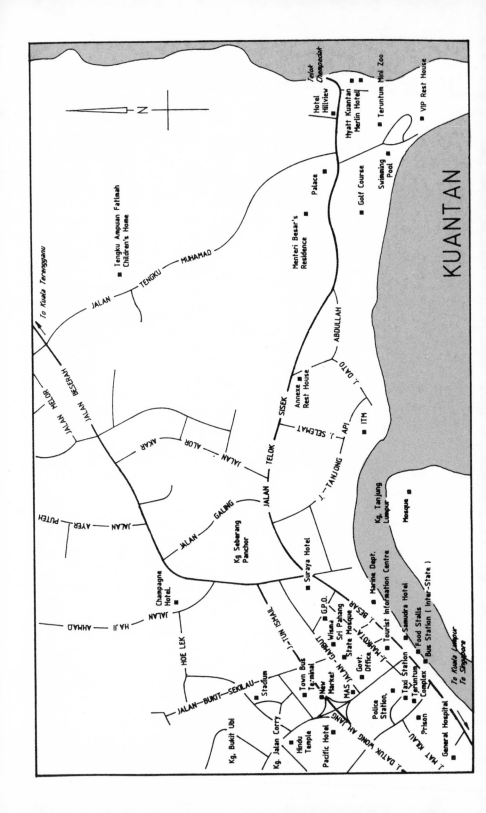

11

The East Coast

1. The General Picture

A short plane ride, or a four-hour drive, from Kuala Lumpur lies Kuantan and the East Coast of Malaysia. If you travel overland, the pace slows appreciably and as you head north along the coast you discover a leisurely and tranquil way of life that has disappeared from much of the world. This is peninsular Malaysia at its most natural, yet it's an area few tourists get the opportunity to explore.

There are more than 800 kilometers of coastline more or less paralleled by a road from Johor Bahru in the far south to the Thai border in the north. Fishing is the main occupation on this sandy shore and you see scores of small stilted villages with wooden fishing boats clustered around the mouths of the coast's numerous estuaries.

Here men in checkered sarongs sit cross-legged, mending their fishing nets, while their shy women in traditional blouse and sarong prepare fish and squid for drying and preserving. Their home is a humble wood and *attap* hut on stilts, huddled into a *kampung*. It is a life-style and tradition that has been hardly touched by the twentieth century.

In between the villages, the golden sands and coconut palms stretch in sweeping curves of almost continuous beach, punctuated here and there by rivers and rocky headlands. There is no shortage of beaches where you will be the only inhabitant, no shortage of quiet picnic spots.

In some areas there is a shortage of shops and restaurants, so you need to be prepared.

Then there are the cities and towns. Kuantan is the major center. It is large, pleasant, and flat, full of shops and industry, but also catering to national and international visitors with a modern airport and several international-style hotels and resorts. Farther north, Kuala Terengganu and Kota Bharu are centers for the states of Terengganu and Kelantan. Each has palaces, mosques, and markets, and plenty of interest for visitors.

It is very easy to be lured by the magical lilt of the seashore and the coconut palms, the delightful timelessness of the *kampungs*, the colorful handicrafts, and the activities of the carefree locals. Without knowing it, you are soon absorbed into the heartland of ancient Malay culture.

Back from the coast, there are coconut, groundnut, and cashew nut crops. Farther north there are tobacco and rice paddies. There is also evidence of devastation and destruction where once grand rain forests have been turned into useless wasteland. This is the dark side of the picture and in places it is still occurring.

Fortunately the large **Taman Negara National Park** provides an area free from damage. It is becoming an increasingly popular destination for visitors. So too are the unspoiled islands off the coast, which until very recently had remained almost hidden secrets.

For the purposes of this book, we consider the East Coast region to extend south as far as the border between Pahang and Johor. Johor is included in the Malacca and the South chapter.

2. Getting There

There are four **airports** serving the East Coast—Kuantan, Kerteh, Kuala Terengganu, and Kota Bharu. All are served by Malaysia Airlines or a subsidiary, and all are linked with Kuala Lumpur and some other ports. Kuantan is probably the most important with services from Kuala Lumpur, Johor Bahru, and Singapore, and feeder services to and from Pulau Tioman and Kerteh. Kuala Terengganu is connected to Kuala Lumpur, Penang, and Johor Bahru, and there are feeder services to Kerteh. Kota Bharu is connected with Kuala Lumpur, Alor Setar, and Penang. Kerteh has a direct service from Kuala Lumpur.

All centers are linked by air-conditioned and non-air-conditioned **buses**. There are regular air-conditioned coaches departing Kota Bharu in the north that travel via Kuala Terengganu, Kertah, and Kuantan to both Kuala Lumpur and Johor Bahru/Singapore. Other services originate in Kuala Terengganu and Kuantan so that there are at least 20

Along the coast of Terengganu, idyllic thatch-roofed villages are a common sight.

Terengganu fishing village. (Courtesy of the Malaysia Tourism Promotion Board)

services a day from Kuantan to Kuala Lumpur and 8-10 services to Johor Bahru. Despite this, at times it can be difficult to get a seat at the time you wish to travel. There are also services from the west coast (Penang) to Kota Bharu via the cross-country Route 4.

Air-conditioned **taxis** also operate these routes at roughly twice the cost of the buses. They can be faster and if there are several people travelling together, they can be extremely convenient because it's not necessary to wait for other passengers.

Kuantan and Kuala Terengganu are not served by **train** but Kota Bharu is. The line doesn't come from Kuala Lumpur, however, but through central Malaysia from Singapore/Johor Bahru, so it is not well used by visitors. This rail line links with the Thai rail system at the border; however, on the Malaysian side no passenger trains actually travel to the border. You have to go the last 20 kilometers or so by taxi or local bus.

3. Local Transportation

All the major centers have local buses that provide fast, cheap, and reliable service to most places that visitors will wish to visit. Some centers have **trishaws**, which are suitable for short journeys. A ten-minute ride should cost approximately M$3.

Buses operate from defined bus stations in each major center. In Kuantan the local buses operate from a terminal on Jalan Besar while the long-distance buses have another bus station also on Jalan Besar. In Kuala Terengganu all buses operate from the central bus station on Jalan Masjid. In Kota Bharu local buses operate from the Jalan Padang Garong bus station; buses to Penang operate from Jalan Sultan Ibrahim; and buses to Kuala Lumpur, Kuantan, and Johor Bahru depart from the bus station on Jalan Hamzah (south of the central city).

Rental car agencies are available for those who want to have the flexibility of their own transportation. In Kuantan there is the choice of **Avis Rent-A-Car** (Tel: 523-659) at 59 Loo Bros Building, or at the Hyatt Hotel Lobby (Tel: 525-211); **Budget Rent-A-Car** (Tel: 587-771) at the Coral Beach Resort at Beserah; or **Thrifty Rent-A-Car** (Tel: 528-400) at the Merlin Inn. These companies will all meet confirmed reservations at the Kuantan airport.

Rental cars are also available in Kuala Terengganu from **WLO Travel and Air Cargo** (Tel: 635-844), and in Kota Bharu from **Avis Rent-A-Car** (Tel: 784-457) at the Perdana Hotel, or **Mars Travel and Tours** (Tel: 785-238). Cars will meet confirmed reservations at the Kota Bharu airport.

Taxis may be hailed or booked by telephone but there is also a central taxi station in each center. In Kuantan it is on Jalan Mahkota, in Kuala Terengganu it is on Jalan Sultan Ismail near the jetty (Tel: 621-581), and in Kota Bharu it is opposite the town bus station on Jalan Pendek (Tel: 747-104).

4. The Hotel Scene

The East Coast has the usual range of accommodation options. The expensive hotels are mainly beach resorts scattered along the coast in the major centers and elsewhere. There are midmarket and budget accommodations both in the major centers and elsewhere, including some in the undeveloped beach areas.

EXPENSIVE HOTELS

There are no expensive hotels on the coast south of Kuantan. In Kuantan, the best hotels are at Teluk Chempedak, a beach about five kilometers from the center of the city.

The **Hyatt Kuantan** (Tel: 525-211), 185 rooms, is the top hotel. It has an absolute beachfront location and many of the rooms in the low-medium-rise accommodation blocks have lovely ocean views. Rooms are brightly furnished with colorful *batik* and stylish rattan furniture, and there are wide balconies for enjoying the outdoors. The large pool with its underwater lighting has a swim-up bar, and lounge chairs under bright umbrellas provide a great setting for a relaxing few hours. You can enjoy spicy Malaysian dishes in the Kampong Cafe, or hone your skills on the tennis courts, the two squash courts, or the nearby golf course. Room prices start around M$200. (Book with the Hyatt organization or direct with the hotel at Teluk Chempedak, Kuantan 25050; Fax: 609-507-577.) This is a very attractive and well-run property.

The **Merlin Inn Resort** (Tel: 522-388), 106 rooms, is built right next door to the Hyatt and shares the same beach. There are noticeable differences in the two properties, however, as indicated by the small lobby at the Merlin compared with the grand timbered affair at the Hyatt. The Merlin has a nice swimming pool and restaurant overlooking the beach but somehow lacks that finishing touch to make it a top resort. I have never stayed here and on my last visit I was unable to convince anyone to show me around. The hotel had also run out of brochures, so frankly my knowledge of the whole place is very limited. Room rates start at around M$160. (Book with the hotel at Teluk Chempedak, Kuantan 25050; Fax: 609-503-001.)

In the city itself, the top hotel is the **Sumudra Riverview** (Tel: 522-688). This is located on Jalan Besar in the heart of downtown near the bus station. Ask for one of the rooms away from the street that overlook the swimming complex, the Kuantan River, and the forests beyond. Fishing boats, anglers, and riverside strollers add to the scene. Rooms here are fairly average but there are good restaurants—the Riverview Lounge at night, and the Sumadra Restaurant for Malay/Chinese/Western dishes—with excellent seafood at reasonable prices. Room prices start at around M$120 a night. (Book with the hotel at Jalan Besar, 25000 Kuantan, Pahang; Fax: 609-500-618.)

Moving north from Kuantan you come to Beserah Beach, 15 kilometers from the city. This is the location of the **Coral Beach Resort** (Tel: 587-544), 162 rooms, on a sweeping beach facing the South China Sea. The resort offers tranquility and privacy under a canopy of casuarinas and palms, but there is also plenty of action for those who need it. The beach is a top windsurfing location and the resort also offers a large swimming pool, a children's pool, a gymnasium, a sauna and spa pool, tennis, squash, badminton, table tennis, a games room, and daily social activities.

There are numerous wining and dining options. The Cafe Bayu overlooks the pool and offers 24-hour coffee house service of Malaysian and Western cuisine. The Nankai Restaurant serves Japanese dishes in a serene ambience, while the Segara Restaurant provides seafood lovers fresh, succulent offerings. For the energetic seeking a livelier beat, there is Force E Discotheque and the Recreational Center lounge. (Book with the hotel at 152 Sungai Karang, 26100 Beserah, Pahang; Fax: 609-587-543.)

There are two new resorts just north of here and another under construction. The **Cherating Holiday Villa Beach Resort** (Tel: 439-500), 200 rooms, has plenty of facilities. There are two pools, a spa, three tennis courts, a gymnasium, a seasports center, a disco, karaoke, and a beach hut restaurant. Room rates from M$150. The luxurious **Palm Grove Beach Resort** (Tel: 439-439), 96 rooms and 56 villas, is similarly equipped. Restaurant choices are the Neptune's Net for seafood; the Five Continents for à-la-carte dining, or the 24-hour coffee shop. Sports facilities include tennis, squash, a gymnasium, a beach club, and a disco. (Book on Fax: 609-439-300.) The **Sunny Beach Resort Hotel Apartment** is under construction on a nice beach front.

It's about 35 kilometers from here to the **Club Méditerranée** at Cherating (Tel: 591-131), 300 rooms. This is the largest resort on the East Coast and one of the nicest. It is located on a private beach tucked beneath a heavily wooded headland. The resort hides behind tight

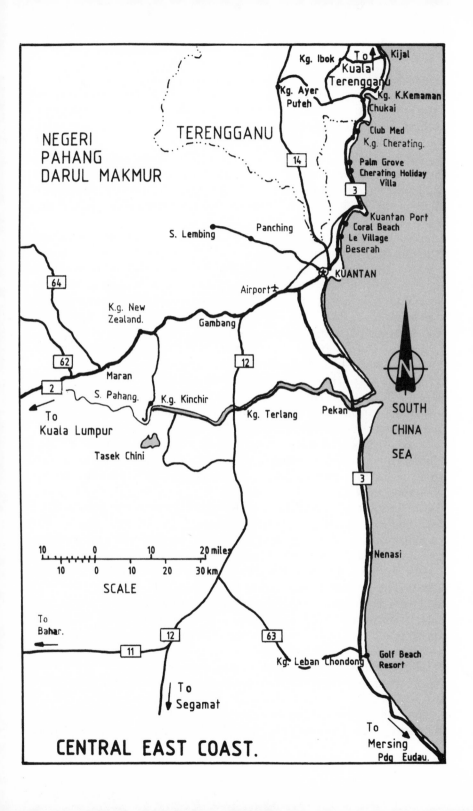

security, and casual day visitors are not permitted. At certain times of the year the supply of overseas packaged tourists slows, so the resort has decided that local packages are OK then, to fill up the empty rooms. You could telephone ahead to see if it is a time that you would be welcome.

The resort has a nice pool, several restaurants, shops, plenty of activities, and the mandatory Club Med beads for payment of drinks and other noninclusive items. The accommodations are all low-rise, close to the beach. (Book with the hotel at Cherating, Kuantan, Pahang; Fax: 609-591-131.)

The Club Med is located right on the border of the states of Pahang and Terengganu and it's another 100 kilometers to the next major resort. The **Tanjong Jara Beach Hotel** (Tel: 841-801), 100 rooms, is, in fact, my favorite East Coast resort. It fronts one of the best stretches of beach on the whole coast, but its great appeal is its architecture, and the use it has made of a small inlet that intrudes onto the site. You need a few days to fully appreciate the beauty and peace of this place.

The hotel is designed in the tradition of the ancient *istana* or Sultan's Palace. Native skills and materials are evident in the carved gable grilles, on steeply pitched roofs thatched with locally made bisque tiles, and the intricately carved balustrades and verandahs. The air-conditioned rooms have traditional louver doors and windows, and towering ceilings. Daily rates start at around M$170.

The heart of the hotel is the spacious lobby that leads to the bar, dining room, and outdoor terrace. All look out on the pool, the lagoon, and the lovely footbridge that links the gardens and sprawling accommodation units. It would be difficult to find a more attractive location. For those sporting enthusiasts, there is swimming, windsurfing, snorkeling, jogging, trekking, boating, sailing, cycling, tennis, and squash. For indoor lovers, there is a games room and a sauna. (Book with the hotel at 8 mile, Off Dungun, 23009 Dungun, Terengganu; Fax: 609-842-653.)

You find the next hotel in this category a few kilometers farther north. The **Rantau Abang Visitor Center** (Tel: 841-533) has 10 chalets that rent for around M$120 in the April to September period and about half of this at other times. This is quite an attractive place built on stilts out over a lagoon behind the beach, and there is a bar and restaurant.

The **Primula Kapas Island Village Resort** (Tel: 622-100) has 40 bugalows, a restaurant, a bar, and a pool on Kapas Island. Room rates are from M$160.

Sixty kilometers farther on, the **Primula K.T. Beach Resort** (Tel: 622-100), 264 rooms, provides good accommodations in Kuala

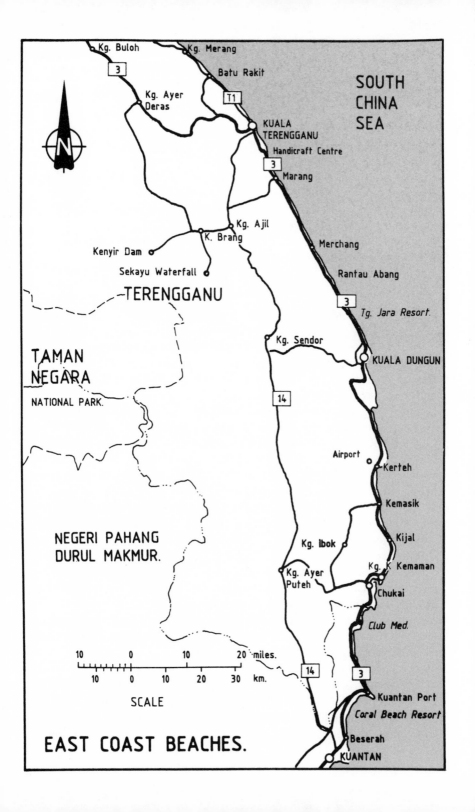

EAST COAST BEACHES.

Terengganu. The hotel is on a beach about one kilometer from the center of town. The beach is not particularly clean but there are windsurfing opportunities and a very attractive swimming pool area. The hotel has three restaurants, a bar, and a disco. Room prices start at M$180. (Book with the hotel at Jalan Persinggahan, Kuala Terengganu, 20904 Terengganu.)

In Kota Bharu, the **Hotel Perdana** (Tel: 785-000), 136 rooms, has a swimming pool, squash courts, tennis, badminton, and 10-pin bowling. Room prices are from M$160. A sister property at the Beach of Passionate Love, the **Perdana Resort** (Tel: 785-222), 120 rooms, has a nice pool, windsurfing, boating, and a restaurant with entertainment. Room prices are from M$120.

MEDIUM-PRICE HOTELS

The choice here is wide, and what suits you will depend to a large extent on what you wish to do—sight-see, laze, or hide away.

Two new resorts have opened south of Kuantan, but they are still struggling to establish themselves. The **Lanjut Golden Beach Golf Resort** (Tel: K.L. 442-3188) and the **Santaburi Beach Resort** will be better in a few years. In the city, four choices that provide reasonable facilities and service are the **Pacific Hotel** (Tel: 511-980), 60 rooms, at 60 Jalan Bukit Ubi; the **Suraya Hotel** (Tel: 524-266); the **Classic Hotel** (Tel: 554-599), 40 rooms, on Jalan Besar; and the **Champagne Hotel** (Tel: 528-820), 50 rooms, at 3002 Jalan Hj. Ahmad Shah. Rooms at the Pacific start at around M$90, at the Suraya at M$80, at the Classic M$75, and those at the Champagne at around M$55. At Baru Beserah, 11 kilometers north of Kuantan, the **Gloria Maris Resort** (Tel: 587-788) has Malay-style wooden chalets right on the beach. They are air-conditioned with attached bathrooms, and the resort has a good Thai/ Chinese restaurant.

Out at Cherating, excellent accommodations and facilities are available at the **Cherating Holiday Villa** (Tel: 508-900), 94 rooms, from M$75. This is a midmarket resort set on the beach with its own swimming pool, gymnasium, sauna, tennis court, and squash court. Some of the rooms are self-contained apartments, ideal for four people travelling together. A short distance north from here, the **Muni Hotel** (Tel: 592-366) at Kemaman has 40 rooms from M$80.

Farther north at the petroleum complex town of Kerteh, the **Perpel Lodge** (Tel: 861-155) provides 48 rooms from $60, while at Kuala Dungun, the **Motel Sri Molek** (Tel: 841-800) has some double rooms from around M$45, chalets from around M$65, and a bungalow at

M$120. A further alternative in this area is the **Merantau Inn** (Tel: 841-131) with 17 chalets from M$50. None of these places is luxurious but they all provide adequate, clean accommodations with some restaurant facilities. The **Liza Inn Marang** (Tel: 632-989) at Kg Pulau Kerengga falls into this same category. Rooms range from M$40-150.

In Kuala Terengganu, the **Motel Desa** (Tel: 623-488), 20 rooms, at around M$80, is at the very top end of this category. It has a swimming pool and is at the summit of a steep hill close to town. In the center of town, on Jalan Sultan Ismail, there are several choices. Look to see which one appeals to you. Try the **Seri Hoover Hotel** (Tel: 624-655), 61 rooms, at No. 49; the **Warisan Hotel** (Tel: 634-622) at No. 65; or the smaller and slightly cheaper **Seri Terengganu** (Tel: 634-622) at No. 120. Room rates in this group start at about M$30 and go up to M$75.

Two other off-the-beaten-track resorts in Terengganu should be included in this category. The first is the **Kenyir Lake Resort** (Tel: 01-950-600), which is a floating chalet and restaurant on the enormous Lake Kenyir, inland from Kuala Terengganu. There are 16 rooms from M$60-120. The second is the **Palau Perhentian Resort** (Tel: 01-333-910) on Perhentian Besar Island, about 20 kilometers off the coast, midway between Kuala Terengganu and Kota Bharu. There are about 80 rooms varying from basic to reasonable. Costs vary between M$20 and M$75. There are also campsites at M$15.

I didn't list any accommodations in Kota Bhuru in the expensive accommodations category but there are plenty in the midmarket class. The best hotel in town is the **Hotel Perdana** (Tel: 785-000), 136 rooms, from about M$90. The hotel has a swimming pool, air-conditioned squash courts, tennis courts, a badminton court, and a bowling alley. There is a coffee house, a poolside terrace, a bar, and a lounge with entertainment.

Down-market from here, there is wide choice. The strange-looking **Murni Hotel** (Tel; 782-399), 38 rooms, on Jalan Dato Pati, is probably the next choice, although there is little to choose between this and the **Kencana Inn City Center** (Tel: 744-388), 34 rooms, which is just around the corner; or the **Kencana Inn** (Tel: 740-944), 36 rooms, on Jalan Padang Garong, a short distance away. Murni rooms start at M$90 while the two Kencana inns start at M$60.

Two other central hotels that are worth trying are **Indah Hotel** (Tel: 785-081), 44 rooms, on Jalan Tengku Besar; and the **Temenggong Hotel** (Tel: 783-130), 36 rooms, on Jalan Tok Hakim. Both have rooms in the M$50-90 price range.

About 12 kilometers from town, at the Beach of Passionate Love, the **Resort Pantai Cinta Berahi** (Tel: 732-307), 29 chalets, has been here for some time and has chalets from around M$100.

BUDGET ACCOMMODATIONS

While there are numerous villages on the coast between Mersing and Kuantan, there are few accommodations for the visitor. Probably the best alternatives are the government **Rest House** (Tel: 565-245) near Kuala Rompin, the small Hotel Kencana, and the **Pekan Hotel** (Tel: 571-378) in Pekan town. All have non-air-conditioned rooms for around M$15.

In Kuantan there is far more choice. The **Baru Raya Hotel** (Tel: 524-953) has 26 fairly basic rooms at prices starting from M$30. Its appeal is the central location and 24-hour check-in. Farther down the same street the **New Embassy Hotel** (Tel: 524-277), 18 rooms, is a better value with rooms from about M$20. There is a nice place called **Annex Rest House** (Tel: 551-455) on Jalan Telok Sisek, about half-way to Telok Chempedak. It is a bit far to walk to anything, but there are plenty of buses passing the door. A room here will cost around M$25.

Out at Telok Chempedak there are several alternatives. The **Hill View Hotel** (Tel: 521-555) is an expensive budget property on the main road with rooms from about M$35. The **Kranton Hotel** behind the Hyatt has basic rooms for around M$30.

About 10 kilometers north at Beserah there are three choices. The **Beserah Beach Rest House** (Tel: 584-935) has a small restaurant and rooms from M$24. **La Chaumiere** (Tel: 587-662) is a bed-and-breakfast place with rates from M$15, while the **Belia Perkasa** (Tel: 588-178) has dormitory accommodation at M$8 and shower-attached rooms from M$13. This latter place is clean, friendly, and half a kilometer from the beach. TV and refrigerators are available for rent.

As you travel north, the first main budget stopover is Cherating. This has become a big backpacker area and the accommodations are being expanded to keep up with demand. I spoke to people who had been there for weeks, so obviously the beach, *kampung* life, and the chance to meet other travellers has appeal to many. The beach is about a kilometer off the main road so I suggest you stay by the beach. There are several budget places with absolute beach front so if this sounds like heaven, try the **Cherating Beach Mini Motel**, the **Kampung Inn** (Tel: 507-744), or the **Coconut Inn**. All have a range of basic-to-reasonable accommodations from around M$15 a night. The **Cherating Inn Beach Resort** (Tel: 439-343) has nice units from M$20, but it is not on the beach. There are several restaurants in the area, including the Cherating Bay Restoran, which has excellent food and a friendly staff; Lianee Cafe; Mimi's Restaurant; and Checkpoint Cherating, which sells bus tickets and rents bicycles and motorcycles. The Pop Inn has live music every evening.

Kamaman is the first town you come to in Terengganu. Reasonable rooms are found at the **Duin Hotel** (Tel: 591-802) on Jalan Kg. Tengah, from M$20. Dungan is the next large center. The main town is a couple of kilometers off the main road and budget accommodations are a bit hard to find. The **Hotel Kasanya** (Tel: 841-704) has 48 large, clean rooms from M$30, and I am told that the **Sri Gate Hotel** (also on Jalan Tambun) has rooms from M$20.

At Rantau Abang there is more choice. Three places can be recommended for location and friendliness although the facilities are fairly basic. **Awang's Bungalows** (Tel: 843-500) has 36 rooms of varying standard from M$5 to $50. The **Ismail Beach House** (Tel: 841-054) has grown to 20 rooms with prices starting at M$12. Reasonable food and cold drinks are available at both. The third is the **Dahima's Guest House**, with 25 rooms from M$15. Those close to the beach are M$55.

Farther north, Marang is another favorite. Some recommendations here are **Kamal Intan Baidui**, which is clean, friendly, and has dormitory beds from M$5; the **Mare Nostrum Resort** (Tel: 681-433) with 19 rooms in the range M$20-50; and the **Island View Resort** (Tel: 682-006) with 20 basic chalets from M$6. Another is the **Semarak Beach Cottage** (Tel: 682-288), about two kilometers south of town. Fan rooms are M$35, air-conditioned ones M$60. Offshore on Kapas Island, the **Zaki Beach Resort** (Tel: 632-989) has some chalets and basic A-frame huts at around M$25.

Kuala Terengganu has many budget hotels but nothing that really stands out from the crowd. **Asrama Seri Pantai** (Tel: 635-766), 10 rooms, has been recommended for cheap accommodations in a good location, from M$10. It is above the TAZ restaurant. The **Terengganu Hotel** (Tel: 622-900), 35 rooms, has fan rooms at M$20 and air-conditioned rooms at M$35. The **Asrama Gelanggang Budaya** (Tel: 622-529) on out-of-the-way Jalan Pasir Pangjang has dormitory accommodations from M$6. At Merang, the **Merang Beach Resort** (Tel: 011-970-853) has 8 rooms with attached bathrooms for M$40, and 12 chalets with outside bathrooms at M$20.

Jerteh has two fairly poor choices. The **Hotel Bertian** (Tel: 971-350), 10 rooms, is probably slightly better than the **Hotel Hoover** (Tel: 971-563), 10 rooms. Both have rooms from M$15. A much better choice is the **Besut Resthouse** (Tel: 976-124) on the coast about 12 kilometers away. Rooms are available from M$14.

Compared to most other East Coast centers, Kota Bharu is crowded with budget hotels and guesthouses. The guesthouses and hostels appear to offer more than the hotels, particularly the ones with gardens. In this category I can recommend the **Rainbow Inn** (Tel: 747-208),

8 rooms, on Jalan Pengkalan Chepa, which has dormitory accommodations from M$16 and rooms from M$10; **Rebana Hostel** on Jalan Sultamah Zairab; and the **De 999 Guest House** near the Hotel Perdana.

If you like staying close to the action, the **Ideal Traveller's House** on Jalan Padang Garong, or the **Town Guest House** (Tel: 785-192) would be suitable choices. Dormitory beds are available at any of these places from around M$6, and most also have private rooms at around M$10-15 a double. All are friendly and have good notice-boards for travellers' information.

Other choices worth considering are the **Johnty's Guest House** (Tel: 748-866) on Jalan Kebun Sultan, which has dormitory beds for M$5, fanned rooms for M$10, and air-conditioned rooms from M$30; **Mummy's Hitec Hostel** (Tel: 787-803), which is nearby and has dormitory beds and fanned rooms for the same price. This is an old-style building with a friendly atmosphere and many repeat visitors; and the **Irama Timur Rest House** (Tel: 771-741) on Jalan Sri Cemerlang where all 35 rooms are air-conditioned and have telephones and prices from M$22; and the **Star Hostel** (Tel: 740-945), 23 rooms from M$30. The **Long House Beach Motel** at Pantai Cinta Berahi has 19 basic rooms from M$20. Don't expect much.

At the Beach of Passionate Love, the **H-B Village Resort** (Tel: 734-993) has dormitory beds from M$5, fanned chalets with bath from M$20, and air-conditioned chalets from M$50. The small restaurant is OK, the chalets are fair, the site is isolated.

5. Dining and Restaurants

Don't go to East Coast Malaysia expecting the gourmet delights of Singapore, New York, or San Francisco. Yes, there are some reasonable restaurants in the major hotels and the main towns, but predominantly there is fairly basic food at very basic prices.

The East Coast is the most Malay part of peninsular Malaysia so you finally get the chance to sample some basic Malay cuisine. For those who don't fancy this fare, the main centers have Chinese and Indian food stalls and restaurants, and there is some influence from Western fast food.

In *Kuantan*, all the major hotels have at least one excellent restaurant. **Hugo's**, at the Hyatt, (Tel: 525-200) is considered to be the best Western restaurant in the city, but the **Merlin Restaurant** at the Hotel Merlin (Tel: 522-388), the **Restaurant Champagne Emas** (Tel: 528-820), and the **Sumudra Restaurant** at the Riverview Hotel (Tel: 522-688) have all been recommended for that special night out.

Somewhat down-market from here are places like **Restoran Tiki** (Tel: 522-272) at 9 Jalan Haji Abdul Aziz, the adjacent **Tawakkai Restaurant** (Tel: 522-637), or the nearby **Restoran Cheun Kee**. These are where the locals congregate but you will be welcome as well. Around dinner time, they can get very busy.

Even further down-market are the outlets in the Jalan Mahkota food center and the small Malay cafes along the riverbank off Jalan Besar. The choice may be limited here but the food is tasty and very cheap.

For those Western bakery lovers, Kuantan provides the best opportunity on the East Coast to indulge in your passion. The **Swan Cafe** (Tel: 521-514) in Jalan Bukit Ubi has some good cakes and pastries, while the **Honeycomb Coffee House** (Tel: 523-434) on Jalan Alor Akar is another possibility.

Out at *Teluk Chempedak*, there are several excellent seafood restaurants on the beach and some good Chinese restaurants on the main road. It's easy to check them out and choose the one that appeals most. **Tan's Restaurant** (Tel: 523-463) has established a great reputation over nearly 20 years with its Malay and Chinese food. **Restoran Pattaya** (Tel: 515-880) is the place to go for excellent Thai and Chinese food, and a great view. **Nisha's Curry House** is tops for north Indian cuisine. There are many restaurants along the road north of Kuantan.

Kuala Terengganu does not have the same number of restaurants as Kuantan but the choice is similar. Popular Malay restaurants are **Zainuddin** (Tel: 633-779) on Jalan Tok Lam and **Miza Restaurant** on Jalan Banggol. The **Sri Intan** on Jalan Sultan Omar, opposite the courts, is noteworthy because it is attractively furnished with deep-blue carpet and white furniture. It offers the standard Malay dishes at good prices. **TAZ** restaurant (Tel: 635-766) on Jalan Sultan Zainal Abidin is noteworthy for its cleanliness and cozy atmosphere.

The **Golden Dragon Restaurant** (Tel: 623-034) on Jalan Bandar has an excellent reputation for top-class Chinese food but don't expect a palace. Cheaper versions can also be found at the **Good Luck Restaurant**, the **Lee Lee Restaurant**, and **Kui Ping Restaurant**, all on Jalan Engku Sar.

Several people have recommended a Chinese place on Jalan Bandar that operates as a semicafeteria where you help yourself to the food on display. It is called the **Cheng Cheng Restaurant** but I have not yet visited myself. The food is supposed to be good and very reasonably priced. Another place to try is the food center adjacent to the beach in Pantai Batu Buruk. There are many good restaurants in this center or adjacent area. The **Restaurant Nil** (Tel: 623-381) is one that can be highly recommended.

Other seafood restaurants are **Awana, Nil** (Tel: 623-381), and **Saujana**, all on Pantai Batu Buruk; and **Pantai Restaurant**, and **Tian Kee Restaurant**, both on Jalan Sultan Zainal Abidin. Good Indian food is available from **Dewi Restaurant** on Jalan Dampung Dalam, and Indian Muslim food from **Tau Fik Restaurant** (Tel: 622-501) on Jalan Masjid Abidin. Close by is the **ACW Restaurant** for those visitors who crave something from the West. You could also try the Mikee Bakery on Jalan S. Ismail. The taxi station food stalls on Jalan Bandar, and the 40 or so stalls at the Taman Selera Tanjung complex, are places to visit for cheap Malay food as enjoyed by the locals.

Kota Bharu is a very Malay town but despite this fact there are good Chinese, Indian, and Thai restaurants available. There are several excellent food centers around town that are highly recommended for easy, tasty, and cheap meals. The night food stalls situated opposite the main bus terminal are particularly good. They are open from sundown and offer *satay*, various noodle dishes, and local delicacies such as *ayam percik*, a spiced chicken dish.

Other open-air alternatives are those near the Pendana Bowling Center on Jalan Mahmud, near Merdeka Square, adjacent to the old market square on Jalan Post Office Lama, and by the bus station on Jalan Hamzah.

Jalan Kebun Sultan near Jalan Padang Garong is the Chinese center of town and there are several good Chinese restaurants here. **Lak Kau Hok Restaurant** (Tel: 723-762) is considered to be one of the best. Another is the **Malaysian Restoran** (Tel: 783-398), which has a wonderful steamboat. You could also try the air-conditioned **Selera Kita** (Tel: 785-262), **Chien Lii Shiang**, or **Restoran Hiang Kang.** They are all good. On Jalan Post Office Lama, the **Chou Choon Huay Restaurant** (Tel: 781-720) is another popular choice.

There are three recommended restaurants on Jalan Hospital. **Syam Restaurant** serves delicious Thai and Malay food—the Baked Shrimp and the Tom Yum soup are both delicious. **Satay Indra** specializes in noodles as well as beef and chicken *satay*. **Satay N' Spice** is another you could try. Seafood addicts will enjoy **Koh Looh Seafood** and **Pata Sea Food** opposite the Istana. **Cherry Hot Bread** cake house will satisfy those looking for pastries.

Finally there are three other suggestions. **Restoran Sakura** is out on Jalan Pasir Putch, south of the Hotel Perdana. **Syed Restaurant** (Tel: 741-624) is on Jalan Dusun Muda, and the **Long House Restaurant** (Tel: 740-090) is at the Beach of Passionate Love.

6. Sight-seeing

The East Coast region has many sight-seeing options but they can be categorized into beaches, islands, rugged mountain scenery, colorful fishing villages, interesting towns, and fascinating handicrafts and culture.

Visitors will either select a beach resort or island for a relaxed stay, or spend a considerable time travelling the 600 kilometers from Mersing to Kota Bharu then exploring one of the inland highways linking this region to the more populated and developed West Coast.

The 100 kilometers from Mersing (see Chapter 10, "Malacca and the South") to Kuantan is either a delight or a disgrace depending on your point of view. If you keep your eyes seaward, there are nice beaches, small fishing villages, and coconut plantations to delight the senses. Unfortunately, if you look inland you will see the devastation caused by the wholesale destruction of towering rain forest. Great stretches of country have been made useless by the total removal of all vegetation. Even today you still have to do battle with heavily laden logging trucks from timber companies that are tearing the remaining forests apart and leaving scarred hillsides and polluted streams in their wake.

This area is thinly populated and it's tempting to travel quickly along the main road with Kuantan firmly in your sights. That would be a pity because the small rural villages on the coast can provide a great insight into the Malaysia of old. Fishing is the principal industry of the people occupying these stilt villages, and dozens of wooden fishing boats cluster around the mouths of numerous sluggish estuaries. Venture into a village and you will see the shy Malay women in traditional blouse and sarong, preparing squid and fish for drying and preserving. The men will often be gathered together, talking, laughing, and mending their fishing nets.

Endar is the first of the larger villages. It is situated at the mouth of the Endar River. Inland from here, there is some delightful untouched countryside with scattered groups of *orang asli* people living in small villages. These riverside *kampungs* have an almost sinister stillness due to the surrounding jungle. Road access is nonexistent but several rivers are navigable and boats can be hired for excursions into the interior. In theory a permit is required but most boatmen ignore this law.

Kuala Rompin is another coastal village farther north. There is a small Chinese hotel here but little reason for most travellers to stay. A road leads inland to the Endar Rompin State Park but development at present is minimal. Much of the park is lowland forest and this is still a breeding area for Sumatran rhinoceros. This is not an area for the casual visitor, but for those interested in the environment and ecology, the area has much charm.

Just north of Kuala Rompin, Route 62 goes left through mangroves, swampland, and forest to Route 12, which is a main highway linking Segamat to Kuantan. This winds through rugged hill country and provides opportunities for rain forest viewing. Jungle runs through the heart of Malaysia but it is somehow closer to the people of the East Coast region than to those who live in the west of the country.

Back on the coast road at **Nenasi** you cross the Bebar River and this provides another opportunity to hire a boat and explore the river and inland *orang asli* villages. The beaches here are deserted and there are plenty of appropriate picnic spots for those with their own transportation. Long-distance buses operate along this road but local bus options are fairly limited so you need to inquire locally before you venture too far by local bus.

Pekan is the first major point of interest north of Mersing. This is the royal capital of the state of Pahang and it is the site of the Sultan's Palace, the State Museum, two nice mosques, a major bridge over the Pahang River (toll applies), and a silk-weaving center. None of these are great attractions in their own right, but together they make Pekan an interesting stopover.

A road leads inland from here along the Pahang River and this will eventually take you to the Segamat to Kuantan highway (Route 12) and then farther inland to **Lake Chini**. Legends tell of an ancient Khymer city that was built on this site and there are stories of mythical monsters that lurk in the deep waters. The lake doesn't need these things to make it interesting. Large areas are covered by lotus plants, and there is some excellent jungle nearby. The lake is famous for fishing and it's also a popular swimming spot. Chalets are available for those who wish to stay overnight. Costs are M$15 for dormitories and M$65 for chalets.

From Lake Chini you should return to Route 12 then follow this to Highway 2, the main Kuala Lumpur to Kuantan highway. If you are planning to visit **Taman Negara National Park** at this time, you would turn left and travel to Maran, take Route 64 to Jerantit, then a local road to Kuala Tembeling.

Kuala Tembeling is the entry point into the park. It's a M$15 per person one-way, three-hour boat trip from here to the park headquarters at Kuala Tahan and reservations for this trip are essential. You should contact the sales office in Kuala Lumpur at Pernas International, Jalan Sultan Ismail, 50250, or telephone 03-905-2872 for further information.

The Taman Negara National Park is by far the largest park in

Malaysia. The 4,300 square kilometers are made up of lofty peaks, green-canopied valleys, and numerous rivers and streams. If your reason for visiting the park is to see wildlife, you could come away disappointed. If on the other hand you need to get away from civilization, would like to try your hand at fishing or hiking, and are prepared to put up with some discomfort, you will probably think Taman Negara is great.

At the park headquarters there are reasonable facilities. There is a reception center, a rest house, a dormitory-style hostel, a camp site, a couple of shops, and some self-contained chalets. There is electricity, water, and sanitation. Outside Kuala Tahan, there are several visitor lodges and fishing lodges that come complete with bedclothes, mosquito nets, crockery, cooking utensils, water, and firewood. These cost about M$5 per person per night. Basic food supplies can be bought at Kuala Tahan.

An attempt has been made to establish several wildlife viewing points throughout the park. Each point has a hide, and some have basic facilities for overnight stays. Your chances of seeing wildlife appear to be better at the hides farthest from park headquarters.

Jenut Tahan is an artificial salt lick just a short way from the park headquarters, while Jenut Tabing is a natural salt lick about an hour away. You are most likely to see deer and wild boar at these locations. Janut Belau is somewhat farther away but it is said that you can see tapir and civet cats here. Perhaps the best hide is at Jemut Kumbang, a five-hour walk from Kuala Tahan. The alternative way to reach it is to take a 45-minute boat ride, then a 45-minute walk. This is recommended to almost everyone. Basic facilities are available at this hide, and even if you see little wildlife, the experience will be worthwhile. Take a powerful flashlight with you. The boat ride is a delight. Sungai Tahan is, in many places, lined with large, leaning *nevam* trees, forming an archway over the water. In other places you see tree trunks and branches festooned with ferns and wild orchids.

I'm told that there are more than 200 species of fish in Taman Negara and that this is an angler's paradise. For the avid fisherman, a camping trip in the upper reaches of the Kenyam and Sepia Rivers would be a great experience, but catches are also said to be good at the fishing lodges at Lata Berkok and Kuala Perkai. Best fishing months are February, March, July, and August.

The walking trails around Kuala Tahan are well marked and many are provided with information on walking times. Some of the more remote trails can be difficult to follow. The park rangers conduct guided walking tours most days and these are recommended for all but the most experienced bush walker. For the really experienced, the climb to the top of Gunung Taham (2187m.) is a challenge. It takes five days from Kuala Tahan and a local guide is strongly recommended.

The best time to visit Taman Negara is between mid-February and September. Note that the park is totally closed from mid-November to mid-January. You can also reach the park entrance at Kuala Tembeling by bus from Kuala Lumpur, or by train from Singapore or Kota Bharu. When travelling by train you alight at Kuala Tembeling Halt (about two kilometers from the boat jetty).

Our destination now will be Kuantan, so we retrace our path to Maran. If waterfalls are your big turn-on, you will want to walk the six kilometers into Berkelah Falls. The falls tumble down eight cascades and are quite attractive, although the track needs more maintenance. You turn off the Maran-Kuantan road at the 42nd kilometer mark.

Kuantan is the largest city on the East Coast of Malaysia and it is also emerging as a significant tourist destination. The airport is served by flights from both Kuala Lumpur and Singapore and hopes are high that other services will be introduced.

The city itself has limited appeal except near the river, but the surrounding area has some nice beaches, some historic interest, and some excellent handicrafts. You can buy some of this handicraft, including lovely *batik* work, at several places in central Kuantan. It is simply a matter of walking along Jalan Besar, Jalan Mahkota, and Jalan Butik Ubi and you will find them.

Telok Chempedak is the major beach in Kuantan and it is quite attractive, but it is not great for swimming. This is where you will find many of the better hotels, restaurants, bars, and handicraft outlets. Balai Karyaneka in particular is a showcase of handicraft from the surrounding area with woven pandanus household articles, wood carvings, shellcraft, and other items at attractive prices. You can reach here by bus No. 39 from central Kuantan.

There are several places of interest to the northwest of Kuantan but very few foreign tourists ever see them or even hear about them. The first point of interest is the **Charah Caves**. These are located a few kilometers from the town of Panching, about 25 kilometers from Kuantan. You can reach Panching on the Sungai Lembing bus. The journey from Kuantan is through interesting country and you see some typical rural sights.

The caves have a long steep stairway leading to them and inside there is a variety of Buddhist statuary. This is a sanctuary for several monks and they make a small admission charge for the public to enter. As caves go, they are not great but it is worth the stop if you are travelling farther in this direction.

It's another 20 kilometers to **Sungai Lembing**, an old tin-mining town which is famous for its very deep workings. There are many historic relics in this area and it is well worth some time just wandering around to absorb some of the unusual atmosphere. Sungai Lembing is being visited by more people these days and one of the reasons is the **Gunung Tapis State Park,** which is 16 kilometers from town. There is a lovely waterfall several kilometers into the jungle.

The park is in the early stages of development but it is located in very attractive country. There is some excellent fishing and one of the rivers is suitable for rafting down rapids. Wildlife is elusive but there is plenty of jungle flora for nature lovers. The park has no accommodations but there are some excellent camping sites. Contact should be made with the Kuantan Tourist Information Center (Tel: 505-566) before you make a visit.

There are two main roads north from Kuantan. Route 3 hugs the coast while Route 14 follows a more direct inland route to Kuala Terengganu. If time is important take Route 14, but Route 3 is far more interesting and will be the sightseer's choice.

Ten kilometers north of Kuantan is the village of **Beserah**. This interesting fishing village is a center for local handicrafts and cultural activities. It has also entered the tourism industry with a *batik* factory and other workshops offering tours and sales to the public. Despite this fact, life remains remarkably unchanged for the villagers. They still use water buffalos to transport fish from the boats to the drying areas and they still engage in traditional top-spinning and kite-flying activities.

Balok Beach is the next point of interest. This is a long open beach flanked by casuarinas, which is excellent for windsurfing. There are a growing number of accommodation and restaurant options here and more are on the way. **Kuantan Port** is just north of here.

The next 25 kilometers to **Cherating** is delightful. There are lovely beaches, patches of forest, several small fishing villages, and offshore Pulau Ular, an island with clear water excellent for swimming and snorkeling.

Cherating has developed into a very popular backpackers' stopover and you will encounter visitors who have stayed for weeks. The appeal is the long beach, the cheap food and accommodations, the few cultural opportunities, and the chance to relax and just let the days slip by.

Chendor Beach is just around the promontory from Cherating. This is home to Club Méditerranée and some other accommodations, and from May to October you can watch giant turtles come ashore at night to lay eggs. The beach is attractive and you can find peace and seclusion despite the existence of the resorts.

Several small towns—Chukai, Kemaman, Kermasik—are passed through on Route 3 before a dramatic change comes about at **Kerteh**. This is a center for a huge petroleum complex—a side of modern Malaysia that is centuries removed from the small fishing villages nearby. Kerteh is vital to the future of Malaysia and it adds a new dimension to East Coast sight-seeing.

Kuala Dungun is the largest center between Kuantan and Kuala Terengganu. It is a sprawling town that spreads between the main highway and the coast. There is little of great interest here but I can recommend the night bazaar near the highway, and a walk along the waterfront in the old part of town. You can take a river safari up the Dungan River, or be more sedate and follow the road that links Dungan to Route 14.

It is now 20 kilometers to **Rantau Abang**, the well-known turtle beach. The beach here is delightful but the real attraction to many is the sight of huge leatherback turtles laboriously climbing the beach, laying their eggs, then returning to their natural habitat and disappearing. There is no doubt that the turtle spectacular is fascinating, but many visitors come away with mixed feelings about the whole affair.

There appears to be two main problems—the general lack of organization to actually see the turtles, and the dubious behavior of many of the locals who see the whole experience as a fun and games activity. Turtles visit the beach here between May and September with late August being the peak of the season. The female turtles can measure two meters long and weigh 700 kilograms (1400 pounds). They crawl up the beach to beyond high-tide mark, dig a hole with their flippers, then with much apparent effort, they lay up to 100 eggs before covering the "nest" and slowly returning to the water.

The turtles are an endangered species, so fortunately the government has started a conservation project to collect eggs and care for them before they hatch. After hatching, the young turtles are returned to the ocean where they are still easy prey for fish and other sea creatures; however, this has dramatically increased successful hatchings compared to a few years ago and hopefully it has saved the species.

There is the Rantar Abang Visitors' Center with its turtle museum that is open all year, but no international visitor will get too excited about this because the content and descriptions are fairly basic.

The road north continues to follow the coast before reaching the picturesque *kampung* of **Marang**. This is a delightful place with a nice beach, coconut palms, brightly painted fishing boats, and friendly

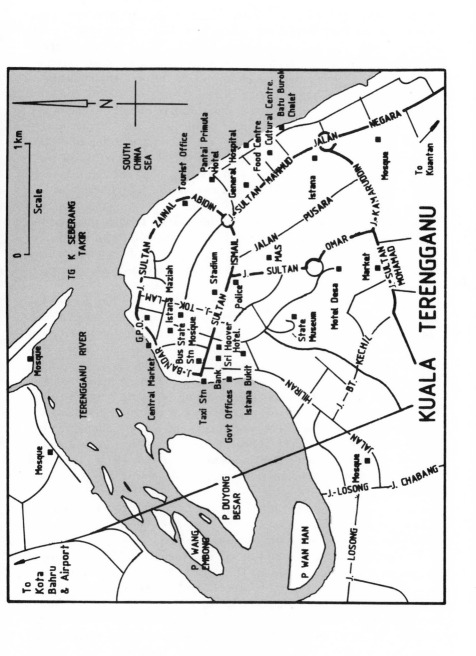

KUALA TERENGGANU

people. There are several places to stay from basic to moderate. Local buses operate from Kuala Dungun and it costs around M$4 for the 1½-hour trip. All along this coast, the *kampungs* scattered at the edge of palm-fringed beaches are charmingly picturesque. Their peacefulness is disturbed only by the noise of children, and the occasional bleating of goats that amble between feeding places.

Offshore (4km.) from Marang is **Pulau Kapas**, one of the better East Coast islands. Boats operate from Marang jetty and charge around M$15 per person for a round trip. The island has numerous white sand beaches with clear water and jungle backdrop. It is a great place for relaxing or for jungle walking, snorkeling along the coral reefs, or fishing. There are three small resorts on the island, each with a restaurant. Most visitors are young.

Kuala Terengganu is the capital of the state of Terengganu, and the largest town between Kuantan and Kota Bharu. This is an old fishing town that is progressing because of the discovery of oil offshore, and the development of tourism along the coast. You can decide yourself if you consider the changes to be positive.

The town stands beside the Terengganu River and has a nice easy pace that will be attractive to most visitors. Like most of the East Coast, there are no dramatic attractions here but it is a logical stopover point and once you do stop you will discover that the friendly people and relaxed life-style make a short visit quite worthwhile.

Downtown Kuala Terengganu is two main streets, a market square, and a small but pleasant esplanade. Walking or riding a trishaw is the best way to get around. The waterfront and central market are the prime attractions in town. The market occupies a modern building, but it sells traditional items such as *batik*, brocade, brasswear, mats, baskets, and *songket*. Fresh produce and souvenirs are also available. The small streets and alleys nearby are worth exploring. You will discover little Chinese shops, a temple, jetties for boats and ferries that crisscross the river, and a colorful atmosphere. In among all this you will find the makers of some of Malaysia's finest brassware. Gleaming bowls and plates shine at you out of the alleyway shadows.

Also in this downtown area you will find the Istana Maziah, which is the venue for formal occasions; the newish Abidin mosque; the state government building; the post office; and the bus and taxi stations. The tourist information office (Tel: 621-433) is at 2243 Jalan Sultan Zainal Abidin. The small state museum, which has a few interesting exhibits, is on Bukit Kecil. Good views of the town and surrounding areas are available from Bukit Besar, a few kilometers south of the central area.

The Gelanggang Seni (cultural center) on Pantai Batu Buruk, about two kilometers south of central Kuala Terengganu, is the cultural platform of the state. Showtime is 5 P.M. on Thursday, Friday, and Saturday and during this time you can see demonstrations of the Malay art of self-defense called Seni Silat, and watch traditional dances, games, and other indigenous pastimes.

A few kilometers farther south you can visit Malaysia's pioneer silk-weaving center. The complex sprawls over 400 hectares and the seasonal silkworm has successfully been adapted to suit Malaysia's single tropical season, resulting in consistent silk production all year. The handwoven taffeta fabrics and the hand-painted products are favorites with buyers.

Inland from Kuala Terengganu, there are two nice locations. The **Sekayu Waterfall** is about 60 kilometers southwest of the town, and Kenyir Lake is close by. Both are reached from Route 14 by turning off at Kg. Ajil. The waterfall is pretty rather than dramatic but the surrounding jungle provides good trekking and flora-viewing opportunities. The area is quite well developed and there is a small entrance fee that appears to be used for visitor amenities. There are some rest houses and chalets, changing rooms, and picnic shelters, and food is available. Contact Jabatan Perhutanun Daerah, Kuala Brang, Hulu Teregganu (Tel: 811-259).

Kenyir Lake is also a peaceful location for trekking, picnicking, and fishing. The lake has a wide variety of tropical freshwater fish and there are organized fishing trips, particularly on weekends. The lake area also has some small waterfalls and swimming holes for those who need a respite from the heat. There are some floating chalets and restaurants to visit.

Back in Kuala Terengganu, it is worth taking the short ferry ride to Pulau Duyong, the largest island in the river estuary. Boat building here has grown from a traditional art form to a commercial enterprise, but very little modern equipment is used and the builders work entirely from memory and experience without set plans. You can also take a boat to *kampung* Seberang Takir on the northern side of the river, or go farther upriver to Pulau Rusa. None of these trips will cost more than M$1 and they give you a good insight into East Coast life.

The main road north (Route 3) now leaves the coast and runs inland, but there is a reasonable road that parallels the coast and serves some lovely beaches at **Merang** and **Rhu Sepuluh**. There are also some islands that can be visited. **Pulau Redang** is the largest of these and can be reached from Kuala Terengganu (about 50 kilometers), or from Merang (about 30 kilometers). Services, however, are rather irregular.

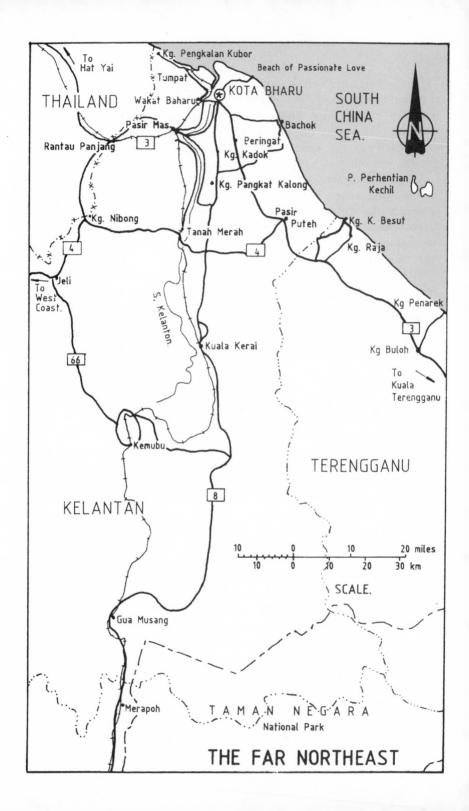

THE FAR NORTHEAST

The island is good for swimming, snorkeling, camping, and trekking. **Pulau Bidong** is closer to the mainland (about 15 kilometers from Merang) but you may find you have to charter a whole boat to reach there.

You must get back on Route 3 to Jerteh before you turn off to **Kuala Besut**. This beachside market town is the access point to Pulau Perhentian and the Bukit Keluang/Dendong Beach Park. The market is a tremendous social event for the wrinkled women with red, betel-stained teeth. **Pulau Perhentian** is a lush tropical island surrounded by crystal-clear waters. The island is about 20 kilometers from Kuala Besut and has some lovely beaches and good coral. Bungalows and chalets are available for those who want to stay overnight. You can also camp on the island, and there are a few shops and restaurants in the fishing village. There are fishing boats from Kuala Besut that take passengers to the island for about M$10 or you can charter a boat for around M$100 a day. More regular services are likely in the future as the island gains in popularity.

The **Bukit Keluang/Dendong Beach Park** is a few kilometers south of Kuala Besut. This very attractive area is being developed for visitors. There are toilet and changing rooms, food and drink vendors, and a boardwalk along the bluff that leads to several small coves and beaches. There are some excellent photographic opportunities, although I have never seen a commercial promotional picture of this area.

The obvious destination now is **Kota Bharu** and the road from Jereh to here runs through attractive rice-growing paddies. Kota Bharu is the capital of the state of Kelantan and is to me the most interesting town on the East Coast. For many years it was isolated from the rest of the peninsula except by sea so there is less outside influence and more "Malayness" here than in most other areas. In many ways it is the nation's storehouse of culture and traditional skills.

Kota Bharu has a population of around 100,000 but it is an easy place to explore. Many of the main points of interest are clustered near the center of town, and walking around this area is a delight. Trishaws are available if you want to go a little farther, then there is a good bus system to all the outlying centers.

A visit to Kota Bharu should start at the Tourist Information Center (Tel: 785-534) on Jalan Sultan Ibrahim. The center has some good local information and maps, and it is also often a venue for cultural, handicraft, and art exhibitions. You should note that in common with most Kelantan organizations, the center closes on Thursday afternoon and all day Friday. It is open for the rest of the week between 8:30

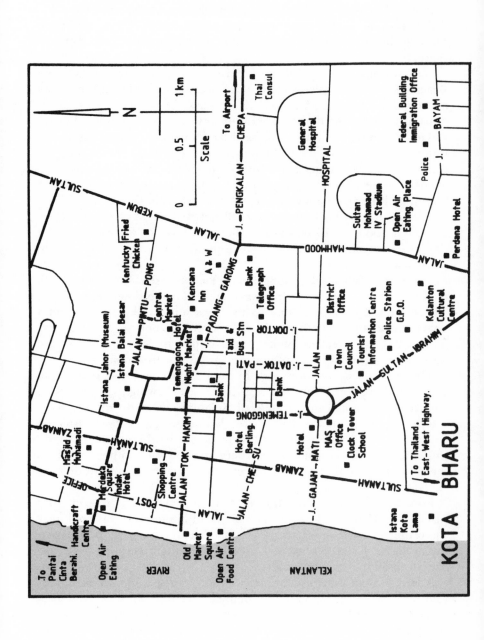

KOTA BHARU

A.M. and 4:30 P.M. The main center of town is directly north of here, while the Kelantan Cultural Center is just to the south.

The Cultural Center (*Gelanggang Seni*) is the place to head on a Wednesday or Saturday between February and October. Performers entertain with *wayang kulit* (a form of shadow puppet theater), and *mak yong* (a dance drama combining elements of dance, opera, drama, and comedy). Locals indulge in kite flying and top spinning while the musically inclined play the *kertok* (coconut percussion instrument) or the *rebana ubi* (giant drum). The audience consists largely of fisherfolk, farmers, and villagers who gather to socialize, watch, and participate for the sheer love of it.

The Central Market is a compulsory morning sight-seeing attraction. This is one of the best markets in Malaysia and it gives you a wonderful insight into local life as well as offering the opportunity to buy some bargain wares. The market starts at around 6 A.M. and subsides about midday. Perhaps the most colorful area is the fruit and vegetable courtyard, which is surrounded by balconies containing curry stalls, restaurants, *batik*, bamboo articles, bags, books, clothes, and shoes.

Most of the traders here are women who chew betel leaves while selling their goods to customers and sharing their moods with other stall holders. Squatting young women dressed in sarongs as colorful as their fruit share messages with serene-faced old women swathed in scarves. There are sounds, sights, and smells to satisfy everyone. A melee of squawking poultry in cages, silvery fish on trestle tables, and baskets on the floor brimming with fruit attract visitors and locals alike. There are also unlimited edible delicacies that look rather too exotic for the Western stomach.

Close by the Central Market, is the Istana Balai Besar. This old palace was built in 1844 and houses the Royal Throne Room, the Hall of Audience, and the State Legislative Assembly Hall. It has a beautifully carved interior and still serves as a venue for some state and royal occasions. Immediately beside it is the Istana Jahar, which was completed in 1889. This magnificent piece of architecture with intricately carved beams and wooden panels is now the State Museum. It is well worth a visit. Hours are from 10:30 A.M. to 6 P.M. Thursday to Tuesday. It is closed on Wednesdays.

The State Mosque, completed in 1926, and Merdeka Square, built to commemorate the Malay warriors and patriots who died during the First World War, are just across the street. This area is good for food stalls at night.

If you walk to the river, you will see clusters of wooden structures anchored to the riverbank. These are rafthouses and some have been here for 30 years. They float on bundles of bamboo that have to be replaced in a difficult exercise every four years or so. Most of the raft people are friendly and will talk to you about river life if you show some interest.

Around Kota Bharu there are some points of interest. Perhaps the most famous is the beautifully named **Beach of Passionate Love**. The name is much more exotic than the reality—the sand is OK and there are some palms and casuarinas, but there are much finer beaches on other parts of the coast. In this strict Muslim area, it is definitely not the place for public passionate love. In fact, the passion is kept heavily under wraps. There are several small cottage industry factories on the 10 kilometers between Kota Bharu and the beach that sell *batik, songket*, brassware, and giant kites.

Pantai Desar Sabak, just south of here, is a similar beach with some attraction. This was where the Japanese landed in World War II during their invasion of Malaysia and Singapore. Farther south again are Pantai Irama (Beach of Melody) and Pantai Bisikan Bayu (Beach of Whispering Breeze). Both have clean sand and clear water and are becoming increasingly popular with visitors.

North from the Beach of Passionate Love is the fishing village of **Kuala Besar**. This is a great example of an East Coast fishing village. You can watch the locals engage in the various activities of fishing, fish preserving, and net mending. From here you can catch a boat to some of the 50 or so islands in the estuary of the Kelantan River. About 15 are inhabited and you can travel the narrow channels to see locals fishing, tending coconut plantations, cockle hunting, or making cigarettes from nipah palm leaves.

If you cross the river you are in the **Tumpat** district, which borders Thailand. This rural area is very attractive with traditional wooden houses built on stilts, buffaloes wallowing in mud, and farmers working hard in the green paddy fields. There is much Thai influence here and in the small village of Kampung Jambu, you will find the Buddhist Wat Phothivihan with an enormous reclining Buddha. It is well worth visiting. The lovely Pantai Kuda is close by and this is a good picnic and swimming spot.

For those visitors moving on to Thailand, there is a border crossing at **Rangau Panjang** about 45 kilometers west of Kota Bharu. Long-distance buses and trains operate regularly from the Thai town of Sungai Golok, just across the border. Thai visas can be obtained from the Thai Consulate on Jalan Pengkalan Chepa in Kota Bharu (Tel: 722-545).

South of Kota Bharu there are some other things worth seeing. At

Reclining Buddha at Phothivihan Buddhist Temple, Kampung Jambu. (Courtesy of the Malaysia Tourism Promotion Board)

Nilam Puri (about 10 km. south) you can find what is claimed to be the oldest mosque in Malaysia. The **Masjid Kampung Laut** was originally built without nails, on a site by the river in Kampung Laut, more than 300 years ago. Due to the threat of flooding and damage, it was moved and re-erected on its present site in 1967. In **Kubang Kerian** (about 9 km. southeast) you will find the **Istana Negeri**, one of the largest and most modern royal residences in Malaysia. In the **Pasir Putch** area (about 35 km. south) there are several waterfalls amid lush greenery.

There are two road choices from Kota Bharu if you don't want to return via the East Coast. The first is Route 4, which is called the northern east-west highway; and the second is Route 8, which travels through the center of the peninsula to Kuala Lumpur. Both pass through sparsely populated jungle country.

Route 4 eventually leads to Gerik in Perak and then to Ipoh or Penang. (See Chapter 9, "Penang and the North.") Along the way you climb and twist over rugged mountains and through deep gorges swirling with mist. Route 8 follows the railway line for much of the way and provides access to the towns of Kuala Kerai, Gua Musang, and Kuala Lipis. A side trip will take you to the small, neat town of Dabong, and on to Kuala Balah. There is also a boat connection between Kuala Kerai and Kuala Balah that travels through some most attractive jungle.

At **Dabong**, it is worthwhile taking the effort to see the **Gua Ikan** (fish cave). The surrounding area has been developed into a small park with cabins and camping ground and it is very popular on weekends. The main cave is about half a kilometer long and there is a shallow stream running its length. Thousands of bats inhabit the cave and there are entrances to other caves and passages. To gain entry to the chambers you must be prepared to crawl a short distance. Not far away is **Strong Waterfall**.

Gua Musang started life as a logging camp but it is now the center for a new agricultural area. The town is developing rapidly and there is a range of accommodations for those wanting to stay the night. **Kuala Lipis** is the next major town to the south and you are now back in the state of Pahang. There are organized treks into the mountains from here, and plenty of restaurants and accommodations.

7. Guided Tours

Tours within the East Coast region are very thin on the ground. There are some extended tours from Kuala Lumpur that travel up the West Coast to Penang then across the northern east-west highway to

Kota Bharu. From here they go south to Kuantan then back to K.L. via Route 2. A typical tour such as this takes 7 to 10 days.

Within individual East Coast regions there are small tour operators who offer specialized trekking and boating tours. The **Roka Outdoor and Survival Academy** (Tel: 784-141) at the Beach of Passionate Love is one of these. **Azizi Rimba Trek Adventures Services** (Tel: 662-268) in Kuala Terengganu is another that can help. These will have limited appeal to some travellers.

For other opportunities, it is best to talk to the local tourist office or travel agent. In Kota Bharu, the **Kelantan Tourist Information Center** (Tel: 785-534) is well organized and helpful. In Kuala Terengganu, I would try **Chong Travel** (Tel: 634-671) and in Kuantan, **Reliance Shipping** (Tel: 502-566). **Kota Gelangi Travel** (Tel: 26-236) in Jerantut can help with wildlife and national park packages.

An alternative is to hire a taxi and organize your own tour. You can do this in Kota Bharu by contacting the **Malay Driver's Association** (Tel: 785-624). There are similar opportunities in Kuantan. Rental cars are available.

8. Culture

The East Coast is the best place in Malaysia to see the traditional culture of the people in its natural form. There are regular performances in Kota Bharu, Kuala Terengganu, and Kuantan, and you will occasionally see less formal happenings in villages elsewhere in the area.

The Gelanggang Seni at Kota Bharu is the best and most reliable place to see many of these cultural events but even here you should check with the local tourist office to ensure that performances occur when you expect them. The major cultural activities include the following:

Mak Yong is a comprehensive theater form combining dance, opera, drama, and comedy. It goes back several centuries when it started out as a popular court entertainment. The *mak yong* or main actress develops the story, usually about legendary princes and princesses, which has been adapted from tales passed down through the years. She is supported by a cast of sixteen performers and the two-hour drama is backed by an orchestra of gongs, drums, and violins (*rebal*). The dialogue will usually be in Malay so the whole affair has limited interest to visitors after the first 15 minutes.

Wayang Kulit is an ancient shadow puppet theater form. Puppets made from buffalo hide and mounted on bamboo sticks are held between a white cloth screen and an oil-lamp light source. The shadows cast on the screen are seen by the audience. Most plays are adaptations of the Indian epic "The Ramayana." The puppeteer, called the *Tok Dalang*, controls the entire performance. He manipulates the puppets, is the voice of all the characters, and conducts the backing orchestra with its resonant melody and sharp staccato rhythm. Invariably the play climaxes with the triumph of good over evil.

The *Kertok* is a drum fashioned from a large coconut with its top sliced off and a piece of nibong wood fastened across the top to form a sounding board. A short wooden stick bound with cloth is used to strike the sounding board. *Kertok* competitions are held between teams of players with points awarded according to the rhythm, timing, and skill of the players.

The *Rebana Ubi*, or giant drum, is made from a hollowed-out log. It is used as a musical instrument but also for competitions. At the end of each harvest season, East Coast villagers challenge each other in the art of drum beating. On these occasions the roll of the *rebana* can be heard all day and often the drummers appear to be almost hypnotized by the proceedings.

Berdikir Barat is a new art form that has come into prominence in the last 50 years. It is a battle of wits between two teams, each consisting of at least ten players. Each team has a leader who makes up impromptu verses ridiculing and mocking the opposing team. These verses are chorused by the rest of the team before the opposing team is given an opportunity to reply. This is a very popular event with the locals, but because of language difficulties it has limited appeal to international visitors.

Traditional dancing is popular through the East Coast states and you will see it at various functions and even in the major hotels. There are several dances that originated in this region and these are among the most popular with the locals.

The *tarian asyik* originated in the royal courts of Kelantan more than 300 years ago and has beautiful movements and dazzling costumes. *Gayong ota-ota* is a warrior's dance from Terengganu performed by male couples carrying swords, shields, and bells. It is accompanied by gongs and gandang drums. The *tarian saba* dance is a combination of music, dance, and song and is sung in contemporary verses.

9. Sports

The major sports for visitors in the East Coast region are water sports and trekking. Many of the major beaches have surfboards, sailboards, and catamarans to rent, while some of the islands have snorkeling and scuba gear available. Most of these activities are controlled by the major resorts as they cater to visitors rather than locals.

Fishing is another popular recreation. You can often hitch a ride with a fishing boat from many of the coastal villages or you can visit one of the lakes or the national park and take an organized tour. You will almost always come back with several meals in hand. Big game fishing is available from Tioman Island.

A few of the major resorts—Hyatt Kuantan, Coral Beach, Tanjung Jara, Primula Pantai, etc.—have tennis courts, and there are some public facilities for basketball, netball, and other sports. It is fair to say, however, that local interest in these international-style sports is low so facilities are rare.

Golfers are reasonably well catered to. The **Royal Pahang Golf Course** (Tel: 527-761), near Kuantan, has been upgraded into a fine 18-hole championship course. It is set amidst swampland but the course is pleasant and the midweek green fee of M$30 is very reasonable. The **Rantai Petronas Country Club** (Tel: 540-027) has a lovely 9-hole course by the South China Sea at Kertah. Green fees are M$30. There is also a driving range open to visitors. The **Royal Terengganu Golf Club** (Tel: 622-111) is situated within the palace grounds at Kuala Terengganu. There are no green fees but you must obtain prior approval to play. The area is often very windy and this makes it a difficult 9-hole course. The 18-hole **Royal Kelantan Golf Club** (Tel: 782-102) is 10 kilometers from Kota Bharu near the airport.

While it is unlikely that you will participate in them, it is interesting to watch some of the local sports:

Kite flying, or *wau*, is a serious activity. The kites are made from bamboo and paper and are heavily decorated—making them flying works of art. Often a bow-shaped device is attached to produce a high-pitched hum when in flight. Kite-flying competitions are often held, with whole villages turning out to support the local competitor. Judging is based on flight, skill of handling, and aesthetic appeal.

One of the favorite kite designs, the *Wau Bulau*, is the logo of the national air carrier, Malaysia Airlines. Some of the ceremonial kites for exhibitions are more than 10 feet long and take weeks to construct and decorate.

Top Spinning, or *gasing uri*, requires great dexterity, skill, and a certain amount of physical strength. The top is about the size of a dinner plate and may weigh up to 5 kilograms (10 pounds). After it is launched, it is quickly scooped up on a wooden bat and transferred to a steel plate on a wooden post. An expert can make a perfectly balanced top spin for more than two hours.

Sepak Raga Bulatan is a game that has been popular with the Malays for centuries. It is played by a group of people standing in a circle. The players try to keep the rattan ball in the air without letting it drop to the ground by propelling it with their feet and heads. The number of times the ball makes contact with the body without dropping to the ground is counted and compared with the efforts of other groups.

Congkak is an indoor game that keeps Malay women absorbed for hours. The game is simple but it requires sharpness of sight and considerable skill. The game has a board with two rows of small depressions and a larger depression at each end. The moves involve filling the small depressions with "seeds," and the winner is the one who collects the most seeds from the opponent.

Silat is the Malay art of self-defense. It has many styles and branches but each depends on two exponents going through a routine of sparring and kicking. The performance is often accompanied by the beating of gongs and drums.

10. Shopping

The East Coast is the best place in Malaysia to buy some of the marvelous handicraft items that are famous around the world. Handicrafts are available in stores in the major towns, but it is often better to buy from local handicraft centers that are scattered throughout the region, or even direct from the craftsmen and women in the *kampungs*. The East Coast states have a rich handicraft tradition. Don't leave this area without some of these exquisite items.

Silvercraft is a traditional craft that has become a thriving cottage industry, particularly in Kelantan. Both fine filigree ornamental silverware, and repoussé, where sheet silver is hammered into relief from the reverse side, are available. Items range from the practical to the purely ornamental—fruit bowls, tea sets, ashtrays, cake servers, spoons, broaches, pendants, and earrings. You can visit small factories to observe crafts people at work in Kota Bharu and in some of the surrounding *kampungs*. Most factories are open every day except Fridays.

Batik **printing** has been around for a long time but it is only in the last 30 years that *batik* printing and painting has generally become a recognized art form. *Batik* means "drawing art with wax." Wax is applied to material in patterns before the dyes are spread, then it is boiled away leaving free-flowing chromatic designs. At many *batik* factories you can follow the printing process right up to the various finished products in the showrooms. Try Samasa Batik factory at

Kampung Puteh, Kota Baru, or Pantas Batik, a store in Komplex MARA in Jalan Dato Pati.

Songket has been aptly called Malaysia's "Cloth of Gold." It is a proud legacy of the courts of the East Coast states. *Songket* came into being during the region's early trade with China (silk) and India (gold and silver). *Songket* is a material richly woven with silver or gold thread that today is used mainly for formal and ceremonial occasions such as weddings. You will be welcomed at any of the *songket* weaving factories near Kota Bharu and in Terengganu. The shop houses along Jalan Sultan Ismail in Kuala Terengganu are also a good place to look.

Bamboo-weaving is an ancient craft that has become a major cottage industry. It requires deft fingerwork and much patience to weave the finely split bamboo strips, so most of the weavers are village women. A wide range of bamboo products are available but baskets, food covers, and trays remain the most popular. Try the Kota Bharu Central Market.

11. Entertainment and Nightlife

Entertainment and nightlife of the Western kind is almost nonexistent on the East Coast outside the major hotels. Within the hotels you will find small bands and groups that provide background music in lounges, and more upbeat tunes for discos and dancing.

The other evening entertainment is provided by the occasional cultural performance at the hotels or the local cultural center. The best of these is in Kota Bharu on Wednesday and Saturday evenings.

12. The East Coast Address List

Airport
    —Kuantan   Tel: 501-291
    —Kuala Terengganu   664-500
    —Kota Bharu   737-000
Bank
    —Kuantan—Bank Bumiputra   527-099
    —Kuala Terengganu—UMBC   622-728
    —Kota Bharu—Malayan Banking   782-803
Doctor/Medical
    —Kota Bharu—Wee Khoon Hock Dental   782-553
    —Kuantan—Pahang Medical Center   524-836
    —Kuala Terengganu—Dr. Wan Saleha Wan Ishak   632-900
    —Kota Bharu—Klinik Paul   746-745

M.A.S.

—7 Jalan Gambut, Kuantan	521-218
—Jalan Paya Bunga, Kuala Teregganu	622-266
—Jalan Gajah Mati, Kota Bharu	747-000

Railway

—Wakaf Bharu Station, Kota Bharu	796-986

Taxi

—Off Jalan Besar, Kuantan
—Jalan Sultan Ismail, Kuala Teregganu
—Jalan Pendek, Kota Bharu

Tourist Information

—L.K.N.P. Komplex Teruntum, Jalan Mahkota, Kuantan	505-566
—TOC Wisma MCIS, Jalan Sultan Zainal Abidin, Kuala Teregganu	621-433
—Jalan Sultan Ibrahim, Kota Bharu	785-534

Tourist Police

—Kota Bharu	785-522

Travel Agent

—S.M.A.S. Travel, Wisma Puriwiran Jalan Segambut, Kuantan	513-890
—Perpel Terengganu S.B., Wisma Maju, Jalan Sultan Ismail, Kota Terengganu	622-700
—Bousted Thomas Cook S.B., Jalan Temenggong, Kota Bharu	741-022

12

Sabah—The Land Below The Wind

1. The General Picture

You go to Sabah for its wildlife, not its nightlife. It's one of those rare places where mountain climbing is more popular than disco dancing. What it offers is found nowhere else in the world in quite the same way. Sabah is different, and for the caring traveller it can be a paradise. It is also probably a place that most people would have great difficulty pinpointing on a blank map, so it gets relatively few visitors. Maybe that is one of the reasons it is ripe with local atmosphere and promising sights.

Sabah occupies the northern tip of Borneo island. It is washed by the South China Sea, the Sulu Sea, and the Celebes Sea and has land borders with Sarawak and Indonesian Borneo (called Kalimantan). The country is mountainous and is intersected by numerous rivers. The highest point is Mount Kinabalu, a granite massif of more than 4100 meters (13,500 feet). It is the highest mountain in Southeast Asia.

The coastal lowlands are a mixture of swamp and tropical forest, while much of the interior is covered by the oldest virgin tropical forest in the world. Unfortunately this is disappearing at an alarming rate as loggers attack large areas, but I am told by locals that the rate of devastation is now being reduced.

The rain forest sustains an amazing ecological community of plants and animals that can best be seen by visitors in the six parks maintained

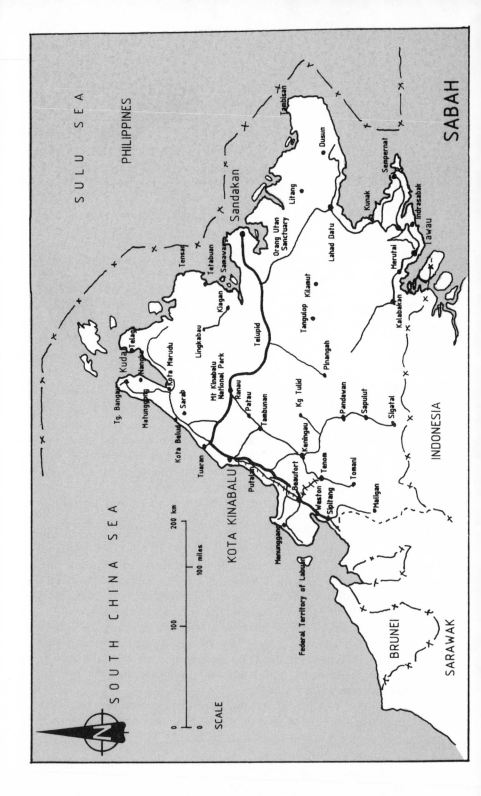

by the state. The best known of the parks is the Kinabalu State Park but others have been established to preserve coral reefs and marine life, mud volcanoes, and green turtles.

The people of Sabah are a unique composite of various ethnic groups, and considerable mixing over the years has blurred tribal differences. In fact, the population of about 1.7 million comprises about 30 different races, about 55 different languages, and more than 100 different dialects. The result today is a wonderful kaleidoscope of color and culture.

Kota Kinabalu is the major gateway, administration center, and financial hub of Sabah. It has been the state's capital since 1946. Other major centers are Sandakan in the northeast, and Tawau in the southeast. Both are linked to Kota Kinabalu by air, but road connections remain poor during the December-February wet season.

Sabah is exotic. It conjures up images of the mysterious, primeval, and awesome, but it also enables visitors to experience "soft adventure" while retaining many of the luxuries of modern civilization. The friendly people of Sabah are hospitable, charming, and welcoming. You could hardly ask for more. No wonder it is becoming a much-sought-after destination for the blasé globe-trotting traveller looking for something really different.

2. Getting There

Kota Kinabalu is the gateway to Sabah. There are some international **airlines** that fly into Kota Kinabalu (from Singapore, Manila, Hong Kong, Seoul, Taipei, Bandar Seri Begawan, and Tokyo) but most visitors will arrive by Malaysia Airlines from peninsular Malaysia.

The service from Kuala Lumpur is excellent with several flights each day on Boeing 737 or Airbus aircraft. Flying time is about two hours. A meal is served on most flights. MAS also has a service from Johor Bahru to Kota Kinabalu. There is a service from Kuala Lumpur to the island of Labuan that continues on to Kota Kinabalu. A network of routes link Kota Kinabalu with various points in Sarawak.

The Kota Kinabalu airport is large and impressive, particularly when you consider the size of the city. You enter the terminal from sky bridges, pass through immigration, even if you are arriving from peninsular Malaysia, then move downstairs to the baggage carousels and customs.

Within the complex there are many facilities. You will find a travel agent for hotel reservations, a branch of the Sabah Tourism Promotion Corporation, a bank, a post office, a highland produce store called the

Mushroom Center, and a book and general store. There are telephone, nursery, and baggage storage facilities, a cafeteria, and an air-conditioned restaurant. All facilities are well signposted in English.

Taxis are available for transportation to the city or major hotels. They operate on a coupon system where you pay at the taxi desk and hand the driver a ticket when you reach your destination. The system works well and, while charges may be a little on the high side, there is no chance of being "ripped off" by unscrupulous drivers. The cost to Tanjang Aru Beach is about M$8 and to the city about M$10.

When departing from Kota Kinabalu, you handle baggage check-in and seat assignment on the second level. There are several different departure halls, so take care that you go to the correct one. It is shown on your boarding pass. There is a departure tax of M$20 for international flights, M$10 for Singapore flights, and M$5 for domestic flights.

There is a bus service from the airport to the city but no one seems to use it, perhaps because it is infrequent and doesn't appear to operate to a well-established timetable. For those really on a budget, it is possible to walk out the airport road to the main highway (about 10 minutes) and easily catch a bus or minibus from there to the city. The cost will be less than M$1. Rental cars are available.

There is no longer any regular **sea** transportation from peninsular Malaysia to Sabah but a few people still arrive by sea. The two common entry points are Tawau, where there are some services from Kalimantan (Indonesia), and Labuan, which has boat connections with Brunei. The occasional cruise liner docks at Kota Kinabalu. There is considerable sea traffic between Sandakan and the Philippines but much of it is illegal or at least suspect. This is not recommended.

Improvements to **land routes** have meant that you can now reach Sabah overland from Brunei and Sarawak. This is an increasingly popular route for young travellers who hitchhike or use local bus transportation between centers. It is not recommended for those who are short on time or for those who place a high value on comfort because it is still in the "soft-adventure" category. Roads are only fair, transportation can be extremely crowded and often breaks down, and there are occasional border-crossing problems for foreigners who cannot produce an onward air ticket and sufficient money to satisfy the authorities.

3. Local Transportation

There are some **bus** services in Kota Kinabalu but little evidence of timetables. Services are operated to Likas and Tuaran/Tamparuli by the

Tuaran United Transport Company, and to Tanjung Aru and Putatan by Luen Thung Transport. These are regular services throughout the day.

Taxis are plentiful and reasonably cheap in Kota Kinabalu. You need to negotiate a fare before you travel. There are several taxi ranks in central Kota Kinabalu but taxis can also be hailed on the street. Most taxis are air-conditioned and you should pay less if you happen to find one that is not. Fares almost double after midnight.

Long distance **minibuses** operate many routes. From Kota Kinabalu there are services to Sandakan (cost around M$35), Tambunan (M$7), Beaufort (M$6), Keningau (M$10), Kota Belud (M$5), Papar (M$2.50), Kinabalu Park (M$6), and Ranau (M$8). You can then change minibuses at these points to reach other destinations. The buses leave when the driver considers he has enough people. If not completely full, he will stop anywhere along the road to pick up additional passengers. You will find yourself squashed in with locals carrying food and household goods, but the atmosphere is friendly and most foreigners enjoy the experience.

Car rental is certainly an option to consider. There are six companies in Kota Kinabalu, all offering a variety of cars at fairly similar prices. Prices start at around M$160 a day for a Malaysian-made Proton, and rise to M$350 for a Toyota Land Cruiser four-wheel-drive. Most companies also offer chauffeur-driven vehicles at about a 50-percent premium. You could try:

• Kinabalu Rent-A-Car, Komplex Karamunsing, KK.88828, Tel: 088-232-602, Fax: 088-242-512

• E & C Rent-A-Car, Wisma Sabah, KK.88814, Tel: 088-57-679, Fax: 088-221-466

• Adaras Rent-A-Car, Wisma Sabah, Tel/Fax: 088-216-010

Rail is an unexpected option. In fact there is only one rail line. It runs between Tanjung Aru (a Kota Kinabalu suburb) and Tenom in the south. Most traffic is generated on the Beaufort to Tenom section, and this is fast-becoming a tourist attraction. I strongly recommend it. (See details in section 6, "Sight-seeing.")

Sea is more or less confined to the services to Labuan. There is a fast boat from Kota Kinabalu that takes two hours and costs M$28 each way. It operates daily round trips. A car ferry operates from Menumbok to Labuan. This takes passengers for about M$6 one way. Power boats also operate this route at a cost of about M$10 per person.

Air services are operated by Malaysia Airlines. The major route is Kota Kinabalu to Sandakan and there are several jet services a day on this route. Flying time is less than one hour. There are also major services from Kota Kinabalu to Tawau, and less frequent services to Lahad Datu and Kudat. There are feeder services from Sandakan to Pamol, Tomanggong, and Semporna. Sandakan is also linked to Tawau, Lahad Datu, and Kudat.

Air is the only way to travel if time and comfort are important to you. The Malaysia Airlines service is efficient and pleasant, and the air network enables you to cover most parts of the state. Roads between some centers become impassable for periods during the wet season so air becomes the only practical way to travel at those times.

Air touring is provided by aircraft and helicopters of Sabah Air, the sole aerial tour operator. Further information is obtainable from Sabah Air Pte. Ltd. Tel: 088-56733 in Kota Kinabalu or Tel: 089-660-527 in Sandakan.

4. The Hotel Scene

Kota Kinabalu, Sandakan, and Tawau have a good range of accommodations but prices tend to be a little higher than you would expect. This is particularly noticeable in the lower midrange properties and in the budget end of the market. There are few luxury hotels in the state but it appears that they are adequate for the present market.

Most towns and attractions have some accommodations, so it is unlikely that you will get caught without a room. Pre-booking, however, is still recommended because most Sabah travellers settle in to their accommodations by midafternoon and public transportation often arrives after that time.

EXPENSIVE HOTELS

There are only three luxury hotels in Sabah. Two are in Kota Kinabalu and one is in Sandakan.

The **Shangri-La Tanjung Aru Resort** (Tel: 088-225-800), 250 rooms and suites with a further 250 under construction, is a delightful beach resort just ten minutes by taxi from downtown Kota Kinabalu, and about eight minutes from the airport. Although the hotel actually has little beach, the green lawns, exotic gardens, palm trees, large swimming pool, outdoor jacuzzi, and floodlit tennis courts are what a seafront hotel should be all about.

A recent visit really impressed me. The newly refurbished rooms with their individual balconies, the choice of restaurants and bars, a fine balance between casual atmosphere and efficient service, all

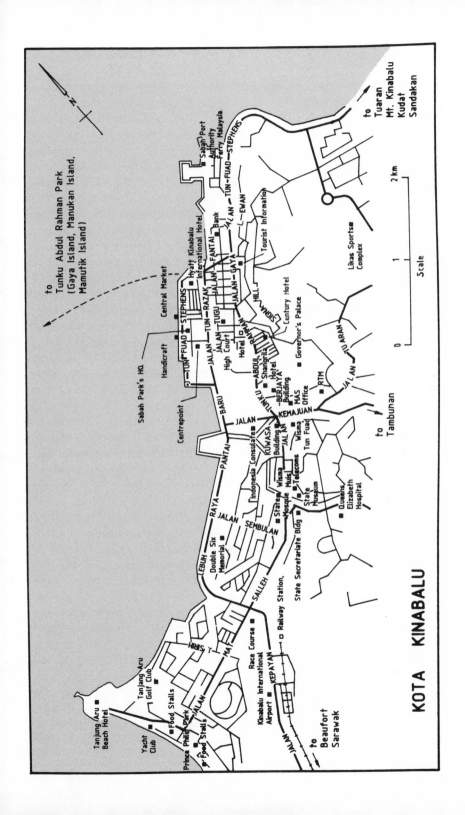

KOTA KINABALU

combined to produce an ambience that just suited my part-business, part-sight-seeing mood.

The spacious open-air lobby is a good introduction to the hotel. It is restrained, functional, yet friendly and classy. The indoors and outdoors merge as they should in the tropics. The low-rise building sprawls on the site so many rooms are a fair walk from the lobby. Most of the bars and restaurants are on a lower level than the lobby and this is where you also find the pool, the shops, and the fitness center. The Coffee Terrace offers both indoor and outdoor dining, the Garden Restaurant operates under the stars, while the excellent Italian cuisine Peppino Restaurant has soft, romantic lights ideal for couples or groups. Nightbirds will gravitate to the Tiong Room for its trendy bar, live entertainment, and dance floor.

The burgundy and sage guest rooms with their rattan furniture come equipped with coffee- and tea-making facilities, minisafe, remote control TV, minibar, IDD telephone, and piped music. The bathrooms have telephone, music, thermostatic-controlled showers, full-length baths, mirror demister, and hairdryer. (Book with the Shangri-La International organization or direct with the hotel at Locked Bay 174, 88999 Kota Kinabalu, Sabah, Malaysia; Fax: 6088-217-155.) Room rates start at around M$380.

The **Hyatt Kinabalu** (Tel: 088-221-234), 315 rooms, is a completely different style of hotel. The 14-story hotel is in the heart of downtown Kota Kinabalu close to business, shopping, and entertainment. The building was the first and only major hotel in Kota Kinabalu for quite some time. It has been under Hyatt management since 1979. In that time it has been renovated and improved so that the public areas and guest rooms have the facilities and amenities expected of Hyatt International hotels. A further 200 rooms in a new building are proposed.

The hotel's three restaurants reflect the cultural heritage of Sabah. The Semporna Grill has a cozy, elegant European atmosphere. Touches of local color are seen in the 24-hour Tanjung Ria cafe where both Asian and Western specialities are served among local furnishings and handicrafts from area tribes. The Phoenix Court presents a rich decor reflecting Chinese designs as it serves the delights of Cantonese and Szechuan cuisine. There is a seafood steamboat dinner poolside each evening. For late-night players there is a choice of soft music in the Atrium Lounge or more heavy atmosphere at the Mikado Night Club.

The hotel also has 35 Regency Club rooms and suites on the 12th and 13th floors. The Regency Club has its own check-in, a concierge, and butler service. Complimentary Continental breakfast is served in the morning, and hors d'oeuvres and cocktails are offered in the late afternoon. Guests receive fruit baskets, personalized stationery and matches, bathrobes, and an extensive range of toiletries. Room rates start at around M$310 and rise to about M$1400. (Book with the Hyatt organization or direct with the hotel at Locked Bag No. 47, 88994 Kota Kinabalu, Sabah, Malaysia; Fax: 6088-225-972.)

The **Ramada Renaissance Hotel Sandakan** (Tel: 089-213-299), 120 rooms and suites, is the newest luxury hotel in Sabah. It is situated in the East Coast town of Sandakan and is the only luxury hotel in the city. The Ramada Hotel integrates the old Sabah Hotel, built around the historic 1911 Governor's House, with a contemporary guest room tower, all situated on five hectares (12 acres) of lush landscaped grounds.

The 120 rooms include 18 in the original colonial-style wing. All rooms have TV with movies, refrigerator with minibar, IDD telephone, desks, and bathrooms with separate tub and shower, hairdryer, and telephone. The Coffee House has a "plantation" theme with an outdoor terrace overlooking the swimming pool and garden. The Chinese speciality restaurant has authentic cuisine, artwork, and decor. Three lounges offer a variety of live entertainment including a discotheque. There is a poolside snack bar and barbecue area.

Recreation facilities include swimming; a health and fitness center with steam bath, sauna, and massage; tennis; and squash. Arrangements for golf can be made with the nearby Sandakan Golf Course. The hotel also has a business center and a tour and hospitality desk. Room prices start at around M$250. (Book with the Ramada sales office or direct with the hotel at P.O. Box 275, 90007 Sandakan, Sabah, Malaysia; Fax: 6089-271-271.)

MEDIUM-PRICE HOTELS

Kota Kinabalu and Sandakan both have a good range of midmarket hotels and there are also some hotels in this category in other centers. (We discuss other towns and their accommodation options in the sight-seeing section of this chapter.) The following are a selection of midmarket hotels in Kota Kinabalu and Sandakan.

KOTA KINABALU

At the top of this range you have the **Hotel Shangri-La** (Tel: 088-212-800), 126 rooms. (This should not be confused with the Shangri-La International organization who operate the Tanjung Aru Resort.) The hotel is situated on the edge of the downtown area, within walking distance of most business, shopping, and entertainment spots.

All guest rooms are air-conditioned and carpeted, with attached bathrooms and have radio, television, IDD telephones, refrigerator, minibar, and hairdryers. The hotel has the popular Grand Palace Chinese Restaurant and an association with the adjacent API Tours and Travel office. There are some nonsmoking rooms. Rates are from M$155 to M$450. (Book direct with the hotel at P.O. Box 11718, 88819 Kota Kinabalu, Sabah, Malaysia; Fax: 6088-212-078.)

Also near the top of this range is the small **Hotel Jesselton** (Tel: 088-55633), 27 rooms, at 69 Gaya Street. Despite its small size there is an excellent restaurant, a coffee house, and a bar, together with 24-hour room service. (Book with the hotel at P.O. Box 10401, 88000 Kota Kinabalu, Sabah, Malaysia; Fax: 6088-240-401.) Prices start at M$165.

The other recommended hotels in this category are all cheaper and perhaps offer better value. The largest of these is the **Hotel Capital** (Tel: 088-231-999), 102 rooms, on Jalan Haji Saman. The hotel has a Chinese restaurant, a coffee shop, room service, and a nightclub. Room prices are in the M$100-180 range. (Book with the hotel at P.O. Box 11223, 88813 Kota Kinabalu, Sabah, Malaysia; Fax: 6088-237-222.)

Another one that I can recommend is the new **Century Hotel** (Tel: 088-242-222), 60 rooms, close to the Hotel Shangri-La. All rooms are air-conditioned, have international-dial telephones, TVs, refrigerators, and bathrooms with bath and shower. The staff is very friendly and the cafe serves Western and Asian cuisine. Room prices start at M$100. (Book with the hotel at Jalan Masjid Lama, 88000 Kota Kinabalu; Fax: 6088-242-929.)

Then there is **Ang's Hotel** (Tel: 088-234-999), 35 rooms, on Jalan Bakau, with its Chinese restaurant and 24-hour room service, and good, clean rooms at M$55-80. (Book at P.O. Box 10843, 88809 Kota Kinabalu, Sabah.) A further alternative is the **Winner Hotel** (Tel: 088-52688), 35 rooms, on Jalan Pasar Baru. All rooms are air-conditioned and carpeted, have TV, telephone, and attached bathrooms. Prices start at M$80. (Book at P.O. Box 11134, 88812 Kota Kinabalu, Sabah; Fax: 6088-215-546.) There are entertainers at the coffee house in the evening.

Also in this category is a group of small hotels that all have reasonable rooms and facilities in the M$60-90 range. The 32-room **Diamond Inn** (Tel: 088-213-222) on Jalan Haji Yakub, the 35-room **Hotel Kinabalu** (Tel: 088-245-599) on Jalan Tugu, the 39-room **Sabah Inn** (Tel: 088-53322) on Jalan Pantai, the 40-room **Park Hotel** (Tel: 088-235-666) on Jalan Sentosa, the 24-room **Town Inn** (Tel: 088-225-823) on Jalan Pantai, and the 16-room **Hotel Rafflesia** (Tel: 088-239-635) on Jalan Sepuluh have all been inspected and would be suitable for visitors looking for clean, reasonably priced rooms.

Three final choices are the **May Plaza Hotel** (Tel: 088-215-418), 20 rooms, in the M$65-90 range (book at P.O. Box 10749, 88808 Kota Kinabalu); the **Borneo Resthouse** (Tel: 088-718-855), which is a motel-style establishment about five kilometers from Kota Kinabalu along the Penampang Road. Facilities are good and room prices are around M$100, but ideally you need a car for this location (book at P.O. Box 14799, 88855 Kota Kinabalu, Sabah; Fax: 6088-718-955); and the new **Hotel Holiday** (Tel: 088-213-116) where air-conditioned rooms have IDO telephones, TV, refrigerator with minibar, and there is friendly staff and good service. Room rates start at M$66. It is on the main road in Block F, Segama Complex in the center of town. (Book on Fax: 6088-215-576.)

SANDAKAN

There are four hotels here worthy of recommendation. The **Hotel City View** (Tel: 089-271-122), 29 rooms, is situated in the center of downtown. All rooms are air-conditioned and have private bathrooms, radio, TV, and minibar. Rooms are small. There is a Western food restaurant on the ground floor, and 24-hour room service. Room prices start at around M$120. (Book at P.O. Box 624, 90007 Sandakan, Sabah, Malaysia; Fax: 6089-273-115.)

I recently spent a few pleasant days at the **Hotel Hsiang Garden** (Tel: 089-273-122), 45 rooms, about 1½ kilometers from the center of Sandakan. While this location is not ideal if all your activities are downtown, the hotel in fact is surrounded by restaurants, bars, and shops; places such as the night market are within walking distance. The rooms are adequate and the service is friendly. There is a restaurant, coffee shop, and 24-hour room service. Room prices start at about M$85. (Book at P.O. Box 82, 90007 Sandakan, Sabah; Fax: 6089-272-988.)

The **Hotel Lee Gardens** (Tel: 089-273-600) on Jalan Leila is a third alternative. All rooms are air-conditioned, have a bath/shower, IDO telephone, and TV with in-house movies. Some rooms have refrigerators. There is a restaurant, a business center, and a small conference room. Room prices start at M$90. (Book at P.O. Box 349, 90007 Sandakan; Fax: 6089-272-930.)

The final choice is the centrally located **Hotel Nak** (Tel: 089-272-988), 43 rooms, in Edinburgh Street near the Malaysia Airlines office. The rooms are fairly basic but they are carpeted, air-conditioned, and have TV, telephone, a long bath and shower. The lobby is clean and pleasant. The large Apple fast-food restaurant off the lobby is one of Sandakan's most popular hangouts for those seeking reasonably priced Western and Asian food. Room prices start at around M$75. (Book at P.O. Box 761, 90008 Sandakan, Sabah; Fax: 6089-272-879.)

BUDGET ACCOMMODATIONS

There are very few low-budget accommodations in either Kota Kinabalu or Sandakan, so some of the suggestions here would be within the low midrange category in other parts. Those are the facts, so it's no use trying to fight it. Accept that Sabah is not a low-cost state and plan accordingly.

KOTA KINABALU

The cheapest reasonable accommodations in the downtown area are found at the **Travellers Rest Hostel** (Tel: 088-240-625). Segregated dormitory accommodations are available at M$15 a night. The male dormitory has 12 beds, the female 10. There is also a room with five beds that can be shared by a mixed group. Single and double accommodations are also available starting at M$28 for a fan room and M$36 for air-conditioned. No rooms have attached bathrooms. All these prices include breakfast. You find it on the third floor, Block L, in the Sinsuran Complex. (Book at P.O. Box 14663, 88853 Kota Kinabalu.) The alternative is the **Likas Sports Complex** (Tel: 088-221-716) about two kilometers east of downtown. A selection of dormitories or rooms is available from M$15.

Jack's B/B (Tel: 088-232-367) is one of those friendly traveller places that are popular worldwide. It's between the airport and city not far from the Sabah Museum. There is air conditioning, a color TV, and bed and breakfast from M$18. The address is No. 17, Block B, Jalan Karamunsing. The **Seaside Travellers** Inn (Tel: 088-750-313) is on the beach at KM20 Papar Highway. Dormitory beds and continental breakfast are from M$20. The **Tourist Rest House** (Tel: 088-245-066) has 10 rooms with two communal bathrooms. It is clean and a good value at M$15 for a fan and M$30 for an air-conditioned room. It is in Block G of the Sinsuran Complex.

The **Hotel Rakyat** (Tel: 088-211-100) is an alternative for those who prefer hotel accommodations. There is a choice of fan rooms with no bathroom for M$25, fan rooms with bathroom for M$37, and air and bathroom from M$43. Three of the rooms are carpeted and all have telephones. Don't expect luxury, but the place is well kept and the people are friendly. You find it on the second level, Block I, Sinsuran Complex. (Book at P.O. Box 13702, 88842 Kota Kinabalu.)

In the same block, the **Hotel Somido** (Tel: 088-211-946) has fanned rooms and air-conditioned rooms with or without bathrooms. Prices start at around M$25. The final really budget selection is the **Mutiera Hotel** (Tel: 088-213-251), 12 rooms, near the Century Hotel. Prices start at M$25. You have a choice of fan, air conditioning, bath, or no bath. It is next to the Uptown Disco.

Going a little up-market from here, we have the **Hotel Sinsuran** (Tel: 088-211-158). There are 11 air-conditioned rooms, all with attached bathrooms and all with TV and telephone. Prices start at M$45 for one or two people. Several reports give this place high praise. The entry is off Jalan Tun Razak and the hotel is at Level 2, Block I, Sinsuran Complex. (Book at P.O. Box 10441, 88805 Kota Kinabalu.)

In the same general area, the **Golden Inn** (Tel: 088-211-581) offers similar accommodations at prices starting at around M$40. The whole place is clean and the management speaks good English. It is a good value and is in Block M, Sinsuran Complex. (Book at P.O. Box 11809, 88820 Kota Kinabalu.) Also worth trying are the **Hilton Inn** (Tel: 088-245-577) and the **Hotel Full Hua** (Tel: 088-234-950), both in Jalan Tugu; **City Inn** (Tel: 088-218-933) in Jalan Pantai; the **Hotel New Sabah** (Tel: 088-224-590) in the Segama Complex Block A; and the **Metro Hotel** (Tel: 088-216-864) in Jalan Berjaya 3. All are small, have acceptable rooms and are in the M$45-55 price range.

A final alternative is the **Hotel Nam Tai** near the night market. This is a typical cheap Chinese hotel. The rooms are bare with not even a hand basin but it seems to get guests at M$29 a night or M$35 for an air-conditioned room.

SANDAKAN

I consider the **Hotel Paris** (Tel: 089-218-488), 21 rooms, on Jalan Tiga, to be the best choice in this category. There is a range of accommodations from fan rooms starting at M$25, to air-conditioned rooms with hot and cold water for M$30. The rooms are not carpeted but all have attached bathroom. The location is good and the people friendly. (Book at P.O. Box 340, 90007 Sandakan, Sabah.)

An alternative is the **Hung Wing Hotel** (Tel: 089-218-895), 29 rooms, on Jalan Tiga. The hotel advertises that all rooms are air-conditioned but in fact you will find some fan rooms on the sixth floor that sell from M$20. That is a good value, if you can survive the stairs. Lower floors have air-conditioned rooms with bathrooms, hot water, and telephone from M$40 up to M$65. The manager was extremely reluctant to show me any rooms but he finally relented so I have doubts about the friendliness of this place. (Book at P.O. Box 1168, 90008 Sandakan, Sabah.)

The **New Sabah Hotel** (Tel: 089-218-711), 28 rooms, is at the other end of the downtown area, close to the night market, and the small red-light district. All rooms are air-conditioned, have a telephone, and an attached bathroom. The hotel is clean and well run and there is no evidence of short-time trade. Room rates are from M$48. (Book at P.O. Box 214, 90007 Sandakan, Sabah; Fax: 6089-271-249.)

5. Dining and Restaurants

Kota Kinabalu has more and better restaurants than any other city on the whole island of Borneo. This doesn't automatically mean that they are great, but there is good variety in cuisine, ambience, and price. Sandakan also has some good restaurants, particularly those specializing in seafood.

KOTA KINABALU

There is a choice of Chinese, Malay, Indian, Thai, Western, Kadazan, Korean, Japanese, and Filipino cuisines together with a wide choice of local dishes at hawkers' stalls, and Western fast food at a number of outlets.

The restaurants within the Shangri-La Tanjung Aru Resort and the Hyatt cannot be faulted, and visitors would do well to try at least one of these during their stay in Kota Kinabalu. **Peppino** Italian restaurant at the Resort or the **Chinese Phoenix Court** at the Hyatt would be good choices. Prices are not cheap but the cuisine, ambience, and service are excellent.

Within the other hotels, the **Grand Palace Chinese Restaurant** at the Shangri-La Hotel (Tel: 212-800) is popular and reasonably priced, while the **Chinese Restaurant** at the Hotel Nan Xing (Tel: 212-988) is considered among the top by Kota Kinabalu locals. I haven't eaten there myself but the **Chinese Restaurant** at the Palace Hotel (Tel: 211-911) has been recommended to me. The **Wishbone Cafe** in the Hotel Jesselton serves both Western and Asian food at reasonable prices.

There are also some recommended restaurants outside the hotels. **Shiraz Restaurant** (Tel: 225-088) in Block B at the SEDCO Complex at Kampong Air is probably the best Indian restaurant in town. It is not cheap but the food is excellent. Good seafood with a Thai flavor is available at **Jaws Restaurant** (Tel: 236-008) on the fourth floor of the

Gaya Center. It is open for breakfast, lunch, and dinner, then carries on with Karaoke until 1:00 A.M. You will find the **X.O. Steak House** (Tel: 237-077) on Jalan Gaya. It is a small cozy restaurant serving imported beef, lamb, and oysters as well as Asian food. It has a range of Californian and Australian wines.

Out at Tanjung Aru Beach there are several favorites. The **Yit Ping Shiang Restaurant** (Tel: 216-120) is a favorite Chinese place. It is not large and is a bit hard to find but tell the driver it's near the Tanjung Aru roundabout. It's worth the effort. A little farther on, you will not be disappointed with the seafood at the **Sea Food Market Restaurant** (Tel: 238-313). This place always seems to be very popular so I suggest you telephone ahead. There are some cheaper hawker outlets close by. Also in this area the **Windbell Seafood Restaurant** (Tel: 222-305) has been recommended. Hidden away in Jalan Aru near the Beach Hotel is the **Dari Senang Restaurant** (Tel: 214-303), serving delightful Korean cuisine. There is a set lunch and dinner of 12 home-cooked dishes served with rice and soup for M\$20, but there are also some exotic and delicious à-la-carte dishes which will tempt you. Try the ginseng chicken soup or the chilli seafood soup for something quite different. The restaurant will send a car to pick you up from your hotel if you telephone ahead.

When it comes to seafood there are several places in town that offer a good choice. At most of these you select your own assortment of live fish, prawns, crabs, and lobsters from a tank, and have it cooked in your favorite style. One such place with a good reputation is the **Port View Seafood Restaurant** (Tel: 221-753), which is on Jalan Haji Saman opposite the old custom's wharf. The **Houng Kee Seafood Restaurant** (Tel: 217-159) in Bandaran Berjaya specializes in steamed seafood. You can eat indoors in air conditioning or outside on the lawn.

Well down the price scale from the seafood places, you can find a selection of other restaurants and cafes offering good food at reasonable prices. One of the most popular is the **Sri Melaka Restoran** (Tel: 224-777) at Jalan Lasman Diki Kampong Air. It has an excellent choice of tasty food, and the staff is helpful and friendly. The **Noodle Inn** (Tel: 219-734) on Jalan Berjaya is another favorite. This unpretentious place has a variety of dishes for around M\$5 and is clean and friendly. In the center of town, the **Sentosa Restaurant** (Tel: 211-658) comes to life when the sun goes down. Tables are set up in the open air and people crowd in to enjoy the food and atmosphere until late at night.

One of the places I particularly wish to recommend is the **Hongkod Seafood Restaurant** (Tel: 718-390) at the K.D.C.A. Cultural Center. This is about seven kilometers out along Jalan Penampang and it specializes in Kadazan cuisine. This will be a great experience for most visitors and I encourage you to make the effort to get out there. A meal for two will cost in the vicinity of M$50. While in the area, the unpretentious **Sri Sakthi Banana Leaf Restaurant** should also be mentioned. Here you eat, with your fingers, a selection of mutton, chicken, fish, or prawn curries with lime pickles, poppadums, and rice. It can be messy but it's fun and a meal for four will cost less than M$25.

In town, the **Nishiki Japanese Restaurant** (Tel: 230-582) on Jalan Gaya and **Korea House** (Tel: 58127) in Bandaran Berjaya are two Oriental favorites.

Apart from restaurants, Kota Kinabalu has a range of eating centers and hawkers' stalls that you should try. Some of these are outdoors like the **Night Food Center** behind the Centrepoint Complex, and the **Night Market** near Taman Bunga Park. I would recommend a little care at these places, however, but they are interesting to visit and you may be tempted to buy. Slightly up-market perhaps are the food stalls upstairs at the central market. These are open till about 10 P.M. and offer Malay, Chinese, and Indian selections. One further step upwards is the Hawker Center in the basement of the **Centrepoint Complex** on Jalan Tun Razak. This is the place if you wish to sample local fare without the heat, noise, and dust of some of the other centers. The food is good, cheap, and safe. There is also a Pizza Hut, an ice-cream and yogurt bar, and other Western favorites.

SANDAKAN

It is claimed that Sandakan has the best seafood on the island of Borneo and if you wish to test this claim, there are several alternatives you can try. The **S.R.C. Restaurant** adjacent to the Padang is a top recommendation. It has a good atmosphere without being too pricey. One of the more popular places is the large **Equitorial Seafood Restaurant** out on Jalan Leila. This is a place that many tourists do not find so its success depends on local patronage. That's always a good sign. My personal favorite, however, is the **Restoran Trig Hill** where you can eat outdoors with a marvelous view of the city and coast. It is a delightful place with good food and attentive service at reasonable prices.

The **XO Steak House** (Tel: 44033) near the Hsiang Garden Hotel is considered to be the best Western restaurant in Sandakan. Prices are not cheap, so take a credit card. A similar comment can be made about the **Golden Unicorn** Japanese restaurant on the 17th floor of the Sabah Bank building, but there is little doubt about the quality. Good vegetarian food is found at the **Supreme Garden** restaurant (Tel: 213-292) in Bandar Ramai.

There are many Indian restaurants in Jalan Pryer opposite the market. I am not an expert on Indian food but I have found **Restoran Buhari**, **Restoran Aysha**, and **Restoran Siray** to be satisfactory. These three restaurants, and probably some others, have a reasonable selection of food, are helpful, and are neat and tidy.

There are scores of small open-fronted Chinese restaurants and it is impossible to give a recommendation for each. I had some wonderful fresh egg custard tarts in **Kai Tan Fu** one afternoon with about half the population of Sandakan. At M$0.50 each and coffee at M$0.60, it is justifiably popular. Another popular place is **Chung Ming Hing** on Jalan Tiga opposite the Shell service station, but there could be many other places that are just as good that I haven't yet tried.

There are many fast-food chains in Sandakan selling Western, Chinese, or Malay food. I had a cheap meal at **Top Cat Fast Food** in Wisma Sabah for less than M$5. Good *satay* can be found at the **Katong Satay House** opposite Suntos Market in Jalan Tiga, while the **Hong Kong Fast Food** provides the opportunity for Chinese food on the run.

Market-style food stalls are found on the second level of the market building. The number of outlets is mind-blowing. I visited late one evening to find them crowded with people, then returned at 8:30 the next morning to see them equally overflowing. Despite all this local enthusiasm, I don't rave on about these for most visitors. I believe better food in better surroundings can be found for little increased cost in some of the more conventional local restaurants around town.

A place many visitors will enjoy is the **Apple Fast Food** outlet in the Nak Hotel. It has a mixture of Asian and Western food including hamburgers, spaghetti, and ice cream, and has reasonable prices and a friendly staff. Not far away the **New Rasa Sayang Drink Bar** has excellent ice cream and sundaes and, like the Apple, it seems to be a good place to meet some locals. Similar fare is offered at any of several outlets of **Superman Icecream**. The name is almost enough to get you in.

A final recommendation is the **Garden Fast Food Center** near the night market. On a pleasant evening, this is a delightful place. There is a variety of food from a number of stalls and there is bar service from friendly locals. This location gives you the chance to watch, at a distance, the antics of local transvestites who try to woo customers in the adjacent streets.

6. Sight-seeing

Kota Kinabalu, often called K.K. by locals, was founded as Jesselton in 1899 as the northern terminal of the North Borneo Railway. The city was almost totally destroyed in World War II during the Allied recapture of Borneo from the Japanese. Kota Kinabalu is a pleasant city with an interesting blend of Western, Chinese, Malay, and local cultures. It has no enormous attraction, but it's worth spending a few days here to enjoy the culture, the cuisine, and the atmosphere of Sabah's capital.

Downtown K.K. is small enough to see on foot and many of the other points of interest can be reached by bus. Taxis are readily available and reasonably cheap if you are looking for more convenience. You can easily spend a day walking around Kota Kinabalu. Visit the Philippines Market on the waterfront to see imitation gem stones, natural pearls, baskets, handbags, clothes, shell chandeliers, souvenirs, and wooden articles of all kinds. Wander along to the new Centrepoint Complex where everything is as modern as tomorrow. Explore the alleys and streets of Sinsuran then venture into the restaurants of KG Air.

If you have the energy, a climb up Signal Hill will reward you with a good view of the city and offshore islands. A visit to the **Sabah Tourism Promotion Corporation** office (Tel: 218-620) in Jalan Gaya is very worthwhile. The staff is extremely helpful and will give you some excellent pointers to seeing and enjoying K.K. and Sabah. While in this area, you could also visit the **Tourism Promotion Board** office in the Wing On Life Building on Jalan Sagunting. The other place worth visiting is the **Sabah Parks** office (Tel: 211-585) on Jalan Tun Fuad Stephens. You can obtain good information on the various parks, and book accommodations at Mt. Kinabalu, Poring Hot Springs, or on the Tunku Abdul Rahman Park.

The **State Mosque** about three kilometers from downtown is a fine example of contemporary Islamic architecture and is worth a visit. Visitors are usually allowed inside provided they are wearing conservative clothes and remove their shoes, but it would be wise to inquire before entering. The **Sabah Museum** (Tel: 50852) is close by and can be visited at the same time. The main building is built in longhouse style with the added symbolism of Islam in the spires, and outstretched arms of Kadazan Sumazau dancers in the eaves. There are displays on natural history, ceramics, and the history of Sabah, and even a small art gallery. I don't believe it is as interesting as the Kutching Museum but it is worth a visit.

The **Sabah Foundation Building** can be seen from much of K.K. and is a startling, unusual building. It is doubtful, however, whether it is worthwhile making the trip out to the site. In my opinion, this is one attraction that is better to view from a distance. If you do go in that direction, you could call in and see the **Likas Sports Complex**, which is one of the best in the Asian region.

Tanjung Aru Beach is the nearest beach to the center of K.K. This is the site of the Shangri-La Tanjung Aru Resort, the Kinabalu Yacht Club, the Kinabalu Golf Club, and Prince Philip Park. The public beach is quite nice and is reasonably clean. The area has food and drink stalls and is very popular with the locals. If you belong to a yacht or golf club back home, you will be welcomed at the local facilities here.

The **Tunku Abdul Rahman Park** comprises five islands and some ocean close to Kota Kinabalu and has become a popular destination for both locals and visitors. Regular boat services are provided to the islands by the Sabah Parks organization and by private firms. The park's ferry service operates from the jetty near the Hyatt Hotel and costs around M$12 for the round trip. Travelling time is about 20 minutes. Good connections are also available from the Tunjung Aru Resort.

The attractions of the park are the good ivory-toned sand beaches, the clear water, and the wealth of coral and marine life. Park headquarters are located on Pulau Manukan, the second largest island in the park. The best beach on this island is on the eastern tip. This is by far the most developed island. There are 20 modern chalets, a clubhouse, a restaurant, a jetty, a marina, a souvenir and diving center, plus a swimming pool, football field, and squash and tennis courts. The island has electricity, water supply, and sewerage. Chalets have no cooking facilities and are M$150 per night on weekdays and M$200 on weekends.

The only other island with accommodations is Pulau Mamutik, the smallest and closest to the mainland. There is an excellent beach and coral reef, which in parts extends to the shore. A fully furnished rest house for up to eight people is available with cooking facilities, electricity, and water. The rate is M$112 per night on weekdays and M$160 on weekends. Camping is allowed on some islands with the written permission of the park warden or the Sabah Parks office in Kota Kinabalu. For lovers of the great outdoors, this is a paradise.

Penampang is a town about 13 kilometers east of K.K. It is inhabited almost exclusively by the Kadazan people and if you visit the graveyards you may still see some burial jars that were once the traditional form of burial. Penampang is the site of St. Michael's Church, the largest and oldest church in Sabah. You may also be able to convince the locals to show you some human heads that survive from the headhunting times. Buses operate from K.K. for around M$1.

On the way to Penampang, you pass the **Hongkod Koisaan** (KDCA

Cultural Center), which is designed to show the different cultures of Sabah. The center has much potential and what is there is a good start, but it is not yet a full-fledged tourist attraction in its own right. The tribal buildings that have been erected here are interesting, particularly for those who will not be travelling extensively in the state. There are displays of musical instruments, a native handicraft shop, a hall that can be used for ceremonies or badminton games, and a popular Kadazan restaurant.

NORTH FROM KOTA KINABALU

The road north from central K.K. passes through the suburb of **Likas** with its large houses, small warehouses and factories, and commercial activity. A couple of "colonial" buildings can be seen on the right before the country changes to semirural. The divided highway continues for some distance and there is considerable traffic because this is also the main road to Mt. Kinabalu and eastern Sabah. You pass the small university on your right, incongruously in the middle of nowhere, and you will see some pottery kilns on your left, then you eventually reach the town of Tuaran.

Tuaran has little to thrill you but the market area is very attractive by the river, under big trees, and there is the opportunity to walk across a pedestrian suspension bridge and test your nerve. As well as the daily market, which is very big on fish, there is a weekly market (or *tamu*) on Sunday. This has plenty of color and activity. The **Restoran Adys** is clean and has good Malay food, while the **Restoran Teh Chung** is recommended for Chinese food. Both are close to the market. The **D'fantesy Karaoke Coffee House** and the **Roses Cafe Disco** offer some evening entertainment and the **Rest House Tuaran** on a hill close to town has four rooms with attached bathrooms, which are available for M$12 for one person and M$24 for two. Two rooms are air-conditioned and two have fans. The town has a large agricultural research station that can be visited.

A few kilometers outside Tuaran you will find the Bajau village of *Mengkabong*, which is built entirely out over the water. The village has existed here for more than 500 years, although the buildings you see today are all modern. Wooden catwalks provide a network of paths linking the various houses with the shore. The inhabitants were formerly pirates, but today they are fishermen. It is possible to rent a boat to explore the village from the water then travel out into the mangroves to see the main fishing and crabbing grounds used by the villagers.

Back on the main road, it's only another six kilometers to *Tamparuli*.

This is where the road to Mt. Kinabalu National Park branches to the right. The town is prosperous and busy. The central area surrounds the compact market and there are several cafes that are satisfactory for a meal. Try the **Kheng Yutting Coffee Shop** for Chinese fare, or the **Kedai Kop Sinar** for Malay food. This area is well known for handicrafts and a small selection is available at the Ru Lim bookstore. A weekly *tamu* occurs on Wednesdays and you may also be able to find some handicraft and ceramics here. Tamparuli has another claim to fame as the location of the longest suspension bridge in Sabah.

The main road now twists and turns its 30 kilometers to Kota Belud. Anyone expecting a smooth ride up a coastal plain will be sadly disappointed but the road does provide some good views particularly towards Mt. Kinabalu. *Kota Belud* is a fairly sleepy rural town with a small market, a hotel, several restaurants, and a range of shops serving local needs. It has reached star status, however, because each Sunday it hosts the largest and most colorful *tamu* in Sabah. The *tamu* is held at a spot about a kilometer out of town. Here village folk meet and mingle with their town cousins amid a collection of cooked food, fruit, vegetables, home-rolled cigarettes, material, clothes, imitation designer watches, and so on. You will see young Kadazan girls wearing short black sarongs as they set up their vegetable stalls next to betel-chewing Bajau women selling tobacco wrappers, and an Indian trader selling cloth and T-shirts. For keen photographers it is a paradise.

A particular attraction of the Kota Belud *tamu* is the water buffalo auctions that are held each Sunday morning. The setting is quite lovely with huge rain trees providing shade for the serious activity of bargaining. Haggling can extend over several hours then the buyer will load the animal on the back of a pickup truck and head off to a remote village with his most important lifetime possession.

The area around Kota Belud has Sabah's main cattle and pony farms and the Bajau horsemen have a big reputation. You will still occasionally see the "cowboys" riding through town although it is no longer common except at festival times. Every evening, however, you will see ponies, along with cars and people, being washed in the river.

If you wish to stay in Kota Belud first try the **Government Rest House** (Tel: 67532) on a small hill just out of town. If you can get a room it will cost M$15 per person per night. The alternative is the **Kota Belud Hotel** (Tel: 976-576), which has nine air-conditioned rooms with hand basin but no bathroom, at M$36 for one or two people. It is more likely that you will be visiting for the day and may wish to try **Restoran Sing Sing** (on the corner near the mosque) where food is about M$3 a dish, or the **Soon Lee Coffee Shop** (on the main road just past the Esso service station) where you can find tasty Chinese and Malay food for lunch and dinner.

It takes about 1 3/4 hours to reach K.B. from K.K. by minibus. Cost is around M$5. It will cost you another M$10 to reach Kudat on the north coast.

The road north is straighter and faster although you need to be very careful because of one-way bridges. There are some extensive rice-growing areas covered with string, plastic bags, and human images, which act to scare away the birds. As you near Kota Marudu you enter coconut and palm oil plantations. *Kota Marudu* is some five kilometers off the main road to Kudat but it can be a good meal stop. The **Good Luck Cafe** will provide a meal for two for about M$12, while the **Hock Guan Restoran** is another Chinese alternative. The town is interesting because it is a fairly new center built by the government to a design that is becoming common throughout Malaysia. The only accommodations are at the **Good Luck Lodging House** (which calls itself a "logging house"). This has five air-conditioned rooms, all with attached bathrooms, which rent for $50 a night without TV, and $60 a night with TV. TV is about the only entertainment after 6 P.M., although the **Texas Cafe** offers some imitation Western food, beer, and recorded music.

Kudat is almost 200 kilometers north of Kota Kinabalu. It is the end of the northern road. This was the first capital of Sabah (North Borneo) from 1881 to 1884. It is still a port and this has an influence on the town. Kudat was the first center for Chinese migration to North Bornea—Hakka and Christian farmers fleeing China. Even in earlier times the East India Company had established a trading post on nearby Balembangan Island, but this was attacked and destroyed by the local people. Today Kudat is the administrative center for the Kudat Division of Sabah and there is quite a bit of development taking place.

The town itself consists of the original old town, a new town, and a further new area being developed along the main road. The old town has a night market but I recommend the new town if you plan to stay or even to eat. Best accommodations by far are at the **Greenland Hotel** (Tel: 62211), 16 carpeted and air-conditioned rooms in the new town. Standard rooms that share bathrooms cost M$35, while deluxe rooms with bathrooms attached and telephone, TV, and video cost M$49-56. In this same area, the **Sungai Wang Restaurant** and the **Prosperous Restaurant** would be good choices for a reasonable meal. The **Dynasty Disco** provides some nighttime entertainment. The **Ocean Hotel** in this area doesn't appear to welcome overnight guests. A few hours will cost M$20.

The only other hotel worth considering is the **Hotel Sunrise** (Tel:

61517) back in the old town. Here rooms with attached bathroom and TV cost M$40, while rooms with outside bathroom and no TV are available at M$28. There is a 9-hole golf course at the new town, however, there are no rental facilities. Visiting members are welcome provided they bring their own gear. The club has a restaurant and lounge.

The Rungus people who live in this region have been able to retain more of their traditional beliefs and ways than many of the other tribes in Sabah. There are still a few thatched-roofed longhouses in this area and it is possible to visit and even stay if you are invited by a local. In practice this is not easy to achieve, so most visitors now rely on arrangements made by tour companies with connections in the area. The Rungus women traditionally wore coils of brass around the neck, forearms, and lower legs, and you can still see women walking the streets with forearm coils. You will also notice the fine beadwork on clothing and bags, and the elaborate weaving. Unfortunately this hand-icraft is not easy to find but you do see items for sale at the Sunday market in Sikuati, about 22 kilometers from Kudat.

One of the other attractions of this region is the beaches, but you need to be very selective in where you go. The beaches close to Kudat are filthy and littered with all kinds of rubbish. The well-promoted Bak Bak beach is better, but I have not left with the feeling of calm and romance that the tourist literature speaks about. A beach worth seeing lies a few kilometers from Sikuati. Here at times you find surf crashing onto the heavily jungled shore. It is a great sight.

SOUTH FROM KOTA KINABALU

The main road south from Kota Kinabalu leads eventually to Sarawak and you can then travel on to Brunei. On the way there is much of interest. This interest starts almost as soon as you pass the airport, about six kilometers south of the city. The countryside is a mixture of coastal flats, small forested hills, and semiurban developments. The road branches after about 15 kilometers with the main highway travelling inland and the well-constructed new road to Papar following the coast.

A few kilometers along the coastal road you find the **Seaside Travellers Inn** (Tel: 750-313), which has 10 rooms situated on a reasonable beach. There is a restaurant and a number of offshore islands. This is a good vantage point for lovely sunsets across the water. Room costs are M$30-60. A little farther on you pass the remains of an old British mansion believed to be about 100 years old, then you reach the small town of Papar.

Papar is one of the neatest and best-kept towns in Sabah. There are rows of shop houses—some modern, some old—but all are well kept and clean. The roads have central gardens that are looked after, and there is a feeling of caring. The town is surrounded by *padi* fields but there are also rubber and palm oil plantations in the area. Just outside town is the popular Pantai Manis (Sweet Beach), which can be a great place for a picnic. The best approach is by a slow boat ride downriver (15 minutes). You can also travel upstream into the jungle where you get glimpses of riverside life.

South of Papar, the road is lined with fruit stalls. You wonder who is ever going to buy the quantity of produce offered. The small center of *Kimanis* was once an American colony set up by the American Trading Company but nothing remains today. A little farther on, a road heads off to the right to the small fishing village of *Kuala Penyu*. This is the starting point for a half-hour boat ride to the **Pulau Tiga State Park**.

You will need permission from the Sabah Parks office in Kota Kinabalu to visit this park but for those who make the effort, the rewards are great. Pulau Tiga has been built up from a series of mud volcanoes. You can see this continuing today and it is a fascinating sight. The main island is a haven for unusual flora and fauna, particularly birdlife. The beach around the island is delightful and the water crystal-clear. I would hope that this area can remain undeveloped and little disturbed forever. On an island a few minutes to the north, you can find hundreds of poisonous striped sea snakes.

Back on the mainland, a road leads to *Menumbok*. This is the departure point for the government car ferry to Labuan Island. There are two departures a day. The ferry also takes passengers without vehicles for around M$6 a person, one way. Speed boats leave more frequently but you will probably be asked for around M$12 for this trip.

Labuan is an island under the control of the federal territory people in Kuala Lumpur. Thanks to its free-port status and barter trade with the southern Philippines, it is an important trade center. Unless you want to buy up big, there is little attraction on the island. The main town is called Victoria and this is where the boats head to. It's where you find the accommodations, restaurants, and shops. Large-scale industries are being developed on the island including oil and gas projects so there is something of a boomtown feel about the place.

The history of Labuan is almost more interesting than the island itself. The British first approached the Sultan of Brunei about using the island as a coaling base, to act against piracy, and to increase trade. In 1848, the Sultan ceded Labuan to the British Crown in perpetuity, and Sir James Brooke became the first governor. In 1890, Labuan came under the control of the British North Borneo Chartered Company and remained so until 1907 when the island was placed under the government of the Straits Settlements.

In 1942 Japanese forces landed in Labuan and occupied the island and all of Sabah until 1945. The Japanese renamed the island "Maida Island." In 1946 Labuan became part of the colony of North Borneo, in 1963 it became part of Sabah and joined Malaysia. Then in 1984 it became part of the Federal Territory of Malaysia.

There are a few nice beaches on the island, a grand Japanese war memorial, a reasonable golf course, and a commonwealth war cemetery. The best hotel in town is the **Hotel Labuan** (Tel: 087-412-502), 150 rooms, on Jalan Merdeka. Rooms are air-conditioned, carpeted, and have attached bathrooms, direct dial telephones, and TV. (Book direct at P.O. Box 354, 87008 W.P. Labuan, Malaysia; Fax: 6087-415-355.) Room rates start at M$130. A new five-star hotel is under construction.

The **Manikar Sheraton Resort Hotel** (Tel: 087-418-700), 250 rooms, is situated on the northwest tip of the island and has become a popular business and holiday hotel. Room rates are from M$180.

Back at Menumbok, you can get a minibus to **Beaufort** for around M$8. Beaufort is a small provincial town with considerable charm. It is built beside the Padas River, which floods at regular intervals. Beaufort has solved this problem by building all its shop houses on stilts above ground. This gives the whole place character that is missing from much of Malaysia. Most of the shop houses are built from timber, which further adds to the appeal. After saying all this, I concede that Beaufort has little to keep you there longer than one day, on your way to somewhere else.

For those travelling south, Beaufort is the last significant settlement before you reach Sarawak. It's a place to stock up on necessities and money. For those looking for a meal, the **Restoran Bismillah** has good Muslim Malay food, while the **Restoran Kim Wah** underneath the Hotel Beaufort is recommended for a wider choice of fare. The best accommodations in town are at the **Hotel Beaufort** (Tel: 087-211-911) where there are air-conditioned rooms with attached bathrooms from M$50 a night. The alternative is the **Hotel Padas** (Tel: 087-212-400), 22 rooms, where a fan room with no bathroom costs M$25 and an air-conditioned room with TV and attached bathroom is M$40.

If you are heading to Sarawak by public transportation, you can take a minibus to Sipitang for about M$5. From there you can get another minibus to Lawas across the border. Even though Sabah and Sarawak are both states of Malaysia, they still operate immigration posts on the border.

The other reason visitors go to Beaufort is to take the train to Tenom. It is a spectacular trip up the Padas Valley through tropical jungle. The train clings to the side of the gorge while the wheels squeal and wail as they scrape around the tight curves. There are small wayside stops in the middle of the jungle where passengers wave down the trains. It is quite an experience. Engineers carry chain saws with them to cut fallen trees from across the tracks.

There are two types of trains operating at different times of the day. The railcar is designated first-class and costs M$8.35 one way, while the diesel train is second-class and costs M$2.75. The seats on the railcar are more comfortable and it travels faster but because it is so small (13 passengers), and hence has such a short wheelbase, the ride it gives is very rough. If you happen to be travelling on this vehicle, try to get the two front seats so you can look down the line ahead. The view is great but forget about taking photographs because of the crazed windows, and constant movement. Listen for the police siren that is used in place of a normal train whistle.

The diesel train is slower, dirty, and you share it with chickens, sacks of rice, and numerous plastic shopping bags, but it has so much local color it's hard not to recommend it. You will find the floor littered with peanut shells, and the smell from the open toilet may be overpowering, but you can stand in the open doorway and watch the river and overhanging jungle just meters away. The present timetable has a railcar departing Beaufort at 8:25 A.M. and 3:05 P.M. and a diesel train departing at 10:50 A.M., 12 noon, and 1:55 P.M. Monday to Saturday. Sunday trips need to be checked with a travel agent in K.K. or with the rail station at Beaufort. The trip to Tenom takes 1½ to two hours.

Tenom is a lively town serving a big agricultural district. It is the center of the Murut community, known for its longhouses, jungle hunting, and blowpipes. In town, of course, you see nothing of this and in fact Tenom looks like a modern Malaysian rural city. The town center consists of several streets of two- and three-story shop houses, a large *padang*, and a few modern buildings. Tenom is in a very pretty setting but the town itself has little charm.

There is actually very little to do in Tenom but the district is worth a look. For about M$5 you can catch a minibus for the 50-kilometer ride south to *Tomani*. Close by you can see Sabah's only rock carvings produced by unknown artists. To travel farther inland, you have to take to the river. There are some traditional longhouses in this region that welcome visitors but you should be aware that facilities are basic. This is an area when you need time and patience. If you get as far as Maligan you can do a two-day walk to the village of *Long Pasia* near the Sarawak and Kalimantan border. There is a simple hut midway along the track where you can spend the night.

The attraction of a place like Long Pasia is the life-style. Everything is done slowly. Communication and interaction among the community is vital. Sharing is more essential than having, and people are accepted for who they are, not for what they have or who they know. In places like Long Pasia, visitors are treated like guests. You will be invited into houses for food and tea. You will not be able to communicate with people but you can feel their hospitality.

Back towards Tenom, there are other things to see. *Kemabong*, about 25 kilometers south, has a traditional *lansaran* dancing platform. This is a wooden platform built on bamboo poles that act as springs to produce an effect something like a trampoline. It can support many energetic dancers, and the noise and activity when a group performs is quite amazing. You can see a replica at the KDCA Cultural Village in K.K.

The other place worth visiting is the **Lagud Sebrang Research Center** (Tel: 088-735-661), where you can see cocoa, coffee, and other plants together with an outstanding orchid collection. Intensive efforts are being made to preserve, propagate, research, and document the orchid species found in Borneo. A minibus goes past this area or you can hire a taxi from Tenom.

There is a surprising amount of accommodations in town. The top-of-the-range hotel is the **Perkasa Hotel** (Tel: 889-511), 63 air-conditioned rooms, which is situated on a hilltop about two kilometers from town. The hotel has rooms with attached bathrooms, TV, telephones, and piped music. There is a restaurant, lounge, cocktail bar, games room, and fitness center. Room rates start at about M$90. Hawkers' food is available on weekends.

Back in town, there is plenty of choice. The **Hotel Tenom** (Tel: 736-378), 12 rooms, has a choice of fan rooms with hand basin for M$20, or rooms with carpet, TV, and attached bathroom for M$28, $30, and $40. The hotel has a restaurant, bar, lounge, and the Heart Throb Karaoke lounge. It could be noisy. The small **Hotel Kim San** (Tel: 735-485) has six rooms with space for up to three people in each. Rooms are air-conditioned and have TV and carpet but do not have bathrooms. Rooms cost M$30. The very friendly Chinese owner has just opened a new hotel called **Kim San Baru**, with 15 rooms, nearer the railway station. All rooms have attached bathrooms with hot and cold water and cost M$30 a night.

The **Siri Jaya Hotel** (Tel: 735-689), 12 rooms, has a reception office at street level and rooms on the third level. All rooms are bright and clean and have air conditioning, carpet, TV, and attached bathrooms.

Prices start at around M$30. The **Sabah Hotel** (Tel: 735-534), five rooms, is the cheapest acceptable place in town with non-air-conditioned rooms from M$20 and air-conditioned ones from M$25. All rooms share a bathroom. You enter the hotel through the Bismillah Restaurant opposite the Chartered Bank near the market.

Tenom has many Chinese restaurants with **Chi Hin Restaurant** and **Fon Him Restaurant**, both on the main pedestrian mall in town, probably good choices. The **Bismillah Restaurant** at the Sabah Hotel serves good Indian-style food.

You could now return to K.K. by minibus via Keningau, the provincial town of the Interior Division. *Keningau* is the center of the interior timber industry. Sawmills abound and log depots can be seen everywhere. The town has grown rapidly in recent years and it shows. The new business premises, shops, and offices have little to recommend them and many people think that the development has ruined what may have once been a nice little community. There is the usual choice of accommodations. The **Hotel Perkasa** (Tel: 31044), 44 rooms, is top of the heap with air-conditioned rooms with all the facilities from around M$90. Middle-of-the-road accommodations are found at the **Hotel Hiap Soon** (Tel: 31541) where there are air-conditioned rooms from M$35. The **Tai Wah Hotel** has basic rooms from around M$25.

There is not a great choice in restaurants. Any of the Chinese ones will provide basic rice and noodles. The **Mandarin Restaurant** offers something a bit better. For local flavor you could try some of the stalls at the night market. To return to K.K. by minibus, there are now two choices—either via Papar on the coast, or across the Crocker Range to Tambunan, then over further mountains to Kota Kinabalu. If you choose this latter route, you should stop off at the **Rafflesia Information Center**, which is on the Tambunan side of Tambunan Hill, 58 kilometers from Kota Kinabalu. Here you can see examples of the world's largest flower and learn of its lifecycle. From Tambunan it is possible to travel by minibus to Ranau and to Kinabalu National Park.

For adventurous travellers with plenty of time, a road leads south from Keningau to Nabaran and eventually to Sapulut. At Sapulut you can hire a boat to travel up the Sapulut River to Tetaluan and Batu Punggus, a 200-meter-high limestone massif with associated caves, found in the middle of the jungle. To reach it you will have to stay overnight in a Murut longhouse beside the river. You will find that there is no problem with accommodations and you will be invited to stay and drink the local wine with the house community. It is customary to leave a gift behind if you have accepted this hospitality. Check with the Rural Development Corporation in Kota Kinabalu (Tel: 088-428-910).

There are many rivers to explore if you have the time and money. All have longhouses and hospitable Muruts, once known as the headhunters of Sabah. This region is far from civilization and even though things like outboard motors and modern clothes have been readily accepted, traditional life-styles have been little eroded. If you visit this area, please leave your Western problems and outlook behind so that you can appreciate the beautiful countryside and the natural culture as it should be seen.

EAST FROM KOTA KINABALU

What has been the biggest attraction in Sabah for many years, lies 1½ hours east of Kota Kinabalu along a good, sealed highway. Mt. Kinabalu is the highest mountain in southeast Asia and draws visitors from around the world. Mt. Kinabalu is many things to many people. To some it is a place of wonderful flora, golden sunsets, and majestic sunrises. To the romantic it is an ever-changing natural wonder to be loved and enjoyed. To the local folk it is the revered place of the dead.

Despite its height, thousands of visitors climb to its summit every year to enjoy the magical view and a sense of personal achievement. The national park also contains some exciting flora and fauna, so it's a great place to visit even if you don't want to climb. It's fun to explore for pitcher plants, which grow in abundance here. They survive by trapping insects and very small animals in their pitchers, which contain some special juices to help the plant digest the nutrients from the victim.

From afar, Kinabalu is an awesome mountain with jagged granite peaks and precipices, however, the trail to the summit can be negotiated by almost anyone who is in good health and is reasonably fit. That's not to say that the climb to the top and back is easy. When you have done it, you will be tired and sore for days but most people believe it is worth the effort.

Minibuses run from Kota Kinabalu to the entrance of the park. Most then continue on to Ranau or to Sandakan on the east coast. The fare from K.K. is around M$9. It's only 100 meters from the main road to the park entrance and reception office. It is best to make advance reservations for accommodations at the park through the Sabah Parks office in K.K. (Tel: 088-211-881). You can, in fact, book accommodations up to 12 months in advance by writing to the Director, Sabah Parks, P.O. Box 10626, 88806 Kota Kinabalu, Sabah, Malaysia, enclosing M$10 as a document fee. Full payment is then made one month before the date of the visit.

Accommodations are available at park headquarters near the main road and on the mountain. At park headquarters the choice is between a reasonably priced hostel or a fairly expensive lodge or chalet. The cheapest is the **Old Hostel** (M$10) while the **New Hostel** costs M$15. Both are clean, are supplied with blankets and pillows, and have cooking facilities. The twin-bedded *cabins* cost M$50 weekdays and M$80 weekends, while the *Nepenthes villas*, which have two bedrooms and can sleep six people, are M$180 weekdays and $250 weekends. On the mountain the choice is between **Laban Rata Rest House** where there are good dormitory accommodations, warmth, and a canteen (cost M$25 a night); or several *mountain huts* (M$10) where there are bunks with mattresses, a gas stove for cooking, and sleeping bags.

There are things to do without climbing the mountain. A 1½-hour guided walk is conducted from the park administration building each morning at 11:15 A.M. There is a multivision show for M$1 at the basement theater each day at 1:30 P.M., and a free slide show at 7:30 P.M. on Friday, Saturday, Sunday, and Monday. The administration building has a small exhibition of plants, birds, and animals that are found in the park, and there are a number of signposted walks around the area. Within the park there are two significant waterfalls. Sungai Langanan is made up of seven separate falls, the most spectacular of which descends from a height of about 150 meters. Sungai Kipungit is a 12-meter-high fall near the Poring Hot Spring.

There are two restaurants. The **Kinabalu Balsam** restaurant is near the reception office. It has an English menu, serves Western and Chinese food, is open from 7 A.M. to 9 P.M., and has a nice outdoor terrace for lunch. Meals start at around M$3.50. There is also a ministore here where you can buy basic supplies. The **Liwagu Restoran**, in the administration building, is a bit more up-market, slightly more expensive, and open from 6 A.M. to 9 P.M. every day.

If you wish to climb the mountain, you must register with the park office. A permit will cost you M$10. Climbers are supposed to have a guide with them and this costs a minimum of M$25/day for one to three people. If you are staying at Laban Rata you will not need a porter but otherwise you may hire one to carry your supplies at M$25/day for up to 24 pounds. Note that the guides and porters are not employees of the park and they vary between poor and excellent. You really just take your chances. Those who reach the top can buy a summit medallion for M$18, a summit badge for M$3, or a certificate for M$1, from the office where they registered.

The recommended climbing routine is to leave at 7 A.M. and take a minibus ride to the power station gate (1 hour if you walk). The real

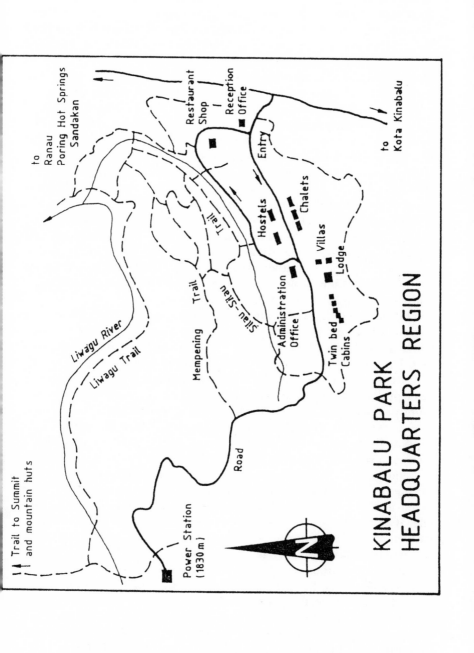

KINABALU PARK
HEADQUARTERS REGION

to
Ranau
Poring Hot Springs
Sandakan

Restaurant
Shop

Reception
Office

Entry

to
Kota Kinabalu

Hostels

Chalets

Villas

Lodge

Administration
Office

Twin bed
Cabins

Trail

Silau-silau

Mempening Trail

Liwagu River

Liwagu Trail

Road

Trail to Summit
and mountain huts

Power Station
(1830 m)

N

climb starts from here and it takes about six hours to reach Laban Rata Rest House. On the way you pass from tropical lowland rain forest, through temperate forest, to alpine meadows. By the time you reach the rest house, despite many stops along the way, you will be very tired, and some people will be already affected by the thin mountain air. You sleep early and arise about 3 A.M. to begin the final ascent. With good luck and good weather you will reach the summit just in time to see sunrise over Sabah. It is a sight you will never forget. The trek down is just as demanding but you will reach the powerhouse and the welcome vehicle by about midday. It's now too late to carry on to Sandakan but you can stay at a nearby hotel to recover or push on to Ranau.

The best accommodations in this area are at the **Hotel Perkasa** (Tel: 088-889-511), 74 rooms, from about M$90, with private bathrooms, heaters, carpet, TV, video, hairdryers, and room service. There is a restaurant serving Malay, Chinese, and Western fare, a cocktail lounge, a small fitness room, and a slot-machine room. The hotel rents golf equipment but anyone needing larger than size-9 shoes will be out of luck. There are several other places of lesser quality and price. One is the **Mountain View Motel** (Tel: 088-889-085) where a room without a bathroom costs M$35 and with M$50.

The surrounding area is known as *Kundasang* and it is quite heavily settled. The forest has given way to terraced hillsides that grow temperate fruits and vegetables. There are many roadside stalls selling produce. Unfortunately the area is now subject to landslides because the forest cover has gone, and the road can be blocked for hours or days after prolonged rain. One slide was so bad that the road was closed for months. It seems we are slow learners when it comes to the environment.

Visitors should stop and visit the **Kundasang War Memorial**. This supposedly contains a British, Australian, and Borneo garden and is a memorial specifically for the men who died in the Ranau death march. In September 1944, the Japanese marched 2,400 British and Australian prisoners of war from Sandakan to the foothills of Mt. Kinabalu. The march took 11 months and only six men survived the war to tell the tale. It is one of the grimmest yet least recorded atrocities of the war. Unfortunately the visitor today will get none of this information from the memorial because there is a total lack of signs or descriptions.

It is about 30 minutes from here to *Ranau*. This small provincial town is the center for a rich agricultural area and it receives some spin-off from the nearby copper mine. Ranau is an attractive, bustling town but there is little to do. It's not a bad place for a meal with the **Leong Leong Restoran** probably the best for Chinese food, and the **Restoran Seri Tanjong** OK for Malay fare. The **Hotel Ranau** (Tel:

876-176) has basic rooms from M$25, and ones with bathroom and air conditioning for M$45. The **Hotel Sepati**, 8 rooms, has some clean fan rooms with no bathroom for M$35. The outside rooms are bright, but the inside rooms are very dark.

One of Sabah's most beautiful waterfalls is located south of here off the Ranau-Tambunan road at Kampung Patau. Unfortunately it involves a two-hour trek with a guide so few visitors take the trouble to get there.

The main attraction in the Ranau area is the Poring Hot Springs, which are part of the Kinabalu National Park, about 20 kilometers north of the town. Infrequent minibuses go there from Ranau, so it's best to try early morning.

The **Poring Hot Springs** is controlled by the Sabah Parks Authority. Admission is M$2. The area was developed by the Japanese during World War II and today you can relax in large outdoor pools where you can adjust the water to your desired temperature. It's a great place to relax tired muscles after you have done the Mt. Kinabalu climb. There are several signposted jungle walks in this area with perhaps the best being the waterfall tour, which takes 1 hour 30 minutes each way.

One of the big attractions here is the canopy walk, a suspension bridge that enables you to walk among the tree canopy, far above the ground. It is not for the fainthearted. The walk is open from 10:30 A.M. to 4 P.M. for M$2 and there is also a camera charge. It is open again from 6:30 P.M. to 10:30 P.M. at much higher cost. A new attraction is the Butterfly Park. There is a hostel at the springs with M$10 dormitory accommodations, and two cabins that rent at prices from M$60 to M$100 depending on the day of the week, but unfortunately there is no canteen.

It is a back-breaking six-hour drive from Ranau to Sandakan at the best of times. In the wet season it can take days. The air service from K.K. to Sandakan certainly has appeal for those who can afford it. *Sandakan* is a charming town in a lovely location. It was the former capital of British North Borneo and today it is a major commercial center with a growing tourism industry.

The Sandakan region was under the control of the Sultanate of Sulu in the eighteenth century and several settlements grew up around the huge bay that dominates the coastline. One of these was at or near present day Sandakan but by the mid-nineteenth century, it had disappeared. In 1889 an Englishman, William Pryer, started a new town on the bay which rapidly grew into an important center. Sandakan continued to grow until it was entirely destroyed during World War II. The present city has re-emerged since that time.

SANDAKAN

We covered Sandakan accommodations and restaurants in the two previous sections of this chapter, but now let's look at the things to see. Downtown Sandakan is a compact area adjacent to the water. The waterfront is dominated by the market. It is one of the best in Malaysia for fish, fruit and vegetables, and cooked food. There are hundreds of food stalls on the second level that are busy all day. Most activity in the other sections occurs in the early morning, when this is the most colorful and lively section of town.

Sandakan is very much a Chinese town so it is no surprise to find several impressive temples. The **Sam Sing Kang Temple** is perhaps the most visual because it stands at the end of the town *padang*. It was built in 1887. The most impressive temple, however, is the **Puu Jih Shih Temple**, high on a hill in the south part of town. The road entrance is through a massive archway. The temple interior is dominated by 34 huge pillars and three teakwood statues of the Buddha. Huge multi-lamped lanterns flank the main altar. It is well worth a visit.

The **Sandakan Mosque** is at the other end of town by the waterfront. It was completed in 1988 and is simple, elegant, and attractive. The **St. Michael and All Angels Church** is an entirely different type of building. It was started in 1893 and construction proceeded in timber, brick, and stone for 20 years. Today it remains one of Sandakan's finest buildings.

There is a fine view of Sandakan from a lookout about one kilometer north of the downtown area. In this same area you can see the **Agnes Keith House** where the author lived from 1934 to 1952 except for periods in the United States and a Japanese prison camp. Her three books, including *Land Below the Wind*, give a penetrating look at life in Sandakan during her period of residency. Even today the house and garden can provoke strong thoughts of another era.

There are two major reminders of World War II. The first is the **Japanese cemetery**, which contains a large memorial for those who died in the war. The cemetery, however, is much older than that. It contains the tombs of many Japanese women who were shipped to Sandakan as young girls and tricked into prostitution. The second reminder is the **Australian memorial** that is at Mile 7 Labuk Road on the site of a major prisoner-of-war camp. At one time the camp held 2,800 prisoners, then in 1944 the 2,400 still alive were marched through the jungle to Ranau near Mt. Kinabalu. Of these only six survived the march to see the end of the war. This event, though not widely reported, claimed more Australian lives than any other single event during the war in Asia.

But by far the most popular attraction at Sandakan is the **Sepilok**

Orangutan Rehabilitation Center. Here amid lovely rain forest you can see apes learning to live in the jungle. Most of the animals you see at the center are young orangutans who have been confiscated from private owners or brought from logging camps. The process of returning these animals to the forest requires patience and understanding in order to revive their buried survival instincts. In time the program teaches the young animals how to integrate socially and independently with the wild population of the forest. They are encouraged to climb, build nests, and gradually learn to forage for themselves. The animals close to the center are fed every day but are eventually sent farther and farther away until they only return infrequently.

Since Sepilok's establishment, more than 100 orangutans have been rehabilitated into the wild. The center is open from 9 A.M. to 4 P.M. daily; admission is M$10. The orangutans are fed at about 10 A.M. and 2 P.M. each day and this is the best time to see these delightful creatures. On the ground they are awkward but in the trees they are completely at home. You are also likely to see some young apes at the center and it's easy to see why they were once so popular as pets. They have personalities similar to humans, and are warm, trusting, and inquisitive.

The center also has a nature education area that is worth a quick look. It has a small theater that has a video on the life of the orangutan, and there is a display hall featuring examples of the various wildlife in the Sepilok area. You can sometimes see other animals at the center. There are two rare Sumatran rhinoceroses, and on my last visit there were two young elephants. The other attraction, of course, is the jungle itself and the various trails allow you to explore the area in safety.

You can reach the center by bus from Sandakan, just look for the bus marked "Sepilok Batu 14," or you can hire a taxi from the airport or the city. The bus costs around M$1.50, while a taxi is likely to be M$15. Local tours also operate from Sandakan and you would do well to consider this option. Whatever you do, don't miss this place.

You may also be interested in going to **Berhala Island**, a rocky outcrop that was once a leper colony, then a prisoner-of-war-camp. Now it is home to several hundred people, and the location of one of the best beaches near Sandakan. Parts of the island are forest reserve and there are some caves in the steep cliffs. You reach Berhala by speedboat from downtown Sandakan.

Another attraction is **Turtle Islands Park**, on Selingan Island, some 40 kilometers northeast of Sandakan. There, close to the border with the Philippines, are three islands that are important breeding grounds for sea turtles. The turtles come up onto the beaches at night, dig a hole in the sand, and lay their eggs. These days the eggs are dug up after the turtles have left and are placed in a hatchery to protect them from man and monitor lizards. There are three visitor chalets on the island that you can book through the Sabah Parks Office in Sandakan (Tel: 089-273-453) or with a tour operator. The cost is M$30 per adult per night. A cafeteria for food and drink is available. There is no regular transportation to the islands, so you may have to charter a boat for the two-hour trip.

Gomantong Caves are south of Sandakan on the other side of the bay. You reach them by boat to Suan Lamba, then taxi to the caves or you can go the whole way overland on the road from Sandakan to Sukau. Either way can be expensive and time-consuming. Travel agents will also arrange trips and, although the cost is high, this can be the most satisfactory way to see this area. The caves and the hill that contains them are interesting to the casual visitor and fascinating for the naturalist. Some of the caverns are huge and there are a series of passageways and subcaves.

The caves are most famous, however, for their swiftlets and their edible nests. Visitors can see the nest-collecting techniques, which involve the use of rattan ladders or bamboo poles to reach up to the 150-meter-high ceiling. It's incredibly dangerous and quite spectacular. The first harvest of nests is taken during February to April immediately after the birds have made their nests and before they have laid eggs. With their nest gone, the birds immediately build another and this is used to raise their young. The used nests are collected from July to September. Unless you are well prepared with hat, powerful light, and good boots with outer covering, you may not enjoy the caves. Tour operators provide this gear so their passengers are well equipped.

Closer to **Sukau** you can ride on the Kinabatagan River into many of its oxbow lakes to observe and photograph wildlife—especially the unique proboscis monkeys that are found only on the island of Borneo and nowhere else in the world. There are now river lodges in this area where you can stay overnight if you book with a tour operator.

From Sukau it's possible to drive to **Lahad Datu**, a busy timber and agricultural town on Darvel Bay. This was an important tobacco area from the 1890s to the 1930s then became a logging boomtown in the 1960s and 1970s. That has now changed to cocoa, oil palm, and other agricultural products particularly in the area to the east. This region receives few tourists but there are reasonable accommodations.

The **Hotel Mido** (Tel: 81800), 61 air-conditioned rooms with attached bathrooms, is the best hotel in town. It has a restaurant, a bar, room service, and the Malaysia Airlines office. Room rates are M$55-120.

The **Ocean Hotel** (Tel: 81700), 20 rooms, is cheaper with rooms at around M$40; while the **Delux Hotel** (Tel: 81500), 12 rooms, has fairly basic rooms from M$30. There are a couple of good beaches east of the town, and the Danum Valley is a virgin forest area to the west. Buses are available to Semporna (about M$7) and Tawau (about M$9).

The **Madai Waterfall** is a lovely place to stop between Lahad Datu and Semporna. The fall is about 30 meters in height and the area is provided with shelters, parking areas, and walkways. The large pool at the bottom is an ideal swimming spot.

Semporna is the next point of interest. It is reached along a good road that passes **Madai Cave** (another source of birds' nests). You can almost drive to the cave mouth, so it is worth a detour. This is an important archeological site because man's presence can be traced back through the layers of guano on the floor. Semporna is a small but thriving town with a growing tourism industry. The attraction is the surrounding islands and coral reefs. Many of the nearer islands can be reached by rented boat. All have beautiful beaches, most have coral, and some are uninhabited. Semporna sports a new floating restaurant and motel called the **Semporna Ocean Tourism Center**. You can stay at the **Dragon Inn** (Tel: 781-088), 22 rooms, for M$60-160. Satisfactory budget accommodations are more difficult to find. Seafood is excellent and any restaurant with fish, prawns, and lobsters on the menu will be satisfactory. **Pulau Bohey Dulang**, an attractive old volcanic island close to Semporna, has a pearl farm.

Pulau Sipadan must be mentioned. This island is developing a good reputation as a diving spot. It is Malaysia's only true oceanic island. In some parts there is a 600-meter sheer drop only 10 meters or so from the shore. The island has 12 hectares (30 acres) of luxuriant forest surrounded by brilliant white beaches. I am not a diver but I am told that the underwater cliffs, reefs, and caverns, and the abundance of fish makes this one of the best diving spots anywhere. There are regular excursions to Sipadan with diving equipment and instruction provided. Dive companies have huts on the island that provide beds, electricity, central showers and toilets, and a dining/bar hall.

The good sealed road now continues west through cocoa and oil palm plantations to *Tawau*. This has taken over from Sandakan as the timber capital of Sabah. The area to the north of here is being extensively logged despite world protests and some action by the Malaysian government. It will be interesting to see how long this continues. The coastline around Tawau is very attractive but there is really little to do in town. The recent growth has spoiled most of the old-world charm that previously existed. Business comes first before everything.

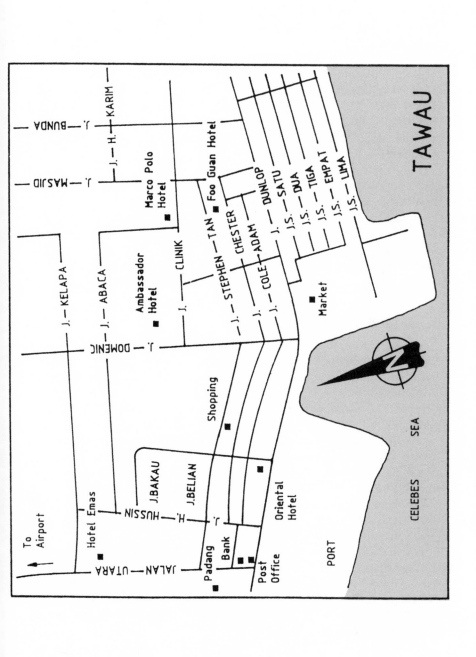

TAWAU

There are some good hotels, with the **Marco Polo** (Tel: 777-988), 150 air-conditioned rooms, being the top choice. This has all the facilities of a first-class hotel with the price to match (M$125-800). The **Hotel Emas** (Tel: 762-000), 100 rooms, is an alternative. Prices here start at M$90. A reasonable midmarket hotel is **The Oriental** (Tel: 771-500), with 20 rooms at M$70-80. Down-market from here, the **Ambassador Hotel** (Tel: 772-700) has 23 air-conditioned rooms for a reasonable M$30-40. The **Foo Guan Hotel** (Tel: 771-700) has 14 fan rooms for around M$25. They are not great, but you won't find anything much cheaper.

The restaurants in the better hotels are the place if you are sick of rice and noodle dishes. Most of them are good. There are also several reasonable Indian restaurants down towards the waterfront. Fast food has reached Tawau so you can indulge in your favorite fried chicken or *satay*. If price is your main consideration, the night food stalls which set up on the waterfront are the place to go. You will also find some excellent, but not inexpensive, seafood in this area. There are avenues of shaded shop houses where you can hunt for souvenirs.

7. Guided Tours

Sabah is a state where the use of some tours as part of your sight-seeing activities makes much sense. It is no coincidence that I have had more direct contact with tour operators here than elsewhere in Malaysia.

Several companies operate a number of standard tours from Kota Kinabalu but will also put together a specific package to meet your needs. Naturally if you have a party of several people, these arrangements will be more economical. Here are four half-day tour suggestions. The first is a three-hour city tour that visits the mosque, the museum, Prince Phillip Park, the Sabah Golf and Country Club, the Sabah Foundation building, Likas Sports Complex, Signal Hill, and downtown Kota Kinabalu. It is an excellent introduction to the city. The cost is around M$30.

The second tour is to Tuaran, Tamparuli, and the Mengakabong fishing village (around M$40). Then there is a tour to Penampang to see the homes of the Kadazan people, the House of Skulls, St. Michael's Church, and the Kadazan and Dusun Cultural Center (around M$45). The final alternative is an island escape to the lovely islands of the Tunku Adbul Rahman State Park.

There are also a range of one-day tours. The most popular is the day trip to Kinabalu National Park (around M$100). There is a longer tour

(10 hours) that combines the park and Poring Hot Springs (around M$120). Some companies have a trip to the Kota Belud Sunday market that departs in the early morning and returns early in the afternoon (around M$55). A much longer day is the trip to Beaufort and Tenom, riding the spectacular railway between the two towns. The longest day of all is the Sandakan. This departs at 7 A.M., does a city and market tour, visits the orangutan rehabilitation center, then visits other places of interest in the city before returning to Kota Kinabalu in the evening. Other options are a tour that climbs Mt. Kinabalu, another that does whitewater rafting, a whole day trip to a longhouse in Kudat, a trip to the Tambunan Rafflesia Center, and others that include bird watching, butterfly catching, and a trip to "Turtle Island" at Selingan.

Of particular interest is the three-days/two nights agro-tourism package put together by **Rafflesia Tours and Travel** (Tel: 088-239-384). You actually stay in lodges where you can inspect rubber plantations, tropical fruit farms, a wild-bird sanctuary, and go swimming, snorkelling, or game fishing. You can get more details on Fax: 6088-231-048. This company will also organize all other touring you may wish to do. I have found them to be excellent.

Popular Express Travel (Tel: 57906) has a day trip to Labuan Island (by air), many of the standard tours, and a six-hour Kinabalu at Night Tour that visits Signal Hill, the night market, and a discotheque. **Api Tours** (Borneo) (Tel: 221-233) has a wide range of options including a day trip to a longhouse in the Kudat region, and a two-day trip to Sandakan that makes a tour of the city, visits the orangutan sanctuary, explores the Gomantong Caves, and searches for proboscis monkeys.

There are also tour operators in Sandakan. I have had personal experience with Roland Ng of **S.I. Tours** (Tel: 089-219-717) and found him excellent. This company handles the Sandakan ground arrangements for several K.K. tour operators, but it also has ex-Sandakan departures that you can pick up if you arrive independently. There is a one-day city and orangutan sanctuary tour that includes lunch, a two-day "Turtle Island" and orangutan sanctuary tour, and a two-day river cruise to see proboscis monkeys and the orangutan tour.

Sabah Air (Tel: 088-56733) has sight-seeing tours from helicopters and fixed-wing aircraft. **Borneo Divers** (Tel: 088-222226) has diving trips and diving/camping vacations on both the East and West Coasts of Sabah. They also provide scuba diving lessons, rent windsurfers, and organize fishing, snorkeling, waterskiing, and pleasure cruises.

For something different, consider a trip to remote Pulau Layang-Layang. It is a two-hour helicopter flight or eight hours by boat. The small island is a paradise for scuba diving and fishing. There are 17 chalets providing air-conditioned accommodation. Contact **Coral Island Cruises** (Tel: 088-223490).

8. Culture

The great cultural mix that you find in Sabah provides many opportunities to experience close contact with people whose traditions and beliefs are very different from our own. The largest indigenous group is the **Kadazans** who make up one-third of the total population. Some Kadazans prefer to be called Dusuns while others are known by tribal or place names. Traditionally, Kadazans have been *padi* farmers but today they can be found at all levels of society. Most are either Christian or pagan.

The **Bajaus** are well known for their expertise at sea and with horses. They are found mostly along the West Coast between Tuaran and Kota Belud, and on the Southeast Coast between Semporna and Tawau. They represent the second largest indigenous group and are involved in agriculture, and buffalo- and pony-raising. The third major group is known as the **Murut**. They live in the lowlands and the hilly regions of the interior. These people have traditionally been shifting cultivators who have hunted and gathered jungle produce. Spears and blowpipes are their chief weapons and many still prefer to live in longhouses as they have done for centuries.

The Cultural Center in K.K. provides an opportunity to see something of the life-style of these people but it is still possible to learn much by visiting the areas where people have remained more faithful to their traditions.

Most of the usual Malaysian festivals and events are celebrated in Sabah but the Pesta Kaamatan or Harvest Festival in May is especially celebrated, particularly by the Kadazans. At this time rice wine flows freely for everyone.

Don't forget a visit to the Sabah Museum (see details in section 6, "Sight-seeing"), and art buffs should also check out the Sebah Art Gallery in Jalan Satu.

9. Sports

Sports play an important part in the life of the modern Sabahan, and the major cities and towns have facilities for soccer, badminton, tennis, basketball, squash, golf, and watersports. In Kota Kinabalu, the **Likas Sports Complex** has excellent facilities for many sports. You should head here if you enjoy jogging, swimming, tennis, or squash. Several other towns have sports complexes where you will be welcomed.

Golf has become very popular and there are courses in K.K., Sandakan, Kudat, Tawau, Ranau, Keningau, Labuan, and at Kundasang at the foot of Mt. Kinabalu. There is a golf driving range at the Likas complex. The **Sabah Golf and Country Club** (Tel: 088-56533) is an international standard 18-hole course set in beautiful landscaped surroundings close to Kota Kinabalu. This longer-than-average course is a great challenge to big hitters and there are several large lakes. The clubhouse has fine facilities including five self-contained rooms that can be reserved in advance. Clubs can be rented and caddies hired. Weekday fees are $50.

The **Sandakan Golf Club** (Tel: 089-660-557) also has a good 18-hole course and tennis, squash, swimming, and restaurant facilities. Visitors are welcome to play weekdays or before midday on Saturdays. Green fees are M$40 and caddies are available. The **Kinabalu Golf Club** (Tel: 088-51615) has a 9-hole layout at Tanjung Aru Beach, which has plenty of traps and challenges for visitors. So too does the **Labuan Golf Club** (Tel: 087-412-810), which is a tight, well-maintained 9-hole course about three kilometers from town. The club has six self-contained rooms for visiting golfers that can be booked in advance.

Yacht clubs exist at Kota Kinabalu, Labuan, and Sandakan. They allow entry to members of overseas clubs and provide swimming pools, tennis or squash, and restaurant and bar facilities. There is a recreation club in Sandakan with a pool, a restaurant, and darts, and pool table facilities.

There are two bowling alleys in Kota Kinabalu. The Merdeka Bowl is on the eighth floor of Wisma Merdeka while the more modern Centrepoint Bowl is on the 11th floor of the Centrepoint Complex.

10. Shopping

Despite the many cultures, there are relatively few opportunities to buy any handicrafts or souvenirs. The air-conditioned shopping complexes are providing clothes, food, and household goods to the locals while the open-air markets and the night markets tend to concentrate on cooked food and fruit and vegetables. The Philippines Bazaar at K.K. and the market at Sandakan have some items that might appeal, or you can get similar items in Labuan. Duty-free goods are available at reasonable prices on Labuan.

Here are a few random shopping suggestions:

Gaya Street Fair—held in the street every Sunday from 6 A.M. to 1 P.M. There are some interesting handicrafts.

Kamang Air Night Market—6:30 P.M. to 10 P.M. every night. Food, audiocassettes, clothes, household accessories.

Yaohan Department Store—Japanese goods in Centrepoint shopping complex.

Borneo Gifts, ground floor, Wisma Sabah—best handicrafts and souvenirs in K.K.

Ace Gift Center, Sinsuran Complex—an alternative source of handicrafts, etc.

Sabah Natives Handicraft Shop—at Kadazan Dusun Association Center.

Mushroom Center—highland produce outlet at Kota Kinabalu Airport.

Lee Man Book Store, Segama Complex—good bookshop.

Arena Book Center, Sinsuran Complex—a reasonable selection of English material.

Ban Loong Jewelry, Wisma Merdeka—wide range of gold and jewelry.

Color Processing Labs, Segama

Complex—film, processing, and other facilities.

Tukang Jahit Singapore, Wisma Merdeka—tailoring.

Top shop, Wisma Sandakan—for male and female fashion.

D'Image Department Store, Sandakan—good range, reasonable prices.

Galleria Gift and Handicraft Shop—Sandakan Airport, upper level.

Semporna on the southeast coast of Sabah is the place to buy cultured pearls.

11. Entertainment and Nightlife

Sabah is not the world's greatest night spot. You will, however, find good lounges in the major hotels. These often have a Filipino band. There are some pubs, discos, and other hangouts in K.K. and Sandakan, and some options in Tawau.

In Kota Kinabalu, **The Cottage** (Tel: 222-559) on Reservoir Road is a good place to start an evening. This is an English-style pub with live piano music and a good atmosphere. From here you could move on to **Strawberry Lounge** (Tel: 234-173), on the 10th floor of Wisma Budaya. There is no cover charge and the drinks are reasonably priced.

Like many other places in the world, the karaoke craze has hit Kota Kinabalu. If you just cannot live without singing to the music, the place to head is the **Hollywood Karaoke** (Tel: 238-976) at Sadong Jaya. It is open from 8:30 P.M. to 3 A.M. An alternative is the **Subaru Karaoke** above the Oriental Bank on Jalan Pantai. **Cafe Yesterday** (Tel: 211-911) at the Palace Hotel also has many devoted fans.

For disco action, head for **Tiffiny Discotheque** (Tel: 218-091) on Jalan Karamunsing. This is currently the hottest place in town. Other local favorites are the **Galaxy Disco Lounge** and the **Uptown Disco** (Tel: 264-148), both at Bandaran Berjaya, and **Venus Disco** near the Winner Hotel on Jalan Haji Saman.

Heartbeat (Tel: 223-880) on Jalan Sembulan Lama likes to combine a disco, lounge, and karaoke, and it succeeds quite well. The **Phoenix Lounge** in Wisma KTS, has a mainly up-market crowd because of its M$15 cover charge. Once you get in, however, drink prices are quite reasonable, and the atmosphere is appealing. **Club Bourgeoisie** is a popular singles bar and discotheque, as is the **Rocky Fun Pub** on the northern end of Gaya Street.

In Sandakan there is less choice but there is still some variety. There are many karaoke places, some pubs and bars on Old Slipway Road, and some action in Ramai Ramai town.

12. The Sabah Address List

Airlines
—MAS Komplex Karanunsing, J. Tuaran K.K.   088-234111
—MAS Kudat   088-61339
—MAS Sabah Building, Jalan Dua Sandakan   089-42211
—MAS Today Travel Service, Block 3 Semporna   089-77616
—MAS 1021 Dunlop Street, Tawau   089-772493
—Sabah Air, K.K.   088-56733
—Singapore Airlines, Kompleks Kuwasa   088-55333

Banks
—Bank Bumiputra Malaysia, Jalan Sagunting,
  K.K.   088-217266
—Standard Chartered Bank, Jalan Pelabuhan,
  Sandakan   089-217522
—Sabah Bank, Jalan Utara, Tawau   089-776483

Emergency
—Ambulance, fire station, or police   999

Foreign Missions
—The British Consul, Wing On Life Bld.   088-54298
—Indonesian Consul, Jalan Karamunsing   088-54100
—Japanese Consul, Wisma Yakim   088-54169

General Hospital
—K.K.   088-218166

Immigration—   088-51411

Opticians
—Crystal Ophtahlenic Opticians, Wisma Sabah   088-233917

Pharmacy
—UMH Pharmacy, 80 Gaya Street, K.K.   088-215312
Police   088-212222
Telephone Directory Assistance   013
Tourist Information
—TPB Jalan Sagunting   088-211698
—STPB   088-218620
—Sabah Parks, Sinsuran Complex   088-211881
—Raflessia Tours   088-239384

13

Sarawak—Unspoiled Borneo

1. The General Picture

When you visit a riverside longhouse in upcountry Sarawak, you see the contrasts that abound everywhere throughout the state. On the one hand you see hunters with blowpipes wearing feather headdresses, and drinking homemade rice wine. But you are just as likely to see a younger man with a rifle, a diver's watch, and sunglasses, drinking canned beer or cola. Smoky human skulls share space with color television sets, while outboard motors power hand-carved log boats.

Sarawak is the largest of the 13 states that make up Malaysia. It stretches along 700 kilometers of northwestern Borneo bordering Kalimanton (Indonesia) on the south, Sabah on the northeast, and completely surrounding the tiny country of Brunei. Kuching, the delightful capital, is as intriguing as its legendary history, as calm as the meandering muddy Sarawak River that wanders through its heart, and as exotic as its multicultured people, and its startling hinterland.

Archaeological excavations at the Niah Caves indicate that this site may have been under human occupation for more than 40,000 years. Certainly it is known that there was barter trade with China prior to the sixth century A.D. The Sumatra-based Srivijaya Empire and the Javanese Majapahit Empire exerted a strong influence on Sarawak in the thirteenth to fifteenth centuries, but finally the area came under the control of the Brunei Sultanate.

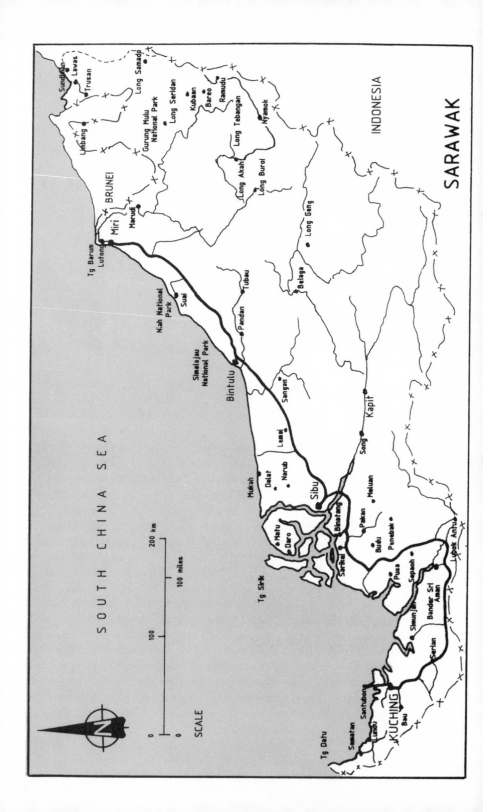

The history of Sarawak as a state began in the 1840s when English adventurer James Brooke helped the Sultan squash disturbances in Kuching and in return was installed as Rajah. For the next 100 years the Brooke family ruled Sarawak in a sort of benevolent dictatorship. It was not until 1941 that the family abrogated their absolute powers by enacting a new constitution to establish self-government. This was nullified, however, by the invasion of Borneo by the Japanese in 1942, and in 1946, after the Japanese surrender, Brooke's descendents were forced to acknowledge that the rebuilding of the country were beyond them, and so Sarawak became a British colony.

Sarawak is a land of rivers and jungles, of flat coastal plains rising sharply to rugged mountains that provide water for large rivers flowing to the South China Sea. These rivers remain vital highways, and despite the improvements in the coastal highway, and the air network throughout the state, the rivers are still the most important means of communication and transportation between many towns. And so it is for tourists.

If you want to experience all of what Sarawak has to offer, you will find that a river trip is essential. You will want to spend a few days in Kuching and maybe another in the surrounding area. Then you should have a longhouse visit high on your list. If you have some time, a visit to Sibu, an excursion into the interior to Kapit, then farther upriver to Belaga will show you the fascinating rural side of the state. It's now possible to go overland from Belaga to Bintulu, then to the Niah Caves, and on to the booming oil town of Miri.

Sarawak is one of those rare places in the modern world where you find fascinating history, beautiful country, pristine nature, friendly people, and few tourists. It almost sounds too good to be true. Outside Kuching, it is perhaps still more a place for the traveller rather than the tourist but that, of course, is part of its appeal. Go before all this changes.

2. Getting There

Kuching is the major gateway to Sarawak but boomtown Miri also has some connections with Kuala Lumpur, Brunei, and Sabah. There are some international flights to Kuching from Manila, Hong Kong, Taipei, Tokyo, Bander Seri Begawan, and Pontianak (Indonesia), but most visitors will arrive by Malaysia Airlines from peninsular Malaysia or Singapore.

The services from Kuala Lumpur, Singapore, and Johor Bahru are excellent with several flights each day crossing the South China Sea. The flight time is 1¼ to 1¾ hours and a meal is served on most flights.

Among the Iban, blowpipes are still used for hunting birds, squirrels, and other small animals.

Likewise there are excellent connections to Kota Kinabalu in Sabah. There are internal flights to several centers from Kuching, Miri, and Lawas in the far northeast.

Kuching Airport is modern and well ordered. You enter the terminal through sky bridges, pass through immigration even if you are arriving from peninsular Malaysia, then move to the baggage carousels, and customs.

As you leave the customs hall there is a tourist office on the left that has a helpful staff and some information about Sarawak. You have to ask specific questions before you get very much information but at least you can get a map, information on hotels, and suggestions on how to get to the city. There is a Sarawak Transport Company bus that operates from the airport to the city at about one-hour intervals. Unless money is super-tight, pay the M$12 taxi fare and use the time to pump the driver for all the information you want about Kuching. You will find it is a good value. There is no apparent payment problem with the taxi drivers although they do not have meters.

When departing from Kuching, you handle baggage check-in and seat assignments on the same level as the arrivals, then go upstairs to the departure lounges. There is a restaurant and a cafeteria on the third level. There is a departure tax of M$20 for international flights, M$8 for Singapore flights, and M$5 for domestic flights. Rental cars are not available at the airport unless you have pre-booked.

Improvements to land routes has meant that you can now reach Sarawak overland from Brunei and Sabah. This is an increasingly popular route for young travellers who hitchhike or use local bus and water transportation between centers.

3. Local Transportation

Kuching city is almost small enough to walk around so transportation is no big problem. If however you are tired, or it is raining, a *taxi* anywhere within the city area will only cost M$2-4. You will have to bargain for the fare because there are no meters but it's all done in a fairly low-key manner. Taxis wait at hotels and around the central market area.

Local buses are a bit of a problem. There is no bus map and no central bus depot. Various companies operate from different street locations but fortunately there is some order to the route numbers. It is wise to ask the hotel or tourist office about specific destinations. Fares vary from about M$0.35 to M$1 depending on the length of travel. There are several operators but these are the ones you are most likely to use.

Chin Lian Long Motor Vehicle Co., Jalan Pending	Tel: 332-766
Kuching Matong Transport Co., Jalan Matong	422-814
Sarawak Transport Co., 2½ Jalan Rock	242-579

Long-distance buses depart from Jalan Jawa near the waterfront. Buses are used to reach places such as Bau, Sematan, Serian, and Sri Aman. There are also twice-daily services to Sarikei, Bintulu, and Miri.

Boats connect Kuching to local villages and there is a ferry service across the river in the downtown area. This latter ride costs around M$0.20, or M$2 if you rent the whole boat.

Rental cars are available from **Mahana Rent-A-Car**, which has an office near the Hilton Hotel (Tel: 411-370). Rates start at around M$150 for self-drive and up to M$220 for chauffeur-driven. You can rent both conventional and four-wheel-drive vehicles.

Long-distance boats service almost all the main towns in Sarawak. Travellers can use these services to ply the coast or travel into the interior. Express boat is the preferred transportation mode between Kuching and Sibu. There are two main companies—**Express Bahagia** (Tel: 421-948) and **Concorde Pertama Union Express** (Tel: 414-735 or 412-551). One service leaves Kuching at 8:30 A.M. and the other at 12:45 P.M. The trip takes about 3½ hours. Return services leave Sibu at 7 A.M. or 11:30 A.M. The basic cost from Kuching to Sarikei is M$29 and from Kuching to Sibu M$33. First-class fares are higher. Both services depart from Bintawa Wharf, which is several kilometers east of the city center. You can reach it by bus No. 17 or 19. From Sibu, there are narrow boats powered by enormous engines which go upriver to Kapit. The 130 kilometers takes about 3½ hours including a few stops. The fare is around M$16. From Kapit there are services on smaller boats to Belaga except when the river is very low. The trip will take at least six hours and will cost around M$16.

Air services around Sarawak are excellent. Malaysia Airlines connects Kuching with Sibu, Kapit, Belaga, Bintulu, Miri, and Lawas. There are also less frequent services (often on Twin Otter aircraft) to the small communities of Marudi, Limbang, Bario, Long Seridan, Ba Kelalon, Long Semado, and Long Lellang. Details are available from **Malaysia Airlines** in Kuching (Tel: 244-144).

Charter aircraft are also available. Helicopters and fixed-wing aircraft can be arranged with **Hornbill Skyways** (Tel: 082-455-737) in Kuching or (Tel: 085-611-066) in Miri. **Boskym** in Miri (Tel: 085-418-449) can also arrange charter planes.

4. The Hotel Scene

Kuching has a couple of top-end hotels that are excellent but the city really shines in the midmarket category where there is enormous choice. There are a number of budget hotels but they tend to be in the upper end of the category, or are very basic and not particularly good value. I have inspected more than 30 hotels in Kuching and recommend the following to you.

EXPENSIVE HOTELS

The first option is the **Holiday Inn Kuching** (Tel: 082-423-111), 320 air-conditioned rooms, all with private bathroom, IDD telephone, TV, in-house movies, radio and minibar. This was the first international hotel in Sarawak and although it has been operating for around 15 years, it is still a great place to stay. It has managed to achieve a nice personal touch even down to a note from housekeeping assuring guests that if any personal essentials have been forgotten, housekeeping will come to the rescue. It's nicely reassuring. The hotel is located on the banks of the Sarawak River, only minutes from the old town center. The original building has had a new wing added to it and this in turn connects to a large shopping center that contains more than 100 shops.

Within the hotel there are several excellent food and beverage outlets. The Serapi Restaurant features a wide range of Western dishes as well as a tempting choice of North Indian *tandoori* specialities. The Meisan Szechuan Chinese Restaurant on the first and second floors has Szechuan and Cantonese cuisine, while the Orchid Garden 24-hour coffee shop has buffets, snacks, and local and Western food. The Poolside Pavilion, overlooking the Sarawak River, serves snacks daily, and a BBQ lunch on Sundays. Adjacent to the lobby is the Rajang Bar, which features a Filipino band each evening, while the Aquarius Discotheque has the latest in music and dancing.

The hotel has a business center with secretarial services, fax and reference library facilities, a health center with gymnasium and sauna, and a floodlit tennis court adjacent to the building. Room rates start at around M$160 and rise to more than M$1000 for the best suites. (Book with the Holiday Inn organization or direct with the hotel at P.O. Box 2362, 93748 Kuching, Sarawak, Malaysia; Fax: 6082-426-169.)

The **Kuching Hilton** (Tel: 082-248-200), 322 rooms, is the most stylish hotel in Kuching. The sparkling white, 15-story building contrasts beautifully with lush green tropical vegetation. The hotel looks out over a road to the gentle Sarawak River and across to Fort Margherita. All rooms have individually controlled air conditioning,

IDD telephone, TV, in-house movies, radio, writing desk, refrigerator with minibar, and private bathrooms. The Executive Floors have a private check-in, a lounge, and library, and complimentary Continental breakfast, and pre-dinner cocktails are served.

The hotel has several fine food outlets. The Steak House is a Western speciality restaurant that features Italian cuisine; the Toh Yuen Chinese Restaurant has Cantonese and Szechuan cuisine; while the Waterfront Cafe has all-day Malay, Chinese, Indian, and Western dining, and a fine view. The Margherita Lounge adjacent to the lobby, has large picture windows that overlook the river, and a Filipino band at night to help pass the hours. The Matang Terrace, located by the pool amid lush gardens, has exotic cocktails and Asian and Western snacks. Ultramodern Pepper's karaoke lounge and discotheque opens each day from 5 P.M. to 2 A.M. Service throughout is excellent.

There is a business center with secretarial services, fax and personal computer facilities, and a business library. On the first floor there is an air-conditioned gymnasium with sauna, steambath, massage, and jacuzzi. On the roof of the podium you find a swimming pool with sunken bar, a pool snack bar, and a floodlit tennis court. Room rates start at around M$260 and go up to around M$2000. (Book with the Hilton organization or direct with the hotel at P.O. Box 2396, 93748 Kuching, Sarawak, Malaysia; Fax: 6082-428-984.) I thoroughly enjoy staying here.

The **Riverside Majestic Hotel** (Tel: 082-247-777), 250 rooms, is Kuching's newest luxury hotel. It is located between the Holiday Inn and the Hilton. There are eight food and beverage outlets, Sarawak's largest ballroom, a business center, and a large shopping center. There are executive club floors and an all-suite floor. Prices range from M$230 to M$2500. (Book with the hotel at P.O. Box 2928, 93756 Kuching, Sarawak, Malaysia; Fax: 6082-425-858.) The rooms at the west end get great views.

The **Holiday Inn Damai Beach** (Tel: 082-411-777), 202 rooms, is a low-rise resort property at Damai Beach, some 35 kilometers from Kuching. There are chalets, studio units, and individual guest rooms, all with attached bathrooms, individually controlled air conditioning, IDD telephone, TV, radio, and in-house movies. All this is set in 35 hectares (90 acres) of land abutting the Teluk Bundung beach and the exotic rain forest of Borneo.

There are two restaurants, the air-conditioned Cafe Satang, which features Malay, Chinese, and Western cuisine; and the open-air Mango Tree Terrace adjacent to the swimming pool. The Santubong Bar off the lobby has a resident band in the evening, while the swim-up bar at the pool is the daytime activity center, and the Sunset Bar provides a perfect place at the end of the day.

The resort offers two squash courts, a golf course, two tennis courts, minigolf, a spa pool, a fitness center with sauna, and the chance to try fishing, waterskiing, windsurfing, sailing, and so on. Unfortunately all this outdoor activity is rather curtailed if it rains, as it did for the entire length of my last visit. Under these conditions, a resort such as this has limited appeal, particularly as little effort has been made to provide all-weather walkways for guests to reach the main lobby/restaurant area.

I'm sure when the sun is shining, it is a different picture. The fact that the resort has recently added an additional 100 deluxe rooms in Sarawakian-style obviously means that it is very successful. Room rates start at around M$130. (Book with the Holiday Inn organization or direct with the hotel at P.O. Box 2870, 92756 Kuching, Sarawak, Malaysia; Fax: 6082-428-911.)

MEDIUM-PRICE HOTELS

The choice of a midrange hotel will be determined by where you want to be and what facilities you specifically want. None of the midrange hotels is adjacent to the river so consequently none has the views or the convenience of the luxury hotels previously mentioned. Room prices are negotiable so ask for a big discount.

The **Telang Usan Hotel** (Tel: 082-415-588), 66 air-conditioned rooms, with IDD telephone, TV, video movies, radio, and attached bathrooms, is a popular hotel with Malaysian business people. To cater for this market the hotel has a business center with secretarial services, and fax and photocopying facilities. There is the Dulit Coffee House serving local and Western dishes; and the Dulit Terrace, which has outdoor eating facilities in the evening. The deluxe and superior rooms have a refrigerator and minibar. Standard rooms are M$85, superior M$120, and deluxe M$150. (Book with the hotel at P.O. Box 1579, 93732 Kuching, Sarawak, Malaysia; Fax: 6082-425-316.)

The **Aurora Hotel** (Tel: 082-240281), 84 rooms, is one of the older of the midrange hotels. Each room has air conditioning, carpet, TV, telephone, piped music, and attached bathrooms. The location on Jalan McDougall is convenient to downtown and the museum, and the hotel offers a good range of restaurants—coffee house, Chinese and Malay restaurant, and Aurora Japanese restaurant. There are shopping facilities close by. I have never stayed here so my comment that the hotel is in need of a brightening up may be too severe; however, my inspection of the restaurants and rooms brings me to this conclusion. Room rates are around M$60 for standard and M$80 for superior rooms. (Book with the hotel at P.O. Box 260, 93704 Kuching, Sarawak.)

The **Borneo Hotel** (Tel: 082-244-122), 65 rooms, has recently undergone extensive renovations. Its rooms are air-conditioned, carpeted, and have telephone, TV, minibar, and attached bathrooms. A dining room serves Chinese and Western cuisine. This location is perhaps not quite as convenient as the Aurora Hotel but most things in Kuching are within walking distance so that's not really a problem. Rates are M$110-190. (Book with the hotel at P.O. Box 1498, 93730 Kuching, Sarawak; Fax: 6082-254-848).

The **Liwah Hotel** (Tel: 082-429-222), 93 rooms, is a modern Chinese hotel at the Ban Hock Road end of Jalan Song Thian Cheok. This area is convenient to the Malaysia Airlines office and the TPB office but it's a fair way from the old center of town. The hotel is modern and the rooms are well fitted out. Basic rooms start at around M$120 but the deluxe rooms are significantly larger and, at around M$145, are probably worth the extra money. The hotel has a restaurant, and a Chinese nightclub that operates from 9:30 P.M. nightly. (Book with the hotel at P.O. Box 1041, 93762 Kuching; Fax: 6082-423690.)

The final choice in this upper midmarket category is the **Hua Kuok Inn** (Tel: 082-429-788) on Ban Hock Road. The rooms are nice with air conditioning, TV, refrigerator, telephone, and carpet. Rates start at M$92. (Book at P.O. Box 2200, 93744, Kuching, Sarawak; Fax: 6082-424-329.)

The **Orchid Inn** (Tel: 082-411-417), 17 rooms, is quite different. This is one of a number of hotels on Green Hill that is adjacent to Lebuh Temple. It is an interesting part of town and these are the best accommodations in the area. The hotel provides fairly basic air-conditioned rooms with attached bathrooms and carpet, telephone, and TV. It has a modern entrance, a friendly staff, and the whole place is very clean. I think it is an excellent value from a discounted M$40 a night. (Book with the hotel at P.O. Box 2466, 93748 Kuching, Sarawak; Fax: 6082-241-635.)

The **City Inn** (Tel: 082-414-866), 33 rooms, is a good value property. Rooms have air conditioning, TV, telephone, and nice bathrooms. Prices start at M$40. Two other small hotels are the **Hotel Victoria** (Tel: 082-218-511), 22 rooms, on Jalan Sentosa (Fax: 6082-218-077) and the **Chung Hin Hotel** (Tel: 082-411-678) on Jalan Padungan with 17 rooms. Both have air-conditioned rooms with TV, telephone, and attached bathroom from M$45.

Two final choices are the Fata Hotel and the **Hotel Longhouse** (Tel:

082-419-333), 50 rooms, on Jalan Abell. This is way down towards the city cat statue and a long way from the old part of town. The hotel has been upgraded in the last few years and the rooms are OK with air conditioning, telephone, TV, and attached bathrooms. The coffee shop and lounge is a popular evening hangout place for the locals. Room rates start at M$55. (Book on fax: 6082-421-563.)

The **Fata Hotel** (Tel: 082-248-111), 35 rooms, is in the same area as the Borneo Hotel. All rooms have air conditioning, carpet, telephone, TV, in-house video, and attached bathrooms. There is a coffee shop and a popular nightclub, a beauty salon, and a travel agency within the building. Room rates start at $55. (Book with the hotel at McDougall Road, Kuching, Sarawak; Fax: 6082-428-987.)

The **Santin Resort** (Tel: 082-488-572), 75 rooms, some 30 kilometers from Kuching also falls into this category. Prices start at M$75. The **Bontal Village Resort** (Tel: 082-416-777), 20 chalets, on a more accessible stretch of beach has fanned rooms from M$70 and air-conditioned ones from M$85 (Fax: 6082-250-567). Neither place is great.

BUDGET ACCOMMODATIONS

Good budget accommodations are a bit hard to find in Kuching, but the following will all be OK if you understand their limitations.

The **Kuching Hotel** (Tel: 082-413-985), 10 rooms, is a good value. It is very clean and it's run by a very friendly group of people. All rooms come equipped with fan and hand basin, and prices start at M$17. You find it upstairs at 6 Temple Street, a handy location close to many of the best attractions of the city. The whole place seems to operate more as a friendly hostel rather than as a formal hotel. Some guests stay for weeks—and why not at this price?

The **Anglican Cathedral Hostel** (Tel: 082-414-027) is the other traditional budget place in Kuching, although it doesn't appear on any official lists because it is not registered as a public accommodations place. It was originally built to accommodate church people and conference delegates, but you can often find that there is a room available for a donation of around M$20. This hostel is on the hill behind the cathedral. It is a good location close to downtown, shops, and the museum.

The **Green Mountain Lodging House** (Tel: 082-246-952), 19 rooms, is another well-run "cheapie." You need to ask to see the room before you take it because there is quite a deal of difference between the best and worst rooms. All have attached bathrooms, some have carpet, all have air conditioning, TV, and telephone. Room rates start at M$33.

Most have small but clean modern bathrooms. You will find this at No. 1 Jalan Green Hill, 93100 Kuching. (Fax: 6082-246-342)

The **Mandarin Hotel** (Tel: 082-418-269) has a few non-air-conditioned rooms and more air-conditioned ones. The people are very friendly and the rooms are clean but the cheapest (M$20) are fairly basic. They do, however, have a hand basin. The other rooms are better and some even have TV, and a bathroom with hot water. This is another place where you need to look at several rooms before you make a choice. The address is 6 Jalan Green Hill, 93100 Kuching.

The **Kapit Hotel** (Tel: 082-244-179) is another alternative. The small property at 59 Jalan Padungan has fanned rooms from M$22 and air-conditioned ones with TV from M$34.

5. Dining and Restaurants

Kuching is unique in my experience in that my two favorite restaurants here are both in hotels. I had one of the best meals in months at the **Steak House** (Tel: 248-200) at the Hilton Hotel. Not only were the food and service excellent but there were several delightful touches that made dining alone an acceptable experience. That is quite an achievement.

The menu has some unique and some traditional items. There is a carpaccio of seabass and salmon, minestrone soup, ravioli, tortellini, lasagna, and, of course, spaghetti. There are also fish seafood items, and prime beef cuts offered from the grill. The Steak House is at the lower level at the Hilton.

The other outstanding restaurant is the **Meisan Szechuan Restaurant** (Tel: 423-111) at the Holiday Inn Kuching. This has a set *dim sum* menu for lunch from 11 A.M. to 2 P.M., six days a week and an all-you-can-eat brunch on Sunday from 8 A.M. to 2 P.M. But it's really at night that the restaurant comes into its own. From 6:30 P.M. to 10:30 P.M. it serves all the usual Chinese favorites plus a few more unusual offerings.

There is Shark's Fin Soup, Bird's Nest Soup, and "live" seafood, but they also have venison, pork, duck, chicken, fish, beef, and prawns. The atmosphere is professional but not daunting and the staff is friendly. Compared to many local restaurants, the prices are high, but you get what you pay for.

The **Aurora Japanese Restaurant** (Tel: 240-281) at the Aurora Hotel is another hotel restaurant worth trying. You can savor Japanese favorites such as *teppanyaki*, *tempura*, *sushi*, and *sashimi*, all washed down with *sake*. A visit here also provides you with entertainment as the chefs go through their routine right before your eyes. There is certainly more than taste to this restaurant.

At the other end of the price scale, there are more than 100 small *Chinese* restaurants scattered throughout the city. Obviously I have not tried all of them but I have some personal favorites that I will pass on to you. The **Green Hill Corner Restaurant** in Lebuh Temple and the nearby **Tiger Garden Restaurant** both serve excellent chicken rice and other simple dishes, as does the **Suan Chicken Rice Restaurant** next to the Pizza Hut near the Holiday Inn.

Indian food is available at many outlets. Naturally Leboh India is one of the better places to find good choices. Along this pedestrian mall, there are numerous restaurants, often side by side, which have to be good to survive the competition. The **Jubillee Restaurant** (Tel: 245-626) at No. 49, the **Malaya Restaurant** at No. 53, the **Madinah Cafe**, and the **Zam Zam Cafe** are some personal favorites. All are excellent. You should try the **riyani** (rice with chicken and vegetables) with the usual curries, and *chappatti* (pancakes). The **Buhari Cafe** on Jalan Satok is another good choice.

Malay and Indonesian food is justifiably popular. It ranges from *Satay* to *Nasi Lemak, Laksa,* and *Rojak.* You will find these dishes at all the open-air markets, and in some restaurants scattered around town. The **Sri Satok Restaurant** (Tel: 411-363) in the Mara Building on Jalan Satok is considered by many to be the best Malay restaurant in town, with the **Minangkaban Restaurant** on Wee Khong Chiang Road being another favorite. The **Long Life Restaurant** on Jalan Petanak is unusual in that it serves both Chinese and Indonesian food. **Thompson's Corner** is also renowned for a wide variety of cuisines at very reasonable prices.

Other Asian cuisines are also available. The **Kikyo-Tei Restaurant** (Tel: 257-886) at the government rest house in Crookshank Road is a popular place for Japanese food. Thai cuisine enthusiasts should head to the **Bangkok Thai Seafood Restaurant** (Tel: 482-181) on Jalan Padungan, or to the nearby **Lok Thian Restaurant**. Filipino food (as well as Malay and Indonesian) is available at the **Permata Food Center**, which is off Jalan Padungan behind the TPB office. The large air-conditioned **Court House Restaurant** (Tel: 247-441) in Jalan Tun Abang Haji Openg, opposite the post office has good Western, Malay, and Chinese food.

For *fast-food* addicts, there are outlets for Kentucky Fried Chicken, Pizza Hut, and Sugar Bun. Many of these are in the major shopping centers such as Sarawak Plaza, Kuching Plaza, and Wisma Saberkas. The **Supersonic Coffee House** (Tel: 250-404) on Jalan Tun Abang Hj

Openg and at the airport, has various Western, Malay, and Chinese offerings and a good selection of seafood at medium prices.

There are a few other places that are worth mentioning. The **Market Street Open Air Market** is a great place for *satay*, and for wandering around to see the sights. The **Batu Lintang Open Air Market** on Jalan Rock on the way to the airport is a great source of cheap food. The **Kuching Food Center** (Tel: 413-361) is by the river near the Holiday Inn. At night it has tables right by the water's edge in a lovely setting under colored lights. **Supreme Corner** next to the Longhouse Hotel is very popular for local food.

6. Sight-seeing

Kuching is a delight to most people. It is a place ideal for walking, enhanced even more by the superb new **Riverside Walk**, and that mode of sight-seeing seems to fit its nineteenth-century atmosphere. Reminders of slower and more genteel days are everywhere in Kuching. The broad, well-kept streets, bazaars, elegant villas, museum, and handsome courthouse, so admired 100 years ago, are still there today. There is a touch of "mañana" pervading the whole place. For casual visitors it is like stepping into the pages of a Somerset Maugham or Joseph Conrad book. Kuching has miraculously kept much of the twentieth century at bay.

There are several points of interest for visitors but to me the real charm of Kuching is to walk the Main Bazaar, Lebuh Carpenter, Lebuh India, and Jalan Khoo Hun Yeang. You will pass countless Chinese and Indian merchants, Malay schoolgirls, and old women inside treasure troves, which have disappeared from most of the world. Dozens of spices, in huge glass jars, mix easily with saris from Madras, tins of corned beef, bottles of Worcestershire sauce, and cassettes of the latest Malaysian pop song.

If you are walking, start at the **Tua Pek Kong Chinese Temple** at the corner where Jalan Tunku Abdul Rahman meets the Main Bazaar. This is the oldest temple in Kuching and although it is crowded on all sides by streets, it is worth a quick visit. From here you should head along the covered walkway of the Main Bazaar. If you are not careful, the next 300 meters could take you all day. There is so much to see and absorb that time becomes unimportant. You pass scores of Chinese shops selling all manner of goods. There are travel operators, bookshops, a few small restaurants, native art shops, goldsmiths, and even a bank.

Midway down this length you should visit the **Tourist Information Center**. Here you can get a reasonable map and a little other information.

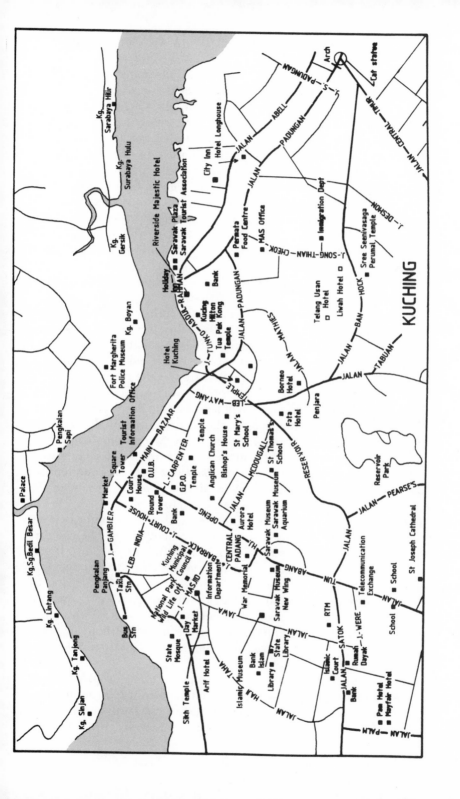

KUCHING

The people are friendly so ask them about buses and other practical information that you need. Nearby is the **Court House**, one of the most attractive buildings in Sarawak. The imposing facade has intricate local art patterns incorporated in its door and window grills, and roof panels. The building was completed in 1874, the clock tower was added in 1883, with the obelisk monument to Charles Brooke commissioned in 1924. Take the time to wander around here.

From the courthouse grounds there is a good view of the **Square Tower**. This building, which resembles the late Renaissance towers in England, was originally built as a detention center for prisoners but it sometimes doubled as a fortress. Near the Square Tower you can catch the ferry that takes you across the river. You land near the **Astana**, a majestic palace built in 1870 by Charles Brooke as a gift to his wife. It is now the official residence of Sarawak's head of state and is not open to the public.

You can, however, visit **Fort Margherita**, which was built in 1878 to defend Kuching against pirate attacks from the river. The Fort is now a police museum that houses a collection of historical items. The contents are not great but it is worth a visit because of the old building and the lovely location. You should also wander around the cultural park and see its art and cultural artifacts, shop, viewing tower, and fountain. From here you need to take the small ferry back to downtown Kuching.

From the landing, continue along the waterfront, then dive into the area around Lebuh India and Lebuh Power. You will discover the long-distance bus stand, the day market, and rows of old shop houses. Go a little farther and you reach the **Sarawak State Mosque** built in 1952, and the **Sikh Temple** on Jalan Mosque. Now walk east to the Central Padang then south to the Sarawak Museum.

The **Sarawak Museum** is one of the best museums in southeast Asia. It is housed in two buildings connected by a footbridge. The old part has recently been renovated and is a wonderful old building. It was built in 1890 in the style of a Normandy town house. The new section was opened in 1983. The buildings house an excellent collection of Borneoan ethnological and archaeological materials, as well as natural history. The displays are varied and interesting. It is a place where you can easily spend several hours. Look in the museum shop for some interesting but expensive items. The museum opens from 9:15 A.M. to 5:30 P.M. each day except Friday.

Farther south from the museum is the modern **St. Joseph's Roman Catholic Cathedral**, then down Jalan Golf Link, you find the impressive **Civic Center** with its art gallery, planetarium, shop, and elevated restaurant/lounge and bar. If you are walking, however, you would do better to head back towards the river along Jalan Tun Abang Haji Openg to **St. Thomas's Anglican Cathedral**. It's only a short walk from here to the **General Post Office** and its magnificent facade of Corinthian columns. Across the road from here is the interesting pavilion building and close by is the curious **Round Tower** built in 1886 for an unknown purpose.

The next section of J. Tun Abang Haji Openg houses many goldsmiths, a good Borneo handicraft shop, and the Bureau de Change of the Hong Kong and Shanghai Bank. You can now return to your starting point by going down Lebuh Carpenter with its many little shops, restaurants, businesses, Chinese temples, and side laneways. This is another area where time has little meaning. You will reach the end of the street when you are ready. Here you will find the **Bishop's House**, the oldest dwelling in Sarawak. It was built in 1849 for Dr. McDougall who later became the first Anglican Bishop of Borneo.

If all this walking has made you tired, a three-hour cruise along the Sarawak River allows you a view of the Sarawakian life-style from a different perspective. It's a good way to finish a long day.

AROUND KUCHING

The Kuching area offers several interesting options that meet the requirements of a wide cross-section of interests.

The **Bako National Park** is probably top of the list. This is the oldest national park in Sarawak and one of the most interesting. It is only 37 kilometers from Kuching but you need to go partway by bus and partway by boat. No. 6 buses of the Petra Jaya Transport Company (Tel: 452-131) leave from Jalan Khoo Hun Yeang to go to Kampong Bako. The cost is M$2.10 one way. From here you have to charter a boat. This costs M$25 for 1 to 10 people for the 30-minute trip.

Bako is not immediately spectacular but within its small area (2700 hectares) there is variety and contrast that is quite amazing. The Bako peninsula is built of horizontal sandstone strata that has weathered in a variety of ways. You can see delicate pink iron patterns on cliff faces, honeycomb weathering, sea arches, sea stacks, and much more. The flora too is diverse. Just 100 meters behind the dry, open beach forest of Telok Assam (the park headquarters area) you find a patch of impenetrable swamp forest. Not far away there is scrubby *padang* vegetation, tropical rain forest, a mangrove swamp, and cliff vegetation. As well you can see a variety of pitcher plants and four types of ant plant, which show an amazing level of cooperation between plant and animal.

Then there is the fauna. The opportunities to observe and photo-graph wildlife are probably better in Bako than anywhere else in Sarawak. Visitors often see long-tailed macques, silvered-leaf monkeys, giant monitor lizards, plantain squirrels, wild boar, and mouse deer. You will probably see the rare proboscis monkey, which only exists in Borneo, and there have been more than 150 species of birds recorded here. You can visit Bako for the day. A canteen sells drinks and meals, and there are public rest rooms, showers, changing rooms, picnic tables, and lockers. An information center offers displays and audiovi-sual programs, there are 30 kilometers of well-maintained trails, and there are opportunities for swimming, beach combing, or just lazing around.

Bako also has accommodations in the form of deluxe rest houses (M$30 per room), standard rest houses (M$25 per room), semi-detached lodges (M$20), hostels (M$2 per adult), campfly (M$3 for up to three people) and campsites (M$1). All rest houses and hostels have mattresses, bedding, cookers, and kitchen utensils. You need to make reservations with the Sarawak Tourist Information Center, Main Bazaar, 9300 Kuching; Tel: 082-248-088.

Santubong and *Damai Beach* are the next points of interest. This location is relatively remote and unspoiled yet it is only a 45-minute drive from Kuching. There are five main points of interest—Buntal fishing village, Kampong Santubong, the Sarawak Cultural Village, Camp Permai, and the Holiday Inn Damai Beach.

Buntal village is famous for its seafood restaurants. Kuching resi-dents travel the 30 kilometers just for a meal. The restaurants are built on stilts out over the mud flats, and are fairly basic, but the seafood is fresh and excellent. My choice from a half-dozen or so good restau-rants is the **Lim Hok Ann Seafood**. Santubong village is somewhat the same but here there are some good beaches. In fact these are the closest good beaches to Kuching so they are very popular with locals on the weekends. The **Holiday Inn Damai Beach** is on a beach a few kilometers farther on and close by is the **Sarawak Cultural Village**.

The village was conceived as a place to portray "live" Sarawak's rich cultural diversity in one single place. The multipurpose reception center houses a theater for cultural dances, a restaurant serving tradi-tional ethnic food, a handicraft shop, and a miniature of the Mulu Caves. Cultural shows are presented on weekdays at 10:30 A.M. and 3:30 P.M. and on weekends at 10:30 A.M., 11:30 A.M., 2:30 P.M., and 4 P.M. There is a cultural show extravaganza each Saturday night at 8:30 P.M.

The village has seven authentic ethnic houses standing around a man-made lake. Some of the houses are occupied by families and others provide the opportunity to try rice wine and ethnic food, and to see coconut dehusking, blowpipe making, top spinning, and other skills. The site is large and it takes several hours to see all the things of interest. It is fascinating to see the big differences in culture between the various tribal people. The Sarawak Cultural Village won the "Best New Tourist Attraction in ASEAN" at the 1990 awards.

Almost right next door is **Camp Permai**, owned by the Sarwak Economic Development Corporation. The camp aims to provide facilities where families can enjoy life together. There are facilities for day trippers (adults pay M$3), lots of water-based recreational activities, and log cabins, tree houses, and tents for those who wish to stay longer. The camp offers a variety of formal challenging courses consisting of Family Adventure Programs, School Courses, Executive Courses, and Leisure Courses. Most involve rock climbing, raft building, jungle trekking, night hikes, and team games. They last from 3 to 14 days and visitors are most welcome to join. More information is available from Tel: 082-416-777 or Fax: 6082-244-585.

Semengoh Sanctuary is well worth a visit, particularly if you are not going to Sandakan in Sabah. This orangutan rehabilitation center is only 22 kilometers from Kuching and can be reached by a half-hour drive on a Sarawak Transport Company bus No. 6, followed by an easy walk through tropical rain forest. You will see rescued orangutans, honey bears, monkeys, and sometimes hornbills, and you learn about their reintroduction to jungle life. To visit here you have to get a permit from the Tourist Information Office in Kuching but this is not difficult. Opening hours are from 8 A.M. to 4:15 P.M. each day. Feeding times are 8:30 A.M. and 2:30 P.M. Farther along the same road you can visit the **Annah Rais Longhouse**, home to 40 Land Dayak families. You will see old women sitting about weaving baskets from ratan while the children are absorbed in watching television. As you would expect, this longhouse, and another at Gaya, are less unspoiled than those farther into the interior, but if this is your only chance to visit a longhouse, you should take the opportunity.

Kuching is relatively close to the Indonesian border but it's still possible to travel west to some lovely coastal villages within Sarawak. You would travel by bus (No. 2) or rental car along the good sealed road to *Bau* then continue on to *Lundu* (bus No. 2B). There is little to see at either of these places so you should continue on to *Sematan* (bus No. 17). The whole journey is about 125 kilometers. As an alternative you could go to the beach at *Siar* (bus No. 17C), which is 10 kilometers from Lundu; or to *Pandan*, which is 15 minutes from Siar. All these places are attractive, relaxed, and ideal for sitting around and doing nothing. There are beach bungalows to rent at Pandan and Sematan.

NORTHEAST FROM KUCHING

Sarawak is not yet a destination where a rental car is the preferred method of travel. Much of the country is inaccessible by road and even the main coastal road leaves much to be desired. Nevertheless, an increasing number of travellers are visiting the major coastal cities and some inland centers, and many are using bus and boat to travel around.

The first major center northeast of Kuching is *Sibu*. Most people prefer to travel there by air or sea, but if you go by land you first head for Serian. At the 29 kilometer mark, near the village of *Siburan*, you can visit **Jong's Crocodile Farm** (Tel: 082-242-790). Buses No. 3, 3A, and 9 come to this area. You can see 1000 or so crocodiles lying around and also see a few monkeys, deer, turtles, lizards, hornbills, and other birds and animals. Admission is M$5 for adults.

Serian is a small town 65 kilometers from Kuching that is popular with locals on weekends because of its nice rock pools and waterfall. You will see many pepper plantations in this area. From Serian there are small villages, rubber estates, *padi* fields, and jungle before you reach *Bandar Sri Aman* and its 1864 Fort Alice. The **Alisan Hotel** (Tel: 083-322-578), 18 rooms, and the **Hosver Hotel** (Tel: 083-321-985), 46 rooms, are the preferred places to stay. The road so far has been good but it deteriorates from here to Sarikei and is dreadful from Sarikei to Sibu. The road now is winding along the fringes of the Kapuas mountain range, which is characterized by deep gorges and dense rain forest.

Those who are travelling to a Skrang River longhouse leave the road at this point and travel upstream by native longboat through sun-dappled jungle to one of many Iban longhouses that now cater to visitors. The attraction is to stay overnight in a longhouse and see something of the culture. If you ask the right questions you can even decide on how "touristy" you wish to go. In a traditional longhouse you will be expected to sleep on the floor with dogs and other people and animals. In some of the Skrang River longhouses you have a basic hut with bunks and simple showers and toilets.

Longhouses can have 30 to 80 families under the one roof and frankly some of them are fairly messy, but it is an experience that you won't get in many other places. In the evening there is likely to be some dancing, a glass or two of the local rice wine, and an opportunity to buy a bag, necklace, or knife. The next morning you will be invited

An Iban tribesman of the Rajang River area of Sarawak. His ancestors were headhunters.

to join the Iban on a fishing or hunting expedition. That is always interesting.

This is also the area where you find 90-kilometer-long Batang Ai Lake, formed by a dam that harnesses the water's power to produce electricity. Here Hilton Hotels will open a 100-room luxury longhouse-style resort in 1994. The resort will offer longboat excursions to the Batang Ai National Park, jungle walks, visits to longhouse communities, and sports facilities. You can drive to *Lubok Antu*, an upcountry township almost to the Indonesian border. The town has a few simple restaurants, a rest house (Tel: 64108), and a number of general stores. The **Pan-LA** is a lodging house above the Kapitan China's Shop. It offers clean, simple accommodations with mosquito nets, a common bathroom down the end of the passage, and a 24-hour news service from the bazaar and the jetty. The road ends at the jetty and from here a few enterprising locals do a brisk trade with their longboats.

Sibu is one of the boomtowns in Sarawak. The city of about 200,000 people is built on a swamp, but it is developing into an attractive center with some tourist appeal. The city is some 60 kilometers up the Rajang River and it lives around its port. Manufactured goods are imported here then distributed into the vast interior. In the opposite direction, lumber, minerals, and agricultural products are brought here for export. The success of the city is largely due to the hard-working, adventurous, and enterprising Foochows who came from southern China, one hundred years ago. They still dominate the town but there are an increasing number of Iban laborers and Malay civil servants moving in.

Most international visitors will be in Sibu because they wish to travel up the Rajang River to Kapit or farther to Belaga, and they will only stay for one or two days. In that time you should visit the native market along the Lembangan River where there are more than 700 stalls selling jungle produce. Many of the hawkers are from rural villages and longhouses, and as well as fruit and edible jungle ferns, they will sell an amazing range of birds and animals, and some handicraft. The market opens every day but is busiest on the weekends. Likewise, visit the night market along High Street, Market Road, and Lembangan Lane. Here hundreds of stalls offer many kinds of goods at very competitive prices. There are some excellent food stalls. The market operates from 6:30 P.M. to 10 P.M.

The waterfront is a constant source of interest. There are all manner of craft—ocean-going freighters, modern express launches, barges of all descriptions, tugboats, houseboats, and motorized dugouts. There is plenty of action, color, and chaos. Just upstream of the main wharves is

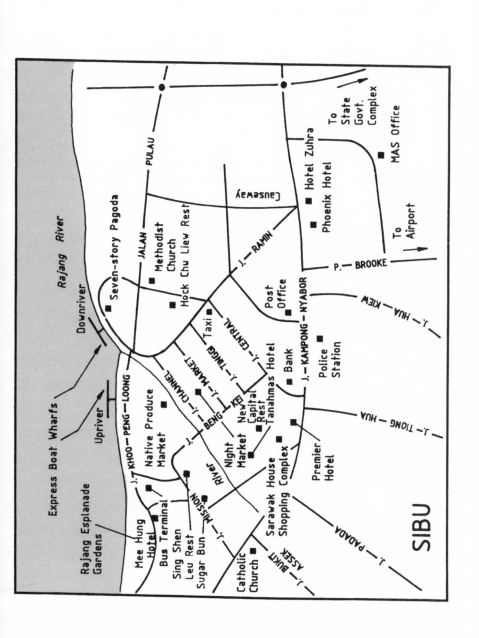

SIBU

the Rajang Esplanade, a fine park built on some reclaimed land. It's a popular place in the evening. Close to the express boat wharf, the new seven-story pagoda next to the Tua Pek Kong Temple, is a prominent landmark. It offers a good panorama from the top.

Sibu has a wide choice of accommodations. The best hotel in town is the **Tanahmas Hotel** (Tel: 084-333-188), with 114 rooms. It has two restaurants, two lounges, a coffee house, and a poolside snack bar. Room prices start at M$140. (Book with the hotel at P.O. Box 240, 96007 Sibu, Sarawak; Fax: 6084-333-288.) The next in line is the slightly larger **Premier Hotel** (Tel: 084-323-222), 120 rooms, which has a restaurant, coffee shop, bar, and health center. Room rates here start at around M$85. (Book with the hotel at P.O. Box 1064, 96008 Sibu, Sarawak.)

The **Hotel Zuhra** (Tel: 084-310-711), 34 rooms, is at the top of the midrange category with prices from M$60 for a reasonable air-conditioned room with attached bathroom. The hotel has a popular coffee shop. The **Malaysia Hotel** (Tel: 084-332-298), 21 rooms, is one step down with rooms from M$50. The **Phoenix Hotel** (Tel: 084-313-871), 25 rooms, is down another step. Rooms here start at M$40. Budget rooms are more difficult to find. The **Diman Hotel** (Tel: 084-337-887) has 20 rooms, some of which are fairly basic but are available for M$20. The nearby **Federal Hotel** (Tel: 084-333-088) is another place worth trying for rooms at around the same price. It's also worth asking at the Methodist Church on Jalan Pulau to see if they have any room in their well-maintained guesthouse. If you can get in, this is the best value in Sibu. The city is also developing some tourist infrastructure. The **River Beach Resort** on Pulau Kerto is up and running and the Bukit Arp and Bukit Lima resorts should be operating by 1994. Sibu has many restaurants but none are particularly outstanding. For Chinese food, the **Hock Chu Liew Restaurant** on Jalan Tukang Bes is quite good, while the **New Capital Restaurant** has some reasonably priced Muslim food. The **Blue Splendor Restaurant** in the same complex on Jalan Kampong Nyabor serves both Chinese and Western food. Try the **coffee shop at the Premier Hotel**, **Peppers Cafe** at the Tanahmas Hotel, or **Sugar Bun** on the corner opposite the Tanahmas, if you want some Western-style snack food.

Buses operate from Sibu to Bintulu (220 kilometers/3½ hours) and to Miri (420 kilometers/7 hours) but most travellers will head upriver to Kapit. Each day between 5:45 A.M. and 1:15 P.M. there are at least 12 express boats leaving Sibu for Kapit. The journey takes 2½ to 4 hours, depending on the number of calls that are made on the way. The trip gives you a good insight into life on Sarawak's most important river. There is no need to book this trip, just wander down to the wharf and you are likely to be away within half an hour. You pay the M$15 fare on board the high-powered, narrow launches.

Kapit is a prosperous river town and administration center for one of the interior divisions of Sarawak. The outstanding landmark is Fort Sylvia, which was built in 1880 and is now used for government offices. This is an important place for many "up-river" people, as a trade, government, and entertainment center, but most visitors will be content to wander around the waterfront, the market, and the shops, then move on. Trips farther upriver have to be approved by the Resident at the State Government complex in Kapit. There is no charge for this but you should allow several hours for the process.

This means that you will spend at least one night in Kapit. The choice of accommodations is clear. The **Hotel Maligai** (Tel: 084-796-611), 41 rooms, is the up-market hotel although at prices from M$35-90 a night you shouldn't expect a palace. The **Kapit Rajang Hotel** (Tel: 084-796-709), 26 rooms, takes the middle ground with clean rooms and Western-style bathrooms from M$25-40 a night, while the **Long House Hotel** (Tel: 084-796-415), 20 rooms, has some rooms from M$15 and other air-conditioned ones up to M$30. The budget market is satisfied by the guesthouse (maybe unofficial) attached to the Methodist Church in the center of town.

Kapit is certainly no gourmet paradise but there are numerous basic Chinese cafes selling noodles and rice with small quantities of meat. I normally enjoy local food but in Kapit I confess to seeking out the bakeries to get some Western-style pastries and cakes as a change from the basic rice meals. The food stalls in the area behind the post office are OK if you are really on a budget.

One of the main reasons for coming upriver, is the chance it gives you to stay at a longhouse. Between Kapit and Belaga there are many opportunities to do this but unfortunately as the number of budget tourists increases, there is some resistance from the local people to-wards open-arms welcomes to people who just turn up and expect to be fed and entertained. It is difficult to do much about this but you can ease your own situation by asking the boatman to recommend a friendly longhouse. Then when you get there, ask to meet the chief, smile a lot, and make it clear you have some food and gifts to help pay for your visit. The Iban are friendly, hospitable people so this will usually ensure that you receive an invitation to stay for the night. The most natural longhouses are those farthest upriver but there is diffi-culty in getting a permit to go beyond Belaga.

Trips from Kapit to Belaga cost around M$16 and take six to eight hours depending on the height of the river. When the river is very low, these trips cease because of the rapids, which have to be negotiated. At these times you will have to use the Malaysia Airlines flight between the two centers. You can, however, probably still reach some of the longhouses by taking a motorized dugout (often at great expense), but if you have made the effort to get to Kapit, this extra cost is worthwhile.

Belaga is a small administration center on the Rajang River. There is now a steady stream of travellers visiting Belaga to explore the rivers, stay in a longhouse, and see the culture. That is slowly changing the area but this is still fairly much frontier country, particularly as far as transportation is concerned. There is no road access to Belaga so that gives some indication of the isolation and the standard of service to expect. Belaga has several hotels, the best of which is the new wing of the **Belaga Hotel** (Tel: 084-461-244). A room here will set you back about M$40. The **Berlian Hotel** is one of two Chinese hotels in town. It is clean but fairly basic. The **Huan Kilah Lodging House** (Tel: 084-461-259), 12 rooms, has a range of room types from around M$30.

It is necessary to obtain a permit from the state government offices if you wish to go farther up the river (even to the famous Bakun rapids, which are about 16 kilometers upstream of the town), or if you wish to travel overland to Bintula, back on the coast. This latter trip is becoming more feasible and popular as logging roads are pushed into the mountains between the two centers, but several travellers have complained about the cost involved in dealing with local boatmen and guides who perceive all foreigners as being rich. For this reason, and for safety, it is best to travel in a group.

The usual route is via the Belaga River till you are blocked by rapids. You then need to hike for several hours till you reach a logging camp or a longhouse. The logging companies have a series of roads that connect their out-camps with *Tubau* on the other side of the mountain. It is often possible to hitch (or buy) a lift with a logging company vehicle. Because the camps are often moved, and different areas are logged at different times, it pays to have a local guide who knows the current situation. From Tubau, you can catch a launch downriver to Bintulu.

Bintulu was a sleepy, little-known fishing village some years ago but today it is a boomtown. The town is evolving as Sarawak's industrial showpiece as oil and timber money pours into the area. Bintulu is being transformed and the totally new township of Kidurong has been developed. A deep-water port, a liquified natural gas plant, and the ASEAN fertilizer plant are ongoing projects with plans for an aluminum smelter and other major developments underway. All this, of course, has little appeal to most travellers.

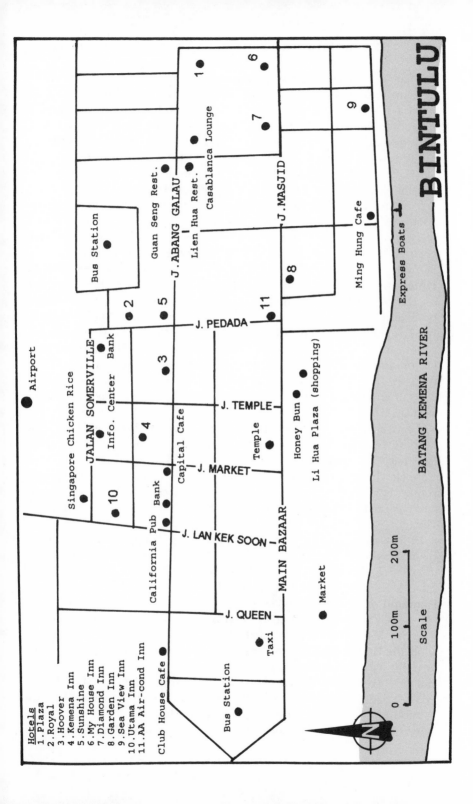

That's not to say that there is no tourist appeal. There are moves to develop easy accessibility to Iban longhouses, to develop a deep-sea fishing fleet, and to have river safaris and other things for visitors. Bintulu already forms the southern gateway to the **Niah National Park** and developments such as the new **Assyakirin mosque** (about 10 minutes drive from the town center) are adding appeal to the area.

As you would expect, the boom has brought an improvement in accommodations. The best hotel is the **Plaza Hotel** (Tel: 086-335-111), 161 rooms, which has two restaurants, a coffee house, a cocktail lounge, a business center, a swimming pool, and a shopping arcade. Room prices start at around M$150 and the best suites will set you back around M$500. (Book with the hotel at P.O. Box 676, 97000 Bintulu, Sarawak; Fax: 6086-332-742.) The other major hotel is the **Li Hua Hotel** (Tel: 086-35000), 90 rooms, which is about four kilometers out on the Miri Road. This hotel also has restaurants, bars, a swimming pool, and a health center. Rooms here start at around M$120. Next in price is the **Royal Hotel** (Tel: 086-332-166), 36 rooms, with elevator, restaurant, and fair rooms with TV, telephone, air conditioning, refrigerator, and carpet priced from M$100. I believe the **Hoover Hotel** (Tel: 086-337-166), 40 rooms, with similar facilities, is a much better value. It is clean and bright and in an excellent location on Jalan Keppel. Prices start at M$90.

There is a variety of accommodations down-market from here, but nothing really budget-priced. The demand for rooms is just too great for that. The **Kemena Inn** (Tel: 086-331-533), 12 rooms, in Jalan Keppel, charges from M$60 a night for reasonable air-conditioned rooms. For M$50 you can get a room with air conditioning, bathroom, and TV at the **Sunlight Inn** (Tel: 086-332-577), 16 rooms, on Jalan Pedada.

In fact, there is a vast choice of small, clean, bright inns with rooms from M$40-50. All have air conditioning, TV, telephone, and small attached bathrooms. There is little difference between them. Along Jalan Masjid you will find **My House Inn** (Tel: 086-336-399), 16 rooms; **Diamond Inn** (Tel: 086-338-911), 15 rooms; Ung Ping Inn (Tel: 086-337-373), 18 rooms; and **Garden Inn** (Tel: 086-339-399), 15 rooms. The **Sea View Inn** (Tel: 086-339-118), 12 rooms, is on the waterfront while the **Utama Inn** (Tel: 086-334-539), 12 rooms, is on Jalan Somerville near the airport. A slightly cheaper option is the pokey **AA Air-cond Inn** (Tel: 086-335-733), 17 rooms, on the corner of Jalan Masjid and Jalan Pedada. Prices start at M$32. Beware of old-style lodging houses in Bintulu. Most are for the "short-time" trade.

It's not difficult to find someplace to eat in Bintulu. The restaurants in the better hotels are OK, and the **Capital Restaurant** on Jalan Abang Galar has good Chinese food. There are many popular local Chinese food outlets along Jalan Bazaar between the taxi station and the Chinese temple. The **Ming Hung Cafe** opposite the express boat wharf, **Singapore Chicken Rice** in Jalan Somerville and the **Guan Seng** and the **Lion Hua** in Jalan Abang Galau are all good. For Indian food, you could try the **Bismi Restaurant** in Jalan Somerville. For casual dining, the place to head is the waterfront food stalls. There is a great selection and everything is comparatively cheap. If you need Western-style fast food, dessert, or cake, there is no better place than **Honey Bun** in Li Hua Plaza. **Kentucky Fried Chicken** has an outlet near the clock tower monument.

If you are seriously into waterfalls, you may like to travel 17 kilometers south along the Sibu road to the **Kampung Jepak Waterfall**. The falls are about a 10-minute trek from the road but they are very attractive. The water, which often is only a small stream, drops over an overhanging rock ledge into a large pool.

Just north of Bintulu is the relatively undeveloped **Similajau National Park**. There are some lovely sand beaches with clean water. The area is currently being developed to provide an access road, information center, day-visitor facilities, and overnight accommodations. A few kilometers offshore, there is a small coral reef with a wealth of marine life. Boats are available to take you out to see the sights. Back on land, the wide-open spaces are perfect for bird watching, and wild boar and macaque monkeys are often seen on the beach. Close to Bintulu town you can see hornbills, orangutans, and Malaysian tigers at the Bintulu Wildlife Park. This is also the home to a collection of Sarawak native plants.

It is possible, but not recommended, to visit the **Niah National Park** in one day. It's much better to travel from Bintulu to the park, sight-see, and spend the night there, then travel on to Miri. There is a bus between Bintulu and Batu Niah. (It takes about 2½ hours and costs around M$12.)

The park comprises about 3,100 hectares of forest and limestone. The center of the park is dominated by 400-meter-high Gunung Subis. Within the park are the world-renowned Niah Caves. You reach the caves on a four-kilometer boardwalk that winds through lowland forest. At certain times of the year, the first part of the walk is subject to flooding and in the rainy season it can be very slippery, so beware.

The Great Cave is among the largest in the world and rarely fails to impress visitors. There is a boardwalk through part of the cave but it's not a bad idea to get a guide if you want to do some more extensive

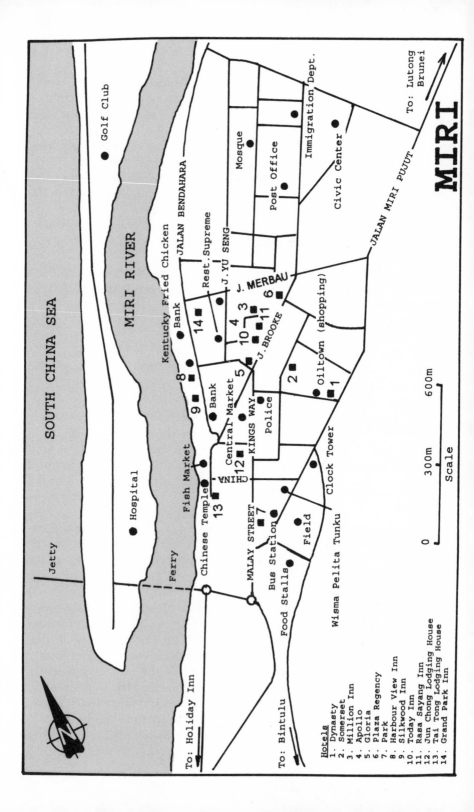

exploring. You will need a pair of sneakers, a strong light, and some spare batteries. The caves are home to millions of swiftlets and bats so there is constant fluttering overhead. A 40,000-year-old human skull was found at the entrance to this cave and the bats have been there longer, so the floor is meters deep in guano—bird and bat excrement.

The other attraction to some are the swiftlet nests that are constructed in crevices in the roof. These are highly prized by the Chinese and are made into bird's nest soup. You will see many flimsy poles stretching from floor to ceiling and men scrambling up them to collect the precious nests.

The Painted Cave is another important part of Niah. Cave paintings have been discovered here that are believed to be at least 1,000 years old. Associated with these paintings are several "ships of the dead," coffins that look like small canoes. You can only visit here with a guide and a permit. These can be obtained from the Forest Department in Kuching or from the ranger at the park.

The Traders' Cave is the other main feature. It contains a "roofless village" or a crude longhouse that was, and is still occasionally, used by bird's nest and guano collectors and buyers. There are two well-marked trails in the park which lead through interesting country. One leads to the summit of Bakit Kasut, while the other is a lowland trail through the swamp forest. Just outside the park's boundary, there is a large Iban longhouse, Rumah Change, which is about a 15-minute walk from the main boardwalk.

The park has an information/interpretation center that displays some aspects of the history, geology, flora, and fauna of the park. A small shop sells food, drinks, and things such as towels, flashlight batteries, cigarettes, etc. There are rest houses, hostels, and campsites for those who wish to stay. All rest houses and hostels are provided with mattresses, bedding, electric fans, gas cookers, and kitchen utensils. Some rest houses have refrigerators. The costs are: deluxe rest house M$30 a room, standard rest house M$20 a room, new hostel M$18 a room, old hostel M$3 per adult. You need jogging shoes, a flashlight, and preferably long slacks and a hat.

When you decide to leave Niah National Park, you can catch a bus to Miri. It costs about M$10 and takes two hours. The last bus leaves in the early afternoon.

Miri is Sarawak's answer to oil-rich Brunei. The area's development is closely linked to oil and mining and by the look of the town there is plenty of money in both these activities. Much of the town is being torn apart by new development, although parts of the old center remain. Like Bintulu, it is an expensive town with little of specific visitor interest. There are some quite good hotels, restaurants, and nightclubs but also some sleaze, particularly in the cheaper end of the market.

The **Holiday Inn** (Tel: 085-418-888) is a new 168-room hotel about two kilometers from downtown Miri. The property is very attractive, but the adjacent beach cannot be used for swimming. Room prices start at M$160. I prefer the downtown **Dynasty Hotel** (Tel: 085-421-111), 140 rooms. It is a very well run property adjacent to a major shopping center and within walking distance of most things in Miri. Rooms are large and are extremely well appointed; there are three food and beverage outlets, and there is a health club. Room rates start at around M$180. (Book with the hotel on P.O. Box 163, Miri 98007 Sarawak; Fax: 6085-422-222.) Also worth considering is the smaller, slightly cheaper **Somerset Hotel** (Tel: 085-422-777), 54 rooms. It has a swimming pool, a restaurant, and music lounge. (Book on fax: 6085-421-234.) At present there are a group of hotels with rooms starting at around M$60-90 and going up from there. These include the **Million Inn** (Tel: 085-415-077), 32 rooms (P.O. Box 237); and the **Apollo Hotel** (Tel: 085-415-235), 19 rooms (P.O. Box 162), both on Jalan South Yu Seng. Then there are the **Gloria Hotel** (Tel: 085-418-800), 42 rooms (P.O. Box 1283); and the **Plaza Regency** (Tel: 085-413-113), 50 rooms, both on Jalan Brooke. The **Park Hotel** (Tel:085-414-555), 95 rooms, on Jalan Raja (P.O. Box 443), has seen better times. I prefer the smaller **Harbour View Inn** (Tel: 085-412-177), 36 rooms on Jalan Bendahara.

Below these, there are a few places that can be recommended. The **Silkwood Inn** (Tel: 085-420-577), 22 rooms, on Jalan Bendahara; and the **Today Inn** (Tel: 085-414-000), 19 rooms; and the **Rasa Sayang Inn** (Tel: 085-413-880), both on Jalan Lee Tak, all have rooms from M$50. Cheaper still are the **Grand Park Inn** (Tel: 085-413-316) in the Beautiful Jade Center near the MAS office, and the very popular **Jun Chong Lodging House** (Tel: 085-412-803) on High Street. The **Tai Tong Lodging House** (Tel: 085-34072), 26 Jalan China, has rooms from M$27 and beds from M$8. There are communal bathrooms.

Eating in Miri is no problem, although prices are higher than many towns. Many of the hotels have reasonable restaurants that serve good Chinese food and mediocre Western fare. The **Kok Chee Restaurant** in the Park Hotel is popular, as is the **Mae Nam Thai Restaurant** at the Dynasty Hotel. For Chinese food the **Kah Hing Restaurant** on Jalan Brooke and the **Restaurant Supreme** and the **Appolo Seafood Restaurant** on Jalan Yu Seng are recommended, but there are undoubtedly scores of reasonable Chinese restaurants that I haven't tried. There are numerous eating outlets—Chinese, Malay, and Western fast food—in the triangle bounded by Brooke Road, River Road, and Merbau Road, in the Wisma Pelita Shopping Complex by the bus station, and in the Oiltown shopping center next to the Dynasty Hotel. **Maxims** has good seafood on the Lutong Road, while the open-air seafood restaurant just past the soon-to-open Royal Rijah luxury hotel is also recommended. **The Ranch** is a country and Western pub and **Purple** is a popular disco.

Although it receives little publicity, the **Lambiu Hills National Park**, about 20 kilometers south of Miri, is worth a visit. The park contains a chain of steep sandstone hills bounded by rugged cliffs, covered by forest. For many visitors the main feature of the park is the numerous waterfalls, with Latak Falls and Pantu Falls, two of the most spectacular. The park has an information center, some marked trails, a canteen, and some recently completed overnight accommodations. Buses are available from Miri to the park. You can also take a tour with Megasia (Tel: 418-663).

The coastal road north from here is sealed to the Brunei border at Kuala Belait. You can book a bus ticket the whole way (M$15) but you actually change buses at the border. If you are heading for Sabah you will find that going through Brunei, then catching a boat to Lawas in northern Sarawak, is the most convenient way. Alternatively if you are heading back to peninsular Malaysia, you would fly either to Kuching, Kota Kinabalu, or take a direct flight from Miri.

For those with time, there are still a few things to see in northern Sarawak. One option is to go up the Baram River to trek in the deep interior, or visit **Gunung Mulu National Park**. To reach the park over land, you first take a bus to *Kuala Baram* (about M$2.50). You then take a launch up the Baram River to *Marudi*. This is a small but busy port, and the surrounding area has some agricultural development. The town has taxis but you will not need them unless you wish to venture out from the city. There are banks, government offices, shops, and several hotels here because it is the regional center for this area. It apparently has been like this for some time because the old fort on the hill was built around 90 years ago.

There are several places to stay in town. Most are on Queen's Square. The **Alisan Hotel** (Tel: 085-55911) is the largest hotel in town with 34 rooms. A few of these are available at M$30 but others rise to M$100. The **Grand Hotel** (Tel: 085-55712) is a good choice, particularly as it has a few rooms for M$25. The **Hotel Zola** (Tel: 085-55991) has 25 rooms available from M$60-85. The budget **Mulu Inn** (Tel: 085-55905) has rooms from M$15.

You need a permit issued by the district office in Marudi, if you wish to go upriver to Barco, Long Lellang, or Long Seridan. You can also reach these small centers by a Malaysia Airlines small plane from Murudi and Miri. The river is fascinating but the long journey becomes a bit tiring after a while and facilities are poor. There are some interesting longhouses, however, at Long Maoh and Leo Mato, which are worth some effort.

If you are heading for the national park, you should take a boat from Marudi to Long Terawan. This will cost about M$15. From Long Terawan you have to hire local longboats to get to Gunung Mulu and this can be both frustrating and expensive. Depending on the number of people making the trip, this last leg can cost M$50. As more visitors explore this area, the price seems to rise but it's now possible to organize a tour with travel agents in Miri or Marudi, and this will take the problems out of the journey. Ask about prices for this. At the best of times, the trip from Marudi to the park headquarters will take around seven hours. If you do not wish to go overland, you can now fly to the National Park from Miri with Malaysia Airlines. This means you can do the trip and see the major caves in two days.

The **Gunung Mulu Park** is dominated by the sandstone mass of Gunung Mulu (2,376m.). To the west is a band of limestone that forms lesser peaks. Much of the area is covered with dense rain forest. On Gunung Api there are some spectacular limestone pinnacles that rise more than 50 meters through the jungle, and under the limestone lie some of the world's most impressive caves. These include the world's largest cave passage (Deer Cave), the world's largest natural chamber (Sarawak Chamber), and at 75 kilometers, the longest cave in southeast Asia (Clearwater Caves). The entire cave system has not yet been explored and only part is open to the public.

Despite the distance from "civilization," and the difficulty of reaching the park, the facilities are remarkably good. There is hostel accommodation, an information center, a canteen, marked trails, and guides. In fact the park authorities insist that all visitors use a guide although they may only be going a short distance from headquarters. Deer Cave is the nearest to the headquarters and the walk through the jungle is quite pleasant. The passage through the cave has electric light and it takes 30-45 minutes to walk the entire length. To reach Clearwater Caves you have to take a two-hour boat ride and there are no real facilities when you get there. You need a strong flashlight and good walking shoes, and be prepared to get wet during the trip.

There is quite some effort involved in seeing the pinnacles, or climbing Gunung Mulu, but those who have made these treks say they are well worthwhile. The pinnacles trip will take two days minimum, and the Gunung Mulu trip, three days. You need to carry food and water and be reasonably fit. Leeches are a problem and you need strong walking shoes. Good luck.

It might be possible to travel overland from the park to either Limbang or Lawas, but I have not heard of anyone who has done it. It seems that you would have to retrace your steps to Miri then go through Brunei.

I have never been to Limbang or Lawes but understand that there is little to attract visitors to either place. You reach Limbang by speedboat from Brunei (M$10) but then there is really nowhere to go. The Tourism Promotion Board tells me that there are several reasonable hotels in town including the **Muhibbah Inn** (Tel: 085-22488) with 34 rooms from M$50-100, and the **National Inn** (Tel: 085-22922) with 35 rooms from M$70-100. The **Southeast Asia Hotel** (Tel: 085-21013) is more of a "cheapie" from M$20.

To reach *Lawes* from Limbang, you get a boat to Punang and a share taxi from there. The total fare is about M$20. There are also some direct launches from Brunei to Lawes. It appears that the **Country Park Hotel** (Tel: 085-85522), 36 rooms, is the top hotel. Room prices are M$75-150. The **Federal Hotel** (Tel: 085-85115) has 9 rooms for M$40, and the **Million Hotel** (Tel: 085-85088) has 12 rooms for the same price.

From here you take a bus to Sabah or fly with Malaysia Airlines to Miri, Kota Kinabalu, or Labuan.

7. Guided Tours

There are half-day, full-day, and several-day tours available from Kuching as well as some extended tours that show you more of Sarawak. Tours are relatively expensive but they eliminate much of the hassle associated with travel in this region.

From Kuching typical half-day tours are:

• **City Tour** of three-hours' duration, which shows you all the places of interest around the city, then visits the museum. The cost is M$40-70 depending on the number of passengers.

• **Orangutan Tour**, which visits the Semonggok Rehabilitation Center and takes you into the jungle in a search of these lovable animals as well as honey bears, hornbills, and monkeys. The cost is around M$70.

• **Sarawak River Cruise**, which shows you the city from a different vantage point. There is a luncheon cruise, a sight-seeing cruise, and a sunset cruise.

• **Land Dayak Longhouse Tour**, which travels through pepper plantations, rubber trees, sago palms, and rice fields before visiting the longhouses. The cost is around M$80-120.

• **Sarawak Cultural Village Tour** to see Sarawak's living culture. You see dancers, handicraft making, and inspect the houses and other buildings.

There are also some full-day tours. The most popular of these is to Bako National Park where you can swim, hike, bird watch, or explore the flora and fauna. Some companies offer a one-day tour from Miri to the Niah National Park. It is a long day but good for those with little time. Unfortunately there are no satisfactory air connections so that you can do this from Kuching in one day.

There are a variety of trips to longhouses on the Skrang or Lemanak Rivers. The basic trip is two days/one night from Kuching but others can be three days/two nights or four days/three nights. These trips will vary from around M$250-700 depending on the number of passengers and the duration. Several companies operate various trips to the Mulu Caves from either Miri or Kuching.

Kuching has an amazing number of tour companies and travel agents. Some of the more well known are **Journey Travel** (Tel: 421-603) in the Hilton Hotel; **Borneo Transverse** (Tel: 257-784), a friendly group in Wayang Street, Kuching; **Sarawak Travel** (Tel: 243-708), which has three outlets including one in the Holiday Inn; **Borneo Adventure** (Tel: 245-175), in Padungan Arcade; and **Borneo Interland Travel** (Tel: 413-595), in the Main Bazaar. I have found them very helpful. There are many more and no doubt most of these also offer good services. At last count there were almost 70 registered inbound tour operators in Sarawak.

8. Culture

The best place to see Sarawak culture together in the one place is at the **Sarawak Cultural Center** at Damai Beach. There is music, dancing, handicrafts, traditional foods and drinks, houses, and so on. Cultural centers may be a bit artificial, but this one is excellent. Here you can see examples of traditional musical instruments such as the *satang*—a bamboo tube with pegged strings; the *sape*—a guitar-type instrument made from a block of soft wood; the flute; the *engkerurai*—a small hand-held organ that can play one or more simple chords; the *jatang utog*—a wooden xylophone; and drums and gongs. You will also see some dances, many of which feature graceful movements of the hands and the feet.

The festivals are another way to see elements of the culture. In Sarawak all the traditional Chinese, Malay, Indian, and Western festivals are observed in varying degrees but there are also a few specific celebrations that are not seen elsewhere. The first one of these is the *Pesta Karl*, held in March/April by the Melanar people. It is organized by the Mukah District Office and is performed to cast out sickness from the villages and to increase the fertility in the fruit gardens.

Melidoh is a festival lasting two or three days in April that is held in the various longhouses and villages around Belaga. It is a time of eating, drinking, rejoicing, blessing, and thanksgiving.

The **Kurah Aran Celebration** takes place on May 1, in the Bidayah village compounds. It is held soon after the *padi* harvest is over to drive away the evil spirits and to hope that the fruit crops produce abundantly.

The **Kapit Cultural Festival** is a big event in May in Kapit. There is a grand regatta and a cultural exhibition among other festivities.

Gawai Dayak is a celebration held throughout Sarawak on June 1 to mark the end of the harvest. It is an opportunity to hold "open house" in many areas. In Kuching, the celebrations start on the eve of Gawai with the crowning of the Gawai King and Queen.

Gawai Sawa is held at the same time in Bidayah villages to offer thanks to God and to pray for the coming year's harvest.

The **Kuching Festival** is an annual event organized by the Kuching Municipal Council, but it appears to change time from year to year. The activities include exhibitions, competitions, sporting events, and traditional games. Many of these activities also occur on September 16, which is the official birthday of Sarawak's head of state. This is a public holiday throughout the state.

9. Sports

Facilities for water sports, golf, tennis, and indoor sports in Sarawak are good. The Indoor Stadium in Kuching has facilities for volleyball, *sepak takraw*, badminton, table tennis, and basketball. In Sibu, similar facilities are provided by the Stadium Pusat Belia Dan Sukan.

Tennis courts are available at the Hilton Hotel, Holiday Inn, Riverside Majestic Hotel, Holiday Inn Damai Beach, and at the Sarawak Club. In Bintulu, courts are available at the Bintulu Development Authority building, the District Office, the Kidurong Club, and the Public Works Department. In Miri, courts are at the Gymkhana Club, the Holiday Inn, and the Pusat Dan Sukan.

Squash courts are at the Ferritel Hotel, the Riverside Majestic Hotel,

Ceremonial longhouse dance, Sarawak.

the Sarawak Club, the Holiday Inn Damai Beach, the Gymkhana Club in Miri, and the Civic Center Miri.

Swimming facilities are found at the Hilton Hotel, the Holiday Inn, the Sarawak Club, and the Bandaraya Kuching Selatton Pool in Kuching, the Holiday Inn Damai Beach, the SMC swimming pool on Bukit Lima Road in Sibu, the Plaza Hotel and the Tanjong Kidurong Club at Bintulu, the Holiday Inn, the Somerset Hotel, and the Gymkhana Club at Miri.

Golf is a growing sport. The **Sarawak Golf and Country Club** (Tel: 082-443-398) in Kuching, has a tricky and scenic championship 18-hole course at Petra Jaya. There is land available to add another 18 holes later. Monstrous bunkers and an array of other hazards add to the challenge of this mostly flat course. The huge pyramid-shaped clubhouse has a bar, restaurant, games room, library, coffee house, tennis courts, and practice green. Weekday green fees are M$50.

There is an 18-hole layout at the **Miri Golf Club** (Tel: 085-416-787) with flowing fairways and well-placed hazards. There is a lovely casual ambience at this course, which is usually relatively uncrowded. Green fees any day are M$50. A 9-hole course has recently opened in Bintulu. The **Tanjung Kidurong Golf Course** (Tel: 086-34198) is situated on the coast about eight kilometers from town. **Sibu Golf Club** has an undulating 9-hole course about 15 kilometers outside town amid rolling hills and lakes. The **Prisons Golf Club** is a 9-hole course in the Penrissen area of Kuching.

10. Shopping

No one would see Sarawak as a place to buy fashion goods, electronic gear, cameras, and so forth. It is the tribal crafts and decorative items that have appeal. The best selection can be brought in Kuching. Handicrafts and antiques can be found in shops in the Main Bazaar, and at Wayang Street and Temple Street. Shops selling arts and crafts are scattered around the city. Many of the indigenous arts are unique to Sarawak. Wood carvings, bags, beads, woven mats, and rugs are prized items. Other good buys are old silver coin ornaments, and silver belts.

Don't forget to check out the Sunday open-market along Jalan Satok. Here antiques can be found together with jungle-type handicrafts like blowpipes and knives. It must be pointed out that no one can take antiquities out of the country unless a license has been issued by the curator of the Sarawak Museum. An antiquity is any object made before 1850.

The best place in town for fine native art and artifacts is **Sarawak House** (Tel: 252-531) at 67 Main Bazaar, Kuching. The shop is an absolute delight and you are welcome to walk around and look without any pressure being put on you to buy. Other places worth visiting are **Borneo Art Gallery** (Tel: 418-312) in the Sarawak Plaza Complex; **Native Arts** (Tel: 424-886), 94 Main Bazaar; and the **Borneo Handicraft Shop** (Tel: 240-875) on Jalan Tun Abg, Hj Openg. The **Sarawak Tourist Information Center** (Tel: 240-620) on Main Bazaar has a good collection of artifacts and souvenir items, as does the **Sarawak Art Shop** in the new wing of the museum. There are many more.

The best general shopping is found in the Sarawak Plaza next to the Holiday Inn. English-language books are found at **H. N. Mehamed Yahia** in the Holiday Inn, and at two branches of **Star Books** in the Main Bazaar. If you are interested in the beautiful Sarawak pottery with its traditional designs, you should try the **Ng Hua Seng Pottery Factory** or the **Ng Lee Seng Pottery Factory**, both on Jalan Penrissen. A surprise discovery is **Fabrika** in Jalan India, where local tribal fabrics are being combined with leather and cottons to create a range of up-market fashion items. Bags, shoes, suits, belts, shirts, and dresses are available.

11. Entertainment and Nightlife

Kuching, Sibu, Bintulu, and Miri all have the usual types of entertainment offered in modern towns—cinemas, nightclubs, pubs, bars, cocktail lounges, and discos. There are a number of pubs or lounges with live music (often a Filipino band). In Kuching, the **Cowboy Lounge** (Tel: 417-005) on Jalan Ban Hock is a current favorite. **My Place Pub** (Tel: 245-335) on Jalan Song Thian Cheok is down-market from here but it's OK, and so is the **D'supreme Coffee House and Pub** on Jalan Tunku Abdul Rahman. I haven't been to it, but the **Mulu Pub** on Jalan Song Thian Cheok has a good reputation.

The best disco in town is the one inside the Holiday Inn. The Holiday Inn, the Riverside Majestic, and the Hilton have lounge bars with imported groups providing excellent music. Peppers Disco and Karaoke Lounge at the Hilton is a good meeting place. For those seeking massage parlors (they are called hairdressing salons in Sarawak), several can be found along Jalan Padungan opposite Permata Hawkers Center.

12. The Sarawak Address List

Airlines
—Malaysia Airlines, Kuching	Tel: 082-244144
—Malaysia Airlines, Sibu	084-326166
—Malaysia Airlines, Bintulu	086-331554
—Malaysia Airlines, Miri	085-414144
—Royal Brunei Airlines, Kuching Hilton	082-243344
—Singapore Airlines, Wisma Bkt Mata Kuching	082-240266

Banks
—Bank Utama, 18 Jalan haji Taha, Kuching	082-259257
—Hock Hua Bank, 51 Jalan Masjid Sarikei	084-652490
—Standard Chartered Bank, Jalan Blacksmith, Sibu	084-336122
—Eon Bank, 27 Jalan Temonggong Jugah, Kapit	084-796413
—Bank Bumiputra Malaysia, Bintulu	086-331320
—Malayan Banking, Jalan Bendahara, Miri	085-412528

Emergency— 999

Foreign Missions
—The British Council, 142 Jalan Abell, Kuching	082-256044
—Indonesian Consulate, 1A Jalan Pisang	082-241734

General Hospital
—Kuching	082-257555
—Sibu	084-313333
—Miri	085-32222

General Post Office
—Kuching	082-242944

Information Bureau
—Kuching	082-410942
—Sibu	084-733052
—Bintulu	086-332278
—Miri	085-33267

Medical
—Kuching	082-248088

National Park & Wildlife
—Miri	085-36637

Police
—Central Police Station, Kuching	082-241222
—Sibu	084-322222
—Bintulu	086-331121
—Miri	085-32533

Telecom Inquiries
—Everywhere	013

Taxi
  —Kuching, 144 Jalan Pandungan   082-242821
  —Sibu, 122 Jalan Maju   084-313384
  —Bintulu   086-332009
  —Miri   085-412277
Sarawak Museum
  —Kuching   082-244232
Worship Directory
  —Roman Catholic, St. Joseph's   082-419897
  —Anglican, St. Thomas's, Jalan McDougall   082-247200
  —Trinity Methodist, 57 Jalan Ellis   082-417015
  —Seventh-Day Adventist, 3 Jalan Rock   082-247746

Index

First Place Winner
1993 Hawaii Visitors Bureau
Travel Journalism Award

THE MAVERICK GUIDE TO
HAWAII: 18th Edition

By Robert W. Bone
Edited by Carol Greenhouse

"One of the most complete guides to these paradisiacal islands in the Pacific . . . An invaluable handbook."

Washington Times

"The best guide to Hawaii, and one of the best travel guides I've ever read, is The Maverick Guide to Hawaii."

Chicago Sun-Times

For more than 15 years this comprehensive book has guided travelers to remote and familiar points on the Hawaiian Islands. Updated annually, it offers the most current information on prices, accommodations, hours, must-sees, and must-avoids. The lively, informative text includes background chapters on each island's history, the people, the language, and how to get the most enjoyment out of a Hawaiian vacation.

With a full complement of landscapes, from beaches to mountains to flowered fields, the islands await you with unlimited outdoor activities. From centers of shopping to the hottest night spots on the beach, you can get the opportunity to see how the Hawaiians live indoors, as well.

472 pp. 5 ½ x 8 ½ Maps Appendix Index
ISBN: 1-56554-022-0 $13.95 pb

THE MAVERICK GUIDE TO
THAILAND: 2nd Edition

By Len Rutledge

"I will always seek to lose myself in Thailand's magic, but with the Maverick Guide close at hand, I can make the most of limited time. . . . Any traveler will benefit from Rutledge's experiences." **Ron Taylor, Travelscope Newsletter**

About five million people travel to Thailand each year, making this unique country one of the most popular destinations in the East. From Chiang Mai and the North to Phuket and the South to Pattaya and the East, Thailand offers romance and adventure to quench the thirst of even the most adventurous traveler. In this land of golden-roofed temples, ancient castles, colorful markets, and beaches with pure white sand and crystal-clear water, the travel possibilities are abundant and diverse.

Updated with new and current information, *The Maverick Guide to Thailand* offers everything the traveler to Thailand could possibly want to know. This comprehensive guide includes where to go and what to do in the countryside and the cities, clearly describing tours, restaurants, sports, and other activities and entertainment available. Aside from the standard guidebook information, details regarding the historical and cultural background of Thailand and its people are provided. A section of profiles of contemporary Thais helps add to the visitor's knowledge as he or she explores this intriguing locale.

384 pp. 5 ½ x 8 ½ Photos Color maps Index
ISBN: 0-88289-942-2 $15.95 pb

Please tell us about your trip to Malaysia and Singapore.
(This page can be folded to make an envelope.)

Cut along this line.

Cut along this line.

_____

_____

_____

re: All New 2nd Edition,
    Malaysia and Singapore

THE MAVERICK GUIDES
PELICAN PUBLISHING COMPANY
1101 Monroe Street
P.O. Box 3110
Gretna, Louisiana 70054